CRANE AND HAGENSICK'S
WISCONSIN GOVERNMENT AND POLITICS
SIXTH EDITION

EDITED BY
RONALD E. WEBER

Wilder Crane Professor of Government
University of Wisconsin–Milwaukee

The McGraw-Hill Companies, Inc.
Primis Custom Publishing

New York   St. Louis   San Francisco   Auckland   Bogotá
Caracas   Lisbon   London   Madrid   Mexico   Milan   Montreal
New Delhi   Paris   San Juan   Singapore   Sydney   Tokyo   Toronto

McGraw·Hill
A Division of The McGraw·Hill Companies

CRANE AND HAGENSICK'S
WISCONSIN GOVERNMENT AND POLITICS

McGraw-Hill's **Primis Custom Publishing** consists of products that are produced from camera-ready copy. Peer review, class testing, and accuracy are primarily the responsibility of the author(s).

3 4 5 6 7 8 9 0   QSR QSR   9 0 9

ISBN 0-07-068829-X

Editor: Tom Lyon
Printer/Binder: Quebecor Printing Dubuque, Inc.

TABLE OF CONTENTS

PART 1: THE SETTING FOR WISCONSIN POLITICS

                                      Ronald E. Weber, University of Wisconsin - Milwaukee
                                         Introduction
                                         Geography, History and Economy of Wisconsin
                                         The People of Wisconsin
                                         Political Development and Political Culture in Wisconsin
                                         Conclusion

                                         Michael Fine, University of Wisconsin - Eau Claire
                                         Basic Features
                                         Political and Ideological Underpinnings of the Original Constitution
                                         Constitutional Development Since 1848
                                         Patterns of Constitutional Change
                                       Conclusion

                                         Edward J. Miller, University of Wisconsin - Stevens Point, and Brett Hawkins,
                                         University of Wisconsin - Milwaukee
                                           Units of Local Government
                                           Counties
                                         Towns
                                         Municipalities: Cities and Villages
                                         Special Districts
                                         Fragmentation of Functions
                                         Financing Local Government
                                         Direct Democracy
                                         State-Local Relations
                                         Local Government Associations
                                         Collective Bargaining for Public Employment
                                         Conclusion

List of Tables

List of Figures

PREFACE

This sixth edition of *Crane and Hagensick's Wisconsin Government and Politics* is dedicated to the memory of the co-authors of the first three editions (1976, 1978, and 1981), UW-Milwaukee Professors of Political Science Wilder Crane (April 7, 1928-December 7, 1985) and A. Clarke Hagensick (November 27, 1933-April 20, 1985). Their names are continued in the title of this new edition in recognition of their earlier contributions to the text and as a mark of the esteem in which their political science contributions are held by their colleagues in Wisconsin.

This edition was edited solely by me using the facilities of the Department of Political Science. The basic organization and coverage of subject matter of the earlier editions have been continued in this version. Changes in the text incorporate significant changes in both the structure and the substance of Wisconsin state and local government that have occurred since the preparation of the 1991 edition. This edition features completely revised chapters on the judiciary and on health and social services policy, as well as an updated concluding chapter that compares Wisconsin politics and policymaking to that of the 49 other states.

My aim has been to have the new edition ready for use in the Fall Semester 1996; consequently, the cut-off for incorporating any changes was mid-July, 1996. This had particular implications for the authors of the chapters on the Legislature (VI) and on Budget and Finance (X), because these authors were able to cover policy and process developments involved with enactment of the 1995-96 Budget Act. Also this publication date enabled the author of the chapter on Health and Social Services Policy to include material on the recently passed W-2 welfare reform legislation. This cut-off also enabled the authors to incorporate material from the recently published 1995-96 State of Wisconsin, *Blue Book*.

Previous editions have been used as texts or supplementary texts in quite a number of Wisconsin college and university courses dealing with state politics and government, Wisconsin politics, and similar topics, plus a few social studies or government courses at the secondary level. Those involved in preparing the present edition hope that it may be of assistance as well to secondary schools and teaching training institutions in meeting the state's increased requirements in the area of social studies education.

The Department of Political Science wishes to thank all of those who helped with this new edition for their many individual and collective contributions. The names and affiliations of the persons who authored the individual chapters are listed in the table of contents with the chapter titles. Authors and affiliations are also indicated in the individual chapters. Contributors to this new edition include current or former faculty from five different higher education institutions within Wisconsin.

This edition was solely edited by me. Political Science Graduate Project Assistants Julie M. Knier and Wendy L. Martinek assisted with the editing and final preparation of the manuscript and updated the bibliography. Meredith W. Watts, Chairman of the Political Science Department, provided administrative support for the project. Donna Schenstrom, Director of the UW-Milwaukee Cartographic Services Laboratory, and her staff created the maps for Chapters I and IV. Reaney Dorsey of McGraw-Hill Custom Publishing Division shepherded this book through the final stages of production and into distribution for the classroom. I wish to acknowledge my debt of gratitude to Professor Emeritus of History, Frederick I. Olson, for his work on the revision of the first chapter of the fourth edition which provided the basis for my revision of the first chapter of this volume.

Ronald E. Weber
Wilder Crane Professor of Government
Department of Political Science
August, 1996

Part I: The Setting for Wisconsin Politics

CHAPTER I

THE SOCIAL, ECONOMIC AND HISTORICAL CONTEXT
OF WISCONSIN POLITICS

Revised by Ronald E. Weber[*]

Introduction

Once upon a time, state and local governments in the United States were thought of as a lost world for study. The U.S. national government was the object of intense study and a presumption was made that the best public policy solutions were national in scope and uniform in design, administration, and impact. Journalists, some academicians, and public officials attacked U.S. state and local governments and their governmental institutions. The attack was widespread, focusing on such diverse institutions as state and local legislatures, executives, bureaucracies and courts. State and local legislatures were denounced as both unrepresentative and unresponsive. State and local executives were attacked as weak and disorganized, lacking in the formal powers necessary to govern modern states and localities. State and local bureaucracies were criticized as too political and too autonomous and independent. State and local courts were attacked as being poorly organized and too slow in decision-making. Thus, some commentators have concluded that existing state borders should be scrapped and replaced by more rational and meaningful political sub-divisions - - presumably subdivisions which would serve principally as administrative arms of the national government. Focusing on dramatic increases in the scope of national authority as well as on alleged defects in the social, economic and governmental bases of many U.S. states, such critics, especially from the 1930s through the 1960s, foresaw the disappearance of the states as an inevitable development.

Practical difficulties obstructing such a fundamental change in the U.S. federal system as well as philosophical objections have, however, left little chance that these changes would in fact be accomplished. Moreover, state and local governments, once condemned as outdated appendages of U.S. life, have confounded their critics by demonstrating renewed energy during the past several decades. States and localities continue to serve as political laboratories, introducing governmental reforms as innovations later copied by other states and even by the national government. State political leaders and the mayors of major cities continue to play important roles, not only in their home states but in the national political arenas as well. The number of state and local government employees has grown steadily at a more rapid rate than the civilian employment of the national government. Since World War II, state budgets have also increased at a more rapid pace than the domestic national budget, as states have taken on new functions or expanded existing ones, while the national government has been forced to rein in discretionary domestic spending. Without question, the states and local governments retain primary responsibility for those governmental programs which have the most direct and immediate impact on U.S. residents.

This revitalization of the U.S. states and localities has paralleled a marked increase in the quantity and quality of scholarly inquiry directed at U.S. state and local governments. The late V.O. Key, Jr.'s pioneering work on politics in the southern states has been followed by an impressive array of works on other regions of the U.S., individual states and localities. The development of urban politics as a field within political science provides another example of an increased emphasis upon the governmental process below the national level. A direct result of this scholarly activity is that a wide variety of institutional and analytical material is available on state and local governments.

---

[*] Wilder Crane Professor of Government, University of Wisconsin - Milwaukee. This chapter is revised from the introductory chapter of the fourth edition which had been revised by Professor Emeritus of History, University of Wisconsin - Milwaukee, Frederick I. Olson.

Among the states, Wisconsin has made many unique and valuable contributions. Its rich heritage provides many examples of institutional and functional innovations which have given it a national reputation as a leader and innovator. The state's motto, "Forward," has been more than a pious hope or a misleading cliche. Indeed, it has served as a meaningful guide for about a century and a half of statehood. The progressive "idea" has led the way to many a governmental innovation. In state services, Wisconsin pioneered in such areas as the regulation of railroads and utilities, worker's compensation, unemployment compensation, state insurance and other programs which guided subsequent action by other states and the national government. The state government has also initiated many institutional changes designed to improve the state's governmental processes. Thus, Wisconsin created the first non-partisan legislative reference bureau, an agency now found in all fifty states. Wisconsin borrowed experts from the state universities to advise elected and appointed officials, long before the national government began to do so in the New Deal era. Wisconsin led in the adoption of municipal home rule and non-partisan elections for local political units. Wisconsin was also one of the first states to adopt a presidential primary. Long before the U.S. Supreme Court prescribed a strict population standard for representation in both chambers of state legislatures, this was the rule in Wisconsin. And, acting on that principle, the Wisconsin Supreme Court was the first judicial body to redistrict legislative districts on its own initiative. Wisconsin has also played a leading role in efforts to reform welfare programs and innovation in educational policy making.

In some cases, Wisconsin's innovations in the process of governing have not stood the test of time and political reality. For example, Wisconsin was a leader in the move to provide a statutory basis for the organization and operation of political parties. The effort was not successful, however, as demonstrated by the story of the statutory parties in Wisconsin and the corresponding creation and dominance of the voluntary political parties in the state. (See Chapter IV.) Similarly, removal of officeholders through recall election procedures, considered a crucial political weapon when that reform was introduced over 75 years ago, has been seldom used, although it received renewed attention when it was used in 1996 to recall Republican State Senator George Petak from Racine County. That recall election restored the Democratic party to control of the State Senate with a 17-16 margin.

Focus upon such governmental innovations tends to stress Wisconsin's uniqueness in comparison with other states. This alleged unique character of the state's political development can be exaggerated. What began as an innovation in Wisconsin may now be found in many if not all other states. Moreover, Wisconsin's role in some institutional or functional areas has clearly been that of a follower rather than a leader. Wisconsin thus reflects the norm of state and local governmental and political activity, especially in more recent decades.

The remaining portion of this chapter is devoted to a brief discussion of the basic setting in which Wisconsin's state and local governments operate. This includes the interweaving of Wisconsin's geography, history, economics and social demographics. Subsequent chapters are built around four main areas. The first is the constitutional framework for state and local governments. The second is the institutions which Wisconsin citizens use to communicate with governments: political parties and elections as well as interest groups. The third is the institutions and processes that are the heart of the governmental process in Wisconsin. This includes the major branches of the state government, including the state bureaucracy. The fourth is the mixture of functional activities performed by the state, with special emphasis given to the major areas of fiscal, educational, human services and environmental policy-making. The combination of these four areas provides a thorough picture of the political and governmental process in Wisconsin.

Geography, History and Economy of Wisconsin

While the focus of this book is on Wisconsin's government and politics, these factors are profoundly shaped by the physical and human environment in which they operate. The underlying ecology of the state shapes and in turn is shaped by the political instruments which emerge within the state. Thus, it is important to examine the geographic, historic and economic factors which have had considerable impact upon the state's political traditions.

The basic physical features of Wisconsin include its location as a northern, Midwestern, Great Lakes state.

Its 56,314 square miles (35.8 million acres) encompass very fertile farm land, areas that are or were rich in mineral resources, and scenic and recreational attractions. Wisconsin's climate, identified as continental, is characterized by marked weather changes common to the latitude as well as to the state's position in the interior of a large land mass. Agriculture, industry and outdoor recreation are adequately supported by the average annual precipitation of about 39 inches.

The most recent cataclysmic changes in Wisconsin's natural terrain were wrought by the massive glaciers of the Ice Age, estimated to have occurred some 17,000 years ago. The glaciers produced the Great Lakes and contributed to the formation of the more than 8,000 lakes and ponds in Wisconsin. Glacial action had contradictory effects upon the state's terrain. It contributed to the fertility of the state's farmland, but in other areas, the glaciers left in their wake quantities of boulders which made it difficult, if not impossible, to carry out profitable farming.

Before settlers began to clear land for residential and farm purposes in the early nineteenth century, more than 85 percent of Wisconsin was covered by forest. Though virgin forests have largely disappeared because of increased population, lumbering operations and forest fires, fully 45 percent of the land area of the state has either retained its forests or been restored as timberland. The logging industry has lost the flamboyant flavor that marked it during the nineteenth and early twentieth centuries, but lumbering and paper production remain significant enterprises within the state. In addition to the economic value of the timber, Wisconsin's forests provided cover for the wildlife which made the area attractive to Native American tribes and also to French and English trappers. The fur trade was the primary fruit of Jean Nicolet's European discovery of Wisconsin in 1634.

While wildlife resources nourished the first European settlements in Wisconsin, mineral resources were instrumental in the area's first population boom in the 1820s and 1830s. The "lead" rush to deposits in southwestern Wisconsin marked the first major extraction of economically desirable minerals in the state. Zinc, present in the same general area, has also been an important mineral resource. In the far northern portions of Wisconsin, mining of iron ore competed with logging as an important economic activity, although the iron mining industry has suffered a serious decline in recent years. The discovery of significant deposits of sulfide, zinc and copper in norther Wisconsin has rekindled interest in mining operations, but no development has currently occurred.

Although lumbering and mining have at times been of great economic significance in Wisconsin, farming has been the basic extractive economic enterprise. The combination of fertile terrain, sufficient rainfall and an adequate growing season for feed crops convinced many of the state's residents that their livelihood would be in farming. At present, about 79,000 farms in the state include approximately 17.1 million acres.[1] There has been a long-run decline in the number of farms and in the amount of land under cultivation. In 1935 there were 200,000 farms covering 23.5 million acres of land, and in 1955 there were 155,000 farms covering 23.2 million acres. There has been a gradual increase in the average farm size. In 1925 the average was about 113 acres which rose to 150 by 1955. At present, the average acreage is about 217. Even with the increase, Wisconsin farms are much smaller than the national average. Another interesting fact about Wisconsin agriguilture is that the price index of farm commodities shows that Wisconsin farmers received higher average prices for their products than the national average. While Wisconsin farms on the whole are relatively prosperous, agricultural prosperity is not uniform throughout the state. In general, farms in the southern half of the state are more productive and prosperous than those in the northern half.

The "America's Dairyland" slogan on some motor vehicle license plates provides testimony to the value of dairy farming as well as the related production of hay, oats, corn, soybean and other animal feed. Other crops gown in significant quantities in the state include potatoes, peas, beans, cranberries and tobacco. Meat animals, poultry and eggs, mink furs and forest products also contribute significantly to farm income. Befitting their economic importance, farmers collectively and dairy farmers in particular have exerted tremendous impact upon the political

---

[1] Statistics on the number and size of farms is taken from the State of Wisconsin, *Blue Book*, 1995 - 96:601-610.

life of the state, until recently far out of proportion to their actual numbers. Not until 1967 did Wisconsin, the last state in the nation to have this prohibition, remove its nearly 80 year old ban on colored oleomargarine. Even in repealing the ban, the state legislature levied a tax on oleomargarine and prescribed that some of the tax proceeds be earmarked for research in dairy farming.

Another major economic use of the land is the growing resort and tourist industry which is built upon the scenic and recreational advantages of the state. This industry has expanded in recent years because of the increased population, its mobility and the affluence of the residents of Wisconsin and its neighboring states, particularly Illinois. Fishing and boating are the basic summer recreational pursuits. Winter sports of skiing, snowmobiling and hunting produce year-round economic gain for some resort areas. Located primarly in the northern half of the state, the industry has counteracted some aspects of the northern region's overall economic depression brought about by the long-term decline in lumbering and mining.

Wisconsin's economy includes a multitude of enterprises and activities. Population expansion in the southern and eastern parts of the state reflects the growing relative importance of urban-based economic activities. The most important industries are light and heavy manufacturing and food and beverage processing. Processes which require an abundant supply of skilled labor predominate. These include the manufacture of paper, heavy machinery, truck and automobile parts and other steel fabrication. Basic industries, such as steel production, oil refining and smelting, which utilize relatively more unskilled labor, are largely absent from Wisconsin.

In addition to the important place of dairy production in Wisconsin, vegetable and meat packing and the brewing of beer are also important food processing industries. Milwaukee, by far the largest city in the state, is the hub of many of these industries as well as the commercial and financial center of the state. Other industries are concentrated in the southeastern quadrant of the state, especially along the shore of Lake Michigan and in the Fox, Rock and Wisconsin River valleys.

Conjoined with the state's major industries, organized labor has strong representation in Wisconsin. Currently, Wisconsin ranks 16th in terms of the percent of the workforce that belongs to unions among the fifty states. In 1994, union members made up slightly more than 18 percent of Wisconsin's workforce, down from 23.8 in 1983.[2] Because of the high degree of skilled labor required by the state's major industries, former AFL affiliates rather than CIO unions are predominant. Public employee and white collar union membership is growing while factory unions decline under the impact of automation and factory relocations to other states and regions of the U.S.

The People of Wisconsin

The history of Wisconsin's people, similar to the nation as a whole, is largely a story of immigration. Successive waves of migration from Europe and other areas of the nation into Wisconsin have had a profound impact on the state's development. Previously mentioned were the French and English fur traders who began to arrive in what is now Wisconsin in the seventeenth and eighteenth centuries. For nearly 200 years, settlement was limited to a few trading posts and forts, most of them along the Fox and Wisconsin river system which nearly bisects the state from northeast to southwest and links the Great Lakes with the Mississippi River. Native American tribes retained their hunting and farming lands during this era. As settlers moved into the state, first in the southwestern corner to tap the lead mineral resources, these tribes were doomed to extinction, expulsion or reservation existence. The major Native American uprising in 1832, the Black Hawk War, ended with the decisive defeat of the Native Americans and prepared the way for rapid entry by European settlers when federal land was offered for sale.

While the lead mines in southeastern Wisconsin attracted persons from southern and border states, the

---

[2] U.S. Bureau of the Census, 1995:444.

tremendous influx of people between 1840 and 1850, when the population of Wisconsin increased nearly tenfold (see Table I-1), was largely an invasion of Yankees and New Yorkers from the East. Foreign immigration, primarily from the British Isles and northern Europe, was also significant before 1850. The impact of the recently arrived foreigner is reflected in the inclusion in the Wisconsin Constitution of 1848 of the right to vote for certain classes of aliens. Immigration from other parts of the Union and abroad continued throughout the nineteenth century and up to World War I. Its importance is reflected in the fact that Wisconsin maintained emigration offices in the eastern states during much of the period from 1852 to 1887. A typical example of the efforts to attract immigrants was seen in the following advertisement in eastern newspapers: "Fifty years' labor in New England or twenty years' toil in Ohio are not equal in their results to five industrious years in Wisconsin."[3]

Table I-1

WISCONSIN POPULATION, 1840 - 90

Year	Population	% Increase	% Urban
1840	30,945	--	--
1850	305,391	886.9	9.4
1860	775,881	154.1	14.4
1870	1,054,670	35.9	19.6
1880	1,315,497	24.7	24.1
1890	1,693,330	28.7	33.2
1900	2,069,042	22.2	38.2
1910	2,333,860	12.8	43.0
1920	2,632,067	12.8	47.3
1930	2,939,006	11.7	52.9
1940	3,137,587	6.7	53.5
1950	3,434,575	9.5	57.9
1960	3,951,777	15.1	63.8
1970	4,417,933	11.8	65.9
1980	4,705,642	6.5	64.2
1990	4,891,769	4.0	65.7

Source: State of Wisconsin, *Blue Book*, 1993-94:777.

Foreign immigration continued unabated into the early decades of the twentieth century, but the national origins of the immigrants changed. Increasingly, southern and eastern Europe replaced Ireland, Germany and Scandinavia as the principal contributors of Wisconsin's foreign-born population. Italians, Poles, Czechs and Russians, among others, made up the new wave of immigration to the state. They brought new customs, languages and living patterns to merge with the mores of the earlier immigrant groups and the old-stock Yankees.

Although the period since World War I has seen a sharp decline in foreign migration, population movements to Wisconsin from other parts of the nation continued to contribute to the population growth of the state and have shaped its political development. Most notably, Wisconsin, as well as other states in the industrial Midwest, were selected by those fleeing from depressed areas in Appalachia and by African Americans fleeing the lack of opportunity in southern states. The latter movement is reflected in the fact that Wisconsin's African

[3] Engler 1964. Wisconsin was the first state to establish an immigration office (Nesbit, 1973:160).

American population increased over sixfold between 1950 and 1990, from 0.8 percent to 5.0 percent of the total population. The 1990 census counted 379,246 non-whites in Wisconsin, of whom 244,539 were African American, 93,194 Hispanic and 52,782 Asian.[4] The African American population is largely--- located in Milwaukee County (almost 80 percent of all African Americans in the state) and other urban counties of southeastern Wisconsin. Hispanic populations are also concentrated in Milwaukee County (about 48 percent of all Hispanics in the state) but not to the degree of African American population concentration.

Migration within the state has also been significant in recent years. This has had two major components: one, migration first from farm to city and then from city to suburb as a result of increasing mechanization of agriculture and the search for jobs; and, two, migration away from economically depressed areas, principally from northern Wisconsin to areas which offer greater economic opportunity. The prevailing pattern of migration, then, has been from Wisconsin's northern areas to its urban centers in the south and east. Over two-thirds of the state's population is within the triangular area bounded by Beloit-Madison-Green Bay-Milwaukee-Kenosha. The population shifts exert an impact upon representation of the state in Congress as well as within the state legislature. During the past two decades, this pattern of intra-state migration has been somewhat modified as some counties in the far northern parts of the state have experienced significant population increases. A major cause of this shift has been the tendency for retirees to move into permanent residence in northern resort areas. There have also been population increases in the far northwest resulting from a spillover from growth of the Twin Cities in Minnesota. (See Figure I-1.)

While major urban areas of the state continue their overall population growth, their central cities have decreased in population. For example, the city of Milwaukee dropped from about 741,000 persons in 1960 to about 636,000 persons in 1980 and down again to about 628,000 persons in 1990. Milwaukee County also lost population between 1970 and 1980 and between 1980 and 1990, with significant population growth occurring in three of the four counties bordering Milwaukee County. Although less dramatic, the same phenomenon is occurring in Madison, Green Bay, Racine, Kenosha and other large cities in the state. The data on population change in Figure I-1 indicates that 19 counties experienced population decreases between 1980 and 1990 and another 20 counties grew at a slower rate than the statewide growth rate of 3.96 percent. The declining counties are concentrated in the northern and southwestern parts of the state. On the other hand, high growth was concentrated in 18 counties including three to the north and west of Milwaukee County, four around Green Bay, three near Madison and two bordering on Minnesota in the western part of Wisconsin.

Personal income growth in Wisconsin seems to track population changes. Larger and growing counties seem to be the wealthiest counties as measured by per capita personal income. Overall per capita personal income in Wisconsin in 1994 was $21,019, ranking Wisconsin as 21st among the fifty states.[5] The data in Figure I-2 show substantial variation across the Wisconsin counties. The poorest counties are most likely to be rural and declining in population. The most affluent counties are located in the suburbs of Milwaukee County and in the far exurbs of the Twin Cities of Minnesota.

---

[4] State of Wisconsin, *Blue Book*, 1993-94:778.

[5] U.S. Bureau of the Census, 1995:461.

Figure I-1
Total Population Growth in Wisconsin: Percentage Change by County, 1980-1990

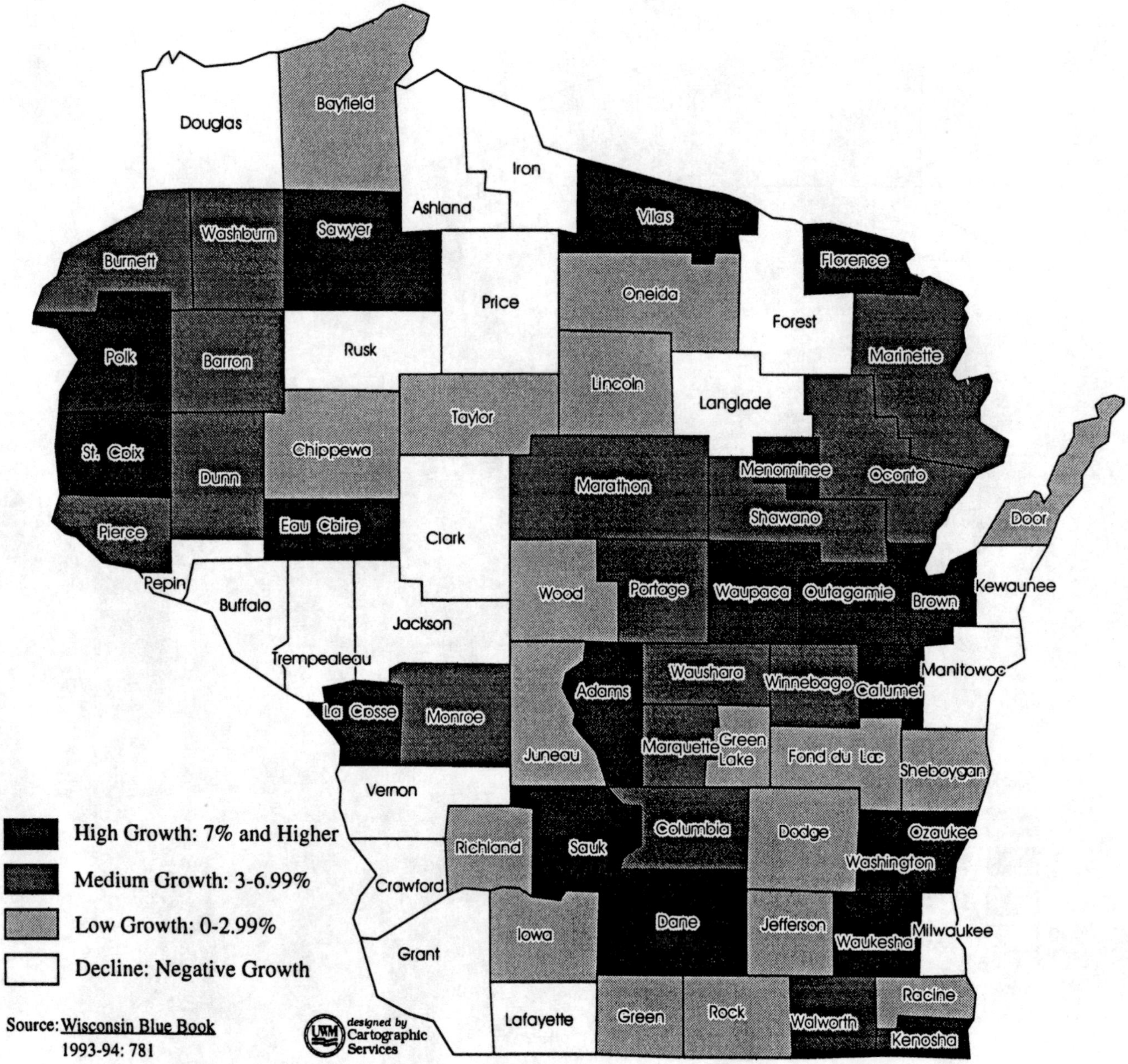

High Growth: 7% and Higher

Medium Growth: 3-6.99%

Low Growth: 0-2.99%

Decline: Negative Growth

Source: Wisconsin Blue Book
1993-94: 781

designed by
Cartographic
Services

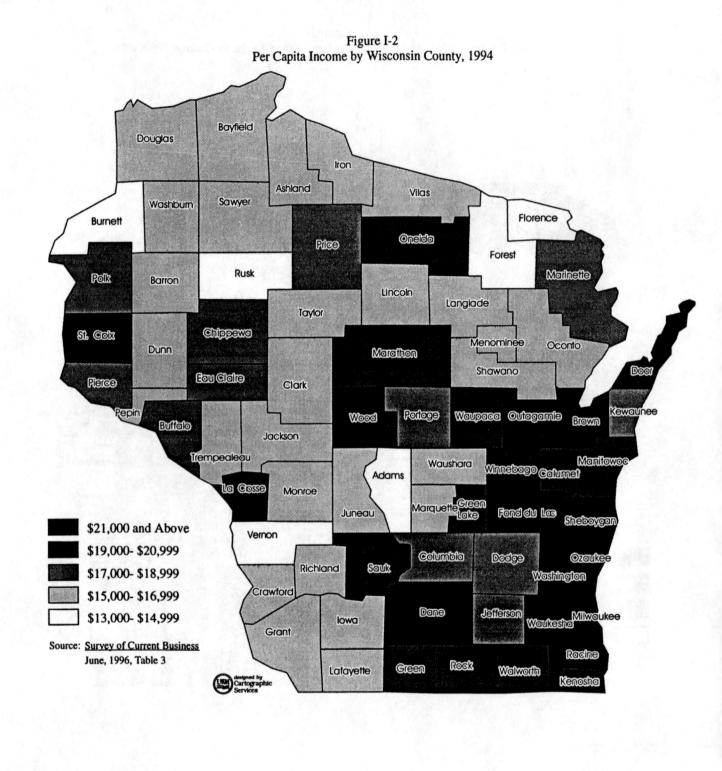

Figure I-2
Per Capita Income by Wisconsin County, 1994

Legend:
- $21,000 and Above
- $19,000- $20,999
- $17,000- $18,999
- $15,000- $16,999
- $13,000- $14,999

Source: Survey of Current Business
June, 1996, Table 3

designed by
Cartographic
Services

Political Development and Political Culture in Wisconsin

Political development in Wisconsin has been inextricably linked to the population changes as well as to the geographic and economic conditions noted above. Originally part of the Northwest Territory, the area was part of the Indiana, Illinois and Michigan Territories successively before the Wisconsin Territory was created in 1836. Twelve years later, Wisconsin was admitted to the Union as the thirtieth state. Reflecting the political preferences and geographical origins of those in the first major settlements in the southwestern portion of the state, Democratic party predominance was apparent from 1848 to 1856. However, the combination of an increase in Yankees, the abolition movement and the Civil War pulled the state firmly into Republican hands. In fact, the national Republican party was founded in Ripon, Wisconsin, in 1854. Republican hegemony rarely was challenged successfully during the remainder of the nineteenth century as immigrants increasingly joined Republican ranks.

The La Follette progressive dynasty, inaugurated in 1901 and pervasive in the state until 1946, marked a new chapter in the basic outline of Wisconsin politics. Progressivism, either as a branch of the Republican party or as a separate party, set a tone for Wisconsin politic which continues to the present. Many of the basic institutions and procedures of state government retain characteristics built into them by "Fighting Bob" La Follette, both a governor and a senator, his sons, one a governor and the other a U.S. senator, and their numerous followers. Since 1946, Progressivism as a distinct and readily identifiable political force has disappeared. Because of the rejuvenation of the Democratic party, Wisconsin has become an intensely competitive two-party state, reflected in the fact that each party has won the major executive offices and controlled the two legislative chambers.

For the last four decades, the state's politics have been more middle of the road than progressive, and there have been few examples of the sorts of structural or substantive innovations that marked the long period of La Follette influence. Democratic candidates for governor have been liberal and labor-oriented, while Republican candidates have been more conservative and business oriented. However, after elections, winners from both parties have gravitated toward a more centrist position. Exceptions to this generalization have been defeated for reelection; e.g., Republican Vernon Thomson in 1958 and Democrats John Reynolds in 1964 and Anthony Earl in 1986.

Recent studies of state political culture by Elazar (1964) and Lieske (1993) confirm the progressive movement's impact upon Wisconsin's political culture. Elazar characterizes the state political culture as moralistic. One of the hallmarks of a moralistic political culture is a belief among the state citizenry in the positive role that government programs should play in a person's life. The role of government is to make things happen and to work toward implementing shared principles. A moralistic political culture is also committed to an open political process, in which political parties compete with each other in an attempt to win sufficient political support to put the party's principles into action through state legislation. Lieske concludes, on the basis of a national study of state political cultures derived from a comprehensive analysis of socio-demographic data at the county level, that Wisconsin is predominantly a Nordic political culture, suggesting settlement by Scandinavians who have kept faith with their native Lutheran church. The second most common political culture pattern in Wisconsin is the Germanic political culture. This designation indicates settlement by German immigrants who have kept faith with either the Roman Catholic or Lutheran churches of their homelands. The Lutheran influences in both groups meant that immigration had brought to Wisconsin a set of peoples whose political values from Europe endorsed a positive government role in society.

Conclusion

This brief view of the basic characteristics of Wisconsin's geography, economy, history, demographics and political development sets the stage for the detailed description and analysis of the fabric of government and politics in Wisconsin that follows. The various authors delineate the legal setting, describe the institutions of interest representation, outline the governmental institutions and discuss the public policies adoped by the state government. The book concludes with a chapter describing the place of Wisconsin among the fifty states of the U.S.

Figure I - 3
Regional Subcultures in Wisconsin

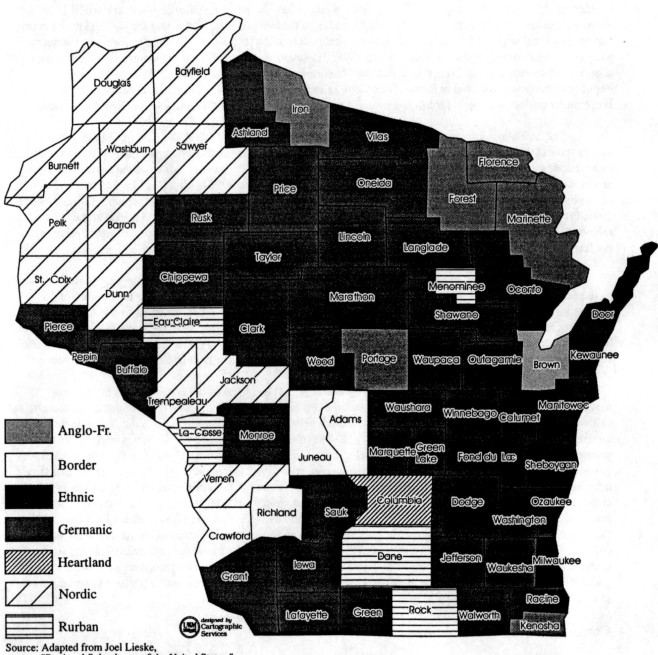

Anglo-Fr.

Border

Ethnic

Germanic

Heartland

Nordic

Rurban

Source: Adapted from Joel Lieske,
"Regional Subcultures of the United States."
The Journal of Politics, Vol. 55 (Nov. 1992): 907.

CHAPTER II

THE CONSTITUTION AND CONSTITUTIONAL CHANGE

By Michael Fine[*]

A constitution is a set of rules about rule making. Its principal purposes are: one, to describe the basic structure and decision-making processes; two, to allocate power among the branches of government; and three, to limit the powers of governments via a bill of rights. Wisconsin's 1948 Constitution, along with more than 100 amendments, has been the state's charter since statehood. This chapter examines the basic features of the constitution, relates them to the political environment at the time of adoption, and explores the ways these features have been altered to meet the changes in that environment.[1]

The 1848 Constitution was Wisconsin's second attempt at constitution making. The first was soundly defeated a year before the state achieved statehood when both Democrats and Whigs considered some of its provisions intolerable (Austin, 1964:107).[2] The second convention convened December 15, 1847. It dropped or modified most of the objectionable features of the first draft, and in March 1848 the second constitution won overwhelming electoral support. Congress promptly passed the act admitting Wisconsin to the Union and President Polk signed it on May 29, 1848. The new constitution took effect that day.

Constitutional law is no more sacred than any other. Its one outstanding characteristic is that it takes precedence when in conflict with other laws of the same level of government. Constitutions are sometimes described as basic law, coming from some sense of natural right. Those who hold this view argue that a constitution should be short and leave day-to-day decision-making to the statutes. While the U.S. Constitution generally follows this rule (despite some lapses such as the two amendments tinkering with the right to sell alcoholic beverages), state constitutions are notoriously long and change frequently, depending on the ease with which they may be amended. Unlike the majority of states which have wholly rewritten their constitutions, Wisconsin has kept the original document from the date of its admission into the Union. Only five states, all in New England, are now operating with older constitutions. This may account for the fact that Wisconsin's constitution has been amended more frequently than most states' present constitutions. Yet at approximately 13,500 words, the length of Wisconsin's constitution is comparatively short; about half of the average length. Other states' constitutions range from the 174,000 words of Alabama's to the 6600 words of Vermont's.[3]

Basic Features

A brief preamble provides a rhetorical introduction to the charter. Apart from mention of gratefulness to Almighty God, the language is virtually identical to phrases of the preamble of the U.S. Constitution. Preambles to constitutions seem compulsory, but are not binding legally. Nevertheless, they may have ideological importance by expressing a basic concept such as the national movement from a confederacy to a union with the statement, "We the People of the United States."

---

[*] Professor of Political Science, University of Wisconsin, Eau Claire.

[1] See Adrian and Fine (1991):Chapter 2, for a general statement regarding the nature of state constitutions.

[2] The Whigs objected to the prohibition against the creation of banks in the state; many Democrats were opposed to clauses providing for the property rights of married women and an exemption from debt provisions for homesteads. There was also a residue of the anti-statehood feelings which defeated proposals for statehood in 1840, 1841, and 1843 referenda. Many people feared taxes would be higher under state government than they would be under territorial status.

[3] Data in this paragraph are taken from The Council of State Governments, *The Book of the States* 1994-95:19.

Constitutions tend to throw in flowery language in preambles and elsewhere which seemingly has no legal purpose. Surely Wisconsin's Article I, Section 22 does not belittle Wisconsin's reputation as the brewery capital of the country when it requires that, "[T]he blessings of a free government can only be maintained by a firm adherence to . . . temperance. . . . "

Declaration of Rights. The legal force of Wisconsin's constitution is most noteworthy for its long Declaration of Rights. Unlike the U.S. Constitution which added a Bill of Rights after passage, the Wisconsin document gives precedence to limiting state power over the individual. Wisconsin's Declaration of Rights is among the longest and most inclusive in the nation. Following a general statement of the equality of all people and their inherent rights to life, liberty, and pursuit of happiness, specific substantive and procedural rights are enumerated. These include most of the provisions of the U.S. Bill of Rights, such as freedom of speech, the right to assemble and petition, and so on. In addition, slavery and involuntary servitude are expressly prohibited, reflecting Wisconsin's status under the Northwest Ordinance of 1787 which prohibited slavery in the Northwest Territory.

A number of economic rights not found in the U.S. Constitution are protected in Wisconsin. Some, which may seem archaic to the modern reader, reflect aspects of economic democracy which gained force during the early decades of the nineteenth century. For example, feudal tenures of land are prohibited. Others, perhaps more pertinent in the modern day, prohibit imprisonment for debt and further decree that the privilege of debtors "to enjoy the necessary comforts of life shall be recognized by wholesome laws, exempting a reasonable amount of property from seizure or sale for the payment of any debt. . . . "

As discussed below, these economic safeguards represented a dominant strain of Jacksonian democracy--an effort to protect agrarian debtor classes against the "predatory gentry." Today they remain in place for the farmer, but also afford protections not found in most states for the urban population (particularly businesses) in bankruptcy proceedings. Wisconsin law provides that,

(1) "[t]he property of no person shall be taken for public use without just compensation therefore," and;
(2) Every person is entitled to a certain remedy in the laws for all injuries, or wrongs which he may receive in his person, property, or character. . . .[4]

These provisions make Wisconsin more liable for torts (personal injury suits) than is the practice in many states where common law exempts the state from such liability. As a result, in this modern period when resort to civil court is widespread and jury judgments are sometimes large, Wisconsin's constitution invites costly lawsuits. On the other hand, many might argue that this liability, which local governments already must bear by common law, should fairly be born by state government also. Lawsuits over property are further encouraged insofar as Wisconsin protects property by extending the right to jury trial in all cases, regardless of the amount in question.

The rights of those accused of crimes are similarly expansive. Protection of those accused of a crime is spelled out in over two pages of specific rights, in far greater detail than and in some areas not protected by the U.S. Bill of Rights. Since the Warren Court decisions of the 1960s, the protections of those accused of crimes have been extended by using the Fourteenth Amendment to apply provisions of the U.S. Bill of Rights to the states. But given that most criminal prosecution and police action takes place at the sub-national level, a state constitution's protection of the rights of the accused may prove to be more important than the national protections. Future court interpretations may limit the application of the national protections to the states. Furthermore, those states which go beyond the national amendments provide greater protection. For example, in Wisconsin it is rare for a police officer to arrest without warrant. This practice is widespread in neighboring Illinois. The distinctions in this regard are not widely known by the average citizen, but can lead a Wisconsinite traveling outside the state to assume that rights exist which, in fact, are particular to Wisconsin's Declaration of Rights. The rights of the accused (too widespread to discuss individually here) and extensive property rights most distinguish Wisconsin's constitution from others.

---

[4] A copy of the Wisconsin Constitution can most easily be found in the State of Wisconsin, *Blue Book*, published biennially by the Wisconsin Legislative Reference Bureau.

Unlike the U.S. Bill of Rights, Wisconsin's Declaration of Rights has been amended. The amendments have been infrequent and have rarely extended state power over the individual. Instead, most further limit state powers over the individual. But there are exceptions. As recently as 1982, major revision was made in the rights of the accused in regard to bail, making it far easier for the state to refuse bail to those accused of crimes and presumed dangerous.

As mentioned below in the section on constitutional change in the 1990s, Wisconsin has added a new twist on rights by adding a lengthy provision to the rights of victims of crimes. This has been increasingly done by statute in most states since about 1980, but the 1990s has seen many states bringing this provision into the constitution. Wisconsin is one of ten states to add the provision between 1989 and 1993.

Suffrage. Following a brief article describing the boundaries of the state, Article III outlines the rights of suffrage as well as restrictions on its exercise. The basic formula granted the franchise to white males, but by a referendum vote in 1849 suffrage was extended to black males. Resident aliens who declared their intention of becoming citizens were also able to vote. Inclusion of aliens within the electorate attested to the growing numbers and political strength of the foreign-born in the state in 1882 when that provision was passed. It was later terminated in a 1908 amendment. National amendments further extended the right to vote to women in 1920 and 18-20 year olds in 1971. The present language, dating from 1934, allows for voting by citizens of the United States, persons of Indian blood who at any time were declared citizens of the United States, and others defined by the legislature and approved by the people in a referendum.

Institutional Framework of Government. Four succeeding articles outline the institutional framework of state government. The composition, powers and procedures of the legislative, executive, and judicial branches are prescribed. These constitutional provisions demarcate the basic ground rules for the major instruments of state governments. Wisconsin follows a practice contrary to the U.S. Constitution, but common to most states, of distinguishing an administrative branch of government with powers partially separate from those of the executive branch. The offices of secretary of state, treasurer, attorney general, and superintendent of public instruction are constitutionally created, and thus are independent from and to some extent in competition with the governor for the scarce resources of state government. Succeeding articles are devoted in turn to three important areas of state activity: finance, eminent domain, and education. Another refers to the creation of municipalities and other corporations. The final three articles cover the procedures for amending the constitution, a series of miscellaneous provisions, and the schedule by which the new constitution was to take effect.

Local Government. Local government is created by constitutional provision in Wisconsin. Wisconsin not only follows the principle of home rule, but gives it constitutional rather than statutory authority. Article XI, Section 3(1) states,

> Cities and villages organized pursuant to state law may determine their local affairs and government, subject only to this constitution and to such enactments of the legislature of statewide concern as with uniformity shall affect every city or every village. The method of such determination shall be prescribed by the legislature.

Dillon's Rule, developed in the nineteenth century, holds that local governments derive all of their legal powers from the state, and, therefore, have no powers that are not delegated by the state. In court, home rule reduces the impact of Dillon's Rule through the principle that holds that the local governments can exercise all of those powers not denied by the state (Adrian and Fine, 1990: Chapter 3). This may seem to negate the general principle of state sovereignty over the locality, but in practice it does not. Home rule is not an inherent power of local government, it is granted by the state. In Wisconsin, it can be withdrawn through constitutional amendment. Furthermore in practice, localities are frequently limited by the state.

Limits on home rule have come from the constitution itself, statute, court rulings, and federal action. Some of the powers denied localities are specified in the constitution; perhaps most important are limits on the powers to raise and borrow money. Others limits are found in statute or by those things implied to have "statewide concern."

For example, in 1989 the Wisconsin Supreme Court ruled that the City of Eau Claire could not create a "public safety officer" by combining certain duties of police officers and fire fighters. The court ruled that the personnel qualifications of each were separately a matter of statewide concern (*Local Union No 487 et al. v City of Eau Claire*, 1989; Fine, 1989).

Localities are further limited by the conditions attached to grants issued by state and national governments. Thus, for example, a local government may choose to build a bridge, but a city will not be fully able to sell bonds because state law limits borrowing power. And should the city seek national or state help in the financing, even final approval of the placement of the bridge may be out of the city's control.

The Amendment Process. Wisconsin uses two of the four formal methods of constitutional change found across the nation. It allows for constitutional change by referendum or convention, but not by initiative or commission. Informally, constitutions may be amended through the practice of government, the action of courts, and by the changes implied by national law.

Changing the constitution by referendum has been used for the adoption of all formal amendments to date. It is a three-step process:

(1) the amendment must be initiated in either house of the legislature, and pass both houses during a given session;

(2) the legislature chosen at the next general election after first passage must again pass the amendment through both chambers in a single legislative session;

(3) After second passage by the legislature, the amendment must be submitted to the people in an election designated by the legislature, and pass by a majority of those voting on the amendment.

Many amendments are written such that fourth and perhaps fifth steps are necessary: enabling legislation from the legislature and court interpretation. For example, in April 1987, an amendment was passed permitting a state lottery and earmarking profits from such a lottery to property tax relief. But such a lottery did not go into effect upon the vote. The state legislature had to decide a variety of questions -- who would run the lottery (a Lottery Board was established), how would the money be earmarked, which property owners would receive the relief, which services provided by property taxes might be funded from the lottery, etc. Even after the lottery was in effect, some of these questions remained to be resolved. And once these questions were answered, the courts may have to decide a number of questions about whether the provisions of the enabling legislation meet the provisions of the constitutional amendment. This discretion to interpret the lottery amendment prompted a second amendment approved in April 1993 that clarified that the state could not use prohibited forms of gambling as part of the lottery. Of course, this amendment will now also require interpretation.

The second method for constitutional revision is by a convention called for that purpose. The legislature begins the process by calling for the convention via majority vote. The question of whether or not to call the convention is then submitted to the voters. If a majority of those voting on the question approve the call of a convention, the legislature at the next session is to provide for it. The resulting convention presumably could then amend the constitution in whole or in part. The present constitution does not provide for the ratification of the new constitution written at the convention; legally the convention could forego a vote of the people as was the case for the U.S. Constitution and as is presently the case for constitutional amendments in Delaware (*The Book of the States*, 1994: 21). But the practice of other states suggests that if a convention was held, a vote of the people to ratify the new document would be necessitated by the language of the new document. Presumably a majority vote of the voters would be needed, given Wisconsin's use of this mechanism for referenda, but conceivably a higher percentage of the vote as defined by the new document itself could be required.

The convention has not been used, although measures have been introduced in the legislature to begin the process. None, however, has ever attained the necessary approval of both houses. Conventions are seen as potentially dangerous because once called, the process is only limited by the U.S. Constitution. In states such as Wisconsin, where the legislature is part of the process of calling a convention, legislators are quite reluctant, realizing that their power might be significantly curtailed by a convention. Usually a convention will be called only when other change is difficult and great demographic or ideological change takes place. As will be discussed later in the chapter, even in the early Progressive Era when constitutional change of greatest importance occurred, referenda rather than convention sufficed.

Constitutional change in Wisconsin is not rigorous in terms of the majorities required for ratification, but it has been time-consuming. When using the referendum, under normal circumstances it could be nearly three years from the time of initial legislative approval of an amendment until final ratification by the voters. An attempt was made in 1914 to change the process to provide for a referendum following approval in one legislative session by three-fifths vote in both houses. The amendment necessary to effect this change was defeated in a referendum vote by greater than a 2-1 margin. Also defeated was an amendment placed on the ballot in 1964 which would have allowed reasonably related items to be included in a single constitutional amendment. This change was deemed necessary because of a Wisconsin Supreme Court decision which ruled an amendment invalid which combined two subjects [*State ex rel. Thomson vs. Zimmerman*, 264 Wis. 644, (1953)].

Thus, Wisconsin has remained somewhat in the middle of the spectrum of states in terms of the ease or difficulty of constitutional change. Eighteen states permit amendment by the initiative process that allows amendments to be placed before the voters through a petition process that bypasses a vote of the state legislature. By less than a 2-1 margin, Wisconsin voters rejected a proposal for an initiative and referendum process in 1914. Where this is possible, such as California, constitutional change is far easier. Conversely, some states make change more difficult. For example in Minnesota, the vote of the people must be by a majority of the people voting in the election, not simply on the amendment. As a result, amendments approved by the voters, but sufficiently obscure to produce less interest and therefore fewer votes than a vote for governor or president, have not passed. Twelve states in addition to Wisconsin require two legislative votes and another four require two legislative votes or one extraordinary majority vote (three-fifths or two-thirds) of the legislature to propose constitutional amendments. Wisconsin, unlike the norm, has not had a constitutional convention after the original document was passed. This is made particularly easy in fourteen states where the electorate is required to vote on whether to have a convention periodically (ranging from every nine years in Hawaii to every 20 years in eight of the fourteen states).

Amendments to the Wisconsin Constitution delete old and add new material from the appropriate sections. They do not append them to the end as is done in the U.S. Constitution and in many state constitutions. This means that the Wisconsin document remains well organized with new language incorporated into the text.

Political and Ideological Underpinnings of the Original Constitution

Meaningful and viable constitutions do not burst forth devoid of an environmental context. Wisconsin's constitution clearly illustrated many political norms and precepts operative at the time it was written. First, it is clear that there was little controversy about many of the most basic characteristics of what a constitution should include. General agreement was present on such fundamental matters as the need for a bill of rights, and what it should contain, the concept of separation of powers with accompanying checks among the major units of the state government, and the value of popular control over the governmental machinery created by the constitution. There were, however, disagreements between the major parties of the time as to how the general principles were to be implemented on specific issues. Understanding the ferment which made up Wisconsin's political character at the time of statehood is essential to a full grasp of the original constitution. Similarly, subsequent political ferment contributed to several patterns of change made in the constitution since 1848.

The most pervasive influence in drafting the constitution came from the body of ideas that made up the dominant political motif of American politics in the first half of the nineteenth century: Jacksonian democracy. This is not surprising in light of the fact that Democrats held an overwhelming majority of the delegates to the constitutional convention. It has already been noted that protection of debtors in the Declaration of Rights was one component of the democratic thrust of the day. In addition, the principles as well as some of the major battles of the

Jacksonian Era exerted an impact upon nearly every article of the constitution.

Universal white male suffrage, based upon the assumption of equality of white men, was one of the Jacksonian norms, and it was the basic standard of suffrage in the constitution. The emphasis upon simple majority rule is seen in the amending process and also in the requirement that the districts for both houses of the legislature be apportioned on the basis of population, rather than area or other political concerns commonly used in other states before the one-person, one-vote rulings of the 1960's. As will be discussed in later chapters, in practice gerrymandering existed in Wisconsin also, but a more restrained gerrymandering emphasizing the belief in the equality of people.[5]

Linked with majority rule and equality was the Jacksonian concept of rotation of office, an idea designed to forestall the development of an aristocratic caste of public servants. If men are equal, then they are equally equipped to hold public office. Moreover if majority rule is supreme, the majority voice should have the opportunity to be expressed at frequent intervals. These tenets surfaced in several provision of the Wisconsin Constitution. Elective status was decreed for many public officers--not only for the governor and legislators, but other for administrators and judges as well. The county sheriff, at the time the most powerful local officer, was expressly prohibited from seeking reelection. Terms of office were short to enable the people to render frequent judgment on their elected representatives and officials. Members of the state assembly served one-year terms, while two-year terms were prescribed for state senators and all executive and administrative positions. The legislature met annually, and the constitution specified that "the doors of each house shall be kept open except when the public welfare shall require secrecy." Clearly the right of the people to know what their representatives were doing commanded a premium.

Many of these principles resisted amendment and remain in practice. For example, Wisconsin today has one of the strictest open meeting laws in the country. Other provisions would have to be broadened as additional parts of the population gained social acceptability. Constitutional equality for some men and all women would take many years. For example, not until November 1982 was the constitution amended to provide some gender neutral language. A second, more-sweeping version of the same amendment was rejected by the voters in April 1995.

While extolling popular control of government, the norms of Jacksonian democracy took root in an era when popular majorities distrusted the entry of governments above the towns into American economic and social life. When governments did enter these realms, they often seemed to do so to the advantage of the well-to-do. In part, differing views of the nature and degree of government in economic affairs contributed to the political battles of the Jacksonian Era. Jackson's attack on the Second Bank of the United States and his opposition to Henry Clay's "American System" of internal improvements is a dramatic illustration of these battles on the national level. Victory in these immediate battles, however, did not result in the victors writing their beliefs into the U.S. Constitution.

The situation differed in Wisconsin in that the substantive targets of Jacksonian ire were singled out for specific prohibition within the state's constitution. In effect, the state's founders were not willing to allow subsequent governors and legislators -- within the confines of the constitution -- to do battle again on certain substantive issues. Thus the constitution prescribed that "the state shall never contract any debt for works of internal improvement, or be a party in carrying on such works." Moreover, the aggregate of any state debts was not to

---

[5] The strict population rule is modified by the requirements that the districts shall be "bounded by county, precinct, town or ward line, to consist of contiguous territory and be in as compact form as possible." Art. IV, Sec 4. Previous to the U.S. Supreme Court's one-person, one-vote rulings of the mid-1960s, this provision of the Wisconsin Constitution often created great departures from one-person, one-vote. In each census subsequent to 1970, this provision of the Wisconsin Constitution has been violated to follow the U.S. Supreme Court rulings. These considerations nevertheless do enter into the political process of reapportionment and were used as grounds to veto one version of the 1980 reapportionment by Governor Dreyfus.

exceed $100,000.[6] After losing in their first effort to prohibit altogether the creation of banks, the Democrats compromised by agreeing to a provision that required a referendum vote on any banking law. Subsequent efforts to ease these limitations required constitutional amendment or, in the case of the debt limit, subterfuge.[7]

The basic governmental organization outlined in the Wisconsin Constitution is consistent with the prevailing pattern of American constitutions. Separate spheres of power with checks and balances between the spheres are expressly provided. As noted earlier, Wisconsin's charter deviates from the U.S. Constitution by adding an administrative sphere of state and county administrators apart from the executive branch. But despite the division between executive and administrative powers, the office of governor is more closely related to the national presidential model than the office of governor established in the earliest constitutions of other states. While the latter were often merely ceremonial heads of state, the Wisconsin governor, from the outset, was granted the set of powers typically accompanying a chief executive, including the veto and other powers which brought him or her into the legislative process, powers of executive clemency, designation as commander-in-chief of the state's military forces, and so on. Furthermore, in the modern world, the informal powers of persuasion, fund raising abilities, and charisma on the television may account for more power than the formal powers found in law. Wisconsin also follows the common practice found in the states in the twentieth century of using an executive budget which gives the governor extraordinary powers over the legislature, despite the Wisconsin practice of using a joint finance committee to streamline the passage of budget bills through the legislature.

Similar to the U.S. Constitution and most state constitutions, the Wisconsin document contains no mention of political parties, though by 1848 the party system was well entrenched in American politics. In part this omission is a result of the voluntary and private character of political parties following the custom of the national document, but it is presumably also the case that the founders did not want mention in the constitution of political organizations customarily held in low repute in Wisconsin. Thus the omission was partly one of custom, partly one of ideology, and partly a sign of the times.

Other political groups or ideologies had an impact on the formation of the 1848 Constitution. Inclusion of certain aliens as qualified electors was previously mentioned as an example of the political impact of the foreign-born population. This impact was also reflected in the Declaration of Rights, where it is decreed that no distinction shall be made between resident aliens and citizens with respect to the "possession, enjoyment, or descent of property."

Constitutional Development Since 1848

At the time of this writing, 146 amendments to the Wisconsin Constitution have been ratified since 1848. In addition, 48 proposed amendments were submitted to the electorate but were defeated in referenda. Countless others have been introduced at legislative sessions but failed to win requisite legislative approval. The fate of amendments submitted to the people for ratification during six periods of state history is presented in Table II-1.

It is significant that over one-half of the amendments have been added since 1960. There were just 63 amendments approved from 1848 through 1960; since then there have been 70. Roughly, three of every four of the proposals placed on the ballot have been approved. However, this ratio is somewhat misleading as a guide to the chances of success of proposed amendments. Discounting a few areas of defeat, the passage rate has been higher until the 1990s. Included within the defeated amendments are ten which dealt with the salaries of elected officials. The original constitution specified the salaries of state officers. Therefore, a constitutional amendment was required

---

[6] Art. VIII, Sec 6, 10; Art. XI, Sec 5. The restriction on state debt was largely eliminated by an amendment ratified in 1969.

[7] The strict constitutional limitations on state debts proved troublesome in the mid-twentieth century when the need for state facilities increased. To get around the debt limitations of the constitution, the legislature authorized the creation of so-called "dummy corporations" which borrowed money for state facilities, such as university dormitories, with the full backing of the state. In 1969 the Constitution was amended to lift the strict limitations on state debts.

whenever any salaries were to be increased, and rejection of proposed salary increases was virtually an automatic response by the electorate. Through subsequent amendments, salaries were to be set by statute rather than by constitutional provision. More recently it took three tries, finally successful in 1967, to exempt judges from the constitutional dictum that a public official's salary could not be increased during his or her term. (Another

---

Table II-1

ADOPTION AND REJECTION OF CONSTITUTIONAL AMENDMENTS
BY THE ELECTORATE, 1848 - 95

	Adopted	%	Rejected	%	Total
1848-1870[a]	4	50	4	50	8
1871-1900	13	81	4	19	16
1901-1930	24[b]	59	17	41	41
1931-1960	22[b]	79	6	21	28
1961-1990	79	86	13	14	92
1991-1995	4	44	5	56	9
Totals	146	75	48	25	194

[a] Denotes the date of a vote by the electorate. Amendments can be put before the electorate at either the November or April election following second passage as designated by the legislature.

[b] Including one declared invalid by the Wisconsin Supreme Court.

Source: Compiled from the State of Wisconsin, *Blue Book*, 1995-96:238-242.

---

amendment was rejected in 1995 which pertained to judges' eligibility to serve in nonjudicial office.) Four other defeated amendments were efforts to remove the restriction on the tenure of sheriffs. In 1929 an amendment passed allowing sheriffs to serve a second successive term but no more than two terms in succession. The limitation was removed altogether in 1967.

Another indication of the fate of constitutional amendments is the fact that most of those defeated in referenda were subsequently ratified. In addition to the salary provisions and the term of office of sheriffs, these included such structural changes as timing of legislative sessions, increasing the term of office of legislators, increasing the size of the supreme court, granting home rule to municipalities, and substantive changes relating to restrictions on municipal indebtedness, authorization of state appropriations for forestry, and state taxation of federal lands.

At least four other proposed amendments met defeat when they appeared on the ballot along with particularly unpopular statewide referenda which were not amendments. Wisconsin law permits referenda statewide for three reasons other than constitutional amendment:

(1) to ratify a law extending the right of suffrage, a constitutional requirement;

(2) to make the effectiveness of a law contingent on ratification; and

(3) to seek the opinion of the electorate through an advisory referendum (State of Wisconsin, *Blue Book*, 1993-94: 246).

About two-thirds of 60 proposals have passed, but some of them have been rejected by wide margins and many are put forth in negative language such that a yes vote is voting against something. Thus, in November 1948, a proposed constitutional amendment dealing with the exercise of eminent domain by municipalities was defeated. Appearing with it on the referendum ballot was an advisory referendum asking the voter's opinion on enacting a three percent retail sales tax in order to provide a veteran's bonus. The advisory referendum was defeated by nearly four to one. Clearly, the negative reaction to a proposed new tax contributed to the defeat of the constitutional amendment. Similarly, at the April 1964 election three relatively innocuous amendments were defeated along with the intensely unpopular "Project 66" advisory referendum. The latter effort to speed highway construction began with the phrase: "Do you favor a 1 cent per gallon increase of the tax on gasoline and other motor fuels? . . . " Voters responded negatively to an increase in taxes, and it is believed that reaction contributed to the defeat of the three constitutional referenda.

Another result which exaggerates the record of unsuccessful constitutional amendments was the defeat of all ten amendments presented to the voters in 1914. Progressive legislatures approved a series of sweeping constitutional changes including the rights of petition, initiative and referendum, recall, and a modification of the amendment process, as well as constitutional authorization of state insurance and municipal home rule. Also included was a salary increase for legislators. Reaction against progressivism was rampant in 1914. A conservative Republican won the party's gubernatorial nomination and the election. The amendments were all rejected, although two were later adopted. The inclusion of these ten amendments, the most ever on the ballot at a single election, distorts the record of voter participation in the amending process.

Thus, counting those declared invalid, the hardy perennials on salary matters and the terms of sheriffs, those rejected mainly because they were voted upon in conjunction with particularly unpopular referenda, those defeated *en masse* in 1914, and those which were ultimately ratified, the record of voter participation on constitution referenda shows overwhelming electoral support for proposals submitted for ratification by the legislature.

Patterns of Constitutional Change

1848-1870: Minor Modifications. From 1848 to 1870 there were relatively few constitutional amendments. Only eight appeared on the ballot during the first twenty-two years of statehood, and four of these were attempted salary changes. Three others, the first amendments presented to the electorate, would have adopted biennial legislative sessions and increased legislative terms. These interrelated amendments proposed in 1854 were defeated, and 27 years elapsed before these changes were adopted, only to be modified again a number of times in the twentieth century. The only other amendment, approved in 1870, removed the requirement of a grand jury indictment in criminal cases.

1871-1900: Constitutional Reform in the Machine Era. The second era of constitutional development, 1871-1900, showed a marked increase in the number of amendments. Sixteen were submitted for ratification; thirteen were approved. The predominant tone of these changes was a reflection of increasing distrust of governing institutions in the state, especially of the legislature and the state's municipalities. Freewheeling political bosses and lobbyists were at the height of their power, and their efforts often ranged from outright bribing of legislators to more subtle influence peddling. State legislators attempted to use their political power at the behest of special interests.

Some of the amendments to control the machine were passed by those same corrupt politicians in an effort to show their honesty. Others were passed during the cycles when reformers came into temporary majority. Realizing the temporary nature of rule, they pushed through constitutional change so that when the popular machines came back, they would have less legislative power. The first amendment approved during this period enumerated nine areas in which the legislature was prohibited from enacting special or private laws. Included were prohibitions against special laws for local highways, for locating any county seat, for granting corporate powers or privileges, for assessing or collecting taxes, and so on. Given the economic impact of the subjects covered, these restrictions were obviously designed to forestall legislative use of devices to grant favors to friends or to harass political enemies. Later in the period the legislature was similarly prohibited from using special laws to incorporate municipalities or change their charters (Art. IV, Sec. 31).

Two amendments designed to reduce corruption in local government were also adopted. Most critically, an amendment passed in 1877 imposed a specific debt limit on local units. The maximum debt for any county, city, town, village, school district, or other municipal corporation was set at five percent of the unit's annual tax assessment. Prior to the ratification of this amendment, the legislature had discretionary authority to control municipal debt policy. The limitation removed legislative determination of municipal debt and specifically bound municipalities to a maximum indebtedness written into the constitution. The brief amendment, designed to inhibit reckless debt policies, subsequently required a series of amendments modifying the five percent limitation. The section is now the longest in the constitution, and its technical specifications of exceptions to the basic percentage limitation make it read more like a statute than a constitutional provision.[8] But its importance cannot be overstated. It is the method whereby the state limits home rule of municipalities and demonstrates state sovereignty over localities.

Fears of corrupt practices in elections held under municipal auspices were also translated into a constitutional amendment. In 1882 voters ratified an amendment which allowed the legislature to set a minimum length of residence for voter registration. The law was deemed necessary for rapidly growing cities where ballot-box stuffing and other fraudulent election practices were assumed to occur.

Other significant constitutional amendments passed during the last three decades of the nineteenth century adopted biennial legislative sessions (1881), increased the terms of members of the assembly and senate (1881), allowed the governor to fill vacancies in county elective offices (1882), increased the Wisconsin Supreme Court from three to five members (1889), and increased the number of circuit judges in populous counties (1897).

1901-1930 Progressive Era Reforms. The election of the senior Robert M. La Follette as Governor in 1900 ushered in the progressive era in Wisconsin politics. The pattern of amendments proposed and adopted between 1901 and 1930 reflects the dominant strains of Wisconsin progressivism. First, it opposed political party bosses and corrupt pressure group activities -- a carryover in constitutional amendment from the previous period. An example is the amendment prohibiting special favors granted by transportation enterprises to public officials. Use of passes, franks and other privileges especially by railroads had incurred the wrath of La Follette and his followers, and they had used the issue effectively in political campaigns. In addition, the state superintendent of public instruction was given a four-year term and placed on a nonpartisan ballot through an amendment ratified in 1902.

Hand in hand with their antipathy toward the smoke-filled rooms of machine politicians was the progressive advocacy of direct democracy. Efforts to give the public greater control of the mechanisms and processes of government were frequently reflected in proposed constitutional amendments. Previously mentioned was the spate of amendments which were submitted to the people in 1914 and ingloriously defeated. They included the initiative and referendum, the petition, the recall of public officers (subsequently adopted in 1926), and a modification in the amending process to bring questions more readily to the public for decision. Municipal home rule, another effort to give the citizenry increased control over its government, was also included in the progressive kit. After an unsuccessful effort in 1914, a home rule amendment was ratified in 1924. Finally it should be noted that the mechanism of greatest impact in this regard, the direct primary, was passed by statute in 1903, not by constitutional amendment.

One amendment, contradictory to the basic progressive impulse of enhanced popular participation in and control over government, was ratified in 1908 to allow only full citizens the suffrage. As previously noted, the original constitution enabled certain aliens to vote.

The third characteristic of progressivism was its emphasis upon the utilization of state resources for the benefit of its citizens. To open the door for the state's entry into many service areas, an amendment authorizing a state income tax was written into the constitution in 1908. To the present time, Wisconsin has relied more heavily

---

[8] Eight amendments have been tacked onto the original limitation. Four others were submitted to the electorate and defeated. Art. XI, Sec. 3.

on the income tax than any other state. Further, Wisconsin's income tax is more progressive than income taxes in most other states. Another mechanism to use greater resources in the public sector was demonstrated when twice during the period, the restrictions on municipal debt policies were successfully modified. Municipalities along with the state also were granted authority to acquire land for certain specified purposes including streets and highways, parks, playgrounds, and sites for public buildings under terms of an amendment adopted in 1912.

The inauguration or expansion of state services in a number of areas ran counter to prohibitions on state action that was found in the original constitution. The requirement that all banking laws must be approved in a referendum was an early target. The referendum requirement was repealed in 1902 along with the approval of a section which specifically authorized the legislature to enact a general banking law by a two-thirds vote of the entire membership in each house (Art. XI, Sec. 4). (The extraordinary majority requirement was removed by a 1981 amendment.) The ban on internal improvements was another obstacle, and in 1908 the first of a series of modifications was made in the prohibition against state involvement in such enterprises. Approved was an amendment allowing the state to appropriate funds for highways. In 1910 authorizations of state participation in programs of water power and forests received voter approval only to be ruled invalid by the Wisconsin Supreme Court.[9] Appropriations for forestry were approved by an amendment ratified in 1924. In 1992 borrowing and spending for railroads would be added (Art VIII, Secs. 7 and 10).

In two related areas progressives attempted to win voter approval of favored parts of their program. Among the ill-fated 1914 amendments were ones that would have authorized the state to operate a state annuity insurance program and state insurance generally. Both of these had and still have a statutory base, but there was a desire to give them the greater permanency of a constitutional provision.

A collection of miscellaneous amendments was also submitted to the people between 1901 and 1930. Eight salary measures, most of which met defeat, appeared on referendum ballots. The sheriff's issue made its appearance, and twice it was referred to the public; the second time (1929) sheriffs were given the right to seek a second successive term. In 1903 the Wisconsin Supreme Court was increased to its present size of seven justices. Two matters related to gubernatorial veto powers received the sanction of the voters during this period. The first, adopted in 1908, specified a six-day limit on the gubernatorial veto; the second granted the governor the partial veto over appropriations in 1929, subsequently modified in 1990. Finally, a 1922 amendment modified the trial by jury section of the Declaration of Rights with the provision that in civil cases a valid verdict could be based on five-sixths of the members of the jury rather than unanimous vote.

1931-1960: Expanding State Government's Role. In the period 1931-1960, tinkering with the basic institutional foundations of government was largely absent. Apart from a rather tardy women's suffrage amendment approved in 1934, and, a more significant attempt in 1953 to introduce an area factor into the apportionment of legislative districts, there were only modest attempts to change the basic fabric of state government. The reapportionment issue, which specified that the senate be apportioned on an area basis, was declared invalid by the Wisconsin Supreme Court.[10] A less significant apportionment question was one rejected by the voters in 1963. It would have allowed the legislature to wait until its second session following a census to reapportion legislative districts. The U.S. Supreme Court's actions on apportionment in the mid-1960s would have overruled these amendments had they prevailed. And following the 1980 round of reapportionment, a series of state and federal court opinions upheld the right to apportion whenever the legislature sees fit, as long as this is done at least once a decade in the first legislative session after the census.

---

[9] *State ex rel. Owens vs. Donald*, 160 Wis. 21, 151 NW 331 (1915). The court declared the amendment invalid on the grounds that the legislature did not follow explicitly the rules governing passage of proposed constitutional amendments.

[10] *State ex rel. Thompson vs. Zimmerman*, 264 Wis. 644 (1953). The court contended that the amendment included changes which should have been submitted separately to the electorate for ratification. The court also objected to the language used to identify the amendment on the ballot.

While basic institutional changes were infrequent, the trend of authorizing state government and its subdivisions to engage in new program areas continued between 1931 and 1960. Three more successful assaults were made on the internal improvements prohibition -- a state aeronautical program (1945), veterans' housing (1949), and port development (1960). An amendment allowing for the improvement of transportation facilities generally was defeated in 1976. One observer noted that the internal improvement section ought to be amended to read,

> "The state shall never be a party in carrying on works of internal improvement. Except that the state may be a party in carrying on such works" (*Milwaukee Journal*, April 2, 1962).

Authorization of state participation in providing public transportation for school children to any school in the state marked another effort to expand the scope of state activities when a provision passed in 1967 to allow the legislature to provide for such busing.

1961-1990: An Era of Major Constitutional Change. Between 1961 and 1990 there were numerous changes in the basic pattern of state government. A series of amendments approved in 1967 granted a four-year term for state officers, provided for joint election of the governor and lieutenant governor, and removed the limitation on the number of consecutive terms a sheriff may serve. In 1968 the electorate ratified an amendment which permits the legislature to meet annually, and a year later the stringent restrictions on state debt were lifted. In 1977 a series of amendments authorizing the reorganization of the judicial system was approved, and four amendments pertaining to the office of lieutenant governor were approved in 1979.

The structure and operating policies of local units were also considerably changed in these three decades. Constitutional status was given to the Milwaukee County executive office (1961), and authorization was made to allow other counties to have a similar office (1969). The offices of coroner and surveyor in Milwaukee County were abolished (1965), and other counties were authorized to abolish the office of coroner (1972). Also in 1972, the requirement that all counties must have the same form of government was modified. A similar effort to remove the uniformity clause for towns was rejected by the voters in 1978. An amendment pertaining to sheriffs arose again in 1982 when counties were made responsible for the acts of sheriffs.

There have been six modifications made in the state's longstanding ban on gambling. The first, approved in 1973, legalized bingo games sponsored by certain charitable and fraternal organizations. In 1977 raffles conducted by such organizations were also legalized. In 1987 the voters allowed the legislature to provide a statewide lottery, with profits going to property tax relief. A second amendment in 1987 allowed for parimutuel betting at Wisconsin tracks. But in the 1990s, there have been mixed signals on gambling. In 1993, the voters approved language to limit the gambling to "bingo, raffles, parimutuel on-track betting and the current state-run lottery," to "assure that the state will not conduct prohibited forms of gambling as part of the state-run lottery." At the same April 1993 election, five non-binding resolutions were also put to the voters on gambling. By a relatively close vote, the voters favored continuing parimutuel on-track betting and, by a wider margin, they favored continuing the lottery. But more than 60 percent approved a resolution calling for a constitutional amendment limiting gambling. And by similar margins, the voters disapproved of extending gambling to casinos on excursion vessels on the Mississippi River, Lake Michigan, and Lake Superior, and through video machines. While these latter resolutions may have reflected opinion on the already-thriving casinos on Indian land, the pattern against widening gambling again was shown in 1995, when an attempt to finance a new stadium in Milwaukee failed when the voters soundly rejected a sports lottery that would dedicate funds to "athletic facilities." Again an ideological vote may have been involved, given the baseball strike at the time of the vote. But for whatever reasons, the voters seem satisfied with the limited lottery and track provisions, but opposed to any greater level of gambling activity.

The original votes on the lottery reflected the hope of lottery sponsors that the amendment process could be used to achieve property tax relief. But amendments which addressed that issue directly, without earmarking funds for some other purpose (with strong interest group support), have traveled a rocky road. In April 1989, one amendment widening the legislature's powers to grant property tax relief failed by less than one percent of the vote. The next legislative session saw a series of proposals to revive the effort, but a second amendment failed in

22

November 1992. This issue demonstrates once again that constitutional change can be similar to statutory change in nature, but is much more difficult in terms of passage procedure. Without the cumbersome passage procedure, much more significant property tax relief in relation to schools passed in statutory form in the early 1990s.

Another amendment was prompted by popular Governor Tommy Thompson's use of the partial veto to strike letters from words (upheld by the Wisconsin Supreme Court), creating new words. This led to the approval of the so called "Vanna White Amendment" in April 1990 which prevents the Governor from creating new words. But Wisconsin's governor still retains substantial partial veto powers.

<u>1991-Present: A Skeptical Electorate?</u>

While we are just beginning the most recent period of constitutional change, two patterns seem to emerge from the first five years of this period: one, there will continue to be frequent referenda, and, two, the voters appear to have grown more skeptical of widening the power of government than they were in the last period.

Five of the nine amendments in the 1990s thus far have failed. As mentioned earlier in this chapter, one would have corrected references to masculine gender, one would have provided a sports lottery, and one dealt with property tax reform. Another would have provided housing for persons of low or moderate income and another would have allowed judges to resign and assume other public offices during their term of office. Only the gender vote was close.

The amendments which have passed in this decade are of limited consequence. As mentioned above, one clarified language on the lottery. A second amendment demonstrated a changing of the times. The fear of the power of major railroads that was felt during the machine days and which led to a number of progressive reforms, including the progressive-era amendments mentioned above, has given way today to a small attempt to assist a struggling industry. The language of Article VIII of the constitution extended the bonding power backed by the full faith, credit, and taxing power of the state to railroads as well as those already mentioned areas (the improvement of land, waters, property, highways, building equipment or facilities for public purposes). This provides state effort to assist AMTRAK in keeping passenger service in Wisconsin and further assists the struggling non-passenger railroad industry.

As noted in Chapter VI, legislative pay is relatively high in Wisconsin, but this is an issue of considerable controversy. In April 1992, the voters approved an amendment to the compensation section of the constitution to require that no salary increase go into effect until after the next legislative election. This followed considerable national debate on Congressional pay increases. Presumably Wisconsin's amendment would allow angry voters to raise this issue in the ensuing campaign, making it even riskier for legislators to allow increases to go into effect.

The most popular amendment to this writing in the 1990s provides a series of "rights" to victims of crimes, including the right to attend court proceedings in most circumstances, protection from the accused, notification of court proceedings, the opportunity to confer with the prosecution, and the opportunity to make a statement to the court. Ambiguous language is also added in regard to restitution and compensation for victims and treatment with "fairness, dignity and respect for their privacy." This amendment reflects the general public antipathy with those rulings by the courts (particularly in the 1960s) which enhanced the protection of those accused of crimes. But the victim's amendment ends with a confusing statement that "Nothing in this section, or in any statute enacted pursuant to this section, shall limit any right of the accused which may be provided by law." Thus, the amendment does not repeal any of the significant protections for those accused of crimes in Wisconsin. As a result, as mentioned above, Wisconsin continues to be more protective than other states, but now the victims of crimes have legal standing in the court procedures.

Conclusion

A summary of constitutional development through the use of the amending process indicates that the ratified amendments have significantly increased the length of the constitution and made it more complex than the original document. Much of the increased verbiage is a direct result of restrictions on state activity included in the constitution at the outset or added in periods when certain governmental actions were suspect. Successive modifications of the section prohibiting state internal improvements are a case in point. So too is the provision relating to municipal debt limitations, as succeeding generations have attempted to modify the restrictions placed in the constitution in 1874. The county and town government uniformity clause has also decreed the necessity for various lengthy exceptions. Other sections written against the backdrop of nineteenth century politics, may be obsolete or irrelevant in the modern day. A number of amendments passed in November 1982 reduce the verbiage a bit by removing some obsolete provisions.

Wisconsin's constitution has shown its capacity to change with the times without the need for the wholesale changes most state constitutions have undergone. Through the years there have been occasional calls for major constitutional revision. This would mean a constitutional convention at which a new constitution would be considered. However, success in passing amendments has largely blunted the demands for more extensive reform. Furthermore, changes in national constitutional law have limited and changed Wisconsin's constitution to further reflect the times. Federal budgetary stringency and changes in public policy enunciated by Congress, the President, and the Supreme Court have resulted in the states being asked to resume their traditional roles as service providers, policy innovators, and protectors of individual rights. So far, Wisconsin's constitution, particularly its extensive Declaration of Rights, has proven to be up to the task of providing for the needs of government while protecting individuals from the might of government. The general conclusion seems to be that the 1848 Constitution, as amended, remains a serviceable document for the state into the next century. This shows the wisdom of the original framers. Later chapters will show how the blueprint of the constitution affects political processes and public policy.

CHAPTER III

LOCAL GOVERNMENT

By Edward J. Miller and Brett Hawkins[*]

Delivery of government services is principally on the shoulders of local government. Whether it's garbage collection, sewer and water provision, street development and maintenance, or education, among many others, local government officials make policy decisions, and local personnel administer them. Local officials are on the front line against the most serious problems of our society such as murder, arson, drug addiction, and homelessness.

With local government in the vortex of policy-making, local officials, especially members of common councils and boards, are deluged by citizens with complaints about service and with opinions about policies. Local leaders face conflicting pressures, such as to provide the best education possible while concurrently minimizing property tax increases.

Despite the predominance of local government delivery of services, financing them represents a complex web of federal, state, and local taxes. Historically, local services were mostly paid for by locally raised revenue. Today, state government contributes a significant portion to local spending through shared taxes with federal grants providing funds as well.

Federal grants illustrate both the advantages and disadvantages of using non-locally generated revenue. Local government and its citizens like grants because they can pay for services with dollars generated elsewhere. Also, the federal taxes that produce the revenue tend to be more progressive than local ones, i.e., taking a larger percent of income from wealthier taxpayers. But federal regulations come with the money, restricting local autonomy, which of course is viewed negatively by local leaders. Further, increasing reliance on money raised by other governments makes it particularly hard when that money is reduced. This is exactly the situation faced by many Wisconsin local governments as federal funds have been cut back. Expansion of federal programs and funding in the 1960s and 1970s left governments ill-prepared for the reductions of the 1980s. The federal policy, called devolution, meant that more reliance was to be placed on both state and local governments to finance their programs. Local governments, in Wisconsin and elsewhere, had to cut back services, raise tax rates, and adopt new taxes. With the national focus on the debt and balancing the budget, it is doubtful that state and local governments can look to the federal level for additional financial assistance.

Citizens repeatedly have affirmed their faith in local government. When asked in 1991 which level of government spends your tax dollars most wisely, 12 percent said federal, 14 percent state, 35 percent local, 27 percent none, two percent all, and ten percent didn't know. In earlier years, local government has alternated at the top with the federal government, but the state government has generally ranked last (ACIR, 1991: 8).

How much autonomy do Wisconsin local governments have in comparison to other states? We have noted that local governments are regulated by Washington. They are regulated even more by their state governments. The Advisory Commission on Intergovernmental Relations, in ranking states as to the degree of discretionary authority of all local governments, ranked Wisconsin in the middle of the states --23rd among the states (ACIR, 1982:262). Focusing just on municipalities, Wisconsin had a similar ranking, 22nd of 49 states ranked. Counties, though, are given more autonomy in Wisconsin than other states, 15th of 50.

---

[*] Professors of Political Science, University of Wisconsin-Stevens Point and University of Wisconsin-Milwaukee, respectively.

This chapter will first focus on the structure and functions of Wisconsin local government. Subsequently, local financing, state-local relations, local government interest groups, and the collective bargaining of public employees will be discussed.

Units of Local Government

Trends in the numbers of various types of local units of government, shown in Table III-1, reveal stability in the number of counties over time, with the only contemporary change being the addition of Menominee County. The numbers of cities and villages, however, have increased mainly because the expanding urbanization of the state has resulted in new incorporations. Some of these incorporations have occurred near existing municipalities despite state efforts to discourage new incorporations near cities. Correspondingly, the number of towns has declined as municipalities have been created. The most startling change since 1952, the first year reported in the table, has been the elimination of nearly 5,000 school districts. Although school districts have been eliminated, there has been a significant increase in other special districts, primarily town sanitary districts and inland lake protection districts. Even with this increase, Wisconsin has fewer special districts than most states.

In 1991 Wisconsin ranked 32nd among the states in the number of state and local employees per 10,000 population, with the state employing 69,302 full time employees (140 employees per 10,000 population) and local government employing 186,720 (377 per 10,000 population). The largest employment category is school districts. In 1992, Wisconsin ranked 9th nationally in the average earnings of state and local government employees (State of Wisconsin, *Blue Book*, 1993-94: 719-721).

Table III-1

UNITS OF GOVERNMENT IN WISCONSIN, 1952 - 92

	1952[a]	1962	1978	1984	1992
Counties	71	72	72	72	72
Cities	166	179	187	189	189
Villages	371	384	392	393	394
Towns	1280	1271	1269	1267	1267
School Districts	5298	1752	436	432	428
Special Districts	73	78	481	437	399
Totals	7259	3736	2837	2790	2749

[a] "Dependent Special Districts" were not counted in 1952.
Sources: Appropriate editions of the State of Wisconsin, *Blue Book*.

Wisconsin, like most states, has a two-tier system of local government. The entire state is divided into counties, and the counties, in turn, contain cities, villages, and towns. This dual jurisdiction of local governments for all areas of the state is one way of providing local services. But the system engenders conflict. For example, the county sheriff may patrol only outside the major cities that have their own police. City residents question, "Why should I pay county property taxes for a service I don't get." In contrast, the counties in New England are not really governing units. In parts of the rural South, the county may be the single unit of local government. Some states allow for city-county consolidation.

The Wisconsin pattern, adopted from New York, included that state's provision for relating town government to county government by having the town chairman serve as the town's representative on the county board of supervisors. As to government structure, the Wisconsin Constitution requires that the legislature establish only one system of town government, but it may establish more than one structural model for county government.[1] The latter variance was introduced to allow counties to have a structure appropriate to their urban or rural characteristics. Early in Wisconsin's history, only counties and towns existed, with cities and villages developing later as the need to govern and service more densely settled populations became evident.

Counties

There are 72 counties in Wisconsin. In recent years some diversity has been introduced in counties' governmental structure with three primary patterns. The *county executive system* (nine counties), pioneered by Milwaukee County, was predicated on the need for central executive authority, viewed as especially important in counties with more services provided at the county level. Thus a chief executive, independent of the county board, is popularly elected for a four-year term. The county executive is considered the chief administrative officer similar to a mayor with supervisory, appointive, removal, and budgetary powers. A county executive frequently makes policy recommendations to the county board. Counties with the executive system cluster in eastern Wisconsin. These counties are:

Brown	Kenosha	Racine
Dane	Milwaukee	Waukesha
Fond du Lac	Outagamie	Winnebago

Some other counties, recognizing a need for a full time general administrative officer, but unwilling to adopt an independently elected executive official, have chosen the route of the *county administrator* (six counties), who is appointed by the county board and can be removed by the board. This official is responsible to the board for the day-to-day management of the county's administrative agencies. The six counties with county administrators are:

Burnett	Marathon	Menominee
Jefferson	Marinette	Rock

County executives and administrators are similar in that both may appoint, with the confirmation of the county board, department heads and non elected members of boards and commissions. The primary difference (other than election) is that the executive has veto power, including partial veto power over appropriations measures, while the administrator does not.

Counties unwilling to give a non elected staff member appointive power (an administrator) or to have an elected county executive are required by law to designate a person to be in charge of administration, known as an administrative coordinator (57 counties). For example, a number of counties designate the county clerk, an employee historically performing administrative functions. Other counties have hired a business administrator to perform these functions, as their administrative coordinator. Still other counties have designated the chairman of the county board to administer functions in the county, making that elected part-time, legislative position into an administrative position as well (Donoghue, 1979:133-134; State of Wisconsin, *Blue Book*, 1989-90:339). As county governments in Wisconsin have expanded their functions and have larger budgets and more employees, a search for more executive leadership has taken place.

---

[1] Wisconsin Constitution, Article IV, Section 23. Originally uniformity required. But in 1885 the Legislature decided it was not practical to treat Milwaukee like other counties, allowing a different structure for that county. The constitutional change in 1972 allowed all counties flexibility in selecting their structure.

Counties, created by the state as an administrative convenience, do not have broad powers to enact programs in the interest of their residents, but are confined to performing functions explicitly set forth in the state statutes.

The most striking feature of county government administration is the diffusion of authority among many elected officials. Consistent with Jacksonian democracy and consistent with the establishment of a plural executive at the state level, Wisconsin's 1848 Constitution provided for the election of eight county officials. Elected for two-year terms in the partisan elections in November are: sheriff, district attorney, clerk, treasurer, register of deeds, clerk of circuit court, surveyor, and coroner. There was no provision in the original state constitution for any overall leadership of these officials, so there was no mechanism for coordinating their activities. In addition, there were no qualifications required for these offices, so any citizen could run for any office. For example, the coroner even now need not be a physician and the surveyor need not know anything about surveying.

The absurdity of the omissions of qualifications in the constitution and statutes led to the abolition of the offices of coroner and surveyor in Milwaukee County by constitutional amendment. Other counties are now authorized to replace the coroner with a medical examiner, but only 13 counties have done so.

Even where there is provision for an executive or administrator, county administration is still diffused. The county executive has veto power over the county board and plays an important role in determining the county budget. However, the executive has no formal authority over the other elected officials of the county. An attempt by the county executive to issue an order on a policy issue to a sheriff or district attorney could be met with the assertion that the other official is responsible to the voters of the county and not to the county executive. This includes controlling the expenditures of the department.

The county board members, or "supervisors," who are elected, traditionally perform both legislative functions (passing resolutions and ordinances) and administrative roles, the latter being fewer in counties adopting the executive arrangement. Members of county boards, part-time positions, are elected from districts within the county in the April non partisan elections for four-year terms in Milwaukee County and for two-year terms in the rest of the state. The size of these Boards varies from seven in Menominee County to 39 in Dane and Outagamie Counties. The election of eight administrative officials on a partisan basis and the county board supervisors on a nonpartisan basis creates further tensions in the relations among these officials. Even though technically nonpartisan, county board members are frequently identified with a political party, which may differ from that of the partisan elected administrative officials (Hagensick, 1964; Crane, 1956).

Under provisions of the 1848 Constitution, town government was linked to county government by having the town chairman serve on the county board of supervisors. One member elected from each village and one elected from each city ward completed the membership of the board. The formula did not take into account population differences among towns, villages, and city wards. Accordingly, after *Baker v. Carr* (1962) and *Reynolds v. Sims* (1964) required apportionment of both houses of the state legislatures on a population base, the Wisconsin Constitution's allocation of county board seats was challenged as unconstitutional under the U.S. Supreme Court's interpretation of the equal protection clause in the Fourteenth Amendment of the U.S. Constitution. The Wisconsin Supreme Court upheld this challenge and invalidated county board apportionment based on towns, villages, and city wards. Subsequently, the U.S. Supreme Court (*Avery v. Midland County*, 1968) and the Wisconsin state Supreme Court (*State ex rel. Sonneborn v. Sylvester*, 1965) reached the same decision with respect to all elective local policy-making boards and councils (Hagensick, 1968). As determined in the 1973 U.S. Supreme Court decision of *Mahan v. Howell* and affirmed in *Brown v. Thomson* (1983), some population deviation in state and local districts, unlike the requirement for Congressional districts, is allowable for justifiable reasons, such as observing municipal boundaries, but population still must be the primary apportionment criterion.

The legislature implemented the state court's decision by requiring all counties to apportion their boards by population and to establish maximum and minimum numbers of members, based on county population. County boards now vary from seven to 39 members; Milwaukee County, which had earlier apportioned by population under a special provision, has 25 members.[2]

Other elected county officials are judges and district attorneys. Virtually all counties have at least one state circuit court judge and a district attorney. The judges have considerable discretion in appointing court officials; thus they, along with other elected county officials, become involved in administrative and personnel matters. In many counties, the district attorney also serves as legal adviser, known as corporate counsel, to the county board while other counties appoint a separate counsel. The state took over responsibility for the entire salary of judges in the late 1970s and of district attorneys as of 1990. The impact of the latter change was to raise salaries of district attorneys and their assistants in most counties, putting them on a par with the state administered public defender system.

Having described the elected officials of counties, let us now examine the functions of county government. The largest single expenditure of county governments is for welfare and related social services. The county administers the largest federal-state public assistance expenditure, the Aid to Families with Dependent Children program (AFDC). The counties at their option may administer general public assistance, a program of financial assistance, mainly property tax supported, for indigent persons who do not receive AFDC benefits. The state has paid about 40 percent of general assistance costs, but the 1995-97 state budget reduces state funding for this program. When counties do not opt to provide general assistance, it is provided by cities, villages, and towns. General assistance has grown with cutbacks in AFDC eligibility.

Additionally, counties provide medical care to indigents without insurance or Medicaid coverage known as General Relief-Medical Program. Many of the working poor, for example, do not qualify for medical assistance under the federal-state Medicaid program and do not receive health insurance as a job benefit, an increasing situation for those involved with smaller employers. In the General Relief-Medical Program the individual counties are responsible for 60 percent of medical costs less than $10,000 and 30 percent of additional costs with the state paying the reminder. But many counties have chosen not to participate in the program, resulting in coverage for the non-Medicaid eligible poor in some counties and not in others. The escalating expense of health coverage, together with the growing number of medically uninsured, has led Wisconsin's local governments to seek a state program. The state has experimented in several counties with alternative approaches to confront the problem of the medically uninsured. Despite frequent discussion at the national level, the federal deficit, interest group opposition, and difficulties in administering some of the plans resulted in the failure to enact national health care financing reforms, which might have provided universal coverage. Consequently, the state and counties must continue to confront the problem of providing health care for the uninsured, albeit with large amounts of federal aid. Often the Medicaid payment to providers is less than the usual charges resulting in few physicians and dentists being willing to see these patients. Where patients are seen, costs not covered are shifted to insured patients. In Wisconsin one of the most severe access problems for the poor is dental care. Additionally, since many poor do not have a family physician, they obtain their medical care in the much more expensive hospital emergency room. This is especially true at county run Doyne Hospital (previously known as the Milwaukee County Medical Center) in Milwaukee. The financial burden of operating the hospital led to the sale of Doyne to Froedtert Luthern Hospital.

The second most important function of county governments, as measured by expenditures, is highways.

---

[2] Maximum membership on county boards is specified by statute on the basis of the following formula (*Wisconsin Statutes* 59.03(3) (a):

County Population	Maximum Number of Supervisors
Under 25,000	21
25,000 - 49,999	31
50,000 - 99,999	39
100,000 - 499,999	47

The counties serve a state function for U.S. and state highways and serve their own purposes in the construction and maintenance of county trunk systems. They may provide highway services under contract to towns, villages and cities.

Although education is the most important function of state and local governments, the county, except in a few minor areas, no longer is involved in this area. Counties once had a role in teacher certification and supervision of rural schools, but these functions are now performed by the state Department of Public Instruction.

Other functions of county governments may include:

1.   law enforcement by the sheriff's department, and, in a decreasing number of counties (only Calumet, Clark, and Kewaunee), a separate county traffic patrol (operating outside cities and villages);

2.   institutions such as hospitals, homes for the elderly, etc.;

3.   health and mental health programs; programs for the elderly;

4.   agricultural extension, involving a unique office supported through national, state (through the University of Wisconsin) and county funding;

5.   zoning and land use regulation (outside cities and villages);

6.   land management, forests and parks;

7.   airports;

8.   veterans' affairs through the county veterans' service officer.

Counties do not collect property taxes directly. Cities, villages, and towns perform these functions--though several counties, e.g., Portage and Dane, now collect the revenue for some of their subdivisions. The county obtains revenue by prorating its needs for property tax money among the smaller jurisdictions within the county. To prorate, the county board must go through a process called equalization, in which an effort is made to determine what percentage of the total true ("full" or market) value of all property in the county is in each city, village, and town. The towns and municipalities must then provide the county with that amount; they have no discretion in paying the tax levy.

Equalization is a very complex process and can lead to many inequities. Further, assessors in villages and towns, especially elected assessors, may be very inexperienced. Accordingly, efforts have been made to establish county-wide assessment, but as noted, Kenosha County is the only one to date to undertake this function. In general, sub-county jurisdictions play the primary role in the collection of property taxes. A 1995 report by the state Department of Revenue recommended that, except in Wisconsin's largest cities that have full time professional assessors, the assessment should be by a county assessor with appeals to a county review board appointed by the county board chair. Kenosha County had been the only model for this but ended the practice in 1995.

Towns

Wisconsin's unit of unincorporated rural government is the town. Usage varies among the states, so it is important to distinguish between towns and townships as these terms are used in Wisconsin (Le May, 1975).

Townships are geographic units established by the land survey provided for in the Northwest Ordinance of

1787. These survey units, sometimes called congressional townships, are six miles square. They are in turn divided into 36 sections, quarters of sections, and quarters of quarter sections. The last are forty acres, the basic unit for conveying rural land.

Towns, a unit of government, may or may not coincide with township boundaries. Variations occur because of 1) survey errors, 2) geographic barriers such as rivers, and, 3) sparse population, especially in northern parts of the state where there may not be enough persons in a 36 square mile area to justify the establishment of a town for only one township. There are more than 1200 towns in Wisconsin. All territory not in a city or a village is under the jurisdiction of a town. In some states the unit of local government that we in Wisconsin call "towns" are called "townships." But that is only in other states.

Because of the uniform requirement for towns in the state constitution, all towns have the same basic form of government. A constitutional amendment to delete the uniformity clause--to allow towns some option in their forms of government--was defeated by voters in a referendum in 1978. All town officials are elected in nonpartisan elections in April for two-year terms. These officers include the town chairman and two to six other supervisors, a clerk, and a treasurer. All towns must have an assessor, who is either elected or appointed. At their option, towns may elect a constable and a justice.

A unique feature of towns, a heritage from New England, is the town meeting. Performing essentially legislative functions, it is one of the few examples of direct democracy for a unit of general purpose government in America. All voters in the town may attend, speak, and vote at town meetings. The law requires an annual town meeting to vote on the budget and the property tax. At the annual meeting, citizens may also bring up any other issues which concern them. Special meetings may also be called to deal with specific issues.

Although advocates of participatory democracy extol the virtues of the New England town meeting, actual experience with this device is generally disappointing. Usually, only a few people bother participating in the annual meetings. Some special meetings, when there is a highly controversial issue, may attract a large turnout. However, since even these meetings attract a small percentage of the eligible voters, it is questionable whether the decisions made reflect the majority more effectively than decisions made by an elected board. Also, the town meeting may only act when a state law specifically requires or allows action. This legal constraint restricts the motions that can be made at town meetings. The town board, however, may be vested by the Town Meeting with the broader powers of a village, except those conflicting with laws applying to towns, facilitating the exercise of urban functions (Wisconsin Taxpayers Alliance, June 1989).

The most important single function of towns is the construction and maintenance of town roads. Other functions include fire protection, ambulance service, zoning, enforcement of weed ordinances, and waste disposal. In those counties in which the county has not assumed the obligations for general public assistance, this welfare function is performed by the town. Usually this assistance takes the form of having the town chairman or the town clerk order groceries and fuel for recipients rather than providing money as is done for recipients of other public assistance programs.

Land in towns may be annexed by adjacent cities and villages with the consent of both the governing board of the annexing municipality and a majority of the voters and property owners being annexed. Annexed land is no longer under the jurisdiction of the town. This piecemeal annexation by municipalities, especially when they seek to take land with a high property value, leaves the town not only with a smaller territory but also a smaller tax base. This problem is particularly acute in fast growing areas in southeastern Wisconsin, especially in counties neighboring Milwaukee.

There are no longer any towns in Milwaukee County. The 1955 legislature enacted a statute, known as the Oak Creek Law, which provided that all rural towns on the border of all first class cities (only Milwaukee) could become fourth class cities, even though they did not meet the usual requirements for incorporation. Towns on the southern boundary of Milwaukee availed themselves of this law. Milwaukee was not successful in opposing the law. If it hadn't passed, Milwaukee would have more than a million people with communities such as New Berlin and Brookfield being part of the city. There was lengthy litigation concerning the Town of Granville on the northern boundary, but ultimately the Village of Brown Deer and City of Milwaukee divided up the town through annexations.

Municipalities: Cities and Villages

Cities and villages are incorporated units of local government in Wisconsin having broad grants of power. In contrast, counties and town have more restricted functions. Further, cities and villages have broad discretion in determining their forms of government, which is more limited for towns and counties.

Originally the entire state consisted only of towns. To understand the development of municipalities, we must understand the processes of incorporation and annexation. The laws for incorporation and annexation have changed some over time, but using present law, we can indicate typical processes by which local governments expand in functions and territory.

As the population of a rural town becomes more dense, there is a need for "urban" services such as water, sewer, and fire protection. The citizens in that area may initiate proceedings in circuit court to become a village. If approved by the court, there is a referendum requiring the approval of a majority of the voters in the affected area. The minimum population for a village is 150 persons in an area of one-half square mile.

As time goes on, the population is likely to sprawl beyond the boundaries of the village. The borders of the village may be expanded by a process known as annexation. That is the right of an incorporated unit of local government (subject to circuit court determination, review by the state, and a referendum of the affected inhabitants) to take adjacent land from unincorporated towns. The annexation does not require the approval of those remaining in the town from which territory is taken. Conflict between the town, which will lose some of its tax base in the annexation, and the annexing municipality is typical. Some people in the area under consideration for annexation may support becoming part of the city or village to gain municipal services such as water and sewer while others may oppose for fear of higher property taxes.

As population growth continues and the population becomes one thousand (and at least one square mile), the village may become a fourth class city. Further growth may lead to becoming a third class city with a population of 10,000, a second class city with a population of 39,000, and a first class city with a population of 150,000.

The legal differences between villages and cities of the second, third, and fourth class are so minor that many municipalities do not bother to change their classifications despite the population being sufficient to warrant it. Thus, for example, Shorewood, Whitefish Bay, and Menomonee Falls, with populations large enough to become third class cities, have remained villages. Similarly, there are cities of one class with populations large enough to become another class that have not taken steps to change classification. Thus, Madison with a population just less than 200,000 could join Milwaukee as a first class city, requiring 150,000 people. Classification changes must be made by local action and are not made at the initiative of state government. Further, once a municipality achieves a certain classification, it does not lose that status, unless municipal action is taken to change a classification or to dissolve the municipality and revert to a town. Consequently, there are villages of less than 150 population, such as Lubin in Taylor County, and cities of less than 1,000 population, such as Bayfield in Bayfield County.

Milwaukee is the only city in the first class category. Accordingly, although the state constitution prohibits bills that change a specific local charter, the legislature can enact general legislation which applies to only the City of Milwaukee by using the formula specifying "In all first class cities." This approach was affirmed in a case growing out of a challenge to the Milwaukee Parental [School] Choice Program (*Davis v. Grover*, 1992).

In any case, as local communities grow, their citizens may acquire needs that cannot be met through existing structures of government. If municipal incorporation and annexation do not meet their needs, communities may turn to other arrangements. Recent years have witnessed a large and creative outpouring of "alternative arrangements" to *provide* services without the local government having to *produce* them itself (Heim, 1991). Examples include contracting for data processing or personnel services with a county, jointly funding and operating a water purification facility with another municipality, having multi-jurisdiction assessors or sharing or hiring private assessors, contracting trash removal services with a private firm, sharing emergency services with several other municipalities, and transferring responsibility for a hospital to a county. By methods such as these, needs are met, and expenses are often held down. Governments seek reduced costs through administrative efficiency, economies of scale (especially for capital intensive functions), and privatization to achieve flexibility often difficult under the rules under which governments must operate.

Privatization of government functions assumes that private firms can produce the service more cheaply and efficiently (Savas, 1982; Rehfuss, 1989) than government, which is often but not always true. Municipal employees typically oppose privatization efforts due to concerns over job loss. Governments considering privatization must balance cost concerns with the possibility that business firms will not be as responsive and accountable as municipal agencies.

The Wisconsin Constitution was amended in 1924 to provide for municipal "home rule" (Article IX, Section 3). The amendment states, "Cities and villages organized pursuant to state law are hereby empowered, to determine their local affairs and government, subject only to this constitution and to such enactments of the legislature of state wide concern as shall with uniformity affect every city or every village."

Proponents of this amendment believed that they had won a significant victory for local autonomy, but the courts have interpreted this provision to allow the legislature to preempt local determination on the basis of a "state-wide concern" except for determining governmental structure. The escape clause, "state-wide concern," has been broadly construed by the courts. The courts have said that a municipality may not exercise a power if the legislature has withdrawn it or if its ordinance conflicts with a state wide statute (*Anchor Savings and Loan v. Madison EOC*, 1984; *Local Union No. 497 v. Eau Claire*, 1989). The state legislature enacts legislation overriding local ordinances when it sees the need for a consistent approach throughout the state. One interesting conflict between state statutes and local ordinances is when there are both a statute and a locally enacted ordinance on the same subject. For example, shoplifting is covered by a statute but may also be included in a local ordinance. An ordinance violation may be brought against a person rather than the statutory charge to keep the individual from having a criminal record since ordinance violations are not considered "criminal" charges. An Attorney General's Opinion states that when there is a state statute, it supersedes an ordinance. Nonetheless, communities still use ordinance charges and it is not in the interest of an individual so charged to have a court test of the issue.

Statutes provide discretion to a municipality to determine its own form of local government. Wisconsin municipalities may choose one of four forms of local government: 1) weak mayor, 2) strong mayor, 3) city manager, or 4) commission. They may also use home rule authority to modify the basic forms. The number of cities and villages with each major government form is shown in Table III-2.

The weak mayor system dominated throughout America until the beginning of the twentieth century. Under this arrangement, the mayor's duties were largely ceremonial. Actual power, such as budget formulation and personnel selection, was shared among the common council, other elected officials, and many independent boards and commissions. Fear of a strong executive, influencing the lack of powers given governors, was evident on the local level as well.

The strong mayor system, developed to focus local administrative leadership, is one in which the mayor appoints officials who are responsible to him or her and has authority to prepare a budget and otherwise exercise control over the city administration. The trend in Wisconsin has been toward giving mayors more authority; but, under home rule, the extent of the mayor's authority is determined by each city.

33

Table III-2

FORMS OF MUNICIPAL GOVERNMENT IN WISCONSIN

| | Cities | | Villages | |
	number	percent	number	percent
Mayors (Cities) or Presidents (Villages)	117	62	328	83
Mayor or President with an Administrator	62	33	57	15
Manager	10	5	9	2
Commission	0	0	0	0
Total	189	100%	394	100%

Source: State of Wisconsin, *Blue Book*, 1995-96:716.

Interestingly, with the exception of Milwaukee, the mayor presides at Council meetings, in some jurisdictions appoints council committee members and chairs, and can vote in case of a tie. Following action by the Council, the mayor can veto ordinances, which can be overridden by a two-thirds majority.

The manager system is one in which the city council or village board chooses a professional as the chief administrator of the jurisdiction. As chief administrator, the manager appoints all heads of departments and other city officials based on the professional qualifications of the individual. The manager is selected by the council and may be removed at any time by it. The manager system has been successful in some medium-sized cities and in some mainly residential suburban villages. It currently operates in nine villages and ten cities. However, the manager form has not been popular in the state's largest cities. In some Wisconsin cities the manager form has been controversial with several cities abandoning it. Significant opposition to the manager form based on a concern about having a non elected person in charge of appointments and city government. Municipalities desiring a professional administrator but one without the statutory powers of a manager, especially appointment power, have instead of a manager added a chief administrator, responsible to the mayor and council. Of the 56 cities with city administrators, 33 of them have their administrators assigned to perform an additional role. These dual position administrators are from smaller cities.

The commission form of government is one in which commissioners are elected at large and serve collectively as a legislative body. Individually, each commissioner is also the administrator of a department, thus fusing legislative and executive authority, in a deviation from the prevailing American concept of separation of powers. It is criticized for not having administrative oversight by an independent body, lacks executive leadership, and encourages logrolling, such as in budgetary allocations, among the commissioners. Wisconsin law allows this form of government; but since its abandonment by Fond du Lac, no Wisconsin city now has it. Similarly, throughout the nation there are fewer commission cities; many that once had adopted it have turned to the manager form.

In addition to the options which cities and villages have in selecting basic forms of government, they have considerable autonomy in determining other aspects of their structure. Under structural home rule, they may decide for themselves whether to elect one or two council members per ward or to elect some or all council members at-large. Some argue that at-large elections encourage council members to view policy from the vantage point of what is good for the entire jurisdiction; others argue that district elections make council members more responsible and responsive to constituents since districts are smaller and more homogeneous than the entire community. Wisconsin Rapids went from district to at-large form of representation in 1994. Cities and villages may make other decisions such as whether to elect or appoint the clerk, treasurer, assessor, or comptroller. They have wide discretion in determining the length of terms of elected officers. Many mayors are now elected for four-year terms, rather than the common practice of two-year terms. All municipal elections must be in the April nonpartisan elections.

Functions of municipalities include police and fire protection, street construction and maintenance, water and sewer, parks, assessment and collection of property taxes, conduct of elections, and many others (Donoghue, 1979). Encouraging businesses to move into and expand in the community has become an increasingly important role of local government officials. The number of services and their level vary widely among local governments because they have broad discretion in determining what functions they wish to provide beyond those required by state law. Thus, for example, some jurisdictions provide garbage collection and sidewalk snow removal and others do not.

Because of financial benefits to local business and prestige, cities work to attract and retain sports teams. Milwaukee and Green Bay have major league teams while several small cities have had or now have minor league teams. Appleton's minor league team, the Timber Rattlers, formerly known as the Foxes, is one of the few in the nation to have a $4.3 million stadium built exclusively through private sector donations. A 1995 referendum to authorize a sports lottery to pay for a new stadium for the Brewers and other sports facilities in the state failed at the polls. However, the governor and state legislature subsequently stepped in with an alternative method of financing the Brewers' ballpark. Several cities have assisted their local college to attract summer training camps of National Football League teams. They have been so successful that Wisconsin training camps have been dubbed the "Cheese League." However, analysts are not in agreement whether the subsidization of privately owned sports teams is an appropriate government function or if the benefits received actually exceed the costs.

Spending varies widely among Wisconsin local governments. Choices whether to provide a service is an important element in the variation as is the level of service of those provided. In some cases a city or village no longer administers a service because the county now does (Wisconsin Taxpayers Alliance, December 1993). In Milwaukee in recent years the museum, emergency government, policing County stadium, and lockup services for people arrested in the city by city officers have been transferred to the county. Cities may also jointly provide a service to be more cost efficient, an outcome more likely for capital intensive and fewer utilized functions, or buy a service from a nearby municipality. The North Shore Water Commission is a joint operation of Fox Point, Glendale, and Whitefish Bay.

Spending is also greater in municipalities with lower income residents who have greater need of public services. Higher population density and a large influx of commuters are two additional explanatory factors of greater service cost among Wisconsin local government (Green and Reschovsky, 1994: 112-113). Some studies, however, have concluded that commuters benefit cities more than they burden them by creating wealth, economic benefits, and revenue through their work, shopping, and taxpaying (Vincent, 1971). Lastly, a higher local wage rate will increase the cost of governmental services leading to more government spending.

Special Districts

Special districts are also units of local government, but they have such a low visibility that few citizens are aware of their existence. Not as widely used in Wisconsin as in many other states, there are nonetheless almost 400 of them in the state. The very fact that the exact number is not known is eloquent testimony to the low visibility of these units.

Special districts are units of government established to deal with one or a very few specific functions. Examples are sewer districts, drainage districts, water districts, and housing and community development authorities. The boundaries of these districts may or may not coincide with other municipal boundaries; but, generally speaking, the purpose of the district is to perform a function not otherwise provided by local government in a particular area. These units have the power to tax, to charge fees, and to borrow money in the bond markets. Because of the complex and diverse methods of choosing officials for these districts and their invisibility to the public, the arrangement is sometimes cited as an example of taxation without representation. Further it is charged that special districts increase governmental fragmentation, making it difficult to coordinate public services provided by different local units and for the people to know who should be held responsible for a specific policy concern. Additionally, some argue that they constitute an end run around state-imposed indebtedness limits on local governments. Some special districts are charged with inequitably serving central city and suburban governments.

In support of special districts is the argument that they are more efficient as their jurisdiction can be made to cover the territory of the problem or service area, extending beyond the boundaries of several political subdivisions. Additionally, having a service provided by a single purpose district removes it from control of local officials of general governments, a principal argument used to justify separate school districts. Their self-supporting nature along with their ease of creation lends further appeal to their formation.

The most important example of a special district in Wisconsin is the Milwaukee Metropolitan Sewerage District (MMSD). Established originally in 1921 and revised in 1981, it provides a mechanism for a unified sewer system for the city of Milwaukee and its nearer suburbs. The District Commission consists of 11 persons, seven appointed by the mayor of Milwaukee and four appointed by the member suburbs in Milwaukee County. The suburban commissioners are actually elected by the Intergovernmental Cooperation Council, a council of governments (COG) for Milwaukee County suburbs (the city itself is now a member, though it was not for many years). MMSD's operating budget is funded by user fees billed to industries directly and for residential users to municipalities, which pass on the charges to their residents. Conflict over the basis for paying for capital charges between MMSD and suburbs outside Milwaukee County which are connected to the sewer system has been intense and prolonged. MMSD's capital budget is financed by a property tax levy based on each municipality's share of the value of all property served by the District. The use of wastewater treatment services is not the basis for capital charges.

Fragmentation of Functions

Concern has frequently been expressed in Wisconsin about the multiplicity of governments in urban areas and the need for more cooperation in the performance of their functions. For example, the existence of city police forces alongside the sheriff's department has been cited as an area for potential change. Should city taxpayers pay for both the city police and the county sheriff's department, not serving the city? But change in this area has been difficult because of the opposition to consolidation. It has become more difficult because academic opinion is no longer overwhelmingly opposed to "fragmented" structures of government. In fact, a considerable body of academic specialists--supported by empirical research and theory (known as public choice theory)--now contend that fragmented systems are more efficient, responsive to citizens, and even equitable (ACIR, 1987; Rafuse, 1991; Hawkins and Hendrick, 1994). Thus multiple governments in a metropolitan area, competing for people and industry, are viewed similarly to competitive markets in the private economy. Competition results in taxes being kept down, and the government being more responsive to citizens.

While the consolidation of governments is not very feasible, limited transfers of functions to counties have occurred. In Milwaukee County, for example, parks, the zoo, the museum, air pollution control, and expressway construction and maintenance are now county, not city, functions. Similarly, the county now administers the library in Stevens Point, previously a city function. Interestingly, when the library function was transferred to the county to allow more area-wide service, the city maintained its authority over the main library building. When the decision was made to build a new library, the split county-city obligation resulted in intense conflict between the city and county over the size and siting of the structure.

In addition to service transfers from municipal to county governments, joint-serving arrangements are common among localities in Wisconsin's metropolitan areas. Those involving Milwaukee north shore communities--water purification, tax assessment, emergency services, and now police--illustrate the pattern.

One attempt at encouraging cooperation among local governments was the formation of regional planning commissions. These commissions with membership appointed by local governments and the governor were designed to bring citizens and officials together to discuss common problems, provide technical planning assistance to local government, integrate planning on an area-wide basis (especially land use, environmental, and transportation planning), and act as the regional review agency for federal grants, a process known as A-95 Review. In this role the regional planning bodies informed the Federal government whether a grant applied for by a local government in the area fitted in with regional needs and priorities. The A-95 Review function was eliminated by an executive order of President Reagan in the early 1980s. Although some of the older councils, such as the seven county Southeastern Wisconsin Planning Commission in the Milwaukee area, have had successes, none has achieved the regional cooperative goals envisioned for them by their advocates. Some, however, do produce high quality advisory plans and provide valuable planning assistance to local governments. Among the obstacles to greater effectiveness in achieving regional cooperation has been opposition to regional planning as a concept, as well as a feeling among some local governments that they were not getting services equal to the dues that had to be paid. Thus, from some regional planning commissions in Wisconsin cities, towns, and counties have withdrawn, although some of these units have since rejoined. Regional bodies themselves have been reluctant to seek greater power--that is, beyond statutory authority for producing advisory plans and performing services for members--out of fear that it would undermine their occasionally shaky support.

Financing Local Government

Local governments in Wisconsin collected more in taxes than the state government until 1963. With the state's introduction of the sales tax, increases in the state income tax, and the decline in the property tax, local taxes were gradually dwarfed by state collected revenue. In line with comparable trends in other states, Wisconsin increased its aid to local government (Lampman and McBride, 1988:48). With increased state revenue, the state also assumed responsibility for several services, including full payment (the non-federal portion) of Aid For Families with Dependent Children (AFDC) and Medicaid.

Historically, Wisconsin local government, consistent with the national pattern, relied primarily on property taxes to obtain revenue. Following the trend in other states, the emphasis in recent years has been on tax diversification with local units being authorized to levy a local sales tax (Bowman and Kearney, 1986:174). In Wisconsin a local sales tax for counties has been allowed since 1970, but proved politically unacceptable in its early form since all the revenue had to be turned over to cities, villages, and towns in the county. Thus, no county adopted it. A 1985 state law directing the money to counties for property tax relief made the tax somewhat more acceptable to counties. A slight majority of Wisconsin's counties have chosen to adopt the local sales tax of .5 (the current legal limit) percent, added to the state tax of 5 percent. It is predicted that most counties will utilize the sales tax in the near future despite its initial rejections in some (Friedrich, 1989:B1). Beyond the statutory change, the decline in federal grant dollars, including the elimination of the federal revenue sharing program, and continued opposition to property tax increases make the adoption of the local sales tax a more viable option. In contrast to the property tax, the sales tax is a less visible tax and is paid by all who purchase items in the county and not just those living in the county. State law requires that receipts from the local sales tax be used to cut property tax but does not specify the connection. Several farm based counties are using it to directly reduce property taxes while other counties initiated the tax with the stated purpose of building a new jail or other facilities. A few counties stated that they would abolish the tax when a specified project is paid off (Walters, 1990:5).

Municipal tax rates vary widely. In 1993 (collected in 1994), city rates ranged from Eagle River with an equalized rate of $15.05 per $1,000 property value to Muskego at $4.66. Maiden Rock located along the Mississippi was the village with the highest tax rate in 1993 at $17.21 while the lowest were the 13 villages that levied no municipal taxes and the 13 additional villages with rates less than one dollar. Those villages with no or very low taxes have small populations. Three towns that are sites of major electric generation facilities receive such large payments from the utility portion of state aid (i.e., "shared revenue") that they not only have no town-purpose taxes, but have a surplus that they are able to reduce the town residents' school district and county property taxes (Wisconsin Taxpayers Alliance, May 1994).

Variation in tax rates is a consequence of the types and levels of services provided as well as the problems facing the municipalities. Thus, local governments with poor citizens typically provide more municipal services, raising the tax rates. But this is not the entire story. Municipalities also differ in their tax base. Those with more significant tax bases can actually finance more services at lower tax rates than local governments with lower tax bases. This leads to the often cited problems of metropolitan areas. The central city such as Milwaukee with greater needs and a lower per capita tax base has, as a consequence, higher tax rates than surrounding more wealthy suburban municipalities. On the other hand, some of the poorer suburbs have higher tax rates than Milwaukee's. Federal and state aids, in addition, significantly reduce the disparities in revenue among jurisdictions by allocating relatively more aid to poorer communities including the central city (MacManus, 1978; Rafuse, 1991). Lastly, cities may have a lower property tax rate because they rely on other tax sources such as sales and hotel taxes.

Municipal taxes are only one element determining the level of local property taxes. School district, county, and vocational school property taxes add to the total obligation. Eagle River, noted earlier as having the highest municipal tax rate actually ranks very low (124th of cities) at $31.23 for all property taxes because its school district, Northland Pines, has the sixth lowest rate in the state in 1993.

Some money, especially for capital items such as sewers and buildings, is borrowed. The amount borrowed is limited by Wisconsin's constitution to five percent of equalized property values for municipalities and counties, ten percent for school districts, and two percent for technical college districts. But unlike many other states, Wisconsin does not require all borrowing to be submitted to a referendum. Municipalities may issue bonds for purposes specified in state law (Wis. Stats. , 67.05) such as for bridges, street improvements, garbage disposal, and band shells among many others, for which a referendum is not required. Citizens though may force an election if they are able to collect signatures on a petition equal to at least 15 percent of the votes cast for governor at the last general election in the city or village.

A notable exception has been school districts, required to hold a bond referendum to borrow in excess of $1,000,000 in one-time borrowing or $5,000,000 in total. The ability to borrow without going to referenda was expanded by the state legislature because citizens in several districts with significant building needs had voted against borrowing, including some that defeated bond referendum year after year. Between 1979 and 1989, 207 school referenda had been approved while 257 were defeated. To provide more flexibility to school districts, state law was amended in 1989 to allow districts to borrow up to a limit without the need to go to the voters. The school board could voluntarily seek voter approval, or voters could petition the borrowing to referenda. The statute was changed because of a state legislative concern with the poor condition of many school buildings and the defeat in several districts of bond referenda. In placing revenue caps on the districts, the legislature changed the way schools account for this borrowing. If the money is borrowed without a referendum, it must be considered part of the operating budget which then reduces the amount available for other items such as textbook purchases under the revenue caps. The consequence has been that districts, despite having enlarged nonvoter approved borrowing power, have chosen to have a referendum even on the smaller amounts.

In 1991 and 1992, 62 percent of school bond referenda were approved by voters. In 1993 it dropped to 42 percent approval, returning to about 60 percent in 1994. The Department of Public Instruction has conducted programs for local school administrations and school board members on explaining the borrowing needs to the public and campaigning for their approval. Consequently, school districts have employed more sophisticated voter appeals than in the past.

The ability of local governments to borrow is also affected by the costs of borrowing. The cost of the bonds fluctuate because of changes in the interest rate for municipal bonds. Thus when the Federal Reserve, for example, pushes up interest rates to fight inflation, local governments pay more for their borrowed funds. Governments may call in these bonds and issue new ones if interest rates fall. A further factor in how much a government will pay for its bonds is how risky the bonds are. If a government is financially shaky, investors in municipal bonds will demand a higher return resulting in these governments paying more interest. Financial stability is rated by two private bond rating services--Moody and Standard & Poor, who use letter grades to evaluate governments. Although Wisconsin municipalities are highly rated, only Madison and Wauwatosa have Moody's top rating (Wisconsin Taxpayers Alliance, November 1994:3).

To encourage development in specific areas, Wisconsin's local governments have made extensive use of Tax Incremental Financing (TIF) Districts. In brief, TIF districts encourage business development by improving the infrastructure (such as roads, sewers and the district's physical appearance), clearing land, and other projects. Increases in the property tax resulting from these improvements(i.e., the increment) rather than going to all property taxing governments such as school district and county, stay with the city or village to pay off the bonds used to finance the development. Once the bonds are paid off, all property taxing governments again receive taxes from the full value of the property in the TIF district. Tax Incremental Financing, used by many governments in Wisconsin, was adopted as a creative way of improving the community and encouraging development. Objections arise from the argument that although the municipal governments benefit, others receive less tax money, resulting in citizens having to pay higher tax rates (Stauber and Wyatt, 1990).

Direct Democracy

Despite the limited participation of citizens in approving local bonding measures, citizens have two important forms of direct action available to them; to hold local government and officials accountable. Recall, available on both the state and local levels, allows citizens to vote to remove an official after a petition is filed before the regular election. The major limitations are that at least one year must have transpired since the official's election and that once a recall has failed, no further attempts are allowed during the term. Prior to 1983, the petitioner only had supply a "good and sufficient reason" for the recall, which could simply be policy judgments. In 1983 a change in the law requires that recall for local officials must only be for "cause," defined broadly as inefficiency, neglect of duties, official misconduct, or malfeasance in office. Interestingly, once a successful petition is filed, other candidates may run in the election as an alternative to the incumbent. Therefore, an incumbent in a recall election not only has to defend his or her record, but also has to convince voters that he or she is better than opponents.

Although infrequently used prior to 1977, a number of recall petitions have been filed since, with several being successful. For example, in 1977 all five members of the La Crosse school broad were recalled. In the same year a county judge was recalled, the first in Wisconsin's history. Several other local officials have been recalled since that time, including the entire board of the Town of Lawrence in Rusk County in 1988, four members of La Crosse's School Board in 1992 over a school busing issue involving economic integration of the schools, and several members of the Wausau School Board recently over a similar integration issue involving the Hmong minority.

A second direct form of democracy available in Wisconsin only on the local level is the initiative, available to cities since 1911 and extended to villages in 1990 [not available on the county level]. The initiative allows citizens to directly propose and vote on local ordinances. Once the petition is filed, the common council could enact it without change. But if they do not within 30 days, the ordinance or resolution will appear on the ballot, allowing voters to directly decide the issue.

Those who support the initiative argue that it allows citizens a safety valve if they don't like what their representatives on the city council or village board are doing. Opponents charge that many initiatives are poorly worded, supported by narrow interest groups, and do harm to representative democracy. Initiatives have not been very frequent in Wisconsin. In 1994 following a national trend, municipal initiatives appeared attempting to limit the terms of local elected officials.

State-Local Relations

State relationships with local units of government take a variety of forms. First, the state is the creator of all local units. Their existence is based upon state constitutional or statutory authorization. In addition, state law prescribes in considerable detail the operational responsibilities and organization of the local units. The home rule movement was an attempt to remove municipalities from the detailed supervision of state law. As previously noted, however, that effort had only limited success. The result is that in many matters the state prescribes what municipalities may or may not do. For example, the revamping of the law requiring that a county sales tax be shared with its municipalities and towns has encouraged several counties to adopt this revenue source as federal aid declines. In a more restrictive vain, school district property tax increases are now limited by state statute.

Second, the state is a crucial source of revenue for most local units of government with 55.5 percent of the state's tax dollar in 1994 (proposed to increase to 61 percent in 1997) going to local governments or to reduce local property taxes. This has become especially important as it has been recognized that local property taxes cannot bear the burden of the increased range and cost of local services. State assistance takes three major forms: 1) shared taxes, and 2) state grants or other aids, and 3) school aids. With shared taxes (ten percent of the 1995-97 biennial budget) the state serves as a collection agency, primarily for income and utility taxes, and returns a portion of the revenue collected to local units on the basis of predetermined, but frequently altered, formulas, based on population, relative property values, and tax effort. Local units seeing their property values increase relative to a state-established standard (other factors being unchanged) see their shared tax allocations fall. Some municipalities receive no allocation at all from the main part of the shared tax program. Shared taxes may be used to support any of the services provided by the local units; local discretion is maximum. The city of Milwaukee receives 21 percent of the shared revenue. State grants in aid are provided for specific local functions where the state has determined that local units of government have requirements which the state has a responsibility to help them fulfill, such as education and transportation.

The state pays 45 percent of the cost of primary and secondary education and the state share is scheduled to increase to two-thirds in 1996 under the recently adopted state budget. This educational assistance is paid according to an equalization formula, measuring the amount of property value in a district per student. Thus, less wealthy districts get more funds. But the equalization formula does not go all the way in requiring completely equal funding in all districts, bringing the poor districts up to the level of others. In several states, state supreme courts have deemed various amounts of inequality among districts a violation of their state constitutions. In a similar Wisconsin case, the Wisconsin Supreme Court did not find that existing differences in school funding violated Wisconsin's constitution. Since the vote of the court was 4-3, we can expect the issue to be brought before the court again.

The Department of Public Instruction and a state task force on the schools have recommended an increased state role in the financing of education. Opposition has centered around two issues--how will the state raise the necessary funds and, if the state becomes a larger financial player, will it choose to exercise even more control over what is taught and how school operates? Former Governor Dreyfus in opposing an enlarged state role often cited what he termed the "golden rule"--who has the gold makes the rules. But in a recent compromise between the legislature and Governor Thompson, it was agreed that the state would assume 66.7 percent of school expenditures by fiscal year 1997 to help reduce local property taxes.

In enacting the change, the legislature did not adopt a method of financing the additional state cost, estimated to be $1.527 billion more in 1996-97 than state school costs were in 1993-94 (Wisconsin Taxpayers Alliance, October 1994:5). The governor and a School Funding Commission were given the job of making a recommendation. To come up with the money, Governor Thompson's 1995-97 biennial budget reduces spending by state agencies and increases fees charged by the state. Other approaches frequently discussed are a tax increase or a broadening of the sales tax to include items not now taxed, such as legal services. However, the legislature adopted Governor Thompson's approach in the 1995-1997 biennial budget.

Third, various state agencies enforce rules and regulations that have a direct impact on local units. A major example is the Department of Natural Resources which applies standards relating to air and water pollution control. It also prescribes rules and regulations governing local refuse disposal. Similarly, the Department of Public Instruction imposes many requirements upon the school districts of the state.

A major concern and irritant for many local units are the imposition of these state mandates. Local units complain that the state often requires that money be spent for state purposes without providing the financial assistance necessary to cover costs. In 1990 at the instigation of the Wisconsin Counties Association an advisory referendum appeared on the ballot in 71 counties (in Menominee county it was inadvertently omitted) asking whether the state should fund all local mandates. The voters, presumably feeling that unfunded mandates result in increasing local property taxes, overwhelmingly supported state funding of mandates. State officials counter that mandates have been funded, but rather than specifically attaching funds to each mandate, substantial money is given by the state to local governments without restrictions. If a portion of the money were to be assigned to each mandate, local government would lose flexibility. This debate, reflecting issues of local autonomy and property taxes, is likely to continue for many years, and one not unique to Wisconsin.

Finally, and in recognition of the growing importance and complexity of state-local relationships, the state in 1967 created the Department of Local Affairs and Development (DLAD). A major responsibility of the agency was to assist in coordinating the many state activities that have an impact upon local governments. It also provided technical assistance in various forms. Most, if not all, of DLAD's activities were advisory or facilitative in nature. Upon recommendation of Governor Dreyfus, in 1980 DLAD was merged with the Department of Business Development to form a new Department of Development. This move appeared to be motivated by controversies surrounding the DLAD and an assessment that DLAD had not fulfilled its mission successfully. It may also reflect a decrease in state interest in state-local relations. The Department of Development has emphasized its economic development mission.

Local Government Associations

Local governments have joined together to form associations which maintain central offices, represent local units before state executive agencies and the legislature, publish newsletters informing members of changes in the law or of pending issues, solicit views from their members, and periodically meet. These associations encourage the interaction of officials throughout the state. The League of Wisconsin Municipalities, the first and largest of the associations, has almost all state municipalities as its members. The publisher of the monthly magazine, *The Municipality*, the League conducts training programs for local officials and staff. Similarly, the Wisconsin County Boards Association, organized in 1935, represents county administrative officers and county boards, and publishes its monthly magazine, *Wisconsin Counties*. Towns have their own organization, the Wisconsin Towns Association, publishing *Wisconsin Towns Report* (Donoghue, 1979:120-22).

Larger cities in Wisconsin, those with more than 30,000 people, decided to form an independent association in 1969, the Alliance of Cities, to concentrate on the interests of the larger municipal units, although smaller cities with "common interests" may join. This association has concentrated its lobbying effort on fiscal matters, especially federal and state aid.

These associations do not always agree. Most notably, conflict has arisen over formulas for the distribution of state funds. Other issues have also brought conflict. For example, the Wisconsin County Boards Association has taken a strong stand against state mandates. Recently, the County Boards Association differed with the state over its handling of Indian Treaty Rights.

Local governments spent $3.3 million on legislative lobbying in the 1991-92 biennium. The largest amount, $1.1 million, was spent by counties with lesser amounts spent by cities, school districts, towns, and sewage districts in that order. Local governments, it is argued, are not just service providers and regulators. They are also lobbyists active in seeking more money from higher levels of government and fewer restrictions on their discretion.

Many other professional and political groups exist including associations of those holding particular offices, such as the Wisconsin Sheriffs and Deputy Sheriffs Association and the Wisconsin Managers Association, as well as regional associations such as the Mid-Moraine Municipal Association in the Milwaukee area and the Dane County Municipal Association. Additionally, several local governments have permanent lobbyists in Madison while others send representatives when issues arise.

Collective Bargaining for Public Employment

Local governmental employees in Wisconsin were granted the right in 1959 to form unions and bargain collectively with their employers, the first such state law in the country. Although private employees were permitted to form unions and collectively bargain, government employees were prohibited from doing so. Among the reasons for the prohibition was the argument that government employees were already covered under civil service laws, therefore it would not be proper to allow them to unionize as well. Further, since the government represented the public interest, it was considered improper for government employees to organize against that public interest. This was reinforced when the possibility of strikes was voiced.

Since the 1959 authorization of public sector unions, union membership has steadily increased. Teachers are among the groups with the greatest percent of unionized employees. Where paid fire departments exist (as opposed to volunteer organizations which exist in many parts of the state), fire fighters are highly organized. The average union membership for local government in Wisconsin is 89 percent, declining to 82.4 percent if Milwaukee is excluded. About 80 percent of cities have one or more unions. Unions representing public employees are typically affiliated with national unions such as the National Education Association, the largest, and the American Federation of State, County, and Municipal Employees, the second largest.

Strikes by public employees, especially teachers, occurred in Wisconsin in the 1960s and 1970s but have significantly declined. Although strikes still may occur if the employer concurs, the adoption of *final offer arbitration* reduced the strike threat. With final offer arbitration, if an agreement is not reached, each party is to submit its final positions. An arbitrator, failing to achieve a voluntary compromise, adopts one of the offers *in toto*. Because of the possibility that an arbitrator will not select an offer that is extreme in its demands, final offer arbitration is presumed to encourage reasonable proposals (Haferbecker, 1978).

It is argued that Wisconsin's compulsory arbitration law did create a resolution of the dispute, avoiding disrupting strikes. It equalizes the power of the parties and provides a face-saving device for both management and labor. Nonetheless, criticisms have been voiced. Most notably, it is argued that the law has provided more expensive settlements than would have otherwise occurred through the negotiations process where compulsory, final offer arbitration was not present as a determinant in an impasse. Governor Thompson charged that the wage settlements resulting from this law are significant in raising local property taxes. Further, the question is raised whether it is acceptable to have a private third party (the arbitrator) imposing a settlement on a government whose officials are responsible to the people. It is argued that this arbitrator has an impact on local government taxes without being elected.

Impartial reviews of Wisconsin's law have been favorable, maintaining that it has achieved goals of resolving disputes fairly and avoiding strikes (Stern et al., 1975). In response to a survey, mediator-arbitrators indicated that the most frequently used guidelines in making awards are the pay and working condition of similar groups of public employees in the immediate geographic area, with other bargaining units of the same employer being the second most frequent basis cited. As to the economic outcomes of the mediation-arbitration process, the mediator-arbitrators believe that there was no discernable difference between settlements outside the process and those within it (Wisconsin Legislative Council Staff, 1985).

In 1994, at Governor Thompson's urging, the Wisconsin legislature limited teacher and administrator compensation to 3.8 percent annually until mid-1996 unless the Board and teacher's union reach a higher contract agreement. With the 3.8 percent in the law, boards feel that this could serve as a limit in their negotiations. The purpose of these changes was to reduce the escalation of property taxes. Governor Thompson argued that teachers' salary raises are a major factor behind the increase in school costs, a large component of property taxes.

The current budget, recently signed into law by Governor Thompson, contains several modifications to employee dispute resolution procedures. For instance, the budget act repeals the scheduled July 1, 1996 sunset of the arbitration law. However, the legislature also included modifications to factors used by arbitrators to settle dispute. Included in these modifications is a requirement that arbitrators must consider state legislative and administrative directives which place limits on local government or school district spending or revenues when settling a case. Again, this limit is intended to help corral escalating local property levies.

Conclusion

Local governments in Wisconsin face multiple challenges. At the root of most is the difficulty of providing high quality services without tax increases. Residents regularly voice concern over rising property taxes. To combat local tax increases, local officials have pressed the state to provide more in shared taxes, but without mandates; sought private firms to provide services more efficiently; and encouraged businesses to expand and to move to their community, thus increasing the tax base. In encouraging economic development, local governments have provided grants and loans to businesses, including issuing bonds, known as Industrial Revenue Bonds, to raise money for these firms.

Whether government should assist business in this manner is controversial. By supporting businesses, jobs are created and more business and personal taxes are paid. These revenues support services that benefit all local citizens. Others suggest that few local jobs are actually developed. Businesses, if viable, would move to the community anyway, and that to assist businesses in this manner constitutes improper public subsidies. Mayors and city councilmen must make decisions on crucial issues such as this.

Although opinions on local issues are not few, as illustrated by Letters to the Editors' column in local newspapers, competition for many local posts is low. Mayors and council members (president and trustees for villages) frequently run unopposed. With the part-time nature of council posts, very low salaries or only per-meeting compensation, plus the pressures of the job, the lack of competition is not surprising. With uncontested seats and low interest among citizens, voter turnout for local elections is typically small.

For the state government, the broad issue concerning equalization of services and revenues among its local subdivisions is enduring. To what extent are poor communities allowed to provide services such as education that are inferior to that provided in other communities in the same state? The question is premised on the idea that spending is a principal determinant of student achievement, a claim that is challenged by a considerable body of empirical research (Hanushek, 1981). In many states, state courts nonetheless are currently pressing the state to step-in to redress this issue as required in their state constitutions. In Wisconsin, the state supreme court has yet to find inequitably distributed service a violation of the state constitution, but whether judicially mandated or not, state government will face this issue regarding its localities in the 1990s.

Part II: Citizen Politics

CHAPTER IV

POLITICAL PARTIES AND ELECTIONS IN WISCONSIN

By John F. Bibby*

Wisconsin is characterized by competitive two-party politics in statewide elections and by political parties that are loosely structured, voluntary associations whose activists reflect an issue oriented style of politics. These parties are not based upon patronage and they do not have the capacity to control nominations. The distinctive character of Wisconsin party politics is derived from the state's open primary, limited political patronage, the development of mass membership party organizations, campaign finance reforms, nonpartisan municipal elections, and a tradition going back to the La Follette progressive era which seems to make mavericks particularly appealing to Wisconsinites. Although Wisconsin has its unique features, its politics has also been molded by national forces.

Patterns of Electoral Competition

Wisconsin's current pattern of vigorous two-party competition is a relatively recent phenomenon (post-1956). Throughout most of the state's history, the Republican party dominated Wisconsin government and politics. The current nature of Wisconsin parties, therefore, owes much to the unique circumstances of its evolution from one-party Republicanism to a system of two-party competitiveness.

Republican One-Partyism, 1855-1934. Nineteenth century Wisconsin politics was characterized by Republican dominance as the party won the governorship in all but three of 19 contests from 1855 to 1894. Republican dominance in national and state elections continued into the twentieth century. In the 1920s, Democratic gubernatorial nominees averaged only 28.4 percent of the vote and in 1922 the party's candidate gained only 10.6 percent of the popular vote. As a result of the Republicans' electoral dominance, the most meaningful competition occurred in the Republican primaries between the conservative stalwart faction and the progressive followers of Robert M. La Follette. Between 1894 and 1934, intra-party struggles between these two factions produced a system of bifactional one-partyism as stalwart and progressive Republicans alternated control of Wisconsin government.

The struggle for control of Republican nominations gave rise to a form of party organization that was later to give both parties their distinctive organizational character. In an effort to nominate their faction's gubernatorial candidates, the stalwart Republicans formed the Republican Voluntary Committee in 1925. This organization endorsed candidates for major state offices and provided the endorsed candidates with financial support and workers in the primaries. The Republican Voluntary Committee with its mass membership and financial resources proved to be an effective campaign resource in gubernatorial primaries. In 1928 it helped Walter Kohler, Sr., win the gubernatorial nomination, and in 1932 it was successful in defeating Governor Philip La Follette in the Republican primary (Sorauf, 1954:695).

The Democrats won statewide elections only under the most unusual circumstances, as during the Great Depression when they carried the state for Franklin Roosevelt, elected a U.S. senator and governor, and gained a majority in the state Assembly in 1932. This electoral sweep was accomplished with the support of the La Follette progressives, who had defected from the GOP after Governor Philip La Follette had been defeated by a stalwart, Walter Kohler, Sr., in the 1932 Republican primary. The La Follettes and their progressive followers did not intend to form a permanent alliance with the Democrats. To the progressives, Wisconsin's Democratic party was electorally weak and no less conservative than the Republicans. A progressive member of the U.S. Congress described the democrats as "a political shell manned by job conscious people" (Sundquist, 1983:243).

---

* Professor of Political Science, University of Wisconsin-Milwaukee.

Multi-Party Politics, 1934-1946. Senator Robert M. La Follette, Jr., who had been elected as a Republican, faced reelection in 1934. However, the Depression had discredited the Republican label whether it was worn by a progressive or stalwart. In addition, his brother Philip's defeat in the 1932 GOP primary demonstrated that he was not assured a renomination as a Republican. Faced with these circumstances, Robert La Follette, Jr. led his family's followers out of the Republican party and formed a separate Progressive party. During the 1934-1946 era, therefore, Wisconsin had three parties contesting elections (Epstein, 1986:125-26; Sundquist, 1983:244-46). The departure of the progressives left the Republican party dominated by conservatives. The Progressives were a moderate to liberal force which was largely supportive of the domestic policies of Franklin Roosevelt's New Deal. The Democratic party had a narrow ethnic base--a coalition of Irish, Polish, and some German Catholics--and a distinctly conservative policy orientation. During this period, major electoral competition for state and congressional offices was between the Republicans and the Progressives. Even the national Democratic party recognized this political reality. It sought to distance itself from the conservative patronage oriented state Democratic party and even supported Robert La Follette, Jr., in his campaigns for the Senate, in 1934 and 1940 (Thompson, 1988:440).

In the mid-1940s, however, an electoral realignment occurred that foreshadowed the development of regular two-party competition between the Republicans and Democrats. Liberal and labor elements in the state started to move into the Democratic party. This movement toward the Democrats was aided by Franklin Roosevelt's fourth term candidacy and popular support for Democratic internationalism rather than Progressive isolationism. In 1944, the Progressives were confronted with Franklin Roosevelt leading the Democratic presidential ticket, no La Follette on the ballot, and a popular Republican governor with some progressive inclinations, Walter Goodland, seeking reelection. In these difficult circumstances, the Progressive gubernatorial candidate received only 5.8 percent of the vote. However, the Democratic nominee, Milwaukee Mayor Daniel Hoan, captured 41 percent of the vote, an indication that Wisconsin politics was moving toward two-party competitiveness between the Republicans and the Democrats.

Caught between an emerging Democratic party and a strong Republican party, the future prospects of the Progressive party were less than encouraging as it confronted the task of securing the reelection of Senator Robert La Follette, Jr., in 1946.

Two-Party Competition, 1946-Present. The events of 1946 had far reaching consequences for the nature of interparty competition in the Wisconsin party system and the character of the Republican and Democratic parties.

The demise of the Progressive party. With their electoral base narrowing and the Democratic National Committee having announced that it would no longer support Progressive candidates (including La Follette) in Wisconsin, and Republican prospects looking highly favorable as the 1946 election approached, the Progressive party voted in 1946 to disband and re-enter the Republican party. Robert M. La Follette, Jr., sought to retain his Senate seat by seeking the GOP nomination. He was, however, defeated in the Republican primary by Joseph McCarthy, who went on to win the general election. La Follette's decision to reenter the GOP and his defeat in the Republican primary killed the Progressive party, which had always been heavily dependent upon the La Follette family's personal following rather than a strong organizational base.

Although many Progressives in metropolitan areas did not follow their leaders back into the Republican party, the return of many older and rural Progressives to the GOP helped the Republicans to maintain their electoral dominance of the state for another decade (Epstein, 1958:51-54; Dykstra and Reynolds, 1978:299-326). The demise of the Progressive party did, however, result in many rank and file Progressive voters shifting their allegiance to the Democrats. As a result, the Democratic share of the gubernatorial vote rose in the 1940s from 12.3 percent in 1942 to 44.1 percent in 1948 as the Democrats became the principal opposition force to the dominant GOP (Thompson, 1988:433-34).

As liberal and labor elements of the Progressive party realigned themselves with the Democrats, the Republicans were left without a strong progressive force within their party that was capable of mobilizing labor and liberal voters for GOP candidates. The post-1946 realignment also meant that there would not be a revival of the bifactionalism that had characterized state politics before the La Follettes had split off from the GOP to form the

48

Progressive party. Henceforth, the divisions within the GOP would be between its conservative and moderate factions. The election of Senator Joseph McCarthy and his emergence as a controversial national figure affected both the Republican and Democratic parties. McCarthy had never been close to the state GOP leadership. Indeed, he had won the party endorsement for the Senate in 1946 largely by default because no well known party leader emerged to challenge La Follette. McCarthy's greatest asset among Republican activists was that he was not La Follette. McCarthy's controversial "red baiting" in the 1950s, however, created a high level of divisiveness within state Republican ranks, as evidenced by his relatively weak showing (54 percent) in the 1952 elections when the GOP presidential and gubernatorial nominees, Dwight Eisenhower and Walter Kohler, Jr., were winning landslide victories.

Although they never succeeded in defeating McCarthy at the polls, the senator did have some beneficial consequences for the Democrats. McCarthy was so controversial and divisive that he proved to be a potent basis for recruiting workers and voters for the Democratic party and thereby contributed in an unintended way to making Wisconsin a two-party state (for an excellent account of the McCarthy era in Wisconsin politics, see Thompson, 1988:528-611).

The Democratic Breakthrough: Proxmire wins McCarthy's Senate seat. The first breakthrough for the Democrats came in the 1957 special election for United States senator to fill the vacancy caused by the death of Senator McCarthy. William E. Proxmire, who had been defeated three times as Democratic nominee for governor, was elected. The following year, he was reelected and Gaylord Nelson became the first Democratic governor since 1932. In addition, three Democrats won state constitutional offices, and the party won control of the Assembly. Wisconsin has had competitive two-party politics in contests for major state-wide offices ever since.

In this competitive, two-party environment, the Republicans have fared better in gubernatorial elections than they have in state legislative elections. Between 1956 and 1994, the GOP held the governorship for 20 years and the Democrats for 18 years. However, the Democrats have held sway for most of the time since the 1970s in the state legislature. Democrats controlled the state Assembly from 1970 until the 1994 elections, when the GOP gained a narrow majority; and Democrats dominated the state Senate from 1974 until a series of special elections in 1993.

The impact of national forces. The collapse of the Progressive party demonstrates that Wisconsin politics, like state politics more generally, does not operate in isolation from national forces. Partisan loyalties are forged in the fires of presidential campaigns and voters tend to support the same party in both national and state elections. These national electoral forces make it difficult for third party movements to survive at the state level. The Wisconsin Progressives and the Minnesota Farmer-Labor party were among the strongest third parties in the country, but both were compelled in the post-World War II era to merge with one of the major parties. The pull of national partisan alignments was so strong that both parties faced inevitable defeat as separate political organizations (Epstein, 1986:124-26).

Patterns of Two-Party Competition Since 1956

Gubernatorial Elections. The Republicans and Democrats have been locked in tight competition to control Wisconsin government since the Democrats emerged as a major electoral force in the 1950s. In the 14 gubernatorial elections between 1956 and 1994, only one candidate, Republican Tommy Thompson in 1994, has received in excess of 58 percent of the major party vote. (See IV Figure-1.) Thompson was the first governor to receive at least 60 percent of the vote since 1952 when Walter Kohler, Jr., won with 62 percent; Thompson's 67 percent in 1994 was the largest majority any candidate had received since 1922 when John J. Blaine (Rep.) garnered 76 percent. Since 1956, the average percentage of the popular vote received by winning gubernatorial candidates has been 54.9 percent, with the GOP winning eight times and the Democrats six.

Figure IV-1

PERCENT VOTE FOR GOVERNOR
Major Parties, 1956 - 1994

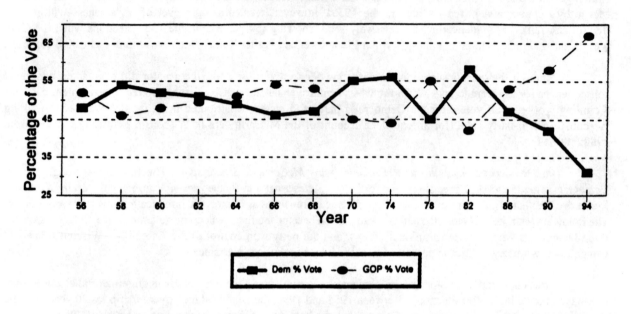

State Constitutional Offices. Although the Democratic party achieved competitiveness with the GOP in gubernatorial and U.S. Senate elections after 1957, it took the party another 17 years before it could assert control over the constitutional offices of lieutenant governor, secretary of state, state treasurer, and attorney general (see Table IV-I).

Table IV-1

PARTY CONTROL OF STATE CONSTITUTIONAL OFFICES, 1956-1994

Year	Lt. Gov.	Sec. of State	State Treas.	Atty. Gen.
		Party Winning the Office		
1956	R	R	R	R
1958	D	R	D	D
1960	R	R	R	D
1962	R	R	R	R
1964	D	R	R	D
1966	R	R	R	D
1968	R	R	R	R
1970[a]	D[b]	R	D	R
1974	D	D	D	D
1978	R	D	D	D
1982	D	D	D	D
1986	R	D	D	R

| 1990 | R | D | R | D |
| 1994 | R | D | R | D |

Party Election Victories

Before	R 5	R 8	R 6	R 4
1974	D 3	D 0	D 2	D 4
After	R 4	R 0	R 2	R 1
1974	D 2	D 6	D 4	D 5
Total	R 9	R 8	R 8	R 5
	D 5	D 6	D 6	D 9

[a] Beginning in 1970 all constitutional officers were elected for four year terms instead of two year terms.

[b] Beginning in 1970 the Lieutenant Governor was elected on a combined ticket with the Governor. Prior to 1970 the Governor and Lieutenant Governor were elected separately.

The state's Republican traditions and well known GOP incumbents, like the ever popular Secretary of State Robert Zimmerman (1957-1975), kept these offices under mostly Republican control until 1974. With GOP fortunes at a low ebb in 1974 due to the Watergate scandals in Washington, Democratic Governor Patrick Lucey coasted to an easy reelection victory and the Democrats began a 12 year period in which they controlled the secretary of state, state treasurer and attorney general offices. Since 1986, the Republicans have managed to at least temporarily reclaim the office of state treasurer (1990, 1994), and attorney general (1986). Due to the low public visibility of the constitutional offices below the governor, a well known political name has been a major asset for candidates of both parties. For example, persons with a last name of Smith have been elected state treasurer in all but two elections between 1938 and 1986; and a Zimmerman or La Follette has won the secretary of state's office in every election but two between 1938 and 1994.

Legislative Elections. The long period of overwhelming Republican dominance in both houses of the state legislature ended when the Democrats won control of the Assembly in 1958. However, it was not until 1974 that the Democrats were able to achieve majority status in the State Senate. (See Figure IV-2.) The 1974 through 1992 elections gave the Democrats uninterrupted control of both chambers of the legislature. It took until 1994 (20 years) until the GOP could again win majorities in both legislative chambers.

In the immediate post-World War II era, there was substantial turnover in the membership of the legislature. Wisconsin had an amateur legislature as members served on a part-time basis with voluntary retirement a commonplace phenomenon. In the ten years between 1946 and 1956, 17 percent of the Assembly membership and 32 percent of the senators did not seek reelection. Nor was it uncommon for incumbents to lose their seats in the primaries or general elections. An average 17 percent of the Assembly members were defeated and 13 percent of the senators lost their seats every two years (Epstein, 1958:198).

By contrast, striking features of the Wisconsin Assembly and Senate since the 1960s have been the low turnover of membership and the high reelect rates of incumbents. With its pattern of high incumbent reelection rates, Wisconsin is part of a national trend in state legislatures (Jewell and Breaux, 1988). As the Wisconsin legislature has become more professionalized, the job of a legislator has become virtually full-time, and the advantages of incumbency (staff support, mailing allowances, opportunities for constituency service, policy advocacy, and fund raising) have expanded dramatically. The vast majority of the members in both chambers now

Figure IV-2

DISTRIBUTION OF SEATS
Percent Controlled by Democrats

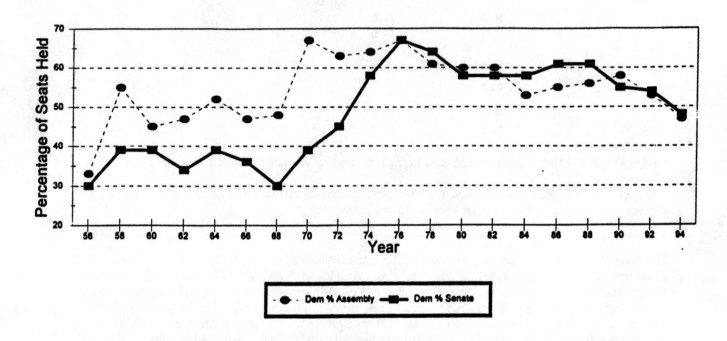

seek reelection and as the data on the 1986-1994 elections illustrate, incumbents are now being reelected in over 90 percent of the cases. (See Table IV-2.) Indeed, in 1994, 39 Assembly incumbents (22 Republicans and 17 Democrats) had no major party opponents in the general election. The tremendous advantages currently enjoyed by incumbents, of course, substantially impede significant shifts in party control of the seats in both the Assembly and Senate.

It appears that the increasing professionalization of the legislature--virtually full-time status, longer sessions, higher pay, larger staffs--has worked to the disadvantage of the Republicans (Fiorina, 1994). Individuals working in the private sector find it increasingly difficult to combine a legislative career with managing a small business or practicing a profession. Full time political careers, therefore, have held limited appeal for many youthful Republican-oriented business and professional people. Yet it has been from among a pool of such individuals that the GOP has traditionally tended to recruit its legislative candidates. Potentially strong candidates from among Democratic clientele groups, by contrast, have tended to find the prospect of full time legislative positions and careers in government to be quite attractive. The Democrats, for example, have been more effective than the Republicans in using legislative staff positions as training grounds for future legislative candidates. After examining candidate recruitment for the legislature, the senior political analyst for *Governing* magazine, Alan Ehrenhalt, concluded:

Every other year, Democrats and Republicans battle for legislative control...in what is advertised as a debate about which party best reflects the views of the electorate. Within the corridors of the capitol, however, the biennial elections are recognized for what they really are: *a competition to attract candidates who have the skills and energy to win and the desire and resourcefulness to stay in office....This is a*

52

competition that the Democrats keep winning. The Republicans know it perfectly well (Ehrenhalt, 1989: 29-30). [Emphasis added.]

Table IV-2

INCUMBENTS WIN: ASSEMBLY AND SENATE ELECTIONS, 1986-1994

	Incumbents Seeking Reelection	Incumbents Winning		Percentage of Incumbents Reelected
		Primary	General Election	
1986 Elections				
Assembly	91	91	88	96.7
Senate	16	15	15	93.8
Totals	107	106	103	96.3
1988 Elections				
Assembly	88	88	83	94.3
Senate	15	15	15	100.0
Totals	103	103	98	95.1
1990 Elections				
Assembly	88	88	86	97.7
Senate	15	15	14	93.3
Totals	93	93	90	96.8
1992 Elections				
Assembly	78	78	76	97.4
Senate	14	14	12	85.7
Totals	92	92	88	95.7
1994 Elections				
Assembly	90	90	88	97.8
Senate	14	13	13	92.9
Totals	104	103	101	97.1

Divided Partisan Control of State Government. The tendency toward extended periods of one party control of the legislature plus competitive contests for governor have made divided partisan control of state government commonplace. Indeed, since 1957 it has been more common for the state to have the governorship and at least one house of the legislature controlled by different parties than for one party to control both the executive and legislature. (See Table IV-3.)

Table IV-3

SINGLE VERSUS DIVIDED PARTY CONTROL OF WISCONSIN GOVERNMENT, 1957-1996

SINGLE PARTY CONTROL
Republican Governor,
Senate, Assembly
1957-58, Thomson
1967-68, Knowles
1969-70, Knowles
1995-96, Thompson

Democratic Governor,
Senate, Assembly

1975-76, Lucey
1976-77, Lucey
1983-84, Earl
1985-86, Earl

DIVIDED GOVERNMENT
Republican Governor/Demo-
cratic Senate & Assembly
1979-80, Dreyfus
1981-82, Dreyfus
1987-88, Thompson
1989-90, Thompson
1991-92, Thompson

Democratic Governor/
Republican Senate and
Assembly
1961-62, Nelson
1963-64, Reynolds

Republican Governor/ One
Chamber Controlled by
Democrats
1965-66, Knowles
1993-94, Thompson*

Democratic Governor/ One
Chamber Controlled by
Republicans
1959-60, Nelson
1971-72, Lucey
1973-74, Lucey

Total Years of Single
Control of Wisconsin
Government: 16

Total Years of Divided Party
Control of Wisconsin
Government: 24

* Republicans gained control of the state Senate in 1993 by winning two of three special elections.

Federal Elections. No clear pattern of partisan advantage emerges from an examination of presidential, United States Senate, and House elections between 1956 and 1994. (See Table IV-4.) In presidential contests, the Republicans have carried the state for their candidate in six of the last ten elections with the Democrats having carried the state in both 1988 and 1992. The electoral competitiveness of Wisconsin is demonstrated by the fact that winning presidential candidates in each election since 1972 have received a smaller percentage of the vote in Wisconsin than they did in the country as a whole. In its presidential voting habits, Wisconsin has tended to follow national trends and has voted for the winning presidential candidate in eight of the last ten elections (the exceptions were 1960 when the state supported Nixon over Kennedy and 1988 when Dukakis carried the state against Bush).

Figure IV-3

WISCONSIN CONGRESSIONAL DISTRICTS

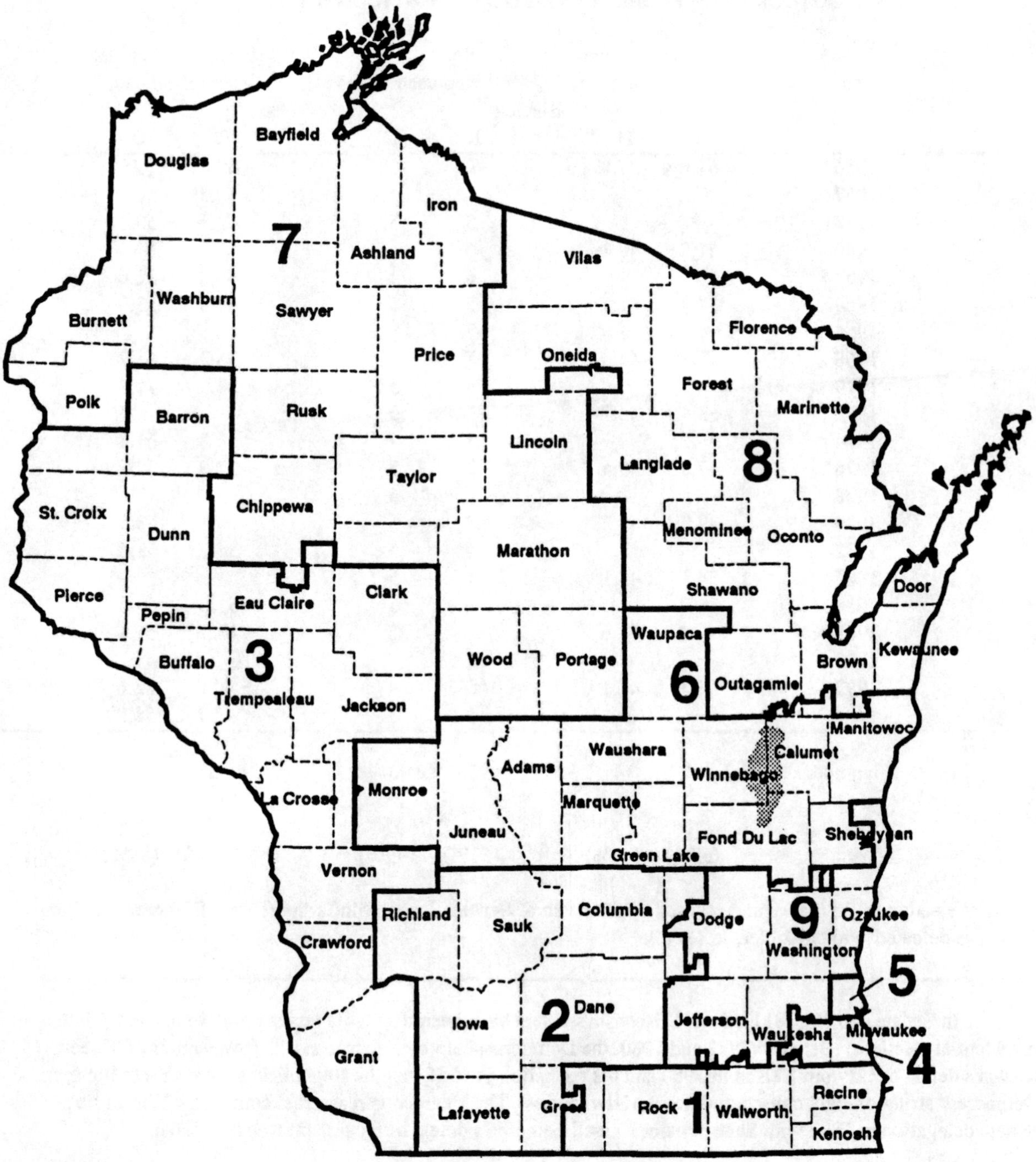

Source: Compiled from the State of Wisconsin, *Blue Book* 1995-96:18.

Table IV-4

OUTCOMES OF FEDERAL ELECTIONS IN WISCONSIN, 1956-1994

Year	Percent of Popular Vote for President		No. of Representatives Elected		Percent of Popular Vote for Senator	
	R	D	R	D	R	D
1956	61.6%	37.8%	7	3	58.6%	41.2%
1957					40.5ᵃ	56.4ᵃ
1958			5	5	42.7	57.1
1960	51.8	48.1	6	4		
1962			6	4	47.2	52.6
1964	37.7	62.1	5	5	46.6	53.3
1966			7	3		
1968	47.9	44.3	7	3	38.3	61.7
1970			5	5	28.5	70.8
1972	53.4	43.7	4	5		
1974			2	7	35.8	61.8
1976	47.8	49.4	2	7	27.0	72.2
1978			3	6		
1980	49.9	43.2	4	5	50.2	48.3
1982			4	5	34.1	63.6
1984	54.3	45.1	4	5		
1986			4	5	51.0	49.0
1988	47.8	51.6	4	5	47.5	52.1
1990			5	4		
1992	36.8	41.1	5	4	46.0	52.6
1994			6	3	41.1	58.9
Number of Elections Won	6	4	95	93	3	12
	(60%)	(40%)	(51%)	(49%)	(20%)	(80%)

ᵃ Special election to fill the vacancy caused by the death of Senator Joseph McCarthy (Rep.). Democrat William Proxmire defeated Walter Kohler, Jr. (Rep.).

In Senate and House elections, Wisconsin's voters have been decidedly less supportive of the GOP than in presidential elections. Between 1962 and 1980, the Democrats held both Senate seats. It was not until Robert Kasten's defeat of Gaylord Nelson in 1980 and his reelection in 1986 that the Republicans were able to break the Democrats' string of eight consecutive senatorial victories. The Democrats reasserted control for Wisconsin's Senate delegation in 1992 with State Senator Russell Feingold's defeat of incumbent Robert Kasten.

The narrowness of Kasten's two elections (50.2 percent in 1980; 51 percent in 1986), Democrat Herbert Kohl's close 52 percent victory over Republican Susan Engeleiter in 1988, and Democrat Feingold's 1992 win with 53 percent of vote, are further evidence of the competitive nature of state-wide elections in the state.

After decades of Republican dominance in the state's U.S. House delegation, the Democrats achieved majority status in 1972 and held control of the delegation until 1990 when moderate Republican, Scott Klug of Madison, defeated incumbent Robert Kastenmeier in the second district. (See Table IV-5.) As is true of congressional elections across the country, an overwhelming proportion of Wisconsin House incumbents win reelection. Between 1980 and 1994, incumbents lost only three elections in which they were seeking reelection for a 95.7 percent reelection rate. Not only have House incumbents been winning reelection, they have been doing so by comfortable margins. (See Table IV-5.) The normal pattern is for Representatives to have one or two competitive elections early in their careers and then to solidify their electoral positions. In fact, between 1980 and 1994, only 24 percent of the elections in which an incumbent was seeking reelection did the incumbent receive less that 60 percent of the vote. Thus Representative Scott Klug (Rep.-Second District) won his initial election in 1990 with only 53 percent of the vote. In his second election (1992), he garnered 63 percent, even though Bill Clinton carried his district in the presidential race. By 1994 Klug had pushed his total to 69 percent of the vote. In addition, incumbents' winning margins are subject to wide swings. For example, between 1984-1986, Aspin posted a +19 percent swing; Petri posted a +47 percent swing between 1990-1992. (See Table IV-5.)

Wisconsin Election Law

Wisconsin's election laws reflect the state's progressive heritage and carry a distinct anti-party organization bias (Epstein, 1958:30-32). Party organizations, of course, operate in Wisconsin, but the political culture and legal climate are not conducive to cohesive organizations capable of controlling nominations, mobilizing voters, or dispensing patronage to the faithful.

Partisan and Nonpartisan Elections. A large number of elected officials are not chosen on a partisan ballot and are thus outside the regular party system. These include all judges, county board members, county executives, municipal councils and village boards, mayors, school board members, town officials, and the state superintendent of public instruction. Nonpartisan elections are held in April of both odd and even numbered years (in 1996, nonpartisan general elections will be held on March 19 in order to coincide with the presidential primary), with nonpartisan primaries conducted in February. Because of the nonpartisan election process, it is normally difficult for large city mayors to use their positions as stepping stones to major state or federal office.

The following state, county and federal officials are elected on a partisan ballot: state officials--governor and lieutenant governor (on a combined ticket), secretary of state, state treasurer, attorney general, state senators, and state representatives; county officials--sheriff, district attorney, clerk, register of deeds, clerk of court, treasurer, coroner, and surveyor (counties may appoint a medical examiner instead of electing a coroner and most counties employ a registered land surveyor in lieu of electing a surveyor); federal officials--president and vice president, United States senator and representative. State constitutional officers are elected for four year terms in non-presidential even-numbered years (i.e., their elections coincide with congressional midterm elections). State senators serve four year terms with half of the Senate elected every two years. All other partisan elected officials serve two year terms and are elected in even numbered years. There is no limit on the number of terms a state or county official may serve.

Ballot Access and Ballot Form. Wisconsin election laws make it relatively easy for parties to qualify for the general election ballot. All that is required for a political party to qualify for a column on the ballot is that one of its candidates for state-wide office in the previous election has polled one percent of the vote for that office. If a party cannot qualify on this basis, it can gain a ballot position by securing a relatively modest number of signatures on a petition. In addition, independent candidates can have their names placed on the ballot by obtaining a stipulated number of signatures on a petition. Unlike many states, Wisconsin does not have a "sore loser" law which bans independent candidacies by persons who lose their party's primary nomination. State statutes bestow no special status upon the two major parties and make access to the ballot for minor parties and independent candidates relatively easy to accomplish.

Wisconsin uses a party column type of ballot in which all of a party's nominees for various offices are arranged in a row or column with the voter permitted to cast a straight party vote by either making a check in a party circle on paper ballots, pulling a party lever on voting machines, or indicating a party line vote on computerized systems. This ballot form tends to encourage straight ticket or party line voting. In presidential years, there is a separate ballot or line on a voting machine for citizens to cast their presidential votes. It is not, therefore, possible to make a single check on the ballot or pull just one lever to cast a straight party vote for all of a party's nominees from president to register of deeds.

Table IV-5

U.S. HOUSE MEMBERS' WINNING PERCENTAGE OF THE VOTE, 1980-1994

District	Candidate	1994	1992	1990	1988	1986	1984	1982	1980	Avg.
1	Aspin (D)	---	58	100	76	75	56	61	56	96
	Neumann (R) [a]	50	---	---	---	---	---	---	---	50
2	Kastenmeier (D)	---	---	---	59	56	64	61	54	59
	Klug (R) [b]	69	63	53	---	---	---	---	---	62
3	Gunerson (R) [c]	56	57	61	68	64	68	57	51	60
4	Zablocki (D)	---	---	---	---	---	---	95	70	83
	Kleczka (D)	54	67	69	100	100	67	---	---	76
5	Reuss (D)	---	---	---	---	---	---	---	77	77
	Moody (D)	---	---	71	64	100	98	64	---	79
	Barrett (D)	62	70	---	---	---	---	---	---	66
6	Petri (R)	100	53	100	74	100	76	65	59	78
7	Obey (D)	54	64	62	70	67	68	57	68	64
8	Roth (R)	64	70	54	67	67	68	57	68	65
9	Sensenbrenner (R)	100	71	73	75	78	73	100	78	84
	Average Winning Percentage	67.7	63.7	71.4	72.6	78.6	70.9	68.6	64.6	71.8

[a] Neumann defeated incumbent Peter Barca (D)., who had won a special election in 1993 after Les Aspin was appointed Secretary of Defense by President Clinton.
[b] Klug defeated incumbent Robert Kastenmeier (D).
[c] Gunderson defeated incumbent Alvin Baldus (D).

<u>An Absence of Patronage</u>. Traditional party organizations have used patronage to reward loyal party workers and contributors and to maintain organizational influence over nominations. Wisconsin political parties are not sustained by patronage. The patronage opportunities for governors and other partisan elected officials are extremely limited. The civil service system is firmly established in Wisconsin. Governors are empowered to appoint most department heads and their key deputies and members of the Public Service Commission, plus a personal staff. Other than these few positions, the only appointments available to the governor are for positions on nonpaid boards and commissions. The absence of patronage is believed to be one of the factors contributing to the issue-oriented style of politics which sets Wisconsin apart from such Midwestern states as Indiana, Illinois, and Ohio, where the patronage system flourishes.

<u>The Open Primary</u>. Party control of the nomination process was severely weakened in 1903 when Wisconsin became the first state to enact a direct primary law to nominate candidates for partisan office. The primary was designed by its progressive sponsor, Governor Robert M. La Follette, to weaken the hold which party organizations had over nominations and to give the voters direct control of nominations. In his successful fight to abolish party nominating conventions and caucuses and replace them with the direct primary, he argued:

> Under our form of government the entire structure rests upon the nomination of candidates for office...If bad men control nominations we cannot have good government...[We] must...place nominations in the hands of the people, and make all nominations by direct vote at a primary election.
> With nominations of all candidates in the control of the people...the public official who desires re-nomination will not dare to seek it, if he has served the machine and the lobby and betrayed the public trust (Torelle, 1920:29-31).

Party primary elections are held in September of even numbered years to nominate candidates for the U.S. Senate, U.S. House, state, and county offices. Primaries are also required to nominate candidates for special elections called to fill vacancies in elective positions. The governor fixes the time for special election primaries.

The particular form of primary used in Wisconsin has especially adverse consequences for party organizations. In order to vote in a Wisconsin party primary, the voter need not register to vote as a Republican or Democrat. Nor is it necessary to make any public declaration of party preference at the polls in order to vote in a party primary. Rather, registered voters decide in the secrecy of the polling booth in which party's primary they wish to vote.

This *open primary* procedure makes it extremely difficult for a party organization to identify its supporters and then turn them out on primary election day to vote for the organization's preferred candidate. By contrast, in those states in which partisan registration is required to vote in a primary, the state is, in effect, providing each party with a list of its supporters. Such lists give the parties a useful tool with which to mobilize both primary and general election voters. Wisconsin's open-primary forces both parties to rely on more expensive and complicated methods (telephone or door to door canvassing) to identify partisan supporters. Wisconsin is one of only nine states that uses an open primary system. Most states require either partisan registration to participate in primaries or some public declaration of party preference at the polls.

<u>Regulation of Political Parties</u>. In an effort to restrain the influence of political parties, La Follette and his supporters enacted severe statutory regulation of party organizational structure and campaign finance. Wisconsin statutes created a *statutory party organization*. The law specified how party officials and committees would be chosen, their terms of office, functions of party committees, and severe limitations on expenditures. The basic principle of this La Follette-inspired legislation was that parties should be controlled by those who won primary elections rather than by leaders chosen through caucuses or conventions.

In an effort to influence the outcome of primaries, create a party organization that operated year around (instead of one, like the statutory party, which came into being after the September primary), and avoid unrealistically low campaign expenditure limitations, conservative Republicans formed a *voluntary party organization* in 1925. This was a dues paying, voluntary, extra-legal organization not subject to the severe restrictions imposed upon the statutory organization. By the 1930s, the voluntary party organization had established itself as the real Republican party of the state. In the post-war years, liberal and labor activists formed a voluntary Democratic Organizing Committee, which like its Republican counterpart, became the functioning Democratic party in Wisconsin (Sorauf, 1954: 692-704).

Although the voluntary Republican Party of Wisconsin and Democratic Party of Wisconsin are the organizations recognized as the official party organizations of the state by the respective national party committees, the statutory parties continue to exist. Their functions, however, are extremely limited. Local committeemen and women elected in the September primary nominate election day poll workers to municipal officials. The statutory party also is authorized to fill vacancies on the general election ballot that may occur due to death or withdrawal after the primary. State level statutory committees select each party's slate of presidential electors.

In reality the distinction between the statutory and voluntary party organizations is insignificant because the statutory party organizations have been merged with the voluntary parties, which are governed by their own constitutions and bylaws. The real organizational muscle of the parties is in the voluntary parties.

The Party Organizations

Political parties in Wisconsin have not been immune from the forces that have affected parties generally in the United States. As American politics has become increasingly *candidate centered*, the party organizations have had to adapt to the existence of a multitude of personal campaign organizations operating in their midst. These highly autonomous candidate organizations raise money, recruit workers, hire staff, and manage the individual campaigns conducted within the state. For example, in the 1994 gubernatorial campaign, both Governor Thompson and State Senator Charles Chvala relied mainly on their own personal organizations to raise money and conduct their campaigns. The regular party organizations' role tended to be supplementary and supportive of the candidates' organizations. The party organizations have also been faced with competition for campaign influence from a growing number of political action committees (PACs), which have assumed a significant role in financing campaigns, especially those of incumbent legislators. The current pattern of candidate centered politics with its attendant role for PACs is quite different than the prior era of party-centered campaigns. This change has not meant, however, that state and local party organizations, both in Wisconsin and across the country, are inactive or in a state of decay (Cotter, et al., 1984; Bibby and Holbrook, 1995). In this state, both parties' organizations have adapted to candidate centered politics by becoming increasingly sophisticated fund raisers and providers of in-kind campaign assistance to candidates.

The state parties also work closely with the Republican and Democratic National Committees, which in recent elections have transferred large amounts of money to their state affiliates for "party building" activities. The most important of these party building activities are voter mobilization operations (voter identification and get-out-the-vote drives) which are both expensive and labor intensive. By working with state parties to support (and sometimes direct) these programs, the national party organizations have been able to use the state organizations to implement their national campaign strategies. Wisconsin's two parties have also derived benefits from the largesse of the national organizations, since they have gained valuable lists of voters who support party candidates, as well as other resources (e.g., computer facilities) which build up the infrastructure of state parties. With the growing involvement of the national party organizations with state parties through fund transfers for party building, Wisconsin's Republican and Democratic parties are being integrated into the national parties' campaign strategies and operations and in the process losing an element of their traditional autonomy.

Mass Membership. Dues Paying. Voluntary Organizations. Although there are variations in the structure and operation of the Republican and Democratic organizations in the state, they share a common organizational base. Membership is composed of individuals who voluntarily join local party units and pay dues to the party. Party members are more than just party voters. They are political activists who are willing to attend party meetings and conventions, contribute money, and often work in campaigns. These activists tend to feel more keenly about political issues than rank and file party voters. In general, Republican activists are more conservative than Republican voters; and Democratic party activists are more liberal than are rank and file Democratic voters.

Membership and active participation in party affairs is largely a middle and upper middle class phenomenon in Wisconsin. The strongest party organizations are, therefore, often found in suburban areas and urban counties where there is a concentration of middle and upper middle class voters. Active local party organizations do not, therefore, necessarily coincide with areas of party electoral strength. For example, an active GOP organization exists in the Democratic stronghold of Dane (Madison) County, while local Democratic units function in Republican dominated Milwaukee suburban areas.

The Local Unit. The basic organizational unit with which party members affiliate is the county organization. Those who attend a county caucus in odd-numbered years and pay dues are the members who elect county party officers, choose delegates to congressional district caucuses and state conventions, and conduct local campaign activities. Because of Milwaukee County's large population, the basic party unit in Milwaukee County is normally an Assembly District, though municipalities and geographic areas also form the basis for organizations (e.g., there are both Democratic and Republican North Shore suburban units). In populous Waukesha County, which is normally a major source of Republican electoral strength, the GOP operates through a series of sub-county units that reflect municipal and regional boundaries.

The Democratic Party of Wisconsin: *County Organization.* County or local unit party members pay annual dues, a small portion of which is sent to state Democratic headquarters. They also elect local party officers and delegates to congressional caucuses and the state convention.

Congressional District Organization. Congressional district officers are elected by delegates to congressional district caucuses held in odd numbered years. An executive committee composed of county and local unit chairs and vice chairs directs the work of the congressional district organization.

State Convention. The state convention meets annually in June and is composed of delegates from each county and local unit. It drafts the party platform, passes policy resolutions, and elects a state party chair, vice chairs, secretary, treasurer, and Democratic National Committee members. The Democrats' constitution bans pre-primary endorsement of candidates for the party's nomination.

State Administrative Committee. The State Administrative Committee is the chief governing body of the state party. It has 42 members including the party chair and other officers, national committee members, congressional district chairs and vice chairs, two additional representatives from each congressional district elected by their respective caucuses, the Milwaukee County chair, the County Chairs' Association chair, representatives of the legislature and Young Democrats, and the immediate past state chair. The state chair is responsible for supervising the staff at party headquarters, maintaining liaison with county units and elected officials, and normally is heavily engaged in fund raising.

The Republican Party of Wisconsin: *County Organization.* Party members are those who pay dues and join a local unit. Dues vary among local units and there is no requirement that a portion of the dues money be forwarded to the state headquarters. County or local unit officers are elected at a caucus held in odd-numbered years. As in the case of the Democrats, the county and local units elect delegates to annual congressional district caucuses and to the state convention.

Congressional District Organization. Congressional district caucuses in odd-numbered years elect a district chairman and vice chairman, who also serve as members of the state executive committee. In even-numbered years, district caucuses may choose to endorse a candidate for the Republican nomination for Congress. Candidate endorsement is, however, optional and it is not practiced in all districts.

State Convention. The annual party convention drafts a party platform in even-numbered years and passes policy oriented resolutions in odd-numbered years. It also elects a national committeeman and woman in presidential election years. Unlike the Democrats, the Republican state convention does not elect the Republican state chairman and other party officers. Rather, party officers are elected by the state executive committee.

Before 1980, the major difference between the two parties' conventions was that the Republicans followed a procedure which required them to endorse candidates for state-wide office in the September primary, while the Democrats' constitution forbad endorsement. One of the reasons for this difference between the parties was the fact that the voluntary Republican Party of Wisconsin came into being as a vehicle of the stalwarts to influence nominations and wrest control of the party from the La Follette progressives. Endorsement was normally quite effective in influencing GOP nominations because it carried with it significant financial and organizational support from the state party. Candidates who failed to gain a party endorsement often declined to run in the September primary believing that they would be unsuccessful or fearing the consequences of alienating the party leadership. The endorsement process was, however, far from invincible and periodically nonendorsed candidates emerged as primary victors (e.g., incumbent Senator Alexander Wiley defeated Second District Representative Glenn Davis, the endorsed candidate, in the hard fought 1956 Senate primary).

Gradually, however, endorsement came to mean less and less as the state GOP failed to provide endorsees with significant financial support and party activists felt little compulsion to support the endorsed candidate. The weakness of the endorsement process was particularly apparent in the 1978 gubernatorial contest between Representative Robert Kasten (Ninth District) and Lee Sherman Dreyfus, the Chancellor of the University of Wisconsin-Stevens Point. Kasten was endorsed by the state GOP convention, but the state party provided him with only modest support in his primary campaign against Dreyfus. This left Kasten with the onus of being perceived as the candidate of the party "bosses" or "kingmakers", while receiving few tangible benefits from the party. Dreyfus exploited Kasten's status as the endorsed candidate and in the Wisconsin tradition of political independence stressed his lack of party connections. Dreyfus won the primary handily.

With Dreyfus installed as governor, the Republicans in 1979 amended their party constitution to make endorsement optional rather than mandatory. Since 1978, the GOP has not endorsed any candidate for state-wide office.

The State Executive Committee. The state executive committee is composed of congressional district chairmen and vice chairmen, the national committeeman and woman, the President of the Federation of Republican Women, representatives of the Young Republicans, the state finance chairman (appointed by the state chairman), the immediate past state chairman, the chairman of the College Republicans, the chairman of the county chairmen, the chairman of the Black Republican Council, and the chairman of the Republican Heritage Groups. The Executive Committee elects a state party chairman, two vice chairmen, a secretary, and treasurer. The state chairman is responsible for headquarters operations, appoints and supervises the staff, and works closely with the finance chairman on fund raising.

The Role of the State Chairman. Wisconsin's state party chairmen have traditionally been unpaid volunteers (though several chairmen in both parties have received compensation), in contrast to the increasingly common practice in other states of chairmen serving as full-time, paid officers. State chairmen here have, therefore, tended to rely heavily on an executive director at party headquarters to handle the day-to-day administration of party business. The chairman is, however, the key leader in the party structure with responsibility for headquarters operations, field staff, finance, and liaison with elected officials and local party leaders. As is true of most state parties across the country, the Republican Party of Wisconsin has consistently operated with larger budgets and staff than its Democratic counterpart. It has, therefore, been a more important campaign resource for its candidates than has the Democratic state party for its nominees.

Governors normally exercise substantial influence in the selection of their party's state chairman, even though neither party's constitution specifies a formal role for the governor in the selection process. The identity of the governor's choice for state chairmen is normally made clear to party leaders, who invariably abide by his wishes. For example, State Senator Donald Stitt (1987-1989) and Michael Grebe (1990) who served as Republican State Chairmen during Governor Tommy Thompson's first term were both his designates, as was David Optiz, who succeeded Grebe.

There has been great variation in the influence wielded by individual state chairmen. Those who have devoted virtually full time to their party duties and were aggressive in fund raising, candidate recruitment, campaign support, and local party building have exerted great influence (e.g., Ody J. Fish in the 1960s for the Republicans and Patrick Lucey in the 1950s and 1960s for the Democrats). The influence of state chairmen is also affected by whether their party controls the governorship and by the nature of their relationship with a governor of their party. Chairmen with a close relationship to a governor of their party have normally found their position substantially strengthened within party circles. When such a relationship exists, the party organization normally benefits because the governor assists the chairman in intra-party disputes, fund raising, candidate recruitment, and campaign efforts. A classic example of a state party chairman with close ties to the governor was Republican Ody J. Fish during the administration of Warren P. Knowles (1965-1970). Fish functioned as a key advisor to the governor and assisted him in liaison with GOP legislators and party leaders across the state.

Not all governors, however, have been supportive of their state party leadership. Some have down-played the role of the party organization and sought to concentrate power within their own personal campaign organizations and the governor's office in order to prevent the party from becoming a rival center of power. Ironically, down-grading of the state party's role was the policy followed by Governor Patrick Lucey (1971-1977), one of the founders of the modern day Democratic party and one of its most influential state chairmen. By contrast, Governor Tommy Thompson has been highly supportive of his state party. Generally, state party chairmen are most prominent and influential when their party does not control the governorship and, therefore, they are not required to share publicity and decision-making authority with the state's chief executive. Out-party state chairmen also have more freedom of action than do those who serve under a governor of their party.

Wisconsin's party chairmen have rarely held elective office simultaneously with their party service. A rare exception was Donald Stitt, who served as Republican chairman (1987-1989) while also a member of the state Senate. Stitt's problems illustrate the difficulty of simultaneously juggling the roles of a legislator, party leader, and gubernatorial supporter. When he felt compelled to take positions (e.g., on Indian treaty rights) as a legislator that were different than those of Governor Thompson, he was placed in an anomalous position of seeming to undermine the Governor's position and of creating intra-party dissention.

The Legislative Campaign Committees. Legislative campaign committees have become increasingly important organizations within both parties. These committees are composed of legislative incumbents chosen by the Republican and Democratic caucuses in the Assembly and state Senate. Their principal function is to help elect fellow partisans to the legislature. Under provisions of a 1979 revision of campaign finance legislation, the Republican Assembly Campaign Committee, Democratic Assembly Campaign Committee, Republican Senate Campaign Committee and Democratic Senate Campaign Committee are each authorized to collect $75,000 per year ($150,000 per two year election cycle). The bulk of their funds tends to be raised from political action committees (PACs).

Backed by leverage which legislative leaders have for raising funds and with the resources to hire professional staff, contract for consultants' services, and make significant contributions to Assembly and Senate candidates, the legislative campaign committees have become the principal party organizations involved in legislative elections. The committees are heavily involved in recruiting candidates, training candidates and their campaign managers, funding candidates, and providing candidates with in-kind assistance. Since the goal of the committees is control of legislative chambers, they tend to use a criterion of "winability," rather than ideological purity, in determining which candidates will receive significant levels of assistance.

Former Assembly Speaker Thomas Loftus described the role of the legislative campaign committees in this way following the 1984 elections:

> I am chairman of the Assembly Democratic Campaign Committee. We raised about $150,000 this year to help Democrats running in marginal seats. In most cases, we recruited the candidate. We provide training through campaign schools. We provide personnel and logistical support, issue papers, press releases, speakers for fund raisers, fund raisers themselves, and phone banks. We pay for the recount, if it's a close race; we pay for the lawyer, if it goes to court; if they have kids, we pay for the baby sitter...We don't have dues paying members, but we are moving toward that concept...(Loftus, 1985:108).

The legislative campaign committees in both parties operate with substantial autonomy from the regular party organizations. They have their own officers and staff and an ability to raise funds among PACs that the state party committees do not have. In each party, the Assembly and Senate committees also operate quite separately from each other, though there are occasional joint fund raising events. The expanding role of legislative campaign committees in Wisconsin is consistent with a pattern that is emerging in other states and reflects the power of legislative incumbency in American politics (Gierzynski, 1992). The increasing importance of legislative campaign committees in Wisconsin also parallels the prominence achieved at the national level by the congressional and senatorial campaign committees, which since the 1970s have become major players in congressional elections (Herrnson, 1995).

Party Differences. Although the Republicans and Democrats have roughly comparable organizational structures, there are significant differences between the two parties and the roles they play in elections. Generally, in state-wide, congressional, and most county races, the Republican party organization is a more important campaign resource than is the Democratic party organization. Although no candidate for major office relies primarily on the party organization to get elected, Republican candidates normally receive more in the way of financial and organizational support from their party than do Democratic candidates.

One of the reasons that party support is less important in the Democratic party is that organized groups allied with the party regularly supplement candidate and party campaign activities (see Cotter, et al.:138-41). Among the organizations in Wisconsin that are closely tied to the Democratic party and which provide its candidates with assistance in fund raising, get-out-the vote drives, precinct targeting, polling, and staffing are the Wisconsin Education Association Council (WEAC), Wisconsin AFL-CIO, and Farmers' Union. WEAC is particularly important. In 1988, the 5400 member association spent $535,516 primarily to support Democratic legislative candidates through direct contributions and independent expenditures (expenditures made by the association without the involvement by the candidate that was being supported).

For interest groups allied with the Democratic party, independent expenditures have become increasingly important. Thus in 1994, labor organizations, led by the state teachers' union, spent almost $325,000 in independent expenditures to help Democratic legislative candidates. In an effort to keep control of the Assembly under Democratic control, Wisconsin Citizens for Responsive Government, a labor PAC, spent $149,000 in three Assembly races that were believed crucial; and WEAC poured $57,000 into television advertizing and direct mail brochures into an unsuccessful effort to defeat Representative Lorraine Seratti (Rep.) of Eagle River in northern Wisconsin. This level of spending is more than the candidates themselves have traditionally spent on Assembly races.

The Republicans, of course, are not without group support. It tends, however, to come mainly from members of the business community and takes the form primarily of financial contributions either to the party or to GOP candidates. This tends to reinforce the importance of the Republican party, since business organizations do not normally engage in independent expenditures or other forms of campaigning.

An additional reason why the state Republican organization tends to be a more important campaign resource than the Democratic party involves the national parties' relationship to their state affiliates. At the national level, the Republican National Committee and the Republican Congressional and Senatorial Committees have been more successful in fund raising than the national level Democratic party committees. As a result, the state Republican party has been receiving more financial support from national party sources than has the state Democratic party.

Neither party is monolithic in character and there are factional divisions within both. Republican factionalism has frequently had an ideological bent as moderates and conservatives find themselves at odds in nominating contests and races for party leadership posts. Electoral successes in the 1980s by Presidents Reagan and Bush, Senator Kasten, and Governor Thompson have, however, tended to bank those ideological fires. Democratic factionalism has tended to be less ideological in its orientation. Instead it has been of a shifting character-- sometimes regional in nature pitting Milwaukee Democrats against out-state Democrats, and at other times centered around either presidential or state-wide candidates.

Interestingly, the state's and the Democrats' most effective post-World War II vote-getter, Senator William Proxmire (1957-1988), operated largely aloof from the party and its allied interest groups. Thus, just two weeks after winning his Senate seat in 1957 with strong backing from organized labor, he went before the Wisconsin State CIO convention to issue what he called his "declaration of independence" from the unions:

> I'll take no dictation, instruction, or discipline from any leader of organized labor. I will not sit down behind closed doors and close out the press and public...I will not submit to collective discipline (Sykes, 1972:95).

Proxmire went on to say that he would do everything in his power to prevent any group, including organized labor from imposing its will on the Democratic party. And for good measure, he advised reporters that he would not submit to influence by the Democratic party. As University of Wisconsin Professor and former Proxmire aide Ralph K. Huitt observed, "No group can contain him long. He does not trust it to take care of him nor make decisions, and he cannot abide the restrictions which would go with his truly belonging (Sykes, 1972:95).

In adopting the stance of an independent and political maverick above parties and organized interests, Proxmire was following in the Wisconsin tradition of the La Follettes and progressives, whom he admired and whose electoral successes he hoped to emulate. Proxmire's successor, Senator Herbert Kohl (Dem.) has also sought to stress an image of political independence by refusing to accept PAC contributions and spending over $6 million of his own money on both his 1988 and 1994 campaigns, while using the slogan, "Nobody's senator but yours". While the Proxmire example is an extreme instance of political independence, most Wisconsin incumbent office holders rely primarily on their own personal organizations and electoral followings, not upon their party's organization.

Campaign Finance

Wisconsin revised its archaic 1911 campaign finance law during the 1970s in the wake of the reform movement that swept the country following the Watergate revelations. A 1977 law enacted by the Legislature limits the amounts all partisan candidates can receive from any one individual, PAC, or another candidate's personal campaign committee. The individual contribution limits are $10,000 for constitutional officers (e.g., governor, attorney general); $1,000 for state senators; and $500 for state representatives. PACs are limited to contributions of $43,128 for gubernatorial candidates; $21,564 for attorney general candidates; $12,939 for lieutenant governor candidates; $8,625 for state treasurer and secretary of state candidates; $1,000 for state Senate campaigns; and $500 for Assembly campaigns.

The act also restricts the percentage of contributions that can be received from PACs to 45 percent of total funds collected. Nor may all PAC contributions total more than $485,190 to gubernatorial candidates, $7,763 to assembly candidates, and $15,525 to state senate candidates. In addition, state law limits contributions from all political committees (including PACs, political parties, and other candidates' committees) to 65 percent of total candidate receipts, with the following cumulative limits on all political committee contributions: gubernatorial candidates--$700,830; assembly candidates--$11,213; and state senate candidates--$22,325.[1]

To further limit the level of campaign spending and the role of PACs, the 1977 law also set up a system of public funding for general election campaigns. In order to qualify for public funding grants, persons must demonstrate their viability as candidates by raising a statutory minimum of funds from individual contributions in amounts of $100 or less. The revenue source for public funding of state campaigns is a one dollar check-off on Wisconsin income tax forms, similar to that used at the national level to pay for public funding of presidential elections.

Candidates who accept public funding of their campaigns must agree to abide by state imposed expenditure limits. However, one of the incentives candidates have for accepting public funding is that the law waives the spending limit for a candidate accepting public funding when an opponent declines to take public funding. Acceptance of public funding was a fairly standard practice for Republican and Democratic nominees for state-wide office and the Legislature during the 1980s. However, beginning in the late 1980s, the proportion of taxpayers using the income tax check-off to direct one dollar of their taxes to the public financing fund dropped off substantially. Approximately 19.7 percent of taxpayers designated one dollar to the fund in 1979, compared to 10.2 percent in 1993. As a result, the effectiveness of the fund as a means of financing campaigns has been reduced. Governor Thompson's campaign committee in 1990 and 1994, for example, declined to accept public funding because it believed (1) there was insufficient money in the fund to help finance a major reelection campaign and (2) that spending limits were too restrictive for a hard fought state-wide race.

Legislation passed in 1986 capped spending for candidates accepting public funding as follows: gubernatorial candidates--$1,078,200; lieutenant governor--$323,475; Attorney general--$539,100; secretary of state and state treasurer--$215,625; State Senate candidates--$34,500; and Assembly candidates--$17,250. Because these expenditure limits are well below what is generally considered necessary in gubernatorial elections or targeted legislative races, candidates are frequently discouraged from taking public funding. Thus, in spite of the fact that Wisconsin's public financing law had as one of goals increasing electoral competition between incumbent legislators and their challengers, there is little evidence to suggest that it has succeeded in achieving this objective (Mayer and Wood, 1995).

Although the law was intended to reduce campaign expenditures and the role of PACs, there is little evidence that it has succeeded. Because of the law's restrictions on the amount and proportion of funds that a candidate may receive from PACs, direct PAC contributions to candidates have been reduced. But PAC money has not been eliminated; it has just been channeled through less direct routes. The legislative campaign committees have been steadily increasing their campaign expenditures and these committees receive a majority of their funds from PACs. Regular features of legislative sessions are Assembly and Senate campaign committees' fund raisers to which lobbyists representing PACs feel obligated to contribute.

Organized interests have also set up conduit systems of campaign financing. Conduits permit special interest groups to collect individual contributions from their members, "bundle" or store those contributions in one account, and then write a single check for all the group members who want to give to specific candidates. Conduits or "bundling" is attractive to both organized interests and candidates. Conduits enable organized interests to increase their level of giving to preferred candidates above the limits imposed on direct PAC contributions. Conduits also permit candidates to accept special interest money indirectly when they have already collected their limit of direct PAC contributions. This highly sophisticated system of campaign finance has grown in recent years and accounted for $2.2 million in campaign contributions in 1993-1994.

---

[1] See Mills (1989) for an analysis of the law and the constitutional issues it raises.

Nominations

State, County, and Congressional Offices. The primary was instituted by the La Follette progressives in an effort to reduce the influence of party leaders and give the voters a more direct say in the selection of candidates for the general election. In this the reformers have achieved success. Party organizations in Wisconsin do not control nominations, although the support of the key party leaders may be extremely valuable to a candidate running in a primary election.

Competition in primaries. Competition has not been as frequent or as intense in the primaries as the reformers had hoped. Primary competition is closely related to a party's prospects of victory in the general election. Thus when Congressman Henry Reuss retired from the House of Representatives in 1982 after holding a safe Democratic seat in Milwaukee (Fifth District) for 28 years, there were 10 candidates for the Democratic nomination to succeed him. With the prospects for general election dismal, there was only one candidate for the Republican nomination. And when the winner of the 1982 Democratic primary, Representative James Moody (Dem.), relinquished his seat to run for the U.S. Senate in 1992, there was a hot six-way primary for the Democratic nomination. Primary contests are frequent for gubernatorial and senatorial nominations because state-wide contests in Wisconsin are normally competitive between the parties. In 1986, for example, there was a spirited contest on the Democratic ballot between Matthew Flynn and Edward Garvey for the right to challenge incumbent Republican Senator Robert Kasten, while Republicans waged a three-way struggle between Tommy Thompson, Jonathan Barry, and George Watts for a chance to face incumbent Governor Anthony Earl. Both parties also had strongly contested primaries in 1988 for the Senate seat being vacated by William Proxmire. Susan Engeleiter defeated Steve King for the GOP nomination and Herbert Kohl beat former Governor Anthony Earl, Secretary of State Douglas La Follette, and the 1986 nominee, Edward Garvey, for the Democratic nomination. However, when the prospects of victory are slim, the likelihood of primaries even for prestigious offices like governor declines. Thus in 1994, State Senate Charles Chvala was unchallenged for the right to be the Democratic nominee against Governor Thompson, who was heavily favored for reelection.

Incumbency. Incumbency carries a distinct advantage in nominating contests, and the presence of an incumbent in a primary is usually enough to scare off serious opposition. As Table IV-2 demonstrates, incumbent state legislators are rarely defeated for renomination. Not one incumbent state senator or representative seeking renomination lost in a primary between 1986 and 1992. However, one state Senator, Republican Barbara Lorman (Fort Atkinson) did lose the primary in 1994.

Similarly, incumbent members of the U.S. House of Representatives customarily coast to easy primary victories with either token or no opposition. The sole instance of an incumbent losing the primary was in the Watergate year of 1974, when Ninth District Congressman Glenn Davis lost the Republican nomination to Robert Kasten.

Cross-over Voting. One of the enduring issues concerning Wisconsin's open primary is the effect of cross-over voting--the ability of partisans of one party to vote in the other party's primary and the ability of independents to vote in partisan primaries. There is strong evidence that voters gravitate to the party primary in which there is a real contest. For example, in the 1992 primary for United States Senator, the Republican share of the total vote was 32 percent and the Democratic share was 68 percent. In that year, there was an intense three-way contest (there were also two minor candidates) for the Democratic nomination, while incumbent Senator Robert Kasten had only token opposition in the GOP primary. By contrast in 1978 and 1986 when there were real battles for either gubernatorial or senatorial nominations in both parties, the Republican and Democratic shares of the total primary vote were approximately equal.

Do voters of one party cross-over in an effort to nominate the weakest candidate of the opposition party? In this controversy, there is conflicting evidence. Most of the evidence, however, suggests that cross-over voters tend to support a preferred candidate and do not engage in partisan maneuvering, or "raiding" of the opposition party's primary.

Turnout and Representativeness of the Primary Electorate. Although Wisconsin has one of the highest voter turnout rates in the nation in general elections, turnout in primary elections is low. Less than 20 percent of the voters normally participate in the September primary. This low turnout rate plus the tendency of political activists to have more extreme ideological views than rank and file voters has caused political scientists to consider whether patterns of voter turnout bias outcomes of primaries. That is, do the patterns of turnout favor conservatives in the Republican primary and liberals in the Democratic primary? Nation-wide, studies of presidential primaries have indicated that such biases do operate. There have, however, been few studies of the effect of turnout on Wisconsin primaries. One study done in the 1960s concluded that Wisconsin primary voters are reasonably representative of the eligible partisan electorate in issue positions or candidate preferences (Ranney and Epstein, 1966).

The primary and the general elections. Party leaders often fear that a divisive primary will leave the party disunited for the general election and result in a victory for the opposition. There are certainly instances in Wisconsin electoral history of divisive primaries contributing to a general election loss. The 1957 special election primary to nominate a candidate to succeed Joseph McCarthy that pitted former Republican Governor Walter Kohler against Congressman Glenn Davis is often cited as an example. There are also observers who believe that Edward Garvey's 1986 campaign against Robert Kasten for the Senate was weakened by the charges leveled against Garvey in the primary by former Democratic State Chairman Matt Flynn.

There are, however, circumstances when a contested primary may help the nominee. Battling for a party nomination normally generates substantial publicity and keeps the name of the candidate before the public during the summer and early fall when most voters are not normally paying much attention to politics. A tough primary fight may even enhance the image of the candidate as an attractive personality, skilled campaigner, and person who is articulate and knowledgeable on the issues. Candidates in contested primaries also get a chance to hone their campaign skills and test out effective campaign themes. However, the absence of a primary fight can push a candidate off the evening news programs and front pages of the newspapers. A primary victory after a heated contest normally gives the winning candidate's campaign a sense of momentum. Campaign workers generate renewed enthusiasm, contributors are stimulated to give, and press coverage increases. In 1986, Republican gubernatorial challenger Tommy Thompson clearly emerged from a contested primary a stronger candidate. He received a surge of favorable publicity, contributions, and volunteer support in September and early October and his standing in the polls shot up dramatically. By contrast, Governor Anthony Earl ran for the Democratic nomination unopposed and, as the favored candidate, got no real boost from his uncontested primary victory.

Presidential Primaries. Wisconsin in 1905 was the first state to adopt the presidential primary as a part of the delegate selection procedure for national nominating conventions. When there were only a few states holding presidential primaries and Wisconsin's was one of the early primaries, the state's primary drew much national attention and on occasion played a major role in determining presidential nominations (e.g., John F. Kennedy's victory over Hubert H. Humphrey in the 1960 Democratic presidential primary). Since 1972, a majority of all national convention delegates in both parties have been chosen in processes that involve primaries. Wisconsin is only one of over 35 states now holding presidential primaries and its importance in presidential nominating politics, therefore, has diminished significantly. Further deflating the importance of Wisconsin's first Tuesday in April primary has been the concentration of other states' presidential primaries in March. This process of "front-loading" the delegate selection process would have meant that in 1996 over 70 percent of national convention delegates would have been chosen before Wisconsin held its primary. Consequently, the state legislature in May 1995 moved the spring primary day for 1996 to the third Tuesday in March to coincide with presidential primaries in Illinois, Michigan and Ohio.

The Wisconsin primary has, however, generated public attention because of a dispute between the Wisconsin Democratic party and the Democratic National Committee (DNC) over Wisconsin's use of an open presidential primary procedure (Wekkin, 1984). In 1974 the national Democratic party banned the use of open presidential primaries. Delegates were to be selected through either closed primaries or party caucuses so that non-

Democrats could not participate in the delegate selection process.

In a case (*Democratic Party of the U.S.A. v. La Follette*, 449 U.S. 89, 1981) brought by the State of Wisconsin challenging the national Democratic party rule against open presidential primaries, the United States Supreme Court in 1981 upheld the right of the national party to compel states to follow delegate selection procedures that were in conformity with national party rules. Previous to this, in 1976 and 1980, Wisconsin Democrats had been able to obtain a waiver of the rule against open presidential primaries from the DNC. No waiver was forthcoming from the DNC in 1984, and state Democrats were, therefore, compelled to select their national convention delegates through a party caucus system. Since the presidential primary law continued on the Wisconsin statutes, the state also conducted a presidential primary in 1984 for Democrats as well as the Republicans (whose national party organization had no rules against open primaries). The 1984 Democratic presidential primary, however, was not legally binding under national party rules and was merely a popularity contest. Interestingly, Senator Gary Hart (D-Colo.) won the presidential primary, but Walter Mondale won a majority of the delegates who were chosen in the party caucuses.

The lengthy and often bitter dispute over the open presidential primary between the state Democratic party and the DNC was finally resolved in 1986 when the DNC revised its delegate selection rules. Wisconsin was permitted to retain its open presidential primary because of its long standing open primary tradition, but the DNC reasserted its legal authority to determine delegate selection standards for the state parties.

The extent and consequences of cross-over voting in Wisconsin presidential primaries has been a source of continuing controversy. Indeed, the large number of voters who crossed-over to vote for George Wallace in the 1964 Democratic primary was a factor in the DNC banning open primaries (Adamany, 1976). An analysis of cross-over voting in the 1968-1984 presidential primaries in Wisconsin revealed that in all but one primary (the 1984 Democratic primary), independent and partisan cross-overs did not have sufficient numbers to alter the plurality winner of the primary, though they may have affected the relative standing of the non-winning candidates. The extent of potential "strategic voting" or "raiding"--that is, voting for a candidate that one would not support in the general election--can be seen in data from the 1984 primaries. In the Republican primary, two percent of the voters indicated that they intended to vote for a different candidate in the November election, while nine percent of voters in the Democratic primary did not plan to support the candidate for whom they voted. Thus, there is potential for cross-over voting and "strategic voting" to affect the results of presidential primaries (Hedlund and Watts, 1986).

Voting Procedures

Elections are conducted by municipalities in accordance with state laws. Poll workers are nominated by ward committee persons of the two major parties. The nominees are then appointed by the appropriate local government officials.

State law requires the use of voting machines in municipalities of 10,000 persons or more. Voter registration is required in every municipality with more than 5,000 population. A Wisconsin first in the continuing effort to achieve greater political participation of citizens was the introduction in 1976 of on-site voter registration. This allows persons to register on election day at the polls by providing appropriate identification and proof of residency.

Another electoral procedure not found in all states is the recall election initiated by a constitutional amendment in Wisconsin in 1926. This amendment authorizes the use of a special election for the purpose of recalling (removing) state, county, legislative, or judicial elected officials. The recall of an incumbent requires signatures on a petition from electors equal in number to at least 25 percent of those voting for governor in the preceding gubernatorial election in the district concerned. An election is then held 40 to 45 days after the filing of such a petition. The incumbent's name is automatically on the ballot unless he/she withdraws. Other persons can file for the office in accordance with the usual filing requirements. The election results then determine if the incumbent is to remain in office or be replaced by a challenger for the rest of the term. Until the adoption of a constitutional amendment in 1981, there was no provision for a primary in conjunction with recall elections. Thus, in 1977 one judge facing two challengers retained his office with less than a majority of votes. However, in that same year, another judge was recalled in spite of having several challengers in the recall election. The 1981 amendment requires a primary if there are more than two candidates for an office subject to the recall proceedings.

The Wisconsin law also authorizes recall of congressmen and senators. However, there is some question whether such a procedure would be effective, because national law does not recognize recall elections, and each house of Congress is itself given the authority to remove members.

Voting Behavior

With the demise of the Progressive party and the revitalization of the Democratic party after World War II, partisan voting behavior in Wisconsin has been consistent with the general trends in other northern states. State-wide elections tend to be competitive between the two major parties. This reflects the relatively close division within the Wisconsin electorate between Republican and Democratic identifiers. (For 1980-1994 party identification and detection data, see Table IV-6 and IV-7).

Table IV-6

PARTY IDENTIFICATION IN WISCONSIN, 1980-1994

Party	Date					
	1980	1984	1986	1988	1992	1994
Democrat	42%	37%	35%	41%	36%	37%
Independent	31	31	28	24	21	22
Republican	26	31	34	34	36	36
Other	1	1	3	2	7	4

Columns may not total to 100% due to rounding.

Source: Professor David Wegge, Director, The Saint Norbert College Wisconsin Survey.

Table IV-7

DEFECTIONS BY PARTY IDENTIFIERS
IN PRESIDENTIAL VOTING IN WISCONSIN, 1984-1992

Party	Percent Defecting[a]		
	1984	1988	1992
Democrats	13%	16%	19%
Republicans	4	7	25

[a] Percentages reflect party identifiers who indicated their intention to vote for a candidate other than their party's nominee. Those who were undecided were not included in the analysis.

70

Source: Professor David Wegge, Director, The Saint Norbert College Wisconsin Survey

The electoral alignments of socio-economic groups within the state are similar to those which exist nationally. In general, higher socio-economic status and educational attainment brings a greater tendency to vote Republican. As Table IV-8 reveals, however, Wisconsin voters are not characterized by sharp class-based divisions. Both parties show a capacity to attract significant levels of support from most major socio-economic groups in the state. The parties, however, do not draw equal levels of support from all groups. Blue collar workers and union members tend to be Democrats, while professional, managerial, and white collar workers are likely to be Republicans. Blacks are overwhelmingly Democratic and persons of Hispanic heritage are strongly Democratic, though not in as pronounced a fashion as Blacks. White Protestants tend to be Republicans, while Catholics (especially those with eastern and southern European backgrounds) are more inclined to be Democrats. Jews are strongly Democratic. Contrary to much conventional wisdom, farmers are not overwhelmingly Republican.

The Political Geography of Wisconsin. In the period of GOP electoral dominance from 1938 through 1956, the vast majority of Wisconsin counties were either strongly or marginally Republican (Donoghue, 1974:56). The GOP was particularly strong in the more prosperous southern half of the state, especially in rural areas, small towns, medium sized cities, and Milwaukee's northern and western suburbs. Democratic electoral strength was concentrated in the southeastern corner of the state--the highly urbanized, industrialized, and unionized counties of Milwaukee, Racine, and Kenosha; Dane County (Madison, the location of the state capitol and the University of Wisconsin); industrial centers of Manitowoc, Sheboygan, and Two Rivers along Lake Michigan and Eau Claire in the northwest; Portage County (Stevens Point); and the economically depressed northern Wisconsin-Lake Superior region. The shift toward the Democrats that began in the late 1950s and ran through the 1970s was particularly pronounced in the northern counties close to the Minnesota border. Counties containing medium sized cities--Green Bay, Janesville, Beloit, Wausau--also moved toward the Democratic column.

During the 1980s, the geographic patterns of party electoral support remained quite similar to those of the 1970s. Democratic support continued to be strongest in Milwaukee, Racine and Kenosha, the Madison area, sparsely populated northern counties, and in selected medium sized cities. Republican strength has continued to be greatest in western and northern Milwaukee suburbs such as Brookfield, Elm Grove, Wauwatosa, Whitefish Bay, Fox Point, River Hills, Bayside, and Mequon; growing suburban/exurban areas in Waukesha, Ozaukee, and Washington Counties; rural and small town areas in the southern half of the state; and the Fox River Valley in the corridor running from Green Bay to Fond du Lac.

Table IV-8

PARTY IDENTIFICATION AMONG SOCIOECONOMIC GROUPS IN WISCONSIN, 1994[a]

	DEMOCRAT	INDEPENDENT	REPUBLICAN	OTHER
STATEWIDE	37	22	36	4
GENDER Men Women	 31 43	 23 22	 40 34	 7 2

AGE				
18-24	34	16	47	3
25-34	39	20	39	2
35-49	37	19	38	6
50-64	27	32	35	6
65 & Over	46	23	28	3
EDUCATION				
8th Grade or less	50	27	18	5
Some High School	50	21	24	6
High School Graduate	43	20	35	2
Some college/ Tech	34	25	36	5
College Graduate	30	20	45	5
INCOME				
Under $10,000	61	25	11	2
$10,000-19,999	40	21	35	4
$20,000-29,999	44	18	32	6
$30,000-39,999	37	17	43	3
$40,000-49,999	30	23	43	5
$50,000-59,999	26	26	44	5
$60,000-Over	28	23	45	4
OCCUPATION				
Prof./Executive	30	23	44	3
Manager/Sales	33	19	41	7
Teacher	48	21	28	3
Other White Collar	47	26	27	**
Skill/unskill labor	37	17	38	8
Farmer	18	36	36	9
Homemaker	25	30	46	**
Student	13	33	53	**
Retired	46	22	30	2
Unemployed	68	11	11	11
RACE				
White	36	23	37	4
Nonwhite	50	13	28	6
RELIGION				
Protestant	24	25	46	5
Catholic	48	21	29	3
Other	43	17	36	3
LABOR UNION				
Blue-Collar Union	35	23	29	13
White-Collar Union	50	23	27	**
Non-Union	37	22	38	4

COMMUNITY SIZE				
Less than 2,500	39	25	33	3
2,500-9,999	35	20	40	6
10,000-49,999	36	22	39	4
50,000-199,999	33	25	38	4
200,000-More	43	19	33	5
POLITICAL VIEWS				
Liberal	56	23	18	3
Moderate	36	29	29	7
Conservative	31	20	45	4

ᵃ Row totals may not sum to 100% due to rounding.

Source: Professor David Wegge, Director, Saint Norbert College Wisconsin Survey.

A basic rule of thumb in Wisconsin politics is that the Democrats must carry Milwaukee County with in excess of 60 percent of the vote in order to win state-wide elections. By contrast, Republican victories require in excess of 40 percent of the Milwaukee County vote, 60+ percent pluralities in the northern and western suburbs (particularly in populous, growing, and normally Republican Waukesha County), and substantial pluralities in the Fox River Valley and other out-state counties in the southern half of the state. When the GOP has scored state-wide victories in closely contested elections, as with Governor Thompson in 1986 and Senator Kasten in 1980 and 1986, the vote has followed these patterns.

The 1990 and 1994 gubernatorial elections were not typical of Wisconsin's competitive, two-party politics. In both elections, Governor Tommy Thompson won reelection by big margins. In 1990, he carried 55 of 72 counties with 58 percent of the popular vote; and in 1994 he won every county but Menomonee while capturing 67 percent of the state-wide vote. However, in Attorney General James Doyle's 52 percent reelection victory, the normal geographic patterns of voting were present. Thus, Doyle rolled up large pluralities in such traditional Democratic strongholds as Milwaukee, Dane, Eau Claire, Kenosha, and Portage Counties, as well as in the more sparsely populated northern region. Doyle's GOP opponent, former federal prosecutor, Jeff Wagner, won his largest pluralities in traditional Republican areas--e.g., Waukesha and Ozaukee Counties, the Fox River valley, and northern and western Milwaukee County suburbs. Compare the geographical pattern just described for the 1994 attorney general election with the 1992 presidential vote as mapped in Figure IV-4.

Figure IV-4

1992 WISCONSIN PRESIDENTIAL VOTE

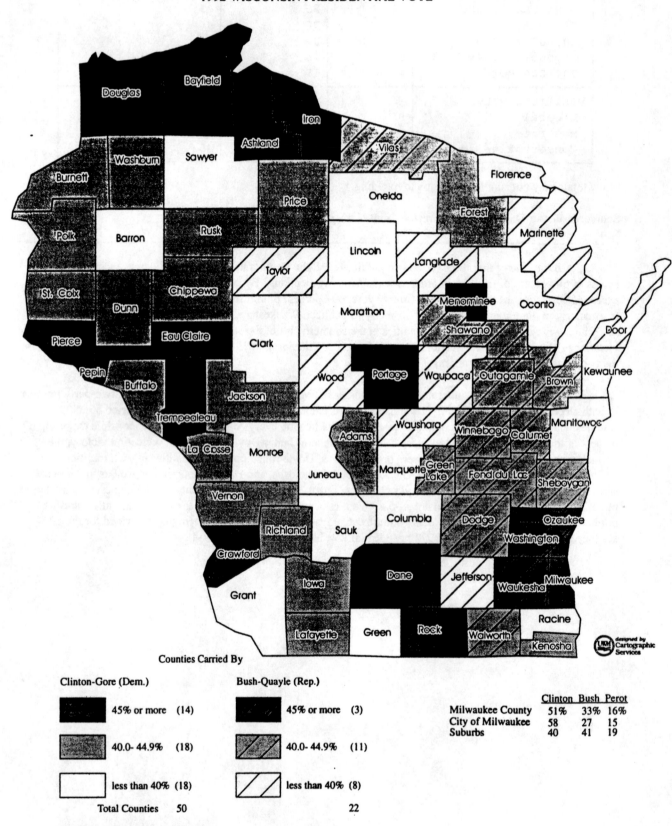

Counties Carried By

	Clinton	Bush	Perot
Milwaukee County	51%	33%	16%
City of Milwaukee	58	27	15
Suburbs	40	41	19

Clinton-Gore (Dem.)

■ 45% or more (14)

▨ 40.0- 44.9% (18)

□ less than 40% (18)

Total Counties 50

Bush-Quayle (Rep.)

■ 45% or more (3)

▨ 40.0- 44.9% (11)

▨ less than 40% (8)

22

Note: Perot did not carry any county.

State-Wide Popular Vote: Clinton 41.1%; Bush 36.8%; Perot 21.1%

Conclusion

The party politics of Wisconsin has unique features that set Wisconsin apart from its sister states. Its statutes and traditions militate against strong, hierarchical, and patronage-based political parties. It is instead a state in which political independence and the style of the maverick have often been a key to electoral success. Politics in Wisconsin tends to be issue oriented and candidate centered. The progressive heritage of the state has affected not only public policies and attitudes toward parties, it has also profoundly influenced the way in which parties are organized on a mass voluntary basis and the manner in which competitive two-party politics finally emerged in the 1950s

While Wisconsin politics has its own distinct flavor, its parties and voting patterns also have much in common with the rest of the northern states. State-wide elections are highly competitive between the two major parties, while congressional and legislative races are generally safe for the incumbents. Divided partisan control of state government occurs frequently. The voting alignments of various socio-economic groups within the state are comparable to those in other states. The web of Wisconsin politics, therefore, combines strands of distinctiveness with strands that are similar to the patterns of political behavior found in the nation as a whole.

CHAPTER V

INTEREST GROUPS

By David G. Wegge[*]

Introduction

Perhaps the most common connotation of interest groups is negative. We often hear that interest groups or the "special interests" have too much power and influence in determining who will serve in decision-making roles, and ultimately what public policy on any given issue will be. In Wisconsin, 62 percent think that interest groups have "too much" influence over political leaders in the state (Common Cause, 1987). While clearly there are negative aspects to the influence of interest groups, it must also be recognized that interest groups perform valuable functions in a democratic system. In fact in the same survey, 52 percent of those interviewed in Wisconsin felt that on the whole interest groups are a "positive force" in Wisconsin politics (Common Cause, 1987).

The debate over interest groups is essentially a debate over two of the primary values in our democratic system: equality and liberty. Democratic theory states that political power within the political system should be widely distributed so that all points of views are represented and all individuals have the same influence within the decision-making process. But democratic theory also states that individuals and groups should have freedom to pursue their self-interests. In the area of interest group politics these two values often clash. The test for democratic systems, both nationally and within state governments, is one of balancing the values of equality and liberty.

This chapter will examine the role that interest groups play in Wisconsin politics. This will be accomplished by (1) summarizing interest group theory, (2) reviewing the functions that interest groups play in democratic systems, (3) delineating the differences between interest groups and other political organizations, and (4) discussing the political action, lobbying and litigation activities that interest groups commonly engage in.

Group Theory

Group theorists believe that if the political role of the interest groups, their functions and the way they exercise power is not understood, it will be impossible to adequately understand the political process as a whole. Group theorists, therefore, begin with the premise that individuals are social beings that live their lives in association with others in groups and that in any society there is a mosaic of overlapping groups of various specialized sorts.

Perhaps the first individual to write on interests in the American context was James Madison in his famous Federalist No. 10. In this treatise Madison defined interests in terms of "faction." He stated:

> By faction I understand a number of citizens, whether amounting to a majority or minority of the whole, who are united and actuated by some common impulse of passion, or of interest, adverse to the rights of other citizens, or to the permanent and aggregate interests of the community (*The Federalist Papers*, p.78).

Madison considered this activity to be the "mischiefs of faction" and was primarily concerned with curing these threats to popular government. According to Madison, numerous factions would emerge based primarily on the distribution of property within the political system and these factions must be held in check.

---

[*] Professor of Political Science and Director of the Survey Center, St. Norbert College.

A landed interest, a manufacturing interest, a mercantile interest, a moneyed interest, with many lesser interests, grow up of necessity in civilized nations and divide them into different classes, actuated by different sentiments and views. The regulation of these various and interfering interests forms the principle task of modern legislation and involves the spirit of party and faction in the necessary and ordinary operations of government . . . (p. 79).

To secure the public good and private rights against the danger of such a faction, and at the same time to preserve the spirit and the form of popular government, is then the great object to which our inquiries are directed (p. 80).

It was through a "republic" form of government, in which the citizenry selects a small number of individuals to represent them in decision-making rather than having all citizens participate directly in the decision-making process, and the separation of powers that Madison believed the "mischiefs of faction" could be controlled. In modern times, however, many question whether these political structures have indeed controlled the "mischiefs of faction."

Over a century later, Arthur Bentley wrote one of the first studies which put interest groups at the vortex of American politics (Bentley, 1908). Among contemporary group theorists, David Truman was one of the first to systematically develop a theory of interest groups (Truman, 1951).

Truman's work, *The Governmental Process*, has become a classic in political science literature. Truman essentially argues that if one is to understand politics in the United States, one must understand the dynamics of interest groups. Briefly, Truman's group theory states that: (1) society is composed of a large number of interest groups, (2) these various groups are constantly in competition with each other, and (3) the public policy which emerges from any decision-making group is the equilibrium reached among competing group interests.

In his work Truman defines a political interest group as "any group that, on the basis of one or more shared attitudes, makes claims upon other groups in society" and makes those claims "through or upon any of the institutions of government" (p.37). Truman's definition emphasizes the notion that individuals with shared attitudes come together in sizable numbers to form an organization. While that clearly is the case with many contemporary groups, it is also possible for interests to be organized with relatively small numbers of members and essentially be staff operations.

One definition that emphasizes the organizational element of interest groups is Berry's definition (1989). Berry defines an interest group as ". . . an organized body of individuals who share some goals and who try to influence public policy" (p. 4). While there are some subtle differences in how various scholars define interest groups, all generally suggest that (1) interest groups emerge out of shared attitudes or goals, (2) some level of organization is necessary, (3) groups are growing both in terms of sheer numbers and amount of activity, and (4) ultimately they all desire to have some impact on public policy.

As we have developed from an agrarian to industrial to information society, we have seen the birth and death of numerous groups. Social, economic and political change bring with it the development of new interests and organizations which support or oppose these new interests. The overall trend has been constant growth.

Walker (1983) documented the growth of interest groups in the United States and found that there was tremendous growth from 1940 to the early 1980's. In Walker's study, 30 percent of the interest groups in existence in 1980 were founded between 1960 and 1980. Wisconsin has also experienced significant growth in the number of interest groups and their activities. One measure of this growth is the change in the number of organizations which have registered to lobby in Wisconsin. In the last six months of 1985 there were 450 different organizations which were represented by lobbyists in Wisconsin. Eight years later in the last six months of 1993 this had increased 22 percent to 551 organizations with registered lobbyists. This growth in lobbying will be covered in more depth at a later point in this chapter.

As interest groups have proliferated, they also find themselves in constant competition with each other. This occurs because each interest group works towards the attainment of its goals which have been defined by the group. When one group attempts to achieve its goals, it will often disturb the goal attainment of other groups. The affected groups will take action to maintain their position and in doing so will affect still other groups. Consequently, each group is fighting to maintain and achieve its goals. For example, in Wisconsin on the recent mandatory seat belt legislation, two groups whose goals directly conflicted with each other were the Wisconsin Safety Belt Coalition and the Seat Belt Freedom of Choice groups. The Wisconsin Safety Belt Coalition lobbied successfully to have the State pass a mandatory seat belt law and the Seat Belt Freedom of Choice lobbies to repeal this mandatory seat belt law.

As interest groups conflict with each other the public policy which emerges from decision-making bodies will often be a balance in the group struggle. Equilibrium, however, does not necessarily mean an "equal" balance of interests. It does mean that those groups which have more political power will get more of what they want and those groups with less power will get less of what they want.

A critical factor in the group process then is the amount of political power that can be exercised by any one interest group or coalition of groups. Truman argues that there are a number of factors which will affect the level of political power which can be mustered by any one group. Some of these factors include the political resources available to the group (e.g., money, status, time, organizational skills, communication effectiveness, etc.), the level of internal group cohesion, the level of access, the quality of leadership, and the current policy mood of the people. Pure and simple, those groups which have these resources will have greater political power and will see the emergent policy to be closer to their desired outcome.

In recent years several scholars have challenged this pluralist point of view, arguing that power in the U. S. is better described as being concentrated in the hand of a few, the elite (Mills, 1956, Parenti, 1988). Although several have questioned pluralism as an accurate description of the American political process, most would see pluralism as the preferred model.

Functions of Interest Groups

Interest groups perform a number of different functions within Wisconsin politics. Berry (1989) suggests that interest groups perform five functions: (1) representation, (2) participation, (3) education, (4) agenda building, and (5) program monitoring.

Interest groups play a very significant role in terms of representation. In Wisconsin all citizens are represented in decision-making bodies by their elected representatives. For example, at the state level individuals are represented in the legislature by elected members of the Assembly and Senate; in local politics people are represented by their elected representatives to the county boards, city councils and school boards. These representatives are selected through an electoral process in which a public official is elected to represent a certain geographical area. While public officials represent the geographical area you live in, the official may not represent the same points of view that you have on various substantive issues.

Interest group representation, on the other hand, is based not on geography but rather on the points of view shared by members of the interest group. Hence an individual could be a member of a labor union and find that she has an elected representative for her district who is anti-union. Under these circumstances she may find that her interests are best represented by her interest group, for example the AFL-CIO, rather than by her elected representative. In this manner interest groups provide a significant link between the citizens in Wisconsin and the institutions of government in the state.

A second function performed by interest groups is that they provide further opportunities for participation in the political process. Some individuals would prefer to participate more frequently than just at election time.

Interest groups provide that opportunity. The policy-making process that interest groups attempt to influence does not stop, it is a continuous process. In order for them to be successful in this process they often need ongoing commitment and active support from their members. Recently, for example, there have been numerous activities scheduled by the interest groups concerned about the issue of abortion. The Wisconsin Right to Life organization and Planned Parenthood of Wisconsin have both been very active. Both of these groups have, in fact, provided participation opportunities for many citizens. Citizens can also participate by contributing money to interest groups. A 1987 statewide survey conducted by the St. Norbert College Survey Center found that 28 percent of the individuals responding had contributed money to an interest group or political action committee in the previous two years.

Educating the public and public officials is a third function that interest groups perform. Most contemporary issues that must be dealt with these days are, by nature, complex. Consequently, one of the first stages of the policy-making process is one of learning about the issue. This is true for both the general public as well as for the public officials who must act on an issue. Because most interest groups have relatively narrow areas of concern, they are often viewed as "experts" in a given policy area. Naturally, however, because they have a specific issue position that they are attempting to promulgate, they are also "biased" in presenting their information. The public and public officials both need to be aware of the interest group's position so that they can take this into consideration when evaluating the information. This does not mean, however, that groups cannot be effective policy educators.

Interest group leaders know that there are boundaries that they must abide by. That is, they know that they cannot present totally fallacious information since this will likely be detected, and eventually will erode the credibility that the interest group has. And, of course, the loss of credibility will lead to a loss of political influence. The watchful eye of other countervailing interest groups also restrains the action of any one interest group in providing information. In Wisconsin, environmental interest groups such as Citizens for a Better Environment and the Environmental Decade have played important roles in educating the Wisconsin citizens regarding the status of the State's environment. Their information is sometimes challenged, as it should be, by other groups which have been concerned about economic development.

Interest groups also perform an agenda-setting function. By agenda-setting we mean getting the issue before the public officials and ultimately placed on their list of problems that need to be resolved. The agenda-setting function can also be performed by keeping certain issues "off" the public agenda. This is a function that often goes hand-in-hand with the education function. In Wisconsin the development of a statewide lottery and parimutuel betting were issues that made their way to the public agenda with considerable assistance from interest groups which would benefit from such activities.

Finally, interest groups often engage in a program monitoring function. This function is performed when groups monitor existing policies as they are being administered and review these programs with the group members' interests in mind. The Citizens' Utility Board is an excellent example of this function being carried out by an interest group in Wisconsin. This group monitors the activities of the Public Service Commission and of the public utilities such as the telephone, gas and electric companies.

Interest Groups and Political Parties

Interest groups and political parties are both political organizations which mediate between the citizens and the public officials in our political system. In that respect they both function as linking mechanisms within our system of government. They are, however, distinct organizations which both have a somewhat different focus for their activities. In very general terms the focus of political parties is to control the positions of government, whereas the focus of interest groups is to control the substance of policy.

In order to control government, parties must concentrate on electoral activities such as recruiting and nominating viable challengers to the opposition party and maintaining their current elected positions in government. To do this parties must be concerned with vote maximization. Since electoral activities are essentially based on geography (the nature of the state legislative districts, etc.) parties are primarily engaged in geographical representation. Political parties are often viewed as part of the legal machinery of government and as a result are usually seen as more legitimate political organizations than interest groups. Furthermore, because a number of different types of candidates with a variety of issue positions run under the same party label and because government is called upon to resolve a multiplicity of problems, political parties tend to have a broad rather than narrow policy focus.

Interest groups on the other hand are most concerned with controlling the substance of policy. Therefore, they concentrate considerable resources on attempting to influence the decision-makers that are in positions of power. Because they represent a group of individuals who have a shared attitude on policy (in some cases groups represent a single position on an issue), they tend to take a much narrower view of public policy. In their attempt to control public policy however, they cannot neglect the electoral process. However, interest groups are generally not afforded the same level of legitimacy within the political process as political parties.

In general terms it could be argued that political parties are coalitions of interests which serve as a unifying force within our political system. Interest groups, on the other hand, are organizations which are concerned about a narrow range of interests and hence are a fractionalizing force within our political system.

There is also a relationship between the nature of the political party system within a state and the nature of the interest group system within that same state. Sarah McCally Morehouse (1981) argues that states which have strong political parties will tend to have weak interest groups and where parties are weak, interest groups will be strong. Using both electoral measures of party strength (Morehouse, 1981) and organizational measures of strength (Cotter, et. al. 1984), Wisconsin is generally felt to have relatively strong political parties. Not surprisingly then Wisconsin is also viewed as having rather weak interest groups. This should not lead one to the conclusion that parties and interest groups do not work together. Actually quite the contrary is true. Interest groups and parties frequently work in unison on policy matters. In Wisconsin there are interest groups which generally tend to align themselves with the Republican Party (e.g., Wisconsin Manufacturers and Commerce) and other groups which are most often aligned with the Democratic Party (e.g., Wisconsin Education Association Council).

In a recent cross-state analysis of interest groups, Thomas and Hrebenar (1990), classify states according to the overall impact that interest groups have in the policy-making process within the state. They suggest that states can be classified into three basic categories, those in which the interest groups system is "dominant," "complementary," "subordinate" or some mix of these three basic categories.

The states in which the interest group system is "dominant" are those in which interest groups are the overwhelming and consistent influence on public policy-making within that state. Interest groups in these states have substantial power and influence in affecting the outcome of public policy-making. Alabama, Florida, Louisiana, New Mexico and Tennessee are some of the states that are classified into this category. In the states with "subordinate" interest groups systems, the interest groups do not exercise a great deal of power in the state's policy process. While Thomas and Hrebenar did not find any states that qualified as pure "subordinate" states they did identify some that fell into their hybrid "complementary-subordinate" category (e.g., Minnesota, Connecticut, Delaware, Rhode Island and Vermont). The states with "complementary" interest group systems are those in which the interest groups collaborate with other elements of the political system or are perhaps restrained by other elements of the state political system in the policy-making process. Using this analysis Thomas and Hrebenar classify Wisconsin as a state in which the interest groups system is "complementary."

Types of Interest Groups

In all states there is a wide range of interest groups which are actively involved in attempting to influence the political process. Table V-1 lists just a small sample of the different organizations that were represented by a registered lobbyist in Wisconsin as of February 1995. A cursory review of these groups leads to several observations.

First, there are many diverse interests represented in Wisconsin. Interests as varied as cranberry growers, bowling alley proprietors, environmentalists, farmers, bankers, nurses, lawyers, realtors, school boards, taverns, wine makers, and students all have their lobbyists operating to protect their special interests in Wisconsin politics. Second, many of the groups represented are industry, trade and professional associations. Groups such as the Wisconsin State AFL-CIO, Wisconsin Education Association Council (WEAC), Wisconsin Hospital Association, Wisconsin Paper Council and the Tavern League of Wisconsin are all examples of these types of groups. Third, several individual corporations or businesses also have lobbyists. A number of these companies include: Anheuser Busch, Ameritech, Fort Howard Corporation, Kwik Trip, Georgia Pacific, Miller Brewing, and Johnson Controls. Many of these corporations are multinational corporations with special interests in Wisconsin, while others are corporations headquartered in Wisconsin. Fourth, several associations which represent governmental bodies also have registered lobbyists. For example, Wisconsin Alliance of Cities, City of Milwaukee, Milwaukee County, Dane County and Brown County have registered lobbyists. Finally, there are a number of groups which are issue specific, such as the Citizens for a Better Environment, National Greyhound Association, and the Smokeless Tobacco Council.

Table V-1

A SAMPLE OF ORGANIZATIONS WITH LOBBYISTS REGISTERED IN WISCONSIN

Wisconsin State AFL-CIO
American Civil Liberties Union of Wisconsin, Inc.
Anheuser Busch Companies, Inc.
Wisconsin Bankers Association
Bowling Proprietors Association of Wisconsin
Wisconsin State Council of Carpenters
Wisconsin Catholic Conference
Wisconsin Cattlemen's Association
Wisconsin Chiropractic Association
Wisconsin Alliance of Cities
Citizens for a Better Environment
Common Cause in Wisconsin
Wisconsin Counties Association
Wisconsin State Cranberry Growers
Wisconsin Dairy Products Association, Inc.
Wisconsin Coalition Against Domestic Violence
Wisconsin Education Association Council
Eli Lilly and Company
Wisconsin Farm Bureau Federation Cooperative
National Farmer's Organization
Fort Howard Corporation
National Greyhound Association
Wisconsin Hospital Association
Wisconsin Manufacturers and Commerce

State Medical Society of Wisconsin
Menominee Indian Tribe of Wisconsin
Miller Brewing Company
City of Milwaukee
Motorcycle Industry Council
Oneida Tribe
Outdoor Advertising Association of Wisconsin
Wisconsin Paper Council
Planned Parenthood of Wisconsin, Inc.
Wisconsin Realtors Association
National Rifle Association
Wisconsin Right to Life
Association of Wisconsin Snowmobile Clubs, Inc.
Tavern League of Wisconsin, Inc.
Wisconsin Women's Network

Source: Wisconsin Ethics Board

Interest Group Activities

In their attempt to meet their group's goals, interest groups generally engage in three primary activities: (1) political action, (2) lobbying and (3) litigation.

Political Action. Political action is any attempt by an interest group to influence the selection of public officials in Wisconsin. This may include attempts to influence the electoral process in the case of elected public officials or attempts to influence the appointment process in the area of appointed positions. Within the electoral process much of the interest group activity is one of providing campaign resources, either directly or indirectly, to political candidates. This is usually in the form of monetary contributions, personnel, and/or other forms of in-kind contributions.

Campaign contributions are perhaps the most widely used form of political action by interest groups. The costs of campaigning have steadily increased at all levels within the U.S. and Wisconsin is no exception. Total spending by state Senate and Assembly candidates in 1981-82 was $3.5 million; by 1991-92 spending had increased to $5.9 million. That represents a 59 percent increase in spending. Care must be taken in interpreting this as a substantial increase however, because over that same period of time there was also a 55 percent increase in inflation. Therefore, in "real" dollar terms there has not been a significant increase over this period of time. In 1981-82 there was only one Wisconsin state Senate campaign that exceeded $50,000 in total expenditures. However, by the 1991-92 election cycle there were 19 Senate campaigns and eight Assembly campaigns that exceeded $50,000 in total expenditures. Because large sums of money are utilized for campaigning and because of the concern that this money may influence public policy, campaign financing is regulated by the state.

In Wisconsin the State Elections Board has the primary responsibility for administering the state's election and campaign finance laws. The State Elections Board was created under Section 15.61, Wisconsin Statutes, in July 1974 when the state legislature passed the campaign finance disclosure law. This board is comprised of eight citizen members appointed by the governor for two-year terms. While officially these eight individuals are "appointed" by the governor, they are actually selected by other political actors. The governor has his designee, of course, and then one member each is designated by the chief justice of the supreme court, the speaker of the Assembly, the majority leader of the Senate, the minority leader of each house of the legislature, and the chief officer of each political party whose candidate for governor received at least 10 percent of the vote cast in the most recent gubernatorial election.

Interest groups participate in the electoral process through their political action committees or PACs. Political action committees (PACs) are essentially the "political arm" of interest groups. Group members contribute funds to the PAC of their group which in turn distributes the funds to candidates that they deem supportive of their group's goals. As defined by state statute, a PAC is "any person other than an individual and any combination of two or more persons, permanent or temporary, which makes or accepts contributions or makes disbursements, whether or not engaged in activities which are exclusively political, except that a 'committee' does not include a political 'group' under this chapter." (Wisconsin Statutes 11.01(4)). Essentially, any political group which specifically advocates the election or defeat of a particular candidate or promotes the passage or defeat of a referenda question *and* expends more than $25 must register with the Wisconsin State Elections Board.

The amount of money that PACs have expended in Wisconsin state elections increased dramatically from 1976 to 1982 when PAC spending increased from less than one million dollars to six million dollars. This six million-dollar figure in 1982 represents the peak of PAC spending. Since 1982 there has been some decline in PAC spending. Although in the 1992 election cycle the figure went up again to $5.1 million. Once again it is necessary to consider the inflationary impact. From 1982 to 1992 there was nearly a 50 percent inflation effect; hence, the 5.1 million spent in 1992 was the equivalent of approximately 2.5 million in 1982 dollars. This indicates that in "real" dollars PAC spending has not increased. Generally PAC spending increases in gubernatorial election years and then declines somewhat in nongubernatorial election years. Another trend that may be developing is a more consistent level of expenditures by PACs. This trend is suggested by examining the "drop-off" of PAC expenditures in the off gubernatorial election years. From 1982 to 1984 there was a $3.2 million drop-off, from 1986 to 1988 a $ 900,000 drop-off and from 1990 to 1992 the drop-off had declined to just $300,000. It would appear that PACs may be moving into a more constant level of expenditures that are less affected by gubernatorial races (see Figure V-1).

Figure V-1

PAC EXPENDITURES, 1974 - 92

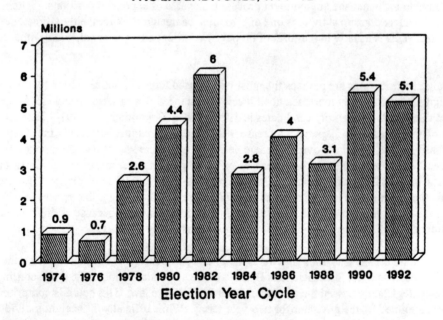

Source: Wisconsin State Elections Board

PACs are limited in the amount of money they can give to individual candidates and candidates are limited in the total amount of money they can receive from PACs. PACs can give single contributions of not more that $43,128 to gubernatorial candidates, $21,560 to attorney general candidates, $8,625 to supreme court candidates, $1,000 to state Senate candidates and $500 to Assembly candidates. Overall candidates are not allowed to receive more than 45 percent of the total campaign spending limit for their race from PACs.

In state legislative campaigns it appears that the patterns of PAC spending are changing. When PAC funds are examined as a percent of the total receipts of state legislative candidates a gradual decline is observed (see Figure V-2). In 1976 PAC funds made up 34 percent of the total receipts of state legislative candidates.

Figure V-2

PAC FUNDS IN STATE LEGISLATIVE RACES, 1972 - 92

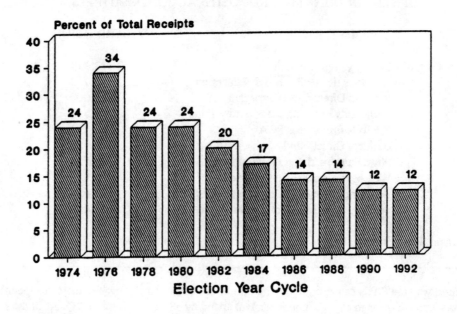

Source: Wisconsin State Elections Board

That figure gradually declined so that in the 1992 election cycle PAC funds made up only 12 percent of the total funds received by state legislative candidates. Clearly there has been a decline in the role that direct PAC contributions are playing in state legislative campaigns. However, there has also been a shift in how interest groups are using their campaign dollars to influence elections. Interest groups are now using two new techniques, conduits and independent expenditures, to channel their campaign dollars into the electoral process.

Conduits are "special interest organizations which collect contributions from individuals, bundle them together, and pass the contributions to candidates and political committees" (Biennial Report of Wisconsin State Elections Board, 1993, p IX). These funds are recorded as being individual contributions, but in reality they are being channeled through the PACs. The primary difference between a PAC and a conduit contribution is that with the conduit the individual contributor decides which candidate receives the money, while with the PAC contributions the PAC directly makes this decision. PACs, however, can "suggest" that the individual contribute to a particular candidate. The end result is that political action committees can provide another source of funds to candidates and they can be sure that the candidate will know who is responsible for them receiving these funds. The political candidates have broadened their contributor base, received additional fund-raising support and can claim they are receiving more individual contributions (this translates into a view of broad-based grass roots support among the people). Thus, interest groups and candidates alike are happy. In 1987-88 $429,348 were channeled through conduits in state elections, by the 1993-94 election cycle the conduit dollars had increased by 419 percent to $2,227,197.

Table V-2 lists the top ten conduits in the 1993-94 election cycle. Far and away the largest conduit in the 1993-94 election cycle was the Majority GOP Conduit which channeled $713,939 to candidates in state elections. The amount from this one conduit is nearly double the amount that all conduits channeled just six years ago.

Table V-2

TOP TEN CONDUITS MAKING POLITICAL CONTRIBUTIONS, 1993 - 94

COMMITTEE NAME	CONTRIBUTION
Majority GOP Conduit	$ 713,939
Chiropractic Health Info & Education	162,753
Realtors Direct Givers Program	144,000
Democrats Ensuring the Majority Fund	94,552
WE/WN Employees PCA	86,359
Builders Direct Fund	82,137
Physicians for Better Government	74,514
WI Chapter Assn. Gen Contractors	72,980
Baird Individual Political Contributors	38,425
Security Savings Conduit Fund	37,092

Source: Wisconsin State Elections Board

A second way the PACs can circumvent the limitations on how much money they can specifically contribute to state campaigns is to engage in independent spending. The U.S. Supreme Court in the *Buckley v. Valeo* case in 1976 stated that political spending is tantamount to political speech and hence is protected by the First Amendment. Therefore, as long as interest groups do not communicate with candidates regarding their spending there is no limit to the amount that the group can spend to elect or defeat a candidate. In the 1987-88 election cycle independent expenditures were at $225,971 and by the 1991-92 election cycle independent expenditures increased 60 percent to $360,599. Table V-3 presents the top ten groups engaging in independent spending during this time period. As Table V-3 indicates the Wisconsin Education Association Council (WEAC) PAC was the most active in this area spending $120,671 or about one-third of total independent expenditures. The changes in conduit contributions and in the independent expenditures indicates that PACs are opting for the conduit path to a much greater extent than they are the independent expenditures.

The changes in how political action committees get money into campaigns suggest three important trends: (1) PACs are raising more money for campaigns in a consistent year around effort; (2) more money is being channeled into campaigns through conduits; and (3) interest groups are gradually increasing their level of independent campaign spending.

Some interest groups provide non-financial resources to political candidates for their campaigns. Labor unions, for example, have for years provided numerous volunteers for candidates for such things as get-out-the-vote campaigns, literature drops and assistance with mass mailings. Groups are also excellent sources for mailing lists, phone banks, office assistance, computer time and the like.

The critical question regarding the campaign contributions to state public officials is whether or not they result in altering a public official's public policy decisions. That is, do the resources contributed "buy" the policy votes of decision-makers. It is extremely difficult to determine if there is a cause and effect relationship between campaign resources and votes. A study by Common Cause found that of the $31,785 contributed to candidates by the Tavern League in Wisconsin, between January 1, 1985 and June 30, 1988 $30,060 or 95 percent went to candidates who voted in favor of a Tavern League backed bill to extend tavern hours (Lueders 1989, p10). However, even this does not demonstrate cause and effect since these legislators may have supported this position in the absence of the campaign contributions. While cause and effect may not be definitively demonstrated, it is apparent that when public officials receive interest group resources certain expectations, exist even if they may be implicit.

Table V-3

TOP TEN COMMITTEES MAKING INDEPENDENT EXPENDITURES, 1991 - 92

COMMITTEE NAME	CONTRIBUTION
Wisconsin Education Association Council PAC	$ 120,671.27
National Riffle Association Victory Fund	72,711.73
Wisconsin Right to Life PAC	52,169.02
Milwaukee Police Association PAC	32,923.94
Volunteers for Agriculture	23,049.06
Concerned Business & Industry	17,924.48
Wisconsin Physicians PAC	7,372.42
Wallace Hilliard	6,200.66
Wisconsin 2000	4,224.90
United Northeast Educators PAC	4,044.45

Source: Wisconsin State Elections Board

Lobbying. Nearly all interest groups are actively involved in lobbying. In fact it is the lobbying activity that has often lead to the public's negative perception of interest groups in general. The perception stems from images of graft and bribery in which "lobbyists" are pictured offering cash "under the table" to public officials in return for a favorable decision in the policy-making process. While this has probably occurred, it is more likely the exception than the rule in Wisconsin politics.

Before proceeding, three significant concepts need to be defined: lobbying, lobbyist and principal. The state statutes define lobbying as the "practice of attempting to influence legislative or administrative action by direct oral or written communication with any elective state official, agency official or legislative employee" (Wisconsin Statutes, Chapter 13.62 (10)). A lobbyist is "an individual who is employed by a principal, or contracts for or receives economic consideration, other than reimbursement for actual expenditures, from a principal and whose duties include lobbying on behalf of the principal." (Wisconsin Statutes, Chapter 13.62 (11)). And a principal is "any person who employs a lobbyist" (Wisconsin Statutes, Chapter 13.62 (12)).

As in most states, Wisconsin attempts to regulate lobbying activity. When compared with most other states Wisconsin's lobbying laws are relatively stringent. It has frequently been the case in recent years that what are viewed as major violations of the lobby law in Wisconsin would clearly be viewed as only minor infractions in many other states. Wisconsin's lobby law has two primary objectives: (1) the disclosure of lobbying activities by requiring the registration and licensing of lobbyists and the reporting of expenditures; and (2) the prohibition of certain types of lobbying activities.

Principals, which spend more than $500 in a calendar year, and their lobbyists, are subject to the licensing and reporting requirements stipulated in the Wisconsin lobby law. The lobby law in Wisconsin states that principals must register with the Ethics Board and provide expenditure reports for the time period in which they were involved in lobbying activities. It is the lobbyists responsibility to forward an expenditure report to their principals prior to the January 31 and July 31 reporting deadlines.

The Wisconsin lobby law also stipulates that certain activities of state officials, lobbyists, and principals are prohibited. The general rule is that principals and lobbyists may not furnish anything of pecuniary value to any state officer or employee, elected official or candidate for elective state office. None of these "restricted recipients" may solicit or accept anything of pecuniary value from a lobbyist or principal. Anything of "pecuniary value" includes such things as: food, beverages, entertainment, lodging, transportation, gifts, money and essentially anything of marketable value. There are numerous exceptions that do exist, however.

One important exception to this rule is that lobbyists can contribute money to the electoral campaigns of public officials. There are timing restrictions which govern when the contributions from lobbyists can be made. Lobbyists can contribute to candidates for elective office to be filled in the November general election during a June 1 through election day "window" period. If they wish to contribute to candidates for the state legislature they can only contribute during the "window" period and only if the state legislature is in recess or adjourned.

Also state agency lobbyists, that is, those individuals who are "officers and employees of the agency who are paid a salary and whose regular duties include attempting to influence legislative action" (Wisconsin Statutes, Chapter 13.695) are not subject to the same prohibited practices as are other lobbyists. State agency lobbyists are not allowed to use any state funds to provide items of value to restricted recipients. However, they are allowed to use their own personal funds if they so desire. The assumption here, of course, is that they will not utilize their personal funds for such activities.

The Wisconsin Ethics Board is charged with enforcing the lobbying law. In most instances violations of this law result in civil cases and penalties as follows:

> Principals up to $5,000 forfeiture;
> Lobbyists up to $1,000 and possibly revocation of lobbying license;
> State agency lobbyists up to $1,000;
> Elective state officials up to $1,000.

The only criminal penalty for the violation of lobbying law is for a lobbyist or a principal who is found guilty of falsifying information on a required report. Falsification of such information can result in a fine of up to $1,000 or imprisonment in a county jail for not more than one year.

In the late 1980s there were a number of violations of lobby law by state officials, lobbyists and principals in Wisconsin. Some of these included:

- One state Senator pleaded guilty to five misdemeanors and agreed to resign from office in exchange for the dismissal of five felony charges. This same state Senator paid $1,221 in fines for civil violations of receiving food and lodging.

- A second State Senator pleaded guilty to five civil counts of receiving illegal gifts from a lobbyist and paid fines of $6,137. Criminal charges against this legislator were dismissed as part of the agreement.

- A number of other state legislators paid fines for accepting food, drinks, and/or lodging from lobbyists.

- One lobbyist pleaded guilty to four felony criminal counts of laundering campaign contributions to lawmakers and paid fines totaling $7,540. As part of a plea bargain agreement the prosecution agreed not to pursue allegations that the lobbyist had provided food, beverages and weekend vacations for ten state legislators.

- Several other lobbyists and principals have paid civil fines for providing something of value to state officials.

In response to these violations Governor Thompson appointed a Blue Ribbon Commission in February of 1989 to review the statutorily established ethical standards in Wisconsin state government. The state legislature did make some minor revisions in the state lobbying and ethics laws in 1990. One change was to consolidate the responsibility for the administration and enforcement of the lobbying and ethics laws under the Ethics Board. This removed the administration and enforcement of the lobbying law from the secretary of state's office as of July 1, 1990.

In spite of the recent lobby law violations, Wisconsin citizens still see state legislators as being generally ethical. In a recent Wisconsin Survey conducted by the St. Norbert College Survey Center eight percent of the public rated state legislators as being "Very Ethical," 66 percent said they were "Somewhat Ethical," 18 percent felt they were "Somewhat Unethical," and three percent indicated that they were "Very Unethical." Since this was the first time this question had been asked in the Wisconsin Survey it is impossible to determine if there has been any change over the past few years. The survey did ask respondents to reflect over the past few years to determine if they felt that the "ethical behavior of Wisconsin State Legislators had generally gotten better or worse?" On this question 37 percent stated they felt ethical behavior of state legislators had gotten worse, 34 percent said it had gotten better and 16 percent volunteered that it had stayed about the same. Hence while there is some feeling that the ethical behavior of state legislators has gotten worse there is an almost equal proportion of the public who think that ethical behavior has gotten better.

Over the past decade there has been an increase in interest group lobbying activities in Wisconsin. Figures V-3 and V-4 below demonstrate some of the growth that has taken place. In the last six months of 1985 there were 450 different organizations which were represented by lobbyists and 317 active lobbyists. Nine years later in the last six months of 1993 these had increased to 551 organizations and 576 lobbyists. Essentially this means that for each state legislator there are 5.8 registered lobbyists.

The most significant increase, however, has been in the level of expenditures on lobbying activities. In 1985-86 groups spent $3,089,867 on lobbying activities. By 1993-94 this had increased 1,045 percent to $35,387,264. This represents an increase that is far above normal inflationary increases. Such a tremendous increase may in part be the result of the gradual shift of programs and policy decisions from the federal government to state and local governments. This shift of authority has also meant that the interest group activity would shift to the level where the decisions are made. This increase in interest group lobbying activities is also a product of increased conflict over scarce resources within the state. With budgets getting tighter and the anti-tax mood among citizens, the battle over who gets what is becoming more intense. Hence, interest groups activity in Wisconsin, as in other states, has increased significantly.

Figure V-3

ORGANIZATIONS WITH LOBBYISTS, 1985-93

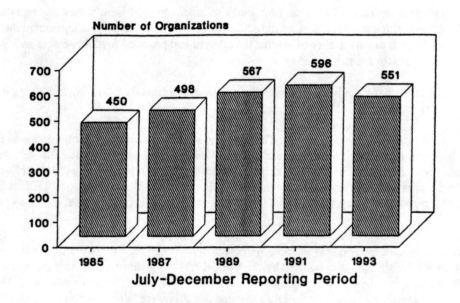

Sources: Wisconsin Secretary of State, Wisconsin Ethics Board

Figure V-4

NUMBER OF LOBBYISTS, 1985 - 93

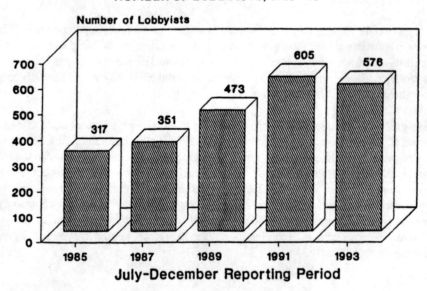

Sources: Wisconsin Secretary of State, Wisconsin Ethics Board

The level of interest group activity is not, however, uniform across all types of interest groups. Clearly, some types of groups are much more active than others. All of the groups registered for the July-December 1989 period, the last time frame for which this data is summarized, are categorized by general type and analyzed in terms of the number and expenditures in Figure V-5.

As Figure V-5 illustrates the industry, trade and professional associations make up approximately 50 percent of the groups registered to lobby and those groups spend about 61 percent of the total funds expended on lobbying activities in the State of Wisconsin. Individual business entities makeup 36 percent of the total number of groups and spend 28 percent of the monies. Other groups (e.g., issue groups, public interest groups, state agencies, etc.) makeup about 13 percent of the groups and spend about 11 percent of the funds.

Figure V-5

TYPES OF INTEREST GROUPS, JULY-DECEMBER 1989

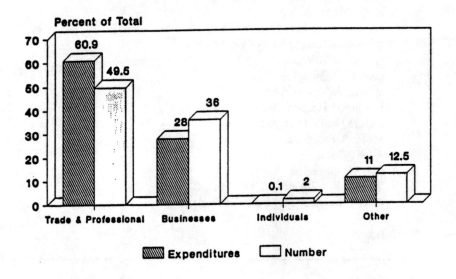

Source: Wisconsin Secretary of State

As Figure V-5 suggests however, spending is not evenly distributed across all groups. Table V-4 lists the top ten principals for the two 1994 reporting periods. Wisconsin Bell, Inc. leads the principals in spending at $681,844 during 1994, followed by the Wisconsin Counties Association ($614,917), Wisconsin Manufacturers & Commerce ($542,257), and Wisconsin Independent Businesses ($531,621). Another way of looking at this data is to say that the top ten groups in terms of expenditures for 1994 represent 1.8 percent of all groups but spent 16 percent ($5,631,571) of the total expenditures.

Table V-4

TOP SPENDING PRINCIPALS, 1994

PRINCIPAL	EXPENDITURE
Wisconsin Bell, Inc.	$ 681,844
Wisconsin Counties Assn.	614,917
Wisconsin Manufacturers & Commerce	542,257
Wisconsin Independent Businesses, Inc.	531,621
Wisconsin Merchants Federation	427,789
Wisconsin Property Taxpayers, Inc.	317,812
Wisconsin Farm Bureau Federation	314,706
Philip Morris, U.S.A.	260,141
Wisconsin Bankers Assn.	186,970
Wisconsin Assn of School Boards, Inc	185,668
County of Milwaukee	173,174
Crandon Mining Co.	168,346
Wisconsin Towns Assn.	163,769
Wisconsin Hospital Assn.	163,765
Aurora Health Care, Inc.	161,066
Miller Brewing Co.	154,016
AT&T Corp.	152,801
City of Milwaukee	147,898
Wisconsin Alliance of Cities, Inc.	146,102
GTE Telephone Operations North Area	136,909

Source: Wisconsin Ethics Board

A more detailed analysis can be made by breaking the groups down into their respective "interest areas." Figure V-6 suggests that the interest areas of commerce and industry and issue advocates are the two areas which are clearly the most active in terms of expenditures for lobbying activities. The interest area of commerce and industry has an economic base while the issue advocate interest area is generally based on much narrower policy matters such as seat belt legislation, abortion policy, and the like. If one examines the trend of expenditures in these issue areas only two areas experienced significant changes during the decade of the 1980s. In 1979-80, for example, the percent of expenditures for the issue advocate area was 9 percent and the expenditures in the area of labor and professional associations represented 23 percent. Hence, there has been a significant decrease in expenditures in the labor and professional associations area and a significant increase in the issue advocacy area.

Figure V-6

LOBBYING BY INTEREST AREA, 1989

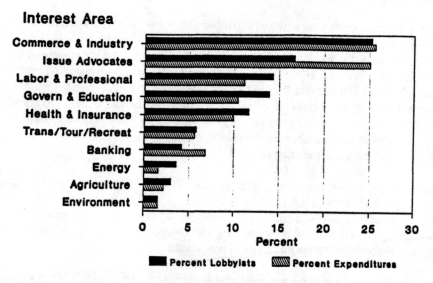

Source: Wisconsin Secretary of State

The key to effective lobbying activity by any group is the individual or individuals who are on the front lines as lobbyist for the group. Hedlund (1993) identifies several characteristics that effective lobbyists need to display. Honesty is perhaps one of the most critical characteristics. Because public officials rely heavily on the information provided by lobbyists they need to know that they can trust the lobbyist and the information that is provided by the lobbyist. One state legislator stated that "Lobbyists have to be 100 percent accurate and 100 percent honest or they are not going to be effective. Once they provide bad information then I don't trust them" (Radloff, 1989a).

Access and knowledge of the political process are also important attributes. Lobbyists must know the intricacies of how the systems works if they are going to be effective. They must know where the "real" decisions are made, who the "influentials" are and what will motivate any given public official to view the policy issue the same way as the lobbyist's client sees it. One lobbyist has stated that, "lobbying is a personal service to our clients. We try to educate legislators and their staff on why an issue is important to our clients" (Radloff, 1989b). Lobbyists also will attempt to mobilize grass-roots support for a particular measure if they feel that technique would be effective. In today's environment of career legislators and their concern for reelection, the grass-roots technique can often be a powerful force for an interest group to use.

It is also important for lobbyists to be able to approach their job with vigor but to not engage in legislator "bashing" or to take things personally. The policy-making process is always a series of shifting coalitions. From a lobbyist's point of view that means that your opposition today may be your ally tomorrow. Therefore, it is necessary to argue and debate policy matters vigorously but not allow them to damage a relationship that would be needed in the future.

Interest groups and more specifically their lobbyists are also very active in lobbying the executive branch of government. In fact, a number of scholars have found support for the notion of a triangulation of relationships between interest groups, legislative committees and executive agencies which then dominate in a given policy domain. While many of these studies have focused on the national level, Hamm (1986) found that these "iron triangles" or "subgovernments," as they are often called, also exist at the state level.

As state governments have taken over new and expanded policy roles the state executive branch has been targeted more and more by interest groups. In Wisconsin some of the most vociferous lobbying of the executive takes place following the passage of the state budget by the legislature. Since Wisconsin's governor has considerable power and flexibility in using the veto power, many groups lobby the governor to protect what they received from the state legislature. The fact that Wisconsin's interest group system is complimentary to the party system also means that there are frequently close relations between the governor and interest groups which have provided support through the electoral process. For example, there is often a close relationship between a republican governor and the Wisconsin Manufacturers and Commerce organization and between democratic governors and the Wisconsin Education Association Council.

Interest groups also directly lobby executive agencies. As Hedlund (1993) points out, extensive agency lobbying occurs in the area of environmental policy which is largely regulated by the Wisconsin Department of Natural Resources (DNR). Since the DNR is responsible for issuing permits for the discharge of waste water, they are frequently being lobbied by manufacturers who are seeking a discharge permit and by environmental groups who want more stringent controls placed on the discharge of waste water.

Overall, members of both the executive and legislative branches believe that lobbying is an appropriate part of the policy process and that lobbyists can contribute in significant ways to this process. King (1984) found that nearly all state legislators (98 percent) felt that lobbying activities were either "Very" or "Somewhat" appropriate in the legislative process. Former state legislator and Governor Anthony Earl stated "I think the vast majority of people, not only currently in the legislative process and executive branch, but those who have been in before, would all acknowledge that lobbyists play a very crucial role in the process" (Radloff, 1989b).

Given these characteristics it is easy to understand why former government officials particularly former state legislators and governors would be effective lobbyists. Table V-5 presents a list of all lobbyists as of February 1995 who represented ten or more principals. Currently there are thirty-one lobbyists who represent ten or more principals. That has increased substantially from 1986 when only twelve lobbyists had ten or more clients. A number of these individuals are former state legislators -- Bill Broydrick, Gary Goyke, Gervase Hephner, and Chet Gerlach (Hephner has recently retired from lobbying) and one is a former governor -- Martin Schrieber. Individuals who have been active in the policy process generally possess most of the characteristics which will make them effective lobbyists. They all have access and excellent knowledge regarding how the systems really works. In 1986 only one women was on the list as representing ten or more clients; by 1993 several women were representing ten or more clients. While women remain generally under-represented in the political process, they are increasing their numbers among the ranks of lobbyists as they are in the state legislature in general.

Table V-5

LOBBYISTS WHO ARE REGISTERED FOR TEN OR MORE PRINCIPALS, 93 - 94

LOBBYIST	NUMBER OF PRINCIPALS
Bill Broydrick	33
JoAnna Richard	21
Peter Theo	21
James Wimmer, Jr.	21
Peter Christianson	20

Sharon Cook	20
Brian Mitchell	20
Michael Vaughan	19
Gary Goyke	17
Anthony Driessen	17
Thomas Hanson	15
Moira Fitzgerald	14
Michael Brozek	14
Lisa Hilbert	14
William Gerrard	14
Cynthia Broydrick	13
Janet Swandby	13
Thomas Coenen	13
Martin Schrieber	13
William Katzman	13
Peter Peshek	13
James Tenuta	13
David Klauser	12
Stephen Bablitch	12
Thomas Krajewski	12
Gervase Hephner	11
James Hough	11
Chet Gerlach	11
Jeffrey Remsik	11
Edward Blume	10
Kelly McDowell	10

Source: Wisconsin Ethics Board

There are basically two types of lobbyists: contract lobbyists and in-house lobbyists. Contract lobbyists generally work for a number of clients on a fee for service basis. The fee for service might be on an hourly or monthly basis or for the entire legislative session. Contract lobbying fees can range from $50 to $175 an hour or as high as $6,000 monthly. Some lobbyists perform a "watch and report" service for their clients in which they simply monitor what is going on in the policy-making process and report on whether any impending proposal will affect the client. A "watch and report" contract would typically cost about $3,500 for the legislative session. Contract lobbyists who are attempting to get a bill passed for a client will charge significantly more. A second type of lobbyist is the in-house lobbyist. These are lobbyists who work for a single organization and are generally in salaried positions within the organization they represent. Organizations with substantial resources and which tend to have a number of policy interests on an ongoing basis are likely to employ in-house lobbyists. Examples of this type of arrangement include the Wisconsin Education Association Council (WEAC), AFL-CIO and Wisconsin Manufacturers and Commerce, all of which have individuals on staff whose primary function is to lobby on behalf of their respective organization.

Litigation

A third activity that interest groups engage in is litigation within the court system. Citizens often view courts as nonpolitical institutions within our system of government. However, courts are important policy-making institutions and as a result are naturally going to end up being political. Many disputes over who gets what in Wisconsin are settled in the courts. Interest groups must also then work within the court system to try and have their policy views represented. One of the most frequent ways that interest groups attempt to influence the court decision is through *amicus curiae* ("friend of the court") briefs. This is a written document in which the interest group presents its position on a particular case before a court. In this way the interest group makes its views known to the court. Common Cause, for example, often submits such briefs on cases that deal with campaign finance issues before the courts.

Interest groups may also decide to take their concerns directly to the courts. This tactic has often been utilized by environmental groups which have sought court injunctions to stop various projects which they felt threatened the environment. Certain groups may find that litigation is the only remedy for their problem. This is particularly true for groups which feel that they have little access to the legislative and/or administrative processes.

Conclusion

This chapter has examined the role that interest groups play in Wisconsin politics. As stated at the outset, the debate regarding interest groups is essentially a debate over equality and liberty within our political system. Do interest groups in Wisconsin have too much political power, so that the special interests and not the public interest are served? Are group activities regulated to the extent that individuals and groups cannot act in their own self-interest? From our analysis it appears that there is a reasonable balance between these two values in Wisconsin. In terms of the trends in their activities, it appears that interest groups are becoming more active in all areas within Wisconsin. The most significant increase is in the area of lobbying. Hence, this activity should be monitored very closely to determine if indeed the influence of interest groups becomes too great. In the area of political action, primarily campaign financing, the focus of interest groups is shifting. Interest groups seem to be putting less emphasis on direct contributions to state legislative candidates and increasing their independent expenditures and their use of conduits. This is also a trend that will require monitoring. Interest group activity is an important and valuable aspect to Wisconsin politics. The balance between equality and liberty must, however, be maintained.

Part III: The Institutions of Wisconsin Government

CHAPTER VI

THE WISCONSIN LEGISLATURE

By Ronald D. Hedlund[*]

As a two-chamber (bicameral) legislative institution, the Wisconsin legislature is elected on a partisan basis at the November general election in each even-numbered year. It is, therefore, one of 49 bicameral partisan state legislatures in the U.S. Nebraska is the lone exception, being both unicameral and non-partisan.

The lower chamber of the Wisconsin legislature is called the Assembly; a term used also by California, Nevada, New Jersey and New York, in contrast with the more common terminology of designating the lower chamber as the house of representatives. Its members, however, are called Representatives to the Assembly, and are elected for two-year terms. Since the redistricting of 1972, there are 99 representatives to the Assembly. The upper chamber of the Wisconsin legislature is called the Senate, the term used in all states. The Wisconsin state constitution authorizes no more than one-third as many members of the Senate as there are members of the Assembly. Its present membership of 33 is, therefore, its permissible size given the size of the Assembly. Senators are elected for four-year terms--one half being elected every two years. The Senate districts are numbered from one to 33, and those in odd numbered districts are elected during the gubernatorial election years (e.g., 1994, 1998, and 2002), while those from even numbered districts are elected during U.S. Presidential elections (e.g., 1992, 1996, 2000). Thus, approximately one-half the Senate districts have elections in each general election. Vacancies in either chamber are filled at the next ensuing election or at a special election called by the governor. There is no provision for filling legislative vacancies by appointment.

In order to understand the Wisconsin legislature and its operations, one must consider specific features like its powers and workload, how it relates to its publics (e.g., apportionment and elections), who serve as members, how legislation is enacted into law, and how the legislature interacts with outside organizations.

A glossary of frequently used legislative terms is found in an appendix to this chapter.

Legislative Structure: Powers and Workload

Since the Wisconsin legislature *can* become involved in resolving *any* issue facing state government, the scope and detail of legislative work, as well as how the legislature has adapted to meet recent changes in public expectations for legislative action, are major issues of concern. Comparative information for alternating legislative sessions between 1953 and 1993, displayed in Table VI-1, illustrates that, since 1953, the legislature has considered between 1515 and 2520 bills and between 228 and 416 resolutions during any of its two-year sessions. Because many bills cover more than one subject and can be very complex, these quantitative estimates of workload are probably conservative regarding the amount of work handled in a two-year session of the Wisconsin legislature. In addition, the range of topics varies in impact and complexity--from designating official state symbols (such as the "Honey Bee" as the state insect) to determining the state budget. Budget items cover everything from the

[*] Vice Provost for Research and Service and Acting Dean of the Graduate School, University of Rhode Island. The author wishes to acknowledge the assistance in preparing this chapter of former Senate President Fred A. Risser; former Assembly Speaker Thomas A. Loftus; former Assembly Minority Leader Betty Jo Nelson; former Senator Walter J. Chilson; former Representative Randall J. Radtke; Representatives Marlin D. Schneider, and David M. Travis; and Pete Cannon, Clark G. Radtz, Richard L. Roe and Gary Watchke of the Legislative Reference Bureau. In addition, Bruce R. Anderson, Emily Van Dunk and Karen M. Hedlund provided invaluable assistance for this chapter.

Table VI-1

WISCONSIN LEGISLATIVE WORKLOAD DATA, SELECTED YEARS
(entries are raw numbers)

Type of Activity	1953 1954	1957 1958	1961 1962	1965 1966	1969 1970	1973 1974	1977 1978	1981 1982	1985 1986	1989 1990	1993 1994
No. Meeting Days (a)											
Senate	97	110	184	161	192	174	94	153	127	120	98
Assembly	98	111	185	157	183	177	122	164	112	121	95
No. Bills Intro (a)	1593	1515	1592	1818	2019	2520	2063	2010	1716	1616	2156
No. Joint Res Intro (a)	175	253	295	293	238	280	196	188	187	251	212
No. Res Intro (a)	70	84	67	86	114	136	56	75	41	45	47
No. Special Sessions	0	1	0	0	2	3	4	3	8	2	2
No Bills Vetoed (a)	31	35	69	24	34	13	21	12	7	35	41
No. Vetoes Overridden(a)	3	0	2	1	1	0	4	2	0	0	0
No Laws Enacted (a)	687	709	689	666	502	350	451	394	342	368	497
No. Standing Comm (b)											
Senate	10	11	11	14	13	13	12	12	11	15	13
Assembly	23	23	23	23	26	26	29	32	28	33	31
Joint	2	2	2	5	3	6	6	9	7	11	10
No of Staff (c)											
Senate	51	50	57	59	79	111	150	190	220	199	199
Assembly	61	66	74	76	151	189	215	222	229	224	261
Joint	---	--	--	36	109	112	150	201	197	197	221
Party of Governor	R	R	D	R	R	D	D	R	D	R	R
Party control Assembly	R	R	R	D	R	D	D	D	D	D	D
Party control Senate (d)	R	R	R	R	R	R	D	D	D	D	R

a. These entries combine numbers for regular session and special sessions held over the two-year session length.
b. For consistency purposes, Joint Standing Committees in each session are excluded from the number of committees for both chambers.
c. Service agencies include Legislative Council, Legislative Audit Bureau, Legislative Fiscal Bureau, Legislative Reference Bureau, Revisor of Statues, Interstate Cooperation Commission, and Council on Home and Family. Depending on what agencies were in existence, information on size before 1966 is not available.
d. At the beginning of the 1993-94 session, three vacancies due to Democratic member resignations left the Senate tied between Republican and Democratic members. In the resulting special elections, two Republicans and one Democrat were elected, thus giving control of the chamber to the Republicans on April 20, 1993.

Sources: Appropriate editions of the State of Wisconsin *Blue Book* and the Council of State Government *Book of the States*.

Department of Administration to the University of Wisconsin System (a total state budget of $19.1 billion in 1985-87 and over $30.4 billion in 1993-5). As a consequence, legislative power, as well as how the legislature organizes given its mandate to complete its workload during the two-year session, is important.

<u>Constitutional Powers</u>. Unlike the U.S. Constitution which delegates specific powers to Congress, the

Wisconsin constitution grants all legislative authority to the state legislature. Accordingly, the legislature may enact statutes on any subject unless prohibited by the national or state constitutions. Compared with most other states, the prohibitions on legislative action are minimal in Wisconsin. The legislature is prohibited from passing special laws granting divorces, chartering corporations, borrowing money to pay for normal state activities, or passing local bills. Only the prohibition against passing local legislation might appear to be a serious restriction. In practice, this restriction has been "overlooked and sidestepped," especially in recent years and most noticeably in the budget process. These prohibitions were envisioned as a means to prevent legislators from becoming preoccupied with local and narrow matters at the expense of attention to state matters--a criticism made by observers about southern state legislatures. However, the expectations of local constituents that the Wisconsin legislature could and should help solve local problems with state resources, plus the nature of the legislative process, have provided ample opportunities for state senators and representatives to involve the state in solving largely local problems.

Regarding the restriction on state borrowing, Article VIII, Section 5 of the Wisconsin Constitution states:

The legislature shall provide for an annual tax sufficient to defray the estimated expenses of the state for each year, and whenever the expenses of any year shall exceed the income, the legislature shall provide for levying a tax for the ensuing year, sufficient, with other sources of income, to pay the deficiency as well as the estimated expenses of such ensuing year.

Thus, the Wisconsin legislature, unlike the U.S. Congress, must raise sufficient revenue during each two-year session to pay for the normal expenses incurred by the state government during that period. However, the Constitution goes on in Section 7 to list several purposes for which public debt by the state is permissible:

- public defense (repel invasion, suppress insurrection, etc.);

- purchase, improve, construct or develop land, waters, highways, railways, buildings and equipment; and,

- veterans housing loans.

These exceptions, added by amending the state's constitution, permit the state to borrow money for several important purposes.

In summary, the legal powers of the Wisconsin legislature are extensive. Through the Wisconsin Constitution as a Jacksonian document (that is, one which extends egalitarianism, democracy, and political involvement to individual citizens), great power and independence have been provided to the legislative branch.

Legislative Sessions. All U.S. legislative bodies meet during specified periods of time, called sessions. A new session of the Wisconsin Assembly and Senate is convened at 2 p.m. on the first Monday of January (if it is not New Year's Day), in every odd-numbered year. At that time, all members of both chambers elected in the previous November's general election are sworn in, joining the existing hold-over senators, and thus forming the membership for the Senate and Assembly for the next two years. Once this swearing-in of members has taken place, chamber leaders in the Assembly and Senate are selected, rules for legislative action are adopted, and then new bills proposing state action can be introduced. (All legislation introduced but not passed in the previous session "dies" at the end of that session). All bills must be introduced by individual legislators, even those considered as part of "the governor's program," including proposed financing for state operations. Bill introduction and the commencement of a new session announces the beginning of what some have called the "dance of legislation," whereby proposals for state action are considered and processed by both chambers. Fewer than half [see the number of laws enacted, in Table VI-1, as a percentage of bills introduced--a high of 47 percent (709/1515) in 1957-58, to a low of 14 percent (350/2520) in 1973-74] have been enacted into law during any session of this 40-year period.

Unlike many state constitutions, Wisconsin's does not set limits on the length of legislative sessions. Until 1959, most sessions lasted from January until June, in the odd-numbered years. The legislature then recessed and came back for a few weeks in the Fall to act on vetoes and a few other matters. Since then, however, the Wisconsin legislature has had longer working sessions. Recent sessions have merely recessed, instead of adjourning, until the day when the next session begins. A constitutional amendment approved in 1968 authorized the legislature, at its own discretion, to institute annual sessions. A legislative review of the state's budget was conducted under this annual session authorization during the second year of the biennial budget in 1972; however, this authorization has remained otherwise unused so that the regular session remains biennial--that is, covering two years. Thus, the net effect of the 1968 change has been to allow the legislature to meet in each of the two years instead of only in the first year of the biennium.

In addition to regular sessions, the governor is authorized to call special sessions. Such sessions are restricted to considering legislation related to the subject or subjects stated by the governor in his/her call. Unlike some state legislatures, the Wisconsin legislature cannot call itself into special session; however, it can call itself *back* into *extraordinary* session, or it can use the recess device, noted above, as a means for legislative leaders to reconvene the legislature into its regular session. Since the legislature controls its own schedule, combinations of these arrangements are possible, thus permitting great flexibility in going about its activities. Special and extraordinary sessions have been used so that both chambers can consider legislation on specified topics without other "distractions." Beginning with 1967-68, the number of special and extraordinary sessions increased, as seen in Table VI-1. Also, since 1969, special and extraordinary sessions have been held while the legislature is in *regular session*. Use of this tactic has thus become one device whereby a governor or a group of legislators can *compel* the legislatures exclusive attention to an important topic or set of topics for a period of time.

Legislative Workload. Because legislative consideration of all introduced bills normally involves extensive review by standing committees in both chambers *prior* to action by the entire chamber, each two-year session for almost 20 years has been divided into alternating periods of committee activity and floor activity. During committee activity periods which start shortly after the convening of each new two-year session, committees meet on a regular basis, holding public hearings for legislation assigned to them, meeting to discuss matters related to these bills, and revising ("marking-up") bills to meet the concerns raised. The purpose is to receive citizen and group reactions, prepare bills for consideration by the entire chamber, and "kill" bills not deemed appropriate for further consideration by that body. During a "floorperiod," the entire chamber meets daily for several hours (usually on a Tuesday through Thursday schedule) and considers bills and other business according to an order of business set out on a daily calendar. Although committees may continue to meet during floorperiod days, most attention is shifted to the daily meeting in each chamber. This is the time when members debate bills and vote on bill passage within each chamber.

From 1985 through 1993, the Democratic leadership scheduled four or five floorperiods in the odd-numbered year, one floorperiod in the even-numbered year, and one three-day veto review period later in that year so that the legislature might attempt to over-ride the governor's veto of bills or parts of bills. When Republicans assumed control of both chambers after the 1994 general election, their leadership implemented a schedule comprised of more floorperiods meeting for shorter periods of time. Eight floorperiods were scheduled for 1995 and three for 1996, with one added for veto review in July, 1996. Each floorperiod was scheduled to last from two to 23 days, with bills being scheduled to be sent to the governor at specified times (1995, Senate Joint Resolution 1). The legislature can, however, continue to conduct business beyond the projected end of a floorperiod, if necessary. A major rationale for altering the schedule was to expedite the flow of legislation through the legislative process by reducing delays, backlogs and end-of-session legislative "log jams" from committee work to final passage. Thus, alternating committee activity and floorperiods are time management devices used by Wisconsin legislative leaders to direct legislators' attention to certain types of legislative activities at specific times in order to facilitate the smooth operation of the legislature.

102

Standing Committees. Much of the work of the Wisconsin legislature is done in its standing committees. In Wisconsin as well as in all other state legislatures, standing committees are given names that designate their areas of responsibility for policy formulation and review. The committee system is created anew at the beginning of each two-year session in both the Senate and Assembly, thus providing each session the ability to create committees compatible with changing needs. Committees are the official "work groups" in the Senate and Assembly, charged with acting on behalf of the entire chamber with regard to writing and revising legislation. Reversing a long-standing trend of increasing the number of committees, the new Republican leadership in the Senate (April, 1993) and Assembly (January, 1995) reduced the number of committees in the respective chambers. Thus for the 1995-96 session, there were eight joint standing committees (10 in 1993-94), 13 standing committees in the Senate (same as 1993-94), and 28 standing committees in the Assembly (31 in 1993-94). When compared with other states for the 1993-94 session (and, including Joint committees), 31 Senates have fewer committees, two the same number, and 16 more committees than Wisconsin. For the lower chamber, 47 states have fewer, while only two have more committees (Council of State Governments, 1994).

The number of committees existing in a legislative chamber reflects an array of complex forces. Most important are the number of legislators serving in a chamber, the range and scope of issues being faced by a legislature, the predispositions and goals of legislative leaders, and the level of member "demands" for "good" committee assignments. Thus, more committees tend to be found in larger legislatures, under conditions of extremely wide ranging legislative issues, and in settings where legislative leaders seek to satisfy member expectations via committee appointments. In Wisconsin, Democratic party leaders, when they were in the majority, attempted to give every veteran member a committee chair or seat on the important Joint Finance Committee. When the Republicans assumed control, such a goal seemed less important so that the number of committees could be reduced. Some experts have argued that a smaller number of committees permits a legislature to operate more effectively, while others point out that a larger number of committees allows members to be more involved in a wide array of policies while also fostering committee specialization and expertise development.

The committee system and the involvement of members are quite different between the Senate and Assembly. With the assumption of Republican control of the Senate in April, 1993, several changes also were made in the committee system and in how committee appointments occur. During the period of Democratic party control of the Senate, January 1975 through April 1993, committee appointments had been made by a five-member Committee on Senate Organization, composed of the President of the Senate and the leaders of each party. Under those rules, that Committee accepted assignments submitted by the Democratic Committee on Committees and the Republican party caucus. Since the early 1980s, the Democratic Committee on Committees had been composed of the three most senior Democratic senators and the party leader, and had tended to preserve the status quo regarding committees (Mayers, 1995a). The assignment of minority party members to committees consistent with their own leadership's recommendations strengthened the position of the minority party leader.

After the 1993 Republican takeover, Senate committees were appointed by the Chair of the Organization Committee--i.e., the majority party leader. The effect of this change was to strengthen substantially the majority leader's power in building a committee system responsive to his/her desires and to weaken the power of influential individual members and the status quo. The minority party was assured proportional allocation of committee seats to reflect their numbers in the Senate, with the important exception of the Joint Finance Committee which retained a six to two split as done previously by the previous majority party. Minority party appointments, although "officially" made by the majority leader, continued to be based on nominations from the minority party. Since about half of the senators are "holdover members" at the beginning of each session (see the beginning of this chapter), there continues to be a tendency to respect preferences of senators who wish to remain on their previous committees. As a consequence, fewer across-session changes occur in the Senate than in the Assembly committee system. Senate committees, varying in size from five to eight members in 1995-96, also provide for division of labor, which tends to build more specialization and expertise in committees. No senator is assigned to so many committees that s/he cannot participate in each one.

Major policy areas are frequently combined under a single committee's jurisdiction so that all major policy areas may be covered with relatively few committees while also accommodating individual senator preferences. In 1989-90, for example, Aging, Banking, Commercial Credit, and Taxation were combined into one Senate committee; Education, Economic Development, Financial Institutions, and Fiscal Policy made up another; and Educational Financing, Higher Education, and Tourism comprised a third. Although assumption of Senate control by the Republicans in April 1993 produced some realignment and simplification of committee jurisdictions, multiple topic responsibilities in a single committee continued--i.e., Financial Institutions and Cultural Affairs; Human Resources, Labor, Tourism, and Veterans and Military Affairs; and, Transportation, Agriculture, and Local and Rural Affairs.

In describing why Senate Democrats had developed such "unusual" combinations of jurisdictions in a single committee, several observers, as well as a former Senate President, indicated that Senate Democrats had "adjusted" the committee structure to their personnel and their predispositions rather than fitting the personnel into the structure, as is done in Congress. Consequently, members' (especially the chairpersons') preferences for combining jurisdictions had been followed by Democratic party leaders in organizing the Senate. While such a practice may have resulted in a greater commitment of members to the legislative process and to increased participation in its operations, it also had a very serious "down side." The emphasis placed on satisfying Democratic members and committee chairs through this structuring of committees weakened Senate Democratic leadership and fostered the creation of policy "fiefdoms" in committees. Because these Senate committees came to reflect the goals and predilections of committee chairs, one legislative observer labeled Democratic committee chairs as "Barons of the legislative process." Legislation emerging from committees was often described as reflecting the chair's own preferences and policy desires. During the 1991-92 session, this sentiment "boiled over" when members openly criticized two Democratic committee chairs because their dictatorial styles had turned their committees into "legislative graveyards" that killed bills not wanted by the chair (*Milwaukee Journal*, March 15, 1991 and *Eau Claire Leader Telegram*, April 3, 1992). This, in turn, produced dysfunctional friction among members regarding "turf," "wounded" Senate Democrats in the eyes of many, and ultimately may have helped produce conditions contributing to the defeat of Democratic senatorial candidates in 1993 and 1994.

After three special elections in April of 1993 gave Republicans control of the Senate, there were several changes in its committee system. The new majority Republican leader--Michael Ellis--initiated steps to "rein-in" the powers Democratic committee chairs had amassed. He did this by determining committee assignments for Republicans, scheduling legislation, and redefining (untangle and simplify) committee jurisdictions. In addition, Ellis implemented tighter leadership controls over committee chairs and committee work while providing proportional minority party membership on all Senate committees except Joint Finance. These efforts were possible because rank-and-file Republicans wanted to alter the legislative process by implementing a more party-based approach to policy making while strengthening party leadership--both inside and outside the legislature. The effects of these changes have been more cooperation from Senate committee chairs with Senate leaders and members and a willingness to move more Republican- rather than chairperson-preferred legislation through committees. The passage of time will reveal if Republicans can resist the tendency for members and committee chairs to develop their own independent bases of power in and through the committee system.

In the Assembly, as Table VI-1 shows, the number of committees increased moderately throughout the 1970s and into the 1980s. One major reason was the growing number of majority Democrats who wanted to be committee chairs and were able to convince the leadership to embrace this approach. Another was the leadership's desire to accommodate members in order to obtain and maintain their own leadership positions--forming four new committees became one means for former Speaker Ed Jackamonis to deal with a "palace revolt" by the more conservative wing of the Democratic Assembly members in the 1981-82 session (see Loftus, 1994: 55-60). Growth in the number of Assembly committees has been facilitated because 1) the number of committees and their titles are set in the chamber rules, adopted (and changed) via chamber resolution at the beginning of each session; 2) the Speaker determines the number, title, and size of committees; and 3) the Speaker is the sole appointing authority for majority party committee members. One consequence has been variation in the size of committees--for example, in 1995-96, the smallest committee had five members while the largest had 18. Also, it has not been uncommon in recent sessions for a representative to have as many as nine committee assignments, or as few as one or two for those assigned to the powerful Joint Finance Committee. As noted above, the Republican takeover of the Assembly in 1995 resulted in a reduction in the number of committees (from 31 to 28). This reduction was possible in part because 23 of the 51 Republican members of the Assembly were in their first or second term and had few expectations about becoming committee chairs. The implications of this reduction are not yet clear.

There never have been clear-cut jurisdictions for Assembly committees based on the subject matter of bills introduced. In some sessions, there were both a Local Affairs and an Urban Affairs Committee; in 1985-86, there was a State Affairs Committee even though specialized policy committees existed for virtually every area of state policy; in 1989-90 through 1995-96, there were three education committees--Education, Urban Education, and Colleges and Universities; and, after the 1970 and 1980 census' when the legislature had to reapportion itself, a separate Reapportionment Committee was selected rather than using the Elections Committee. (After the 1990 census, redistricting was assigned to a Special Reapportionment Committee rather than to the Elections and Constitutional Law standing committee). This absence of simple and clear-cut committee jurisdictions, together with variation across sessions, allows the leadership impressive freedom in assigning bills and also permits them latitude in dealing with members and issues.

Seniority has not been an explicit factor in making Assembly assignments to committees nor in naming chairpersons; but members who have served in previous sessions appear to have preference. A recent study showed that members with previous service who *requested* to remain on the same committee were virtually assured of continuing on that committee (Hedlund, 1992). Speaker candidates, when seeking election or re-election to this position, have used committee assignments as "bargaining stock" prior to party caucus meetings where leaders are selected. Since each Speaker puts together his/her own coalition to win this position, there may be turnover in chairpersons, even when one party maintains its majority across sessions.

Traditionally, and unlike Congress or the Wisconsin Senate (post 1993), the minority party in the Assembly has not been assured a number of committee positions proportional to their numbers in the chamber. Assembly Rules before 1995 did not require the Speaker to provide the minority party seats on committees in proportion to their representation in the Assembly or to accept minority leaders' preferences for their members' committee assignments; however, between 1973 and 1994, Democratic Speakers had voluntarily honored the nominations for committee assignments provided by the minority party. The consequence of voluntarily accepting the minority leader's recommendations was a strengthening of the minority party leadership since *it was responsible* for minority party committee appointments. One byproduct of a strong minority leader was his/her ability to negotiate for party members and deliver votes on any promises made to the Speaker. At the beginning of the 1995 session, new Republican Speaker Prosser formalized both changes in the rules by requiring the Speaker to " . . . make all committee appointments of the minority party as nominated by the minority leader except that the Speaker may appoint any member of the minority party as chairperson of a committee" (1995 Assembly Resolution 2, p.8). This provision for minority party members to serve as chairs was seen as an initiative to weaken the resolve of some minority party members. Consistent with this rule, Speaker Prosser appointed one minority party Democrat as a committee chair in 1995, although rumors circulated that other Democrats had declined overtures to appoint them as chairs. (Presumably, the "political strings" attached to accepting such an appointment made many Democrats unwilling to be participants).

In order to minimize the potential threat of minority party committee appointments, Speakers have been known to "manipulate" committee size and their party's appointments in order to assure adequate control over committee action. (One former Speaker always reviewed the minority party's appointments in order to be able to counter, in his majority party appointments, the predispositions represented among minority members. If the minority appointed an especially vocal and outspoken critic of the majority party, the Speaker would balance that off by appointing an even more forthright supporter of the majority position). Asserting influence by limiting the minority party's appointments has been especially prevalent regarding the very important Joint Finance Committee, where the number of minority party members is proportionately small. This under-representation produced an ongoing debate and some change with regard to minority party representation on the Joint Finance Committee in the early 1990s--a temporary increase from two of eight to three of eight members. This increase was made permanent in 1995. Thus, through their appointments of members and determination of committee size and scope of responsibility, Speakers have been able to wield important influence over the work of committees.

The 1995 Republican Assembly rules changes enhanced further the powers of the Speaker *vis-a-vis* committees. The changes permitted the Speaker to withdraw (bring back to the chamber) any administrative rule referred to a committee and to limit committee hearings held outside of the state capitol during critical election periods. Consequently, a Speaker could prevent a committee from delaying consideration of administrative rule-making and restrict chairs from using committee hearings to enhance their re-election efforts (a charge made against Democratic chairs in previous sessions).

Because members have varied policy interests and their preferences are often honored in committee assignments, committee composition does not reflect the makeup of the legislature and certainly not the state in general. Farmers seek to be on the Agriculture Committee and educators on the Education Committee. Insurance agents and bankers seek membership on the Financial Institutions Committee, while union members pursue appointment to the Labor Committee. Attorneys tend to be over-represented on the Judiciary Committee. As a result, most committees tend to endorse policies favored by the majority party's interests on the committee. (For example, when Democratic teachers dominated the Education Committee before 1995, the committee was pro-education and favored teachers' interests). Thus, if an Assembly committee rejects a bill related to its interests, another committee rarely assumes a lead role in advancing that bill. If, however, a subject matter committee recommends passage for a bill, other committees and legislators frequently remain skeptical in their consideration of the proposal, questioning the true merits of the bill. The assumption seems to be that a committee's endorsement may come only to a bill favoring the committee members' or the relevant pressure group's own special interests.

In order to expedite and unify across chambers the treatment of certain important topics, the Wisconsin legislature makes use of several *joint committees*. Members are appointed to these committees from each chamber in the normal manner and have these committee memberships treated as standing committee assignments. The primary difference is that when the committee convenes, members from both chambers attend and serve as full committee members. Joint standing committees have all of the powers and duties of a chamber standing committee, but differ in their composition. In 1995-1996 eight joint standing committees were formed--Review of Administrative Rules, Audit, Employment Relations, Finance, Information Policy, Legislative Organization, Survey on Retirement Systems, and Survey on Tax Exemptions. Each chamber appointing authority designates a chair who then shares responsibilities with his/her co-chair for the joint committee.

In recent sessions, the leadership of both chambers (especially the Assembly) has opted to use a small number of *special committees* to direct attention to certain limited scope problems. Thus in 1995-96, the Assembly Rules specified formation of three special committees--Controlled Substances, Gambling Oversight, and State-Federal Relations. Each of these operates much like a standing committee with regard to legislation review and oversight of administrative agencies. In addition, there are regional and national study committees (many of them associated with organizations like the Education Commission of the States, the National Conference of State Legislatures and the Council of State Governments) that are highly sought by many members as a source of recognition and possible travel opportunities while working with national experts.

Statutory Committees. The vast majority of legislative committees in Wisconsin are created by the legislature itself under chamber rules, as described above. In addition, the Wisconsin legislature also participates in committees created by state statutes and designated as decision making bodies in certain areas. Some of these statutory committees are composed solely of legislators and operate as joint committees while others include non-legislators and work in a manner which tends to blur the traditional concept of separation of executive and legislative functions. Four such statutory bodies which designate both legislators and non-legislators as members are the State Building Commission, the Retirement Research Committee, the Transportation Projects Commission and the Commission on Uniform State Laws. (The Legislative Council, described below, is also a statutory committee). The Building Commission--formed in 1949 and composed of legislators, the governor, and one appointee of the governor--plans and monitors the state's building construction program. This entity has veto power through its authority to refuse approval of specific construction plans previously authorized in principle by the legislature. Service on the Commission is a much coveted legislative appointment since all state building construction is its responsibility and having state building projects funded in one's district is a factor contributing toward re-election and constituent service.

The Transportation Projects Commission--formed in 1983 and composed of the governor, legislators and three citizen members--reviews the Department of Transportation's recommended major highway projects prior to the submission of these projects to the governor or legislature. Since state supported highway construction money is a critical factor in many legislative districts, service on this commission provides an important means for influencing possible highway construction projects in one's district as well as the state. Needless to say, service on either the Building or Transportation Commission can also place a member in a position to help other legislators and interest groups.

The Wisconsin legislature has also established the Retirement Research Committee composed of legislators from the Joint Survey Committee on Retirement Systems, administrative personnel having responsibilities in the state retirement system, representatives from employee groups, and public members. This committee reviews and oversees the state's retirement program, including benefits and retirement program features. Given the tens of thousands of state workers covered under this program and the multi-billion dollar investment portfolio, service on this committee includes substantial responsibilities.

Since all 50 states consider legislation on many similar topics, concern is often expressed that uniformity of provisions is desirable. For example, if Wisconsin offers better benefits under some of its public welfare programs, the state may attract new residents seeking only to benefit from those programs. Consequently, a number of strategies are used by the Wisconsin legislature to monitor legislation as enacted in other states. One such strategy is the appointment of the Commission on Uniform State Laws composed of legislators, legislative staff involved in the preparation and revision of state laws, and public members. Members of this Commission attend the annual meeting of the National Conference of Commissioners on Uniform State Laws and interact with their counterparts in other states regarding model legislation prepared in certain policy areas. The goal is to share information regarding possible legislation in certain policy areas.

These statutory committees, together with the Legislative Council described below, provide useful opportunities for legislators. They create a setting in which members can interact with agency personnel and citizens regarding solutions to public policy issues more informally and with less pressure than that associated with standing committee hearings in the Senate and Assembly. In addition, these statutory committees tend to transcend some of the traditional barriers established between the legislative, executive and judicial branches of state government. This facilitates a unified approach to issues.

Legislative Staff. Assistance for the Wisconsin legislature in processing the increasing number and complexity of legislative proposals, as well as in meeting other needs and demands for action, has occurred by increasing the number and competencies of support personnel--staff for individual legislators as well as legislative agency staff. Like most other state legislatures, the Wisconsin Senate and Assembly have increased the number of professional and support staff available to individual members, to legislative leaders, to committees, to political parties in the legislature (caucuses), and to legislative service agencies. Such increases are intended to help legislators be more effective in handling the increasing number and diversity of requests being made, both from individual constituents and from organizations. The availability of staff makes it possible for legislators to delegate many of the more routine legislative activities to staff and to hire well-qualified experts in some of the specialized and technical policy areas (for example, disposal of hazardous materials, or utilizing science and technology in solving state problems) requiring legislative attention.

Four types of legislative staff can be found in Wisconsin--individual legislator staff, partisan caucus staff, chamber staff, and legislative agency staff. Individual legislators, depending on their responsibilities, may share staff or have staff assigned solely to them. Included here may be secretarial as well as policy-oriented professional staff. Each party in the Senate and Assembly meets periodically as the Republican and Democratic caucuses. These four caucuses each have staff to help party members analyze bills and formulate positions from a partisan perspective. In addition, these caucus staffs have had increasingly important roles in developing and implementing partisan electoral strategies with the goal of electing more Republicans or Democrats in that chamber.

Chamber staff, on the other hand, are less partisan than caucus staff and are assigned to a wide range of responsibilities related to keeping the chamber working and on schedule. Individuals working in the offices of Chief Clerk of the Assembly or Secretary of the Senate are responsible for generating and maintaining many of the official documents required for conducting public business. In recent years, persons in these positions have had specialized training and experiences and have tended to have long tenure. The selection of a replacement Assembly Chief Clerk after the 1995 Republican takeover resulted in a person being chosen who had strong professional credentials rather than a close association with Republican politics. A second type of chamber staff--the Sergeants-at-Arms--assist in maintaining order and decorum in the chamber and "running errands for members" under the direction of the presiding officer. While both the Chief Clerk/Secretary of the Senate and the Sergeant-at-Arms are elected by legislators in each chamber from outside their membership, the former tend to have professional credentials and specialized experience while the latter have been more known for their ties to the majority party.

Substantial non-partisan expertise is also found in a series of independent legislative service agencies composed of highly-trained, professional staff who specialize in designated task and policy areas. In 1901 Wisconsin was the first state to establish a Legislative Reference Library. Subsequently, all other states have established such an agency, sometimes called by another title. This agency, now known as the Legislative Reference Bureau (LRB), has grown to include much more than the library. The important bill-drafting service of this agency is described below. Its other important functions include providing information to legislators and to committees as well as to the public, when requested. This research service enables Wisconsin legislators to be informed by an impartial agency.

Wisconsin also has a Legislative Council, an institution created by statute--which Kansas began, but which Wisconsin expanded. The Council initiates studies on problems which require more comprehensive study than could be done during a regular legislative session. Legislative leaders may establish Council committees, comprised of both legislators and non-legislative members, which conduct in-depth studies, usually during the interim time between sessions. Nineteen special and two statutory Council Committees reported to the 1993-94 session of the legislature. These committees have the right to introduce their proposals as bills at the next legislative session. The Council has a permanent staff which functions throughout the year, and also serves as staff to standing committees while the legislature is in session. Use of the Council provides the Wisconsin legislature a way to conduct long-term research on policy problems without the press of daily legislative concerns.

Other legislative staff agencies include the Legislative Fiscal Bureau (staff to the Joint Finance Committee), the Legislative Audit Bureau, and the Revisor of Statutes. These provide important fiscal/ audit and statutory clarification services to legislators.

As Table VI-1 shows, there has been an increase in *all* types of legislative staff since 1954. This growth has leveled off in recent years, as "adequate" staffing levels were reached. The largest increases have been in the fiscal and audit functions. This reflects both the importance placed on these aspects of government operations by contemporary legislators and on the size/complexity of the state's fiscal responsibilities. One fact-of-life learned by most U.S. state legislators has been that to be effective and independent in any policy area, and especially in those having a fiscal component, legislators must have *their own* financial experts. Relying only on outside groups having a "stake" in a policy area for fiscal information (be they representatives from pressure groups or bureaucrats from state agencies) has sometimes proved very embarrassing for legislators. Information from legislative-based agencies helps to assure that the Senate and Assembly will be able to function independently and without undue influence either from executive agencies or from pressure groups on the important money matters.

A balance must be achieved, however, regarding the continuing legislative and public policy pay-offs from ever-increasing number of staff. For example, concerns have been expressed about the spiraling costs incurred when staff size continually increases, about their possible intrusions into the legislative process in order to demonstrate their value, about the potential for increased focus on minute policy details (sometimes called "over-legislating") due to an "over-abundance" of expertise, and about their increasing role in securing the election/re-election of their party's members. While unquestionably, legislative staff are a critical element in an effective legislature, it seems unlikely that there will be any great expansion of legislative staff in Wisconsin during the near future.

During the early weeks of the 1995-96 legislative session, concerns emerged in the press regarding the compensation provided to certain personal and partisan legislative staff--both Republican and Democratic. Reports appeared indicating that seven Assembly and six Senate staff (personal, caucus and chamber staff) had salaries in excess of $50,000 while members of the Senate and Assembly elected in 1994 received $38,056. In defense of this situation, legislators themselves noted that, technically, being a legislator in Wisconsin is a part-time position and that the skills and experience required of these particular legislative staff necessitated remuneration at this level. Other sources were more skeptical and criticized these salaries. None of the staff resigned their positions or had their salaries reduced. Nevertheless, public concerns about the advisability of such a situation have persisted.

A different concern, but one also important in assessing legislative staff, is the role they sometimes play in policy making. In some instances, it has been charged that staff have become legislators without benefit of election by a constituency. In fact during the 1970s and 1980s, many staff became so involved and skilled at legislative activities that they were prime recruits to run, subsequently, for legislative office. (In the 1995 session, five senators and 16 representatives had prior experience in a legislative staff position.) While in Wisconsin the prominence of staff playing these roles has not been as common as noted in some other states, many Wisconsin legislators have become increasingly sensitive to these staff issues.

<u>Legislative Leadership: Chamber Officers</u>. In order to assure the smooth operation of the legislative process, each chamber elects its own leaders. The Senate and Assembly are each led by a presiding officer who is selected from among the chamber's members by the majority party caucus and then elected, usually on a straight party line vote, by the entire chamber. Political parties in the legislature also select their own leaders who advance the party's agenda in the legislature and provide consultation across party lines so that chamber operations are facilitated. Party leaders (called majority and minority leaders) and their assistants, as well as caucus officers, are selected by the respective party members within each chamber.

The presiding officer of the Senate is called the President and is elected from its members through nominations made by each party at the start of every two-year session. While all senators vote for the President, the real election takes place in the majority party caucus after the November election and before the beginning of the January session. The President presides over the daily meetings of the Senate, managing legislative procedure and assuring its smooth operation. Prior to 1979, the lieutenant governor, who was elected state-wide by all voters along with the governor in the general election, was the presiding officer. Since 1979, however, the lieutenant governor has had virtually no power in the Senate. This constitutional change enhanced the Senate's independence and altered its power structure by strengthening its own internal leadership.

The presiding officer of the Assembly is the Speaker, who has been described as the second most powerful public official in the state--second only to the governor. Like the Senate President, the Speaker is responsible for presiding during daily Assembly meetings; however, in addition, s/he is responsible for organizing and managing all aspects of the legislative process in the Assembly. Since the Speaker is selected by the majority party in the Assembly at its pre-session organizational meeting and elected by the entire membership on the first day of a new session, s/he has a large power base for influencing decisions and public policies. As the leader of his/her party in the Assembly, s/he exercises considerable influence because of that responsibility. The Speaker's power is further increased through the ability to appoint his/her party's members to standing committees, to determine the size and jurisdiction of committees and to refer bills to committees. (As noted above, the 1995 Assembly Rules formally gave to the minority leader the power to appoint minority party members to their committees although these appointments are "passed through" the Speaker). In a body which has no seniority rules nor norms which require that members continue to serve on the same committee, the discretion which the Speaker exercises regarding committee assignments gives him/her considerable authority.

Speakers from both parties have exercised great discretion in appointing committee members and chairpersons, sometimes using this power to achieve other ends, as noted above. In 1981, however, a series of committee assignments by Speaker Jackamonis were regarded by the conservative wing of the Democratic Assembly as retaliatory for their non-support and foreboding to their future in the upcoming reapportionment. They threatened to form a coalition with the Republicans and take control of the Assembly. Since their numbers were sufficient, this possibility could not be dismissed, especially with many Republicans openly encouraging such a move. Ultimately, a compromise was worked out which placated the dissidents by changing some committee assignments and by creating four new committees. The resulting loss of trust in the Speaker weakened his position and influence and served as a warning to future Speakers about the need to maintain the trust and confidence of members through committee assignments. As successor to Jackamonis and learning from this 1981 experience, former Speaker Tom Loftus wrote "I often told the members of the caucus to think carefully about what committee assignment they asked me for because they might get it" (Loftus, 1994: 59).

The area and scope of a committee's policy jurisdiction is purposely imprecise and nebulous. This provides the Speaker with wiggle room and opportunities to influence committee decisions on policies since s/he assigns bills to committees. Because the Speaker often knows how a committee will react to a given proposal, s/he can sometimes determine the results by his/her bill assignment. If s/he favors a proposal, s/he can refer it to a more "sympathetic" committee and since s/he appoints committees, s/he can determine how supportive committees will be for various types of proposals. For example, many years ago when a Speaker assigned a bill to allow the sale of colored oleomargarine in direct competition with Wisconsin's own butter to a committee other than the Agriculture Committee, it was clear the Speaker favored the bill. When the same proposal was assigned to the Agriculture Committee in the Senate, it was clear that it would "die" in committee.

The Speaker and President preside at all floor sessions of their chambers unless they designate someone else for a "short" period of time. In this capacity, the presiding officer must comply with certain forms of impartiality, but great latitude is permitted. For example, the presiding officer can interpret rules or make new rulings favorable to his/her own interests. While courtesy and good sense are usually followed by presiding officers, the latitude available even in the presiding officer's power to recognize members to speak on the floor provides considerable power. Legislative rules tend to favor the majority party and a clever presiding officer can increase that advantage.

The ability of Assembly Speakers to adopt differing approaches to leadership in discharging their committee responsibilities is epitomized in a leadership style identified with former Speaker Loftus, sometimes labeled "Zen Leadership." Under this approach, Loftus shared power by "parceling out" responsibilities to members and committees with few "strings" or restrictions; he then would "step back" and permit matters to proceed, even if they unraveled and "chaos" ensued. Loftus had an uncanny ability to manage whatever happened and still develop acceptable strategies and solutions even under conditions of great uncertainty and tension (see Loftus, 1994: Chapter 4 "Legislative Leadership: Apprenticeship in the School of Chaos"). While such an approach has been lauded for fostering individual member responsibility and involvement, it has also been criticized for the growth of highly individualized Democratic approaches to policy making (the antithesis of a unified party approach) and of general inefficiency. The selection of a new Democratic Speaker in 1990--Wally Kunicki--saw the evolution of a different leadership style, one that still relied on individual member initiative, but tolerated less member freedom, ambiguity and chaos in the search for legislative solutions to problems.

The Republican victories in the 1994 general election resulted in eight term (three as minority Assembly leader) David Prosser assuming the Speaker's position and implementing his leadership style. Given the relatively sizeable number of Republican representatives with limited legislative experience plus a commitment to accomplish a new and different legislative agenda (one reflecting the Republican governor's program), Prosser seemed to use a more conventional goal-oriented leadership style, while emphasizing fairness and consultation. This goal was to support the Republican governor and his program. The Speaker's leadership in garnering support for the governor was facilitated by the selection of a majority leader--Scott R. Jensen--who had been a high-ranking member of Governor Tommy Thompson's staff and was committed to advancing the governor's agenda. The Republican leaders' success in generating members' support for the governor became obvious during the chamber's revision and approval of the state budget bill in May and June, 1995. At the same time, defeats for other legislation (most notably a $3 billion road construction package) raised questions and Prosser's style was criticized for being too lenient and forgiving. Late in the floorperiod, the press asked if he was really tough enough to forge the voting coalitions needed to pass "unpopular" legislation? (Bice, 1995). Nevertheless, the power of leadership based on partisan ties to the governor became apparent in the Assembly.

Presiding officer responsibilities are complemented by the majority leader, caucus chairperson, and other leaders who assist in coordinating and directing legislative activities. The minority party also has a set of leaders headed by the minority leader, responsible for coordinating their activities *in response* to the majority party. While the precise duties can change, these persons comprise the formal party leadership in that chamber.

The Legislature and Its Publics

U.S. state legislatures are an integral part of their environments, drawing resources, and support, from their publics. Included as relevant publics are all persons residing within a state, those who vote for state legislators, those who are affected by decisions made in the Wisconsin legislature, and those who pay ongoing attention to what happens in the legislative arena.

Legislative Interaction with the Public. In its law making activities, the Wisconsin legislature is very sensitive to its publics and the image it projects. Thus, extraordinary efforts are made to solicit input and support from the public, to respond to citizen concerns, and to avoid alienating constituents. Legislators spend considerable time with constituents--in their districts as well as in the state capitol--talking and listening to what they have to say. In addition, some unusual steps have been taken which illustrate the degree of effort going into constituent relations:

- The legislature has a toll free legislative "hotline" so that any citizen can contact his/her legislator on any issue. This line has been maintained even though pressure groups have advised their members to use this number for pressuring legislators on behalf of group issues.

- The legislature has not acted formally to repeal Section 940 of the Wisconsin Statutes banning

111

abortions in the state, despite the likelihood that it is unconstitutional since it is similar to provisions declared invalid by the U.S. Supreme Court in *Roe v. Wade* (1972). Legislative sentiment seems to be that any action on their part formally to repeal this section would only open new and unneeded public debate on this divisive and emotional issue for no good public reason. Thus, the provision remains in the statutes even though it is not enforced and contains a note regarding the U.S. case.

- The legislature has become an active participant in the civics education of many public schools. More than one innovative teacher have taught their classes about state law-making by having students approach their legislator about introducing a bill of interest to the class or by becoming involved in law-making activities. By observing and participating, the class learns first-hand about the legislative process. Examples of resulting laws include designation of the badger as the state animal (1957), the honey bee as the state insect (1977), and the American water spaniel as the state dog (1986). Other efforts have resulted in corn being chosen as the state grain (1989) and the polka as the state dance (1993). Some efforts, such as a formal designation of the cranberry muffin as the state muffin, failed to become law. (An effort to prevent the introduction of "meaningless" bills, including designating state symbols and memorials to Congress, failed at the start of the 1995 session).

- The legislature has procedures whereby constituents can receive official legislative recognition. When constituents sit in the galleries surrounding the chamber, notification to their legislator can result in an "official introduction" during the chamber's proceedings. Meritorious actions by private citizens or groups including local sports teams may result in an official legislative citation or possibly a resolution being prepared and given to the recipient on behalf of the legislature.

- Substantial time from personal and caucus staff as well as the legislature goes into developing and maintaining contact with constituents. The means used for these contacts include legislator newsletters, personal correspondence, and individual meetings. Legislators know the necessity of "staying in touch" with their constituents. The single most important strategy is the "casework" role played by legislators. Any constituent having a problem with any state agency will find a sympathetic and helpful response from their senator and representative.

- Many legislative committees in recent sessions have scheduled hearings on bills across the state to facilitate constituent input; however, the use of such hearings close to election time as a means to assist an incumbent's re-election were curtailed by the Assembly rules adopted at the beginning of the 1995 session.

Constituent contact and service are important legislative activities between, as well as during, election campaigns.

Legislative Reapportionment. From the adoption of the U. S. constitution in 1787, U.S. legislators have been selected by voters through elections in geographically defined legislative districts. Since people are neither randomly nor evenly distributed across parts of the state, differences across legislative districts are expected. Also, the types of people living in a district are very likely to be reflected in who is elected and in what policy interests s/he pursues in the legislature. (A legislator elected from a rural, agricultural area composed of farms and small towns will be different from a legislator selected from an inner-city area in terms of perspectives and policy interests). Thus, the composition of legislative districts, as determined by the drawing of district boundaries after every decennial census, is very important to legislators, interested groups, and political parties. In fact, most politicians conclude that the redistricting/reapportionment process (i.e., the redrawing of legislative district boundaries in order to create districts of approximately equal population size) determines much of the nature and scope of all governmental activities for the next decade.

All Wisconsin legislators are elected in single-member districts; that is, there is one, and only one, legislator per district. This system is often regarded as the norm in U.S. legislative bodies; but, in fact, some states elect some legislators from multi-member districts--usually several from one county. In Wisconsin, Assembly districts cannot be split in making Senate districts. Accordingly, each Senate district is composed of three Assembly districts. The districts are to follow county, city, village, town, and ward lines to the maximum extent possible in achieving population equality. From 1892 to 1972, the State Supreme Court did not permit combining part of one county with another county nor with part of another county to create an Assembly district; but the 1972 reapportionment ignored this restriction because court decisions have increasingly placed a higher premium on equal population in districts.

Aside from the population discrepancies which resulted from following county lines, the Wisconsin Constitution required that reapportionment of both chambers of the legislature be based on population (*Baker v. Carr* 1962; *Reynolds v. Sims* 1964). Thus, the state required using population long before the U.S. Supreme Court decided that all state legislative districting follow this criterion. Unlike Wisconsin, many U.S. state constitutions provided for using other criteria like geography for legislative reapportionment.

Apportionment based on population has not always been automatically achieved in Wisconsin. Population shifts from rural to urban areas and, more recently, to the Milwaukee suburbs have led to many controversies on legislative reapportionment. Before the U.S. Supreme Court ruled that state legislatures must be apportioned on the basis of population, Wisconsin was one of two states which most nearly coincided with this standard. This resulted because the Wisconsin Supreme Court, consistent with its tradition of judicial activism, ruled in 1954 that a proposed constitutional amendment, which would have included area as well as population in apportioning one chamber of the legislature, was unconstitutional. As a consequence, a reapportionment plan based solely on population, which had been approved *pro forma* by the legislature on the assumption that it would never go into effect, became the Wisconsin law.

The Wisconsin Supreme Court again intervened in reapportionment after the 1960 census due to an impasse between Democratic Governors Gaylord Nelson and John Reynolds, on the one hand, and the Republican-controlled legislature on the other. In the 1961 and 1963 sessions of the legislature, the Republicans passed reapportionment bills which the Democratic governors vetoed, and the governors proposed reapportionment measures which the Republican legislators defeated. While both parties agreed that the fast-growing Milwaukee suburbs should be given more representation at the expense of declining rural areas in northern and western Wisconsin, the parties differed on how the lines should be drawn and on whether Milwaukee County should receive one or two additional seats. Finally, the state supreme court gave the legislature and the governor an ultimatum: reapportion the state or the court would. When further attempts at agreement failed, the state was reapportioned by court order (*Thomson v. Zimmerman*, 1964).

Accordingly, beginning in 1964, elections were held under a reapportionment based on the court's order, although the old reapportionment remained in the statutes. The court ordered a reapportionment more drastic than any of the politicians would have contemplated. While the basic shift in political power was not great, many traditional districts were changed and political boundaries were crossed.

Following the 1970 census, many observers believed that the legislature might again fail to reach agreement on reapportionment. With a Democratic governor and Assembly and a Republican Senate, it seemed likely that there would be another partisan impasse. However, in 1972, the legislators visibly demonstrated the principle of personal advantage. After many months of negotiating and after the failure of several proposals, a majority in each chamber of the divided legislature found a remapping on which they could agree and which the governor signed. The stratagem was to devise a map which provided reelection advantages for the greatest number of incumbents, thus protecting the Democratic majority in the Assembly and the Republican one in the Senate. Assembly Republicans were strongly opposed to the plan because they knew its adoption would keep them in the minority for the entire decade. Admittedly, the result conformed to more accurate population equality than any preceding reapportionment, but meeting this requirement and the requirement of protecting incumbents resulted in a confusing hodgepodge of district boundaries. This reapportionment was challenged in the state supreme court, but the court refused to invalidate it. *(Seefeldt et al. v. Zimmerman,* 1972). Unfortunately for one major force supporting this plan in the legislature (Senate Republicans), the 1974 election was conducted against the backdrop of Watergate and featured a United Auto Workers (UAW) assault to replace certain Republican incumbents. The result was a loss of their assumed advantage for the rest of the 1970s, the 1980s, and into the 1990s until the special Senate elections of April, 1993.

After the 1980 census, reapportionment disputes again erupted, and on a scale rivaling earlier disputes. The major problem centered around an on-going partisan dispute between Republican Governor Lee Dreyfus and the Democratically-controlled legislature in which reapportionment was simply the latest issue. Before district boundaries were finalized in mid-1984 (three plus years after the census figures were available), bills had passed in two legislative sessions (1981-82 and 1983-84) redistricting the state to meet the one-person one-vote dictum; two governors (one from each party) had vetoed legislative redistricting bills a total of three times; a three-judge federal panel had imposed its own redistricting plan which was used for one state legislative election; a three-judge federal panel had ruled one legislative redistricting plan unconstitutional; and the U.S. Supreme Court had "stayed" (halted) the decision of the three-judge panel, thus permitting one legislative plan to stand. In summary, a confusing and protracted situation had again characterized the redrawing of legislative districts (Legislative Reference Bureau, 1984).

Reapportionment after the 1990 census took place against the backdrop of Democratic control of both the Assembly and Senate, with a strong and confrontative Republican governor--former Assembly minority leader Tommy Thompson. The two political parties, in the form of the Democratic legislative leaders versus the Republican governor and the Republican legislative leaders, had been unable to develop an acceptable reapportionment plan. Creation of an independent or bipartisan panel to create an acceptable plan was rejected by the Democrats in the fall of 1991. Fearing an excessive delay that could jeopardize the timely creation of legislative districts for the 1992 November election, Republican legislators and representatives from minority groups in Milwaukee sued in federal court for relief. A three-judge panel began work in April 1992, with agreement from the Wisconsin legislature, to redistrict the state. Various groups including the Democratically controlled legislature, the Republican legislative leadership, minority groups, and other interested pressure groups submitted alternative reapportionment plans to the court. The panel reviewed these plans and heard testimony from interested parties on all plans submitted. With technical help from an employee of the Wisconsin Legislative Reference Bureau, the panel selected portions of the plans submitted and issued its redistricting plan in June, 1992. Although there was talk of an appeal to the U.S. Supreme Court, nothing happened and the court produced plan went into effect for the September 1992 primary elections. (For descriptive information on legislative districts see, Wisconsin Legislative Reference Bureau, *Research Bulletin* 94-4).

The success of the federal court's 1990 reapportionment effort is apparent when one reviews the results. Wisconsin's population according to the 1990 census was 4,891,755. The task was to divide this population, residing in thousands of census "blocks," into 33 Senate and 99 Assembly districts. The ideal Senate district would have a population of 148,235 and the Assembly 49,412. The resulting 33 Senate districts differed from the ideal by a *total* of 4,704 or an average deviation of 143 persons per district--+/- 0.10 percent. (The largest deviation was -436 and the smallest + 2 persons). For the Assembly, the resulting 99 districts differed from the ideal by a total of 8,261 or an average deviation of 83 persons per district--+/- 0.17 percent. (The largest deviation was - 261 and the smallest +/- 1 person). In addition, the court plan resulted in only 16 incumbents for both the Senate and Assembly having to run against each other. Six races would have candidates running against one another from the same party--four Democrats and two Republicans (State of Wisconsin, *Blue Book*, 1993-4: 284-5). Given the Republican party's improved electoral success beginning in 1992, one can speculate as to whether this reapportionment helped weaken Democratic electoral control of the Senate and Assembly in ways the Republicans were able to exploit.

This analysis of five reapportionment efforts after the 1950, 1960, 1970, 1980, and 1990 censuses suggests that redistricting plans in Wisconsin:

- bring out strong partisan feelings;
- are "hotly contested," divisive issues;
- sometimes stretch across several legislative sessions;
- frequently involve differences of opinion and policies across legislative, executive and judicial branches of government; and
- are seen as very important because they are thought to largely determine what policy approaches will be followed by state government for the next decade.

Legislative Elections. Although the creation of legislative districts after each decennial census through reapportionment is a critical backdrop for every election, the outcomes of a two-year campaign struggle also reflect other factors. For example, recent election studies have shown that once elected, state legislators in Wisconsin are likely to be re-elected even if their party identification differs from that dominant in their district. In describing this situation, former Speaker Loftus noted:

When an incumbent leaves office (an open seat race), predicting the vote becomes more difficult. Unless a district is extremely partisan, it is up for grabs. In this circumstance there are more than enough voters who can easily vote for the "right" person in either party. . . .

A decision to vote for one of the two candidates in an open seat for the state legislature is a serious decision that is not really rethought for the next time around. The persuadable voter is wooed by two suitors and, having chosen one, does not two years later divorce and choose again between the incumbent and a new Romeo. Incumbents are hard to beat partly because of the bond they form with voters during their first campaign.

The next campaign, and others that will follow, will be a choice for voters between the known incumbent and the unknown challenger. Asking voters to vote against the incumbent is like asking them to discard an old friend in order to gain a new friend. Most of us will stick with the old friend (Loftus, 1994: 14).

Consequently, continuity of members in the Wisconsin Assembly and Senate is an expectation.

One type of evidence supporting this conclusion was presented above in Chapter IV, in Table IV-2, showing the success rate of Assembly and Senate incumbents when seeking re-election. The data show that, at least since 1986, an overwhelming majority of both senators and representatives have sought re-election--about 90 percent, except in 1992. The Court ordered reapportionment plan, as noted above, resulted in 16 incumbents being placed in the same districts in 1992 thus producing an incentive for many to retire voluntarily. In addition, the district boundaries that had become familiar to many legislators were changed so that districts became less "hospitable" to many incumbents. Consequently many fewer incumbents sought re-election in 1992. In addition, of those incumbents who sought re-election, over 90 percent in every election except the 1992 Senate were re-elected. Thus, the overwhelming majority of Wisconsin legislators seek re-election (with the rate being understandably lower following reapportionments), and are successful in that effort.

Table VI-2 presents information about the margins of victory experienced by members of both parties, first for the Assembly and then for the Senate, 1968-1994. These data reinforce what both parties know--most election contests are one-sided in Wisconsin, with the winner garnering over 60 percent of the vote. More than half of the legislative general election contests for both parties in all but four years show the winner being elected by at least 60 percent of the popular vote. (The exceptions are all for the Republicans: Republican representatives 1982; and Republican senators 1970, 1974 and 1982.) Conversely, relatively few elections in legislative districts, usually less than one in five, show the winner receiving less than 52.5 percent of the popular vote. (Most cases in which the margin of difference within districts exceeds 20 percent involve Senate races and are thus based on relatively few races.) These findings reinforce other research (Weber, *et.al.*, 1991) and indicate the degree to which the vast majority of legislative districts in Wisconsin are relatively safe, once a member has been elected. One important consequence is that most legislators have relatively great flexibility when discharging their legislative activities because they have fewer serious concerns about being replaced due to competitive election districts. (Obviously actions by a legislator contrary to the mood in one's district poses risks at election time; but great latitude usually is given to incumbents).

One very real consequence of this situation is that political parties can concentrate their resources on the marginal elections in relatively few districts in hopes of securing control of the chamber. Recently, the leadership of each party in both chambers has assumed increased responsibility for recruiting and helping elect members of their party to the legislature because the political parties and others showed little interest. In describing this, former Assembly Speaker Loftus noted that electioneering activities are required because the regular political parties *are not* interested in electing their party members to the legislature. Instead, parties focus on gubernatorial, congressional, and national races. As a consequence, party fortunes in the legislature have been left to a series of forces outside the legislature—notably to Political Action Committees (PAC) and to wealthy influentials willing to provide the resources needed to run for office. Loftus concluded:

> The basic point is the political party has let the legislative candidates fend for themselves.... Under any party circumstances, the idea of winning and keeping a partisan majority in a legislative body is a rather sophisticated goal which is more appealing in the abstract. People may give money to elect a local hero, but getting money to "keep-the-majority" is a little tougher (Loftus, December 9, 1984).

Thus, a new activity has been added for legislative leaders—recruiting and helping elect persons to the legislature who will be willing to support their party's fortunes. In this, the legislative leadership assumes responsibility, including assessing sitting legislators for campaign contributions to a central election fund for winning marginal seats, recruiting legislative candidates, training legislative candidates in campaign techniques, providing personnel and logistical help for campaigns, and raising campaign money both locally and statewide. The explicit purpose is to win more seats for the party in each chamber and to have people in those seats who will vote with the party to organize and control that chamber. In recognition of this change, Legislative Campaign Committees (LCCs) now exist for each party in both chambers and report their contributions to candidates as required by the State Election Board.

When implementing a party's legislative election strategy, the leaders target so called "marginal" or competitive districts—those districts where the successful candidate has won by less than 55 percent of the vote. (Obviously, attention must be given to the effects of reapportionment on district boundaries when examining the election history of a district. With precinct-level election data readily available, however, such a task is not too difficult). Consequently, Republicans and Democrats are targeting the same districts for special campaign attention and resources. Within this list of targeted seats, priorities are then established by considering factors like the absence of an incumbent in the race (higher priority for attention), districts that have elected both Republicans and Democrats in the past (higher priority for attention), and an "over confident" incumbent (again, higher priority for attention). Also, "gut political" feelings enter into the equation (what "kind of people" live in a district and how will different candidates appeal to these voters). Analysis of the number of districts (upon which Table VI-2 is based) indicates that in the Assembly since 1968, approximately 15 districts constitute the competitive category (one election, 1982, had a high of 29 districts where the margin of victory was less that 55 percent of the popular vote; 1970 had 22; 1972 and 1978 had 21; while the remainder had 16 or fewer). In the Senate no election has had more than five seats won by less that 55 percent of the vote. Targeting competitive districts in Wisconsin legislative elections for special attention and resources is common practice for both parties in each chamber.

Republican Governor Thompson introduced a new element into legislative elections, with a consequent

Table VI-2

WISCONSIN LEGISLATIVE GENERAL ELECTIONS, 1968 - 94

ELECTION	PARTY	PERCENT VOTE VICTOR RECEIVED					TOTAL	N
		0-52.49	52.5-54.99	55-59.99	6.0-74.99	75-100		
ASSEMBLY								
1968	D	10.4	10.4	25	39.6	14.6	100	48
	R	3.8	7.7	23.1	44.2	21.2	100	52
1970	D	13.4	9	16.4	38.8	22.4	100	67
	R	15.2	6.1	27.3	51.5	0	100.1	33
1972	D	4 8	16.1	17.7	33.9	27.4	99.9	62
	R	13.5	8.1	5.4	64.9	8.1	100	37
1974	D	4.8	4.8	25.4	25.4	39.7	100.1	63
	R	16.7	8.3	19.4	44.4	11.1	99.9	36
1976	D	3	6.1	19.7	37.9	33.3	100	66
	R	9.1	12.1	18.2	33.3	27.3	100	33
1978	D	11.9	8.3	10	36.7	33.3	100.2	60
	R	17.9	5.1	12.8	38.5	25.6	99.9	39
1980	D	6.9	3.4	15.5	39.7	34.5	100	58
	R	7 9	5.1	15.4	25.6	46.2	100.2	39
1982	D	12.1	8.6	19	20.7	34.7	95.1	58
	R	14 6	26.8	19.5	36.6	2.4	99.9	41
1984	D	1 9	9.6	9.6	44.2	34.6	99.9	52
	R	10.6	10.6	17	44.7	17	99.9	47
1986	D	7 4	1 9	13	57.4	20.4	100.1	54
	R	2.2	2.2	13.3	33.3	49.9	100.9	45
1988	D	3.6	7.1	12.5	32.1	44 6	99.9	56
	R	7	11 6	14	44 2	23.3	100.1	43
1990	D						0	
	R						0	
1992	D						0	
	R						0	
1994	D	10 4	10 4	8 3	47 9	47 9	124 9	48
	R	3 9	2	11 8	52.9	52.9	123.5	51
SENATE								
1968	D	0	0	50	25	25	100	4
	R	8 3	0	16 7	25	25	75	12
1970	D	11 1	11 1	11 1	22.2	22.2	77 7	9
	R	25	12 5	50	0	0	87 5	8
1972	D	0	33 3	16 7	33.3	16 7	100	6
	R	9 1	18 2	18 2	54 5	0	100	11
1974	D	15 4	0	30 8	15 4	38 5	100 1	13
	R	0	50	25	25	0	100	4
1976	D	0	18 8	18 8	36 4	27 3	101 3	11
	R	0	0	33 3	50	16 7	100	6
1978	D	9 1	0	18 2	45 5	27 3	100 1	11
	R	16 7	0	16 7	33 3	33 3	100	6
1980	D	0	22 2	22 2	22.2	33 3	99 9	9
	R	14 3	0	14 3	28 6	42 9	100 1	7
1982	D	22 2	11 1	0	33 3	33 3	99 9	9
	R	12 5	0	50	25	12.5	100	8
1984	D	9 1	0	27 3	27 3	36 4	100 1	11
	R	0	33 3	16 7	50	0	100	6
1986	D	10	0	20	50	20	100	10
	R	14 3	0	0	57 1	28 6	100	7
1988	D	0	8 3	16 7	25	50	100	12
	R	0	0	20	80	0	100	5
1990	D	11 1	0	11 1	22.2	55 6	100	9
	R	0	0	37 5	25	37 5	100	8
1992	D	33 3	0	0	22.2	44 4	99 9	9
	R	14 3	0	14 3	57 1	14 3	100	7
1994	D	14 3	14 3	14 3	28 6	28 6	100 1	7
	R	0	0	0	70	30	100	10

Sources: The 1968-88 data were generated from information provided by the Inter-University Consortium for Political and Social Research, University of Michigan. The 1990-94 data were generated from the appropriate editions of the State of Wisconsin Blue Book. Table prepared by Bruce R. Anderson.

narrowing of chamber party margins in each chamber, through his use of carefully targeted appointments of Democratic legislators to administrative positions. In 1987, the beginning of his first term as governor, Thompson identified likely Republican districts represented by Democrats and convinced some sitting Democratic legislators to accept better paying positions in administrative agencies. This created open districts which could then be filled through special elections called by the governor. Since Republican-oriented voters are more likely to vote in special elections and since these were thought to be Republican-leaning districts, Thompson increased the odds for a Republican victory. His first use of this strategy was to appoint Senate Majority leader Tim Cullen as Secretary of the Department of Health and Social Services in 1987. Cullen had been re-elected as senator on November 4, 1986 with 63.4 percent of the vote. His successor, Tim Weeden a Republican representative, was elected on April 7, 1987 with 58.3 percent of the vote and continues to represent that Senate district in 1995. At the same time, Governor Thompson rebuffed many job-seeking overtures from his Republican former legislative colleagues because he did not wish to diminish Republican legislative ranks prior to resolution of the 1987-89 budget (Friederich, July 7, 1987).

The most significant use of this strategy occurred after the 1992 election. Two Democratic members of the Wisconsin Senate (Russ Feingold and Tom Barrett) ran and were elected to the U. S. Congress in the November 1992 general election. The two vacancies created were supplemented in December 1992, when Governor Thompson appointed Democratic Senator Marvin Roshell as the administrator in the Safety and Buildings Division of the Department of Industry, Labor and Human Relations. With three vacant positions, all formerly held by Democrats, the Senate was tied--15 Republicans, 15 Democrats. Special elections were scheduled for April 6, 1993. The election of two Republicans and one Democrat turned control of the Senate over to the Republicans after 18 years of Democratic control. At the end of the 1993-94 session (March 1994), Thompson repeated this tactic by appointing 12-term Democratic Representative Larry Swoboda as Executive Director of the state's National and Community Service Board. Swoboda's seat was won by a Republican in 1994. While Democratic leaders and the press openly criticized this tactic from the outset, as long as Democratic legislators were willing to accept such positions, Thompson seemed willing to oblige (Rinard, 1994).

Legislative Campaign Finance. Financing legislative campaigns has become a continuing effort for both legislative members and their leaders. A recent analysis of races for the Wisconsin Senate found that campaign spending is a major factor in winning an election. This analysis concluded:

> ...spending is strongly related to the percent of vote received, competition and winning a state Senate seat. In fact, the relative impact of this variable [amount of money spent by a candidate] in explaining percent vote and district competition indicates that spending explains a large amount of the variance [in the percent of vote a candidate receives] ...In spite of the large amount of variance explained by spending, candidate quality and being a state representative were found to be positively related to competition, percent vote and winning.... The results also indicate that being an incumbent is strongly related to winning and the percent of vote received.... Finally, the analysis of the spending data suggests that Republicans, especially non-incumbents in Wisconsin spend more than the Democratic candidates to run for office. In concluding, neither party seems to have an advantage in having quality candidates run for office (Van Dunk. 1994: 23-24).

Money for legislative campaigns is thus a critical concern.

For his first legislative election in 1976, former Speaker Loftus reported spending a little over $11,000 to be elected to an open seat (Loftus, 1994: 27). A mid-1994 newspaper report indicated that the average spending by a winning Senate candidate was $43,209 in 1990 and $67,240 in 1992; in the Assembly the comparative costs were $19,932 in 1990 and $25,835 in 1992. Average spending in 1992 for the *marginal* districts was $77,457 in the Senate and $30,842 in the Assembly (Pommer, 1994). The three 1993 special elections to the Senate received much public and press attention when it was reported that the candidates for former Senator Feingold's seat spent a total of

$540,291; for former Senator Barrett's seat, $390,116; and for former Senator Roshell's seat, $345,931 (Kelley, 1994). With an annual legislative salary in 1994 of $38,056, questions emerge regarding the expenditure of up to ten times this annual salary to win election to the legislature.

Of course, candidates for legislative office do not pay all of these election costs. Campaign contributions from individuals is one source for funding. In addition, Wisconsin is one of three states which provides public financing for legislative campaigns; but, the strings attached to accepting public financing and the relatively small amount of money available make public money of limited interest to many candidates. In addition, a recent study of public financing for legislative elections in Wisconsin found that although spending gaps had been narrowed, there was no evidence that such financing made the elections more competitive (Mayer and Wood, 1995: 83-86). Therefore fund raising has become an occupational necessity for Wisconsin lawmakers and their leaders as well as for aspiring legislators (Daley, 1993).

One major source of funding are the party caucuses LCCs, described above. For these organizations, each party leader in both chambers initiates a number of fund raising events attended by lobbyists, interested groups and loyal supporters. Many of these are scheduled throughout the legislative session and are well attended. (As one lobbyist said, "I can't afford to miss the Speaker's--or the minority leader's--fund raisers. They know who was there and remember. While I can't tell you about any issue or vote I got because I attended one of these, I sure know I'll get better entry if I'm there and I bring a lot of my people along"). The money raised goes to support candidates selected by the leaders of the appropriate LCC and not by the contributors. In describing one such event, former Speaker Loftus noted:

> One primary election night at a party organized to watch the election results, I stationed myself inside the doorway and asked each person entering (I knew most of them) to give me a small check made out to a specific Democratic Candidate for the Assembly.... When enough was raised for one candidate, I started on the next. Then I started to collect checks with payor left blank in order to be able to have some flexibility

> ...By 9:00 P.M. I had well over one hundred checks stuffed in my inside coat pocket, and I hustled up State Street to the Capitol two blocks away. Gathered there from various parts of the state were about a dozen candidates or their treasurers, milling about the staff office of the Democratic caucus. I distributed the checks so each would have enough money to reach the $1,000 threshold required to qualify for the grant [state supported public campaign financing] (Loftus, 1994: 31).

Critical money, important to initiate a campaign, is thus often provided by the LCCs.

A second source of funding is direct contributions from individuals and groups to specific candidates. Certain groups have a traditional affinity for candidates from one party or the other (unions, teachers, lawyers lean toward the Democrats while business, so-called "old-money," banks, insurance and physicians lean to the Republicans) and provide support to those party's candidates. At the same time, some groups contribute to candidates from both parties, and sometimes even to opposing candidates in an election, in order to assure access for their interests. In addition, most candidates solicit support from their friends and acquaintances, especially those living in their district. In a recent court decision, a federal judge ruled that lobbyists can work in individual election campaigns, thus providing another type of resource to a candidate. (Buelow, 1993)

Two special types of organizations geared to contributing to legislative campaigns can be found in Wisconsin--Political Action Committees (PACs) and "conduits." PACs are groups of individuals, businesses and/or organizations who have a common interest and agree to "pool" their money to increase their clout through more substantial contributions. Democrats seem to have benefitted more from PACs in the Wisconsin legislature than Republicans. Recently, several Democratic-oriented PACs got together and formed a "super PAC," Wisconsin

Citizens for Responsible Government, that contributed heavily to the three special Senate elections in 1993; however, PAC activities are regulated by the state and limited in how much they can contribute directly to a campaign. PACs can also provide services that assist a campaign such as telephone banks, printing and literature drops. Conduits are a special type of group that collects checks from sympathetic supporters, written out for specific candidates. Obviously, the conduits select candidates to receive their support who are thought to be sympathetic to their interests. The courts have ruled that conduits are exempt from the restrictions faced by PACs. As a consequence, conduits have assumed special importance as a source of campaign funds. Recent disclosures indicate that Republicans get more support from conduits than do Democrats. A total of 49 conduits reported contributing to legislative races in 1993, with the largest conduit being the Republican Party followed by the Chiropractors and Realtors (Rowen, 1993).

Concerning the relative contributions of these sources for campaign funding, an analysis of nine *special* legislative campaigns in 1993 is found in Table VI-3. Conduits provided over 28 percent of the total spent, while PACs provided 27 percent (11 percent to the candidates and 16 percent through independent spending), candidates raised/provided 22 percent, and LCCs another 22 percent. Thus, the majority of funding for these campaigns was provided through third party fund raising.

Table VI-3

SOURCES OF CAMPAIGN FUNDS FOR NINE SPECIAL ELECTIONS
(entries are dollar figures)

SOURCE OF CAMPAIGN FUNDS	SENATE REPUBLICANS	DEMOCRATS	ASSEMBLY REPUBLICANS	DEMOCRATS	TOTAL
LEGISLATIVE CAMPAIGN COMMITTEES TO CANDIDATES	$84,745	$51,043	$16,257	$59,939	$211,984
LEGISLATIVE CAMPAIGN COMMITTEES OTHER SPENDING	$48,023	$92,190	$10,454	$34,595	$185,262

	REPUBLICANS	DEMOCRATS	OTHER	TOTAL
PACs	$102,505	$103,445	N/A	$205,950
CONDUITS	$419,706	$98,868	N/A	$518,574
INDEPENDENT SPENDING BY PACs	$17,227	$261,150	$2,507	$280,884
RAISED BY CANDIDATES/OTHER	$259,966	$143,109	N/A	$403,075
			TOTAL	$1,805,729

120

Source: Calculated from Tim Kelly, "Politicians For Sale? Big Spending Special Interests Wield Increasing Clout in State Elections," Wisconsin State Journal, January 16, 1994, page 1. Some changes and imputations made from report by author.

Regarding the effects of campaign contributions, the consensus is that financial support helps provide individuals and groups with access to legislators. As one contributor noted, "Making a contribution gets me in 'through the door.' What happens after that depends on a lot of things, but without getting a hearing for my side, I'm noplace." A newspaper report of an atypical case in 1994 noted that a group lobbying on behalf of a pesticides bill gave $50 campaign checks and thank you notes to 76 legislators who voted for that bill. Many legislators returned these checks because of the appearance that they were paid in return for their vote. Few similar instances have been reported in Wisconsin.

A Profile of Member Attributes

Who is elected to the legislature is also an important factor in determining what issues will be resolved and with what approach. The traditional norm in U.S. politics has been a "citizen legislature" who gives a portion of his/her time to make policies in the best interest of all. Time and again, however, studies show that legislative bodies do *not* mirror the state nor necessarily the constituencies they represent. Table VI-4 provides information on Wisconsin legislators for selected sessions from 1957 to 1995.

Table VI-4

PERSONAL DATA ON WISCONSIN STATE LEGISLATORS, SELECTED YEARS
(entries are raw figures)

PERSONAL TRAIT	1957 SEN	ASSEM	1967 SEN	ASSEM	1977 SEN	ASSEM	1987 SEN	ASSEM	1991 SEN	ASSEM	1995 SEN	ASSEM
AGE												
OLDEST	72	79	77	77	77	74	63	74	66	78	67	69
YOUNGEST	29	25	28	26	26	22	31	26	32	27	31	26
AVERAGE	50	48	56	47	43	42	44	44	47	45	48	45
OCCUPATION												
ATTORNEY	9	30	12	19	14	12	9	12	9	10	6	10
FARMER	5	14	5	24	0	13	4	13	3	13	1	14
OTHER	16	45	10	54	19	69	17	73	21	76	26	75
RETIRED	3	11	6	3	0	5	0	1	NA	NA	NA	NA
EDUCATION (b)												
NOT BEYOND HIGH SCHOOL	6	29	6	36	0	20	3	12	3	11	2	15
BUSINESS/TECH SCHOOL	3	9	4	13	1	3	1	6	1	7	NA	NA
ATTENDED COLLEGE	24	62	22	51	32	79	27	87	30	88	31	84
ACADEMIC DEGREE	18	45	21	44	27	58	23	73	25	73	19	40
HIGHER DEGREE	11	29	11	23	20	2	11	29	11	29	8	26
MARITAL STATUS												
SINGLE	4	7	2	8	11	24	1	22	5	24	5	28
MARRIED	28	90	30	88	22	71	28	76	28	73	28	70
WIDOWED	1	3	1	5	1	4	1	1	0	2	0	1
VETERANS	21	39	19	42	10	33	8	17	6	15	6	14
WOMEN	0	0	0	3	2	10	4	24	5	26	8	24

PARTY												
DEMOCRAT	10	33	12	46	23	66	9	54	19	58	16	48
REPUBLICAN	23	67	21	54	10	33	11	45	14	41	17	51
NO SERVING PRIOR TERMS												
IN SENATE	10	1	27	0	27	0	28	0	29	0	32	0
IN ASSEMBLY	7	72	13	76	11	85	17	87	28	85	21	87
TOP NO OF PRIOR SESSIONS												
IN SAME HOUSE	10	14	16	11	14	10	12	15	14	16	16	12
NO WITH PRIOR EXPERIENCE IN LOCAL GOV'T												
COUNTY BOARD	10	29	7	27	5	21	3	18	3	15	2	22
OTHER MUNICIPAL BOARD	11	26	7	29	8	21	5	21	4	19	8	24

a. Three vacancies occurred at the start of the session.

b. Beginning in 1993-94, the LRB revised the categories for reporting education level and dropped the category of "Business/Tech School."

Sources: Wisconsin Legislative Reference Bureau, Bulletin 87-1 and appropriate editions of the State of Wisconsin *Blue Book*.

Composition The types of individuals who seek and are elected to state legislative offices in Wisconsin tend to be from higher economic and social backgrounds and to have been more involved in public and political affairs. Such a profile has clear implications for the types of policies adopted by the Senate and Assembly.

Age. The average age of members declined during the 1970s and 1980s, from 56 to 43 in the Senate and 48 to 42 in the Assembly, and has increased slightly during recent sessions. The generally decreasing average age resulted from a lowering of both the oldest and youngest ages found among members. A detailed examination of the age distribution indicates that large groupings of members occur at several ages, with smaller concentrations being found in recent years at both younger and older ages. In the past, young persons served briefly in the legislature until they established themselves in their careers and older persons found legislative service attractive and possible as they moved toward retirement and reduced other activities. This pattern has changed considerably with the advent of full-time, professional legislators, however. Now, an increasing number of persons find that serving in the legislature is an acceptable occupation that can be pursued on a full-time basis.

Occupations. Unlike Congress, in which about two-thirds of the members are attorneys, the Wisconsin legislature has been averaging about one-third attorneys in the Senate (down to six of 33 in 1995) and about 10 percent in the Assembly. In recent sessions, teachers have comprised sizeable proportions, especially in the Assembly. Eight senators and 10 representatives listed teaching as a former or current profession in 1995-96. For a state with a large agricultural sector, one might expect a large contingent of farmers in the legislature; however, this portion of the state's population has been decreasing in recent years. In fact, the figures must be viewed with caution regarding farmers since many legislators from out-state Wisconsin list farming because this designation is still thought to be politically attractive and advantageous for election purposes. The most frequently listed occupation is full-time legislator--12 senators and 40 representatives in 1995-96. This reduction in the numbers of attorneys and farmers, together with the increasing number of members listing legislator as their occupation, can be found in several states. These trends seem indicative of the degree to which service in legislative bodies and the representation of constituent interests is moving toward a specialized occupational status as a profession and away from the meaning of citizen legislature.

Education. Wisconsin legislators are much more educated than the state average. Between 90 percent and 95 percent of the members in each chamber attended college. A sizable proportion, more than one quarter, have received some type of advanced degree. Most legislators have attended colleges and universities in Wisconsin, with the University of Wisconsin being most frequently mentioned. These levels of educational attainment show growth over the last 30 years, more so than has occurred for the general public.

Marital Status. Military Service. Gender and Race. Table VI-4 also displays information on several other demographic variables. While the vast majority of members in each chamber are married, a sizable number in more recent sessions--especially in the Assembly--have been single. Similarly, fewer veterans have served in recent sessions than served during those decades immediately after major international conflicts (the 1950s, 1960s and 1970s), when large numbers of legislators were elected who had military experience during World War II, Korea, or Vietnam.

Increasing numbers of women and racial minorities have also been elected to the legislature and selected to leadership positions. While representation by gender still does not approach the proportion of women in the general population, there are now eight senators and 24 representatives who are women. This indicates a sizable growth over the 1950s, and 1960s, when few, if any, legislators were women. In fact, during the 1987-88 session, the Republican minority leaders in both the Senate and Assembly were women. Regarding racial minority members, there are eight African-Americans (two in the Senate and six in the Assembly) in the 1995-96 session of the legislature, but no Hispanics nor native Americans. Thus, African-Americans make up 6.1 percent of the membership of each chamber, while being only 5.0 percent of the total population in the state.

Mobility. While the socioeconomic and geographic mobility patterns of Wisconsin legislators are of interest, no recent data are available. In Wisconsin, as in all other states, the position of legislator typically is ranked fairly high on occupational prestige scales. Legislators have tended to be geographically less mobile than the general population. It is likely that Wisconsin legislators today are somewhat more mobile in both these respects than those of previous generations, but the last legislator socioeconomic mobility study was in 1957. At that time, only 31 percent of then incumbent legislators had fathers who were businessmen or professionals, while the great majority of the remaining fathers had been farmers or workers. Geographic non-mobility is suggested by the finding that 65 percent of those legislators had lived in the districts they represented and 72 percent in the county they represented for over 30 years (Epstein, 1958). Relative stability in residence is to be expected since many voters highly value having an elected representative who has "deep roots" in the district.

Partisan Makeup. Until the Democrats won control of the Senate in the 1974 election, they had not had a majority in that chamber since 1891. The Republicans, except for the Progressive Party majorities in 1934 and 1936, had controlled that body since 1895. This had occurred without any overt "gerrymandering" to give the Republicans such an advantage. Rather, it happened because Republicans were able to win most marginal districts, while the Democrats "wasted" their "strength in numbers" on areas (like Milwaukee) with heavy concentrations of Democratic voters. Beginning with the 1972 redistricting, Democrats were able to "spread their votes out" over a larger number of districts, permitting more Democratic senators to be elected. In addition, Wisconsin became a more competitive state between the two parties.

Democratic party fortunes in the Assembly over the past one hundred years were only marginally better than in the Senate. Until the 1970 election, they had been a majority in the Assembly only during the two-year periods of 1933-34, 1959-60, and 1965-66. The Republicans, except for the Democratic Party majority in the election of 1932 and the Progressive Party majorities in 1934 and 1936, had controlled the Assembly from 1895-1958. Democratic fortunes in the electorate finally produced Assembly control by the Democrats from 1971-94. Republican control of the Assembly from 1895-1957 (except for the six years during the Depression) occurred without any blatant population gerrymandering, but it happened because Republicans were able to win most marginal districts, while the Democrats "wasted" their "strength in numbers" on areas with heavy concentrations of Democratic voters. Beginning with the 1972 redistricting, Democrats were able to "spread their votes out" over a larger number of districts, permitting more Democratic Assembly members to be elected. Also by the 1970s, Wisconsin had become a more two-party competitive state.

A recent analysis of the Democratic leaders in the Assembly during the 1980s pointed out that a large number of them have been committed "professional politicians" all of their adult lives. Many of them became involved in politics as a result of the Vietnam War and were elected to the legislature in the 1970s. Since that time, they have supported a variety of liberal policies, and have also worked hard at being reelected and at moving up in the legislative leadership. At the same time, they have mastered the art of electing Democrats and controlling the legislative agenda. Consequently, their influence on the state's policies far exceeded their numbers; however, several no longer serve in the legislature (Ehrenhalt, 1989).

The election of Governor Thompson in 1986 and his success in raising campaign money had a stimulating effect on Republicans in both chambers. They rallied behind him and supported his positions, especially in upholding his vetoes. On the contrary in earlier sessions, Democratic legislators sometimes found themselves opposing a governor of their own party and overriding his vetoes. One legislator noted, "Sometimes we felt that [Governor] Tony Earl had gone too far. He was vetoing things that he shouldn't. In the caucus we decided to stand up to him and show him that we could be independent. He didn't like it, but we proved our point." This was not true of the Republicans; they never voted in any numbers to override any of Governor Thompson's vetoes. As a consequence, Thompson's vetoes became "override proof" and he was able to advance Republican causes despite numerical majorities for Democrats in both chambers until 1993.

Prior Service. Turnover in the Wisconsin legislature, as noted above, is lower than in most states. In some states, more than half of the members are new in each session. In Wisconsin, the highest recent turnover was in 1961, when 35 percent of the representatives were new members. In the last 15 years, fewer than 15 percent of the representatives have not had previous legislative service at the state level. Many members, moreover, have had long years of service. In 1995, for instance, one member of the Senate had 32 years of prior service (16 sessions) in the Senate and six years (three terms) in the Assembly. Two representatives had 24 years prior legislative service. Such a pattern helps assure development of consistency and stability across time in terms of approaches and sometimes even policies.

Local Government Experience. Several trends are of interest (in Table VI-4) regarding prior experience of legislators in local government. In recent sessions, the proportions of legislators having prior experience on county or municipal boards have been lower than they were in the 1950s and 1960s, except for a resurgence among Republicans in 1995. This reduction suggests that legislator familiarity with local problems and the attendant political issues gained by service in local government may be less in recent years. In addition, most legislators having such experience have come from out-state rather than from Milwaukee County and the other urban districts. In 1995, 46 representatives had held prior elective positions in local government. To the extent that such service in local governmental positions prepares future state legislators for policy making with regard to local problems and approaches, this trend suggests that for Milwaukee (and perhaps other urban) local interests may be at some disadvantage. Possible factors influencing Milwaukee County officials to remain in local offices may be that these local positions generally pay better than service in the legislature, carry higher levels of prestige and recognition in their communities, and are more amenable to maintaining a home and family life. Thus, city aldermen and urban county board members seem to prefer continuing service where they are, rather than seeking election to the state Assembly or Senate.

Compensation for Legislators. Wisconsin legislators are far better paid than legislators in many other states. Beginning in 1995, they received $38,056 per year. This salary level is reviewed by the Secretary of Employment Relations who makes recommendations for compensation to the Joint Committee on Employment Relations, so that this amount can increase without requiring legislators to vote separately on their own salaries. In addition, they receive up to $75 per day for living expenses while in Madison on legislative business and reimbursement for one weekly round trip home. Each senator and representative also receives funding for general office expenses, printing, and postage. Legislators are eligible to participate in state health insurance and retirement plans as well. Thus, compensation for service in the legislature is much more comparable to other professions than has been true in other states (Legislative Reference Bureau, 1986). Also, recent moves of several state departments and offices from the Capitol has increased the space available for legislators and their staff. Even legislative support agencies have been moved out of the Capitol into office buildings. Legislative leaders, committee chairpersons, all senators and several representatives (especially those in the majority party) have private offices, permitting them to conduct their business in a much more congenial setting. These benefits, services, and facilities exceed those provided in many U.S. states.

Professional Legislators. One widely discussed change in the composition of the Wisconsin legislature has been the great increase in persons who call themselves "full-time, professional legislators." These so-called "new-breed" legislators have no other employment, and many have never held employment other than some type(s) of government service. In the current political rhetoric, "they have never had to meet a payroll nor had any real life experiences." The increase in salary and other compensation has made it possible for a middle class person, especially one with a working spouse, to devote full-time to legislative activities. In addition, it has become increasingly difficult for legislators (because of the extent of required legislative activities) to pursue concurrently some other occupation such as practicing law, selling real estate or insurance, or operating a business. Further, legislative salaries are now equal to or better than the salaries of some other professionals.

The critical questions about such a trend relate to possible consequences on policy making and government. Some observers have argued that having full-time legislators is an advantage to the public. Because they work at being legislators all the time they are different from their predecessors and more independent from many economic interests. Some argue that these legislators can become more competent and skilled at representing their constituents in policy making and are better able to avoid conflicts of interest, especially those arising from competing occupational/economic/social interests. In commenting on this trend, Former Speaker Loftus argued that the new breed of legislator is much better educated and is as able to represent the popular will as well as any previous generation of legislators (Loftus, October 3, 1984). Others argue, just as persuasively, that practical experience in non-legislative activities *improves* a legislator's understanding of "real world" problems and broadens one's perspective. One legislator noted, "If they've never met a payroll or had to compete in the private sector, how can they make laws?" Persons totally dependent on an elective office for their livelihood, who have never worked outside the public realm, are thought by some to be more susceptible to pressure on even the most basic issues (Rinard, 1995).

Further evidence of the changing nature of the legislative profession can be seen in post-legislative experiences. Many former legislators have been appointed and/or elected to important state administrative positions. Between 1965 and 1986, at least 29 appointments of legislators to full-time governmental positions were made by governors and 15 appointments by state boards or departmental secretaries. In 1995, three of the state's six constitutional officers (including the governor), two state supreme court justices, and eight of the eleven members of Congress (one senator and seven representatives) are former state legislators. Also, at least 12 more former legislators held some type of executive position in state agencies. Some of these appointments have probably been rewards to legislative friends and supporters; and some, as noted above, have been calculated efforts to remove partisan opponents from marginal legislative districts, thus providing an opportunity for one party to regain a legislative seat. Several former legislators have also become well-known lobbyists, working in and around state government on behalf of clients--something similar to what they did as legislators for their constituents, but for much better compensation.

Conflict-of-Interest. Ethics associated with legislative service has received increasing press attention in Wisconsin. Using one's official position and clout to bestow special advantages on one's relatives or friends or their interests, that is, conflicts-of-interest, have resulted in federal and state investigations. The most frequent charge is that a legislator sought and advanced legislation that would result in pecuniary gains for self, family, friends, associates, or clients (Bice, 1995a).

A new "twist" on possible conflict-of-interest was reported during the 1995 session when Assembly Republican majority leader Jensen resigned his non-legislative position with a well-known Milwaukee public relations firm. Jensen's relationships to the firm had been criticized because the firm maintained an extensive lobbying practice on behalf of several clients. During this debate, it was noted that Jensen's wife as well as family members for two other legislators and half a dozen other public officials were registered lobbyists (Daley, 1995). Thus, potential conflicts-of-interest due to legislator and family-based associations with lobbyists was not unique to one person. In commenting on this situation, one long time legislative observer noted, "It was inevitable that [Scott] Jensen would resign [from the PR firm]. You can't be an effective leader while you're getting a lot of bad press. Sometimes you can 'ride it out,' but it detracts from your role in the legislature. If you're always defending yourself, you can't be out in front on the issues." While Wisconsin has a State Ethics Board whose job it is to provide advice and guidance to public officials on matters like this, frequently the appearance of impropriety in Wisconsin renders rulings and advisory opinions on ethics meaningless. In Wisconsin, there is a long tradition of public officials being held to a high standard of conduct.

Processing of Legislation: How A Bill Becomes A Law

Since one of the principal activities of a legislative body is to enact laws, the process by which vague ideas for public policy become specific bills which are considered by both chambers is important (see Theobald, 1985 and Roe, et al., 1993). The Wisconsin LRB-prepared diagram (Figure VI-1) and the sample bill history [1991 Assembly Bill 655 (AB-655), Figure VI-2] illustrate the legislative process. As noted above, bills may be introduced *only* by legislators or legislative bodies, such as the legislator's committees, and the Revisor of Statutes or the Legislative Council. Hence, the process by which ideas and proposals for policy decisions become law centers around legislators. And, although many proposals emanate from the governor, other executive officials, organized interest groups, and individual citizens, the formal introduction must be by one or several legislators and passage must involve both chambers. [With regard to AB-655, it was introduced on October 24, 1991 with 16 co-sponsors at the request of Governor Thompson.]

Any legislator seeking to introduce a bill has it drafted by the bill drafting section of the LRB. During the 1991-92 session, the LRB received 14,707 bill drafting requests. Typically, a legislator will provide written or verbal instructions to a lawyer trained in drafting bills. This use of professional drafting services ensures that bills are written as clearly as possible, that a bill's language accomplishes the desired change in the law, and that constitutional conflicts and difficulties are avoided. (Bill drafting attorneys always seek to write bills that accomplish what the sponsor requests). Unlike other states which may permit lobbyists and outside parties to draft bills in their own ways, Wisconsin legislators can introduce only those bills drafted or "cleared" by this impartial and specialized agency. Admittedly, the ideas for many bills emanate from citizens, lobbyists, agency staff, and even national legislative organizations, but the *language* in every bill must be reviewed by professional bill drafting attorneys in the LRB.

After a bill or resolution has been drafted by the LRB, a brief analysis is prepared, also by the LRB, and attached to the bill or resolution. (Typically, this analysis is included at the beginning of a bill or resolution. For AB-655, the summary is included in Figure VI-2 after the Bill Title). It provides a clear and concise summary of the bill's major components and a description of how the bill would change existing law. It is especially helpful to have this analysis with respect to the many lengthy and technical proposals considered. (Legislators and legislative observers point out the invaluable assistance that such an analysis provides as they "wade through" all the legislation to be considered). In addition, every proposal which increases or decreases the financial liability of the state or local governments must include a "fiscal note" setting forth its fiscal effect. (For AB-655, three fiscal notes were provided on 10-28 and 10-29, after the bill was introduced, see Figure IV-2).

Figure VI-1

1991 ASSEMBLY BILL 655 FLOW CHART

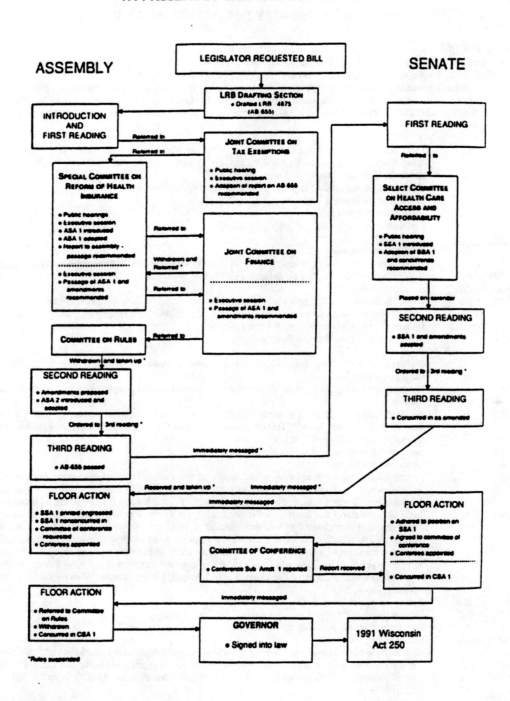

Source: State of Wisconsin, *Blue Book* 1993-94:180.

Figure VI-2

PROCEDURAL HISTORY FOR 1991 ASSEMBLY BILL 655

Assembly Bill 655

AN ACT to amend 185.983 (1) (intro.), 600.01 (2) (b), 613.03 (3) and 631.01 (4); and to create 15.07 (2) (I), 15.07 (5) (z), 15.07 (5) (zm), 15.735, 20.145 (8), 71.05 (6) (b) 17 and 18, 71.07 (5) (a) 9, 185.983 (lg), 227.01 (13) (om), 609.85, 628.36 (3m), 632.70 and subchapter II of chapter 635 of the statues, relating to establishing a group health insurance plan for employees of small employers, creating a board to oversee the plan, creating a fund for catastrophic claims and a catastrophic claims fund board, creating an individual income tax deduction for certain medical care insurance costs paid by certain self-employed persons, granting rule-ruling making authority and making an appropriation. (FE)

1991

10-24	A.	Introduced by Representatives **Clarenbach, Rosenzweig, Underheim, Kunicki, Prosser, Brancel, Hauke, Cullen, Hisrich, Carpenter, Baldus, Fortis, Johnsrud** and **Urban**, cosponsored by Senators **Van Sistine** and **Rude**, by request of Governor Tommy G. Thompson.
10-24	A.	Read first time and referred to joint survey committee on Tax Exemptions 596
10-28	A.	Fiscal estimate received.
10-29	A.	Fiscal estimate received.
10-29	A.	Fiscal estimate received.
10-30	A.	Public hearing held.
10-30	A.	Executive session held.
10-30	A.	Report adoption of report recommended by joint survey committee on Tax Exemptions, Ayes 9, Noes 0. 622
10-30	A.	Referred to special committee on Reform of Health Insurance. 622
10-30	A.	Executive session held.
10-30	A.	Assembly substitute amendment 1 offered by special committee on Reform of Health Insurance.
10-31	A.	Report assembly substitute amendment 1 adoption, Ayes 11, Noes 0, passage recommended by special committee on Reform of Health Insurance, Ayes 9, Noes 2. 629
10-31	A.	Referred to joint committee on Finance. 629
11-5	A.	Rules suspended. 639
11-5	A.	Withdrawn from join committee on Finance and referred to special committee on Reform of Health Insurance. 639
11-5	A.	Executive session held.
11-5	A.	Assembly amendment 1 to assembly substitute amendment 1 offered by special committee on Reform of Health Insurance.
11-5	A.	Report assembly amendment 1 to assembly substitute amendment 1 adoption, Ayes 10, Noes 1, assembly substitute amendment 1 adoption, Ayes 11, Noes 0, passage recommended by special committee on Reform of Health Insurance, Ayes 10, Noes 1. 641
11-5	A.	Referred to joint committee on Finance. 641
11-6	A.	Executive session held.
11-6	A.	Assembly amendment 2 to assembly substitute amendment 1 offered by joint committee on Finance. 658
11-6	A.	Assembly amendment 3 to assembly substitute amendment 1 offered by joint committee on Finance. 658
11-6	A.	Assembly amendment 4 to assembly substitute amendment 1 offered by joint committee on Finance. 658
11-6	A.	Assembly amendment 5 to assembly substitute amendment 1 offered by joint committee on Finance. 658
11-7	A.	Report assembly amendment 1 to assembly substitute amendment 1 adoption, Ayes 10, Noes 6, assembly amendment 2 to assembly substitute amendment 1 adoption, Ayes 16, Noes 0, assembly amendment 3 to assembly substitute amendment 1 adoption, Ayes 16, Noes 0, assembly amendment 4 to assembly substitute amendment 1 adoption, Ayes 16, Noes 0, assembly amendment 5 to assembly substitute amendment 1 adoption, Ayes 12, Noes 4, assembly substitute amendment 1 adoption, Ayes 13, Noes 3, passage recommended by joint committee on Finance, Ayes 12, Noes 4. 673
11-7	A.	Referred to committee on Rules. 673
11-7	A.	Rules suspended. 683
11-7	A.	Withdrawn from committee on Rules and taken up. 683
11-7	A.	Read a second time. 683
11-7	A.	Assembly substitute amendment 2 offered by Representatives Clarenbach, Underheim and Rosenzweig. 684
11-7	A.	Assembly amendment 1 to assembly substitute 2 offered by Representatives Fortis and Van Dreel. 684
11-7	A.	Assembly amendment 1 to assembly substitute amendment 2 laid on table, Ayes 79, Noes 17. 684
11-7	A.	Laid on table. 684
11-7	A.	Taken from table. 685
11-7	A.	Assembly amendment 2 to assembly substitute amendment 2 offered by Representative Fortis. 685
11-7	A.	Assembly amendment 2 to assembly substitute amendment 2 laid on table, Ayes 75, Noes 22. 685
11-7	A.	Assembly amendment 3 to assembly substitute amendment 2 offered by Representative Antaramian. 685
11-7	A.	Assembly amendment 3 to assembly substitute amendment 2 laid on table, Ayes 67, Noes 30. 685

2-27	S.	Ordered immediately messaged. 686
3-3	A.	Received from senate amended and concurred in as amended (senate substitute 1 as amended by senate amendments 2, 3, 5, 6, 10, 13 and 14 adopted). 900
3-3	A.	Rules suspended and taken up. 900
3-3	A.	Senate substitute amendment 1 ordered printed engrossed by direction of Assembly Chief Clerk. 900
3-3	A.	Senate substitute amendment 1 nonconcurred in. 900
3-3	A.	LRB correction (assembly substitute amendment 1). 903
3-3	A.	LRB correction (assembly substitute amendment 2). 903
3-3	A.	Assembly requests a committee of conference and appoints Representatives Kunicki, Clarenbach and Underheim as conferees on its part. 902
3-3	A.	Ordered immediately messaged. 902
3-4	S.	Received from Assembly, Senate substitute amendment 1 nonconcurred in, Assembly requests a committee of Conference and appoints Representatives Kunicki, Clarenbach and Underheim as conferees on its part. 701
3-5	S.	Senate adheres to its position on Senate substitute amendment 1, agrees to a committee of Conference and appoints Senators Van Sistine, Moen and Rude as conferees on its part. 712
3-5	S.	Acton ordered immediately messaged. 716
3-25	S.	Report of committee of Conference received (Conference substitute amendment 1). 789
3-25	S.	Rejection of committee of Conference report refused, Ayes 5, Noes 26. 789
3-25	S.	Committee of Conference report adopted, Ayes 26, Noes 5. 790
3-25	S.	Ordered immediately messaged. 790
3-26	A.	Received from senate committee of conference report adopted. 1080
3-26	A.	Referred to committee on Rules. 1081
3-26	A.	Rules suspended. 1087
3-26	A.	Refused to lay committee of conference report on the table, Ayes 31, Noes 67. 1087
3-26	A.	Committee of conference report concurred in, Ayes 66, Noes 32. 1087
3-26	A.	Action ordered immediately messaged. 1088
4-7	A.	Report correctly enrolled. 1138
4-14	A.	LRB correction (conference substitute amendment 1). 1148
4-28	A.	Report approved by the Governor on 4-27-92. 1165

1991 Wisconsin Act 250. Published 5-11-92

Source: State of Wisconsin, *Blue Book* 1993-94:179-79.

Official introduction into the Senate *or* Assembly can take place once the bill drafting is complete. After introduction and assignment of a bill number, the bill is referred to a standing committee. It is at this point that the Speaker, if it is in the Assembly, can determine a bill's fate, as noted above. (Note that AB-655 was referred by the Assembly Speaker to the Joint Survey on Tax Exemptions on 10-24, the day it was introduced). Once a bill has been assigned to a committee, the chairperson will usually schedule a hearing on it. (For AB-655, the public hearing was scheduled for 10-30). The time, place, and content of hearings are a matter of public knowledge, and hearings scheduled for the following week are usually announced the previous Thursday. Thus, all organized groups, interested citizens and others, including the press, have an opportunity to appear at the hearing. (Although most legislative hearings are held in Madison, increasingly both chambers are scheduling hearings around the state to foster citizen interest and involvement. While some skeptics argue that this is purely a public relations "gimmick," large numbers of citizens have appeared at certain times. Even the important Joint Finance Committee has held hearings around the state since 1985). The Wisconsin legislature is especially generous in allowing testimony before its committees. While lobbyists for interested groups and experts tend to be the most important witnesses at hearings, any person can present his/her views. What uninformed citizens say at hearings probably has little effect on legislators' actions, but citizens have the opportunity, not easily available in many other states and certainly problematic in Congress, to appear and tell public officials exactly what they think.

Another important group of people likely to appear at hearings are state officials from the agencies involved in the policy area being considered. These individuals wield considerable influence, given their knowledge of the area and existing policies. A special relationship sometimes develops among legislators, lobbyists, and public officials in the formulation of public policy--called "iron triangles" because of the cohesion and strength they can impose on decision making.

Also in attendance at committee hearings will be lobbyists and group representatives likely to be affected by a bill's provisions. Often, prominent group members will testify on a bill in order to provide additional information as well as opinion. In describing the rationale for testifying at committee hearings, one lobbyist noted, "I don't expect that what we [group representatives] say at a hearing will necessarily 'carry-the-day.' What I want is for committee members to know where my group stands on a bill and to listen to someone who is very knowledgeable and respected. I and some group leaders will approach members individually and discuss our concerns later in private without the glare of publicity. We have to be there and participate, but the hearing is only the beginning of my work with a committee."

After the committee has held the hearing(s) on a bill, it conducts reviews in executive sessions, which are open to the public, to reach decisions. Frequently, amendments are proposed in these sessions to make a bill more acceptable to affected groups. In fact, it is not unknown for legislators to adopt amendments formulated and deemed acceptable by all those groups and state agencies affected by a bill. Such an approach provides considerable influence to those groups in obtaining the types of provisions they want. The committee may then vote to recommend the bill for passage or for indefinite postponement by the entire chamber--Assembly or Senate. (This is a committee recommendation to the entire body). Like the procedure in Congress where most bills are defeated by "pigeonholing" (i.e., failing to act), Wisconsin legislative committees or the chairperson may hold a bill in committee, effectively "killing" it for that two-year session. (The executive session for AB-655 was held on 10-30-91 resulting in a report recommending adoption by a 9-0 vote). A review of committee recommendations for recent sessions indicated that most bills reported out have a positive recommendation. Thus, committee action to stop a bill usually involves holding it in the committee until the session ends. If a committee fails to act, the legislative chamber *may* vote to place the bill on the chamber's calendar anyway. (However, this a little used procedure). Thus, the vast majority of bills which do not pass are killed in committee. Bills reported out late in a legislative session typically face more extensive hurdles before floor consideration than do those reported out early.

Once a committee has concluded its deliberations on a bill and has "voted it out," the bill may be referred to another committee depending on its content, to the Joint Finance Committee, or may be placed on a calendar by the Rules Committee for Assembly bills or by the Committee on Senate Organization for Senate bills. (AB-655 was referred to a second committee--Reform of Health Insurance on 10-30-91 and to Joint Finance on 10-31-91). Consideration by a second committee may or may not involve public hearings.

After a bill has finished all committee reviews, it then goes to an "organizational committee," Rules or Senate Organization, which schedules it for floor action. These committees, controlled by the leadership in each chamber, determine much about a bill's fate on the floor of that chamber. Bills are placed on the calendar in the order determined by these committees and may or may not correspond to the order in which they are reported out by committees. (AB-655 was referred to the Assembly Rules Committee on 11-7-91, but was then taken directly to the floor through a suspension of the rules procedure, also on 11-7).

In the absence of other procedures, bills are taken up according to the calendar; however, the Assembly in 1973 and the Senate in 1975 adopted new rules to expedite consideration of "more important" bills. The Assembly authorized its Rules Committee to recommend rules under which bills could be made special orders of business and to provide for specific times and debate limits for the consideration of a bill on the Assembly floor. The Senate granted its Committee on Senate Organization authority to draw up calendars which would determine the order in which bills would be considered. Toward the end of a session, when so many bills are being reported out of committees and there is great competition to bring bills to the floor, only those bills which are given special status by the leadership through these procedural committees will have much chance of even

131

being considered. This setting of priorities for bill consideration is an important power for the leadership.

When a bill comes to the floor so that the entire chamber can consider it, the precise question being considered is "should the bill be engrossed?" (Engrossment means that the bill will be put into final form so that it can no longer be changed through amendments). At this stage ("should the bill be engrossed?"), amendments can be proposed by any legislator and must be voted on by the entire membership. Legislators may propose clarifying amendments intended to straighten out any possible vagueness, constructive amendments intended to change and "improve" (sometimes weaken) the bill, or delaying amendments intended to hold up consideration of the bill. Debate takes place on these amendments, not on the bill itself. (AB-655 had five substitute amendments offered during second reading on 11-7-91, with Substitute Amendment 2 being adopted 81-16). After all amendments have been dealt with, the chamber votes to engross the bill and order it to a "third reading consideration." Third reading usually takes place two legislative days later and is the time for final consideration and voting. Over time, however, both chambers have developed means for "speeding" a bill through this stage and messaging (sending) the bill to the other chamber in an expedited fashion. Such accelerated action requires more than a simple majority vote by the initiating chamber. (With AB-655, the Rules were suspended for a third reading on the same day as second reading, 11-7-91, passed on the third reading by a vote of 81-16, and immediately messaged to the Senate, 95-2). If the bill is passed at third reading, it is sent to the other chamber where all of these steps have to be repeated. (Actually, much of the committee work may take place concurrently in both chambers so that consideration is expedited in the second chamber).

In the Assembly, a computerized voting machine is used to provide for a rapid tally of the 99 members in roll call votes. The smaller Senate uses a "voice" roll call vote, where each member responds when his/her name is called, indicating his/her vote. At times, the presiding officer of either chamber may try to use a general voice vote, asking that all members present vote verbally, saying "aye" or "no" when asked to do so by the presiding officer. This procedure speeds up the voting process but provides no record on how individual members voted. A member, backed by one-sixth of the members, may force a recorded roll call, although in most instances the leadership will comply with a single member's desire to have a roll call.

If there are differences in the versions passed by each chamber, and each chamber insists on its own version, a conference committee composed of members of both chambers is appointed to iron out the differences. (On AB-655 a Conference Committee was needed and reported back, 3-25-92). A conference committee report can only be accepted or rejected; it cannot be amended. In recent years (such as 1983), the leadership of each chamber has sometimes met to work out differences, especially on very important issues like the budget, *without* a formal conference committee. These sessions have featured delegations from each chamber sitting around a table with perhaps 50 or 100 staff, press representatives, lobbyists, and citizens watching negotiations over bill language. This is a prime example of government decision making in the open.

After a bill has been approved in identical form in both chambers, it is designated as an "enrolled" bill and sent to the governor. (AB-655 was enrolled on 4-7-92 and approved by Governor Thompson on 4-27-92). The constitution provides that s/he has six days in which to sign or veto it; however, the constitution does not say when the bill must be sent to the governor. Over the years an accommodation to the governor developed so that the chief clerk or Senate secretary would *not* send an enrolled bill to the governor until s/he was ready for it. This process gives the governor more time for making her/his decision than the constitution authorized. Beginning in 1975, the legislature, in setting its timetable for a session by designating floorperiods, also set deadlines specifying when the chief clerks were to send bills to the governor. For example, the deadline for bills passed in the session which ended March 31 was set at May 22. In establishing floorperiods for the 1995-96 session, the legislature specified certain target dates for forwarding legislation to the governor.

The Wisconsin governor, unlike the President of the U.S. but like the governors of 42 other states, has a partial or line item veto on finance bills. This means that s/he can reject part of a bill while accepting other parts. As a consequence, governors have been able to become exceedingly powerful through the creative use of the partial line item veto. According to former Assembly majority leader David Travis, the governor's veto in Wisconsin has made the legislature "...the weakest legislature in the country" (Jones, 1995). The practice of partial line item vetoes, initiated by Democratic Governor Patrick Lucey in 1971 and refined by Governors Martin Schreiber (1977), Dreyfus (1981), Anthony Earl (1983) and Thompson (1987), has evolved into a powerful, pro-active force especially for changing the legislative budget to a governor's liking. In a series of cases, the Wisconsin Supreme Court has ruled that a partial veto can be used to change bill content as well as budget amounts as enacted by the legislature. Such a position is based on the wording in the Wisconsin Constitution which states that, "Appropriations bills may be approved in whole or in part by the governor, and the part approved shall become law" (Wisconsin Constitution, Art. V, Sec. 10). This practice has been called "writing with an eraser" or the "Vanna White" veto. Under this interpretation, the governor not only can strike-out entire sections, but also words and even letters and numbers, thus *creating* entirely new content and new provisions via new words formed with letters from existing words. Between 1987 and June 1995, Governor Thompson exercised approximately 1300 partial vetoes on budget bills. He precipitated a crisis in 1987 through a record 290 partial vetoes to the 1987-89 budget. The Senate responded by suing the governor in order to overturn this type of veto use. The suit failed; but opponents of this type of veto power finally succeeded when, in April of 1990, the voters passed a constitutional amendment prohibiting the governor from creating new words by striking letters from existing words (Legislative Reference Bureau, 1990).

In vetoing portions of the 1994-95 budget (SB-44), Governor Thompson "struck through" amounts of money approved by the legislature and wrote in different ones. This action of writing in a new amount was challenged in the state supreme court (*Citizen's Utility Board, et. al. v. Klauser and Thompson*). In June 1995, the court upheld the governor's right to insert a lesser amount and dismissed this challenge (Jones, 1995). This decision increased considerably the power of the governor's partial veto and led some legislators to consider initiating another limiting constitutional amendment.

Given the legislative process in budget building (described in greater detail in the next section), "private or local" provisions can "creep into" the budget bill and "pork barrel" projects (i.e., government supported projects having only limited local interest and support, but funded by the state) are sometimes included. One consequence is that many additional, special interest expenditures of a narrow focus get included. Through the governor's line item veto as interpreted by court decisions, the amount of special interest provisions and pork barrel projects included in the budget bill may be reduced in the final legislation as enacted into law (Friederich, June 21, 1987).

If the governor signs the bill, it becomes law. If s/he vetoes the bill, in whole or in part, it is returned to the legislative chamber of origin. If this chamber and the other chamber both pass the bill by two-thirds votes, thus rejecting the governor's action, the governor's veto is overridden and the bill becomes law without the governor's signature. Overriding a governor's veto, however, is very difficult, as noted in Table VI-1.

A bill which will become law is sent to the Wisconsin secretary of state for publication. The secretary of state assigns a "publication" date to the bill. The day after the publication date, the bill becomes law, unless the legislation specifies a later effective date. Laws in Wisconsin are included in the *Wisconsin Statutes*, published biennially. Any bill passed must indicate what it adds or repeals in the existing statutes, so it is always clear exactly what the law is. In addition, Wisconsin has a Revisor of Statutes whose task it is to see that the statutes are always current and reflect exactly what the legislature has done. When the Revisor detects problems, s/he may submit Revisor's Bills directly to the legislature, which "tidy up" and correct these uncertainties. This system, called permanent revision, attempts to ensure that the law is always clear. Many states lack this system; and thus elsewhere, until the courts rule, it is not always clear whether a new statute has repealed or modified a statute enacted previously.

The Budget Process in the Legislature. Special attention must be paid in Wisconsin to the budget process, and especially to the critical role played by the Joint Finance Committee. (As its title indicates, the Joint Finance Committee is a single committee, composed of *both* senators and representatives who together are responsible for all finance matters handled by the legislature). Next to the majority party leadership, especially the Speaker and the governor, this committee is credited with being the most influential factor in *legislative* policy making. (In recent sessions, several steps including formation of a Ways and Means Committee, introduction of a modified budget process, and assumption of greater responsibility in final budget formation by the majority party caucus have been introduced to reduce domination by the Joint Finance Committee; however, the effects of these steps on the Committee appear minimal). A new and effective challenge to the role of the Joint Finance Committee came with the passage of the 1996-97 budget in May and June of 1995. At that time, the Republicans in the Assembly rejected many of the budget provisions developed by the Committee and passed a bill closely resembling what Governor Thompson had requested originally. This was an unprecedented rejection of the Joint Finance Committee's work.

The Joint Finance Committee is composed of eight senators and eight representatives who are appointed in the same manner as are other committee members in their respective chambers. The majority party in each chamber appoints six of their members while the minority appoints two. All bills concerning revenue, appropriations and expenditures are sent to this committee, some after they have been sent to and recommended by a subject matter committee. In cases of double consideration, one committee will theoretically review the desirability of a bill from a substantive perspective (the subject matter committee), while the other considers its fiscal impact (the Joint Finance Committee). In fact, however, the Joint Finance Committee considers substantive issues as well as fiscal ones and is, thereby, more important than any of the subject matter committees, since it makes the ultimate recommendation on every bill having a fiscal impact. Because many subject matter bills include some fiscal impact, the role of this committee extends to almost every area of state government policy.

The Joint Finance Committee's tasks are so formidable that it has been given an extensive and very skilled professional staff, the Legislative Fiscal Bureau, to assist it in studying the budget. This was the first standing committee to have such staff available to it. The Bureau's staff is composed of a wide variety of fiscal experts specializing in financial and program analysis, state budget and taxation policy, and all aspects of state operations; its importance to the legislature and to the state's fiscal affairs cannot be overstated. Among their many duties, staff members attend all Joint Finance Committee meetings, advise Assembly and Senate leaders during budget negotiations, and provide information and analysis to legislators as requested. The Bureau is regarded as a service office for the whole legislature.

The Joint Finance Committee's major task is studying and altering the governor's budget proposals. This process occurs over several months and takes precedence over consideration of proposals coming from individual legislators. Typically, this committee meets from early February to late May or early June in every odd numbered year, focusing almost entirely on the governor's budget; however, work on formulating the budget begins in the executive agencies many months earlier. The initial step begins as agency personnel project what it will cost to provide existing programs for the next fiscal year, what new initiatives are appropriate, and their cost. These projections usually begin within a context of public policy set by the governor and given to the agencies in writing. At the same time, units within the Department of Administration begin to assess amounts that existing taxing programs will yield and what building and development programs are necessary for the state. All of these are presented to the governor, and an executive budget is formulated, typically in the summer and early fall of each even-numbered year.

The executive budget, as prepared in bill form, becomes known as the biennial budget bill and has always been an important document for two primary reasons: 1) it sets out state expenditures for the next two years, and 2) it indicates how the money is to be raised. When the budget is passed, it becomes part of the state's

134

statutes and is law itself until a subsequent budget bill is passed and replaces it. Thus, failure of the legislature to pass a new budget will <u>not</u> result in the state having no budget nor in a crisis whereby bills can be held hostage until a budget is passed. This is an important difference between Wisconsin and the federal government.

In recent sessions, governors began to experience difficulties in obtaining portions of their substantive programs from the legislature, especially when they were of a party which did not control the legislature. Gradually, a practice began whereby governors, and eventually legislators, have used the budget bill as a means to implement changes in *substantive policies*, as well as a means to establish the state's budget. Former Speaker Loftus described the budget bill as the primary vehicle for the governor to initiate changes in public policy and a means for the legislature to review the performance of agencies and programs (Loftus, 1986). Thus, the budget bill has evolved into a major vehicle for the governor, the opposition party, and individual legislators to accomplish matters of policy substance, as well as to set the fiscal policy for the next biennium. Clearly, the budget is a partisan document intended to achieve policy goals as well as to establish state fiscal policies.

The governor's practice of including substantive provisions in his executive budget continued for years until the spring of 1993 when the Joint Finance Committee co-chairs acted to remove 110 policy items and introduce them as separate bills. This bipartisan effort focused the budget bill on state spending and revenue issues, with a minimum of policy provisions left in (Pommer, 1993). The strategy was repeated in March of 1995 when the Republican co-chairs again acted to remove 89 substantive provision; but, even with this action, a large number of substantive provisions remained in the 1996-97 budget bill (Walters, 1995).

In Wisconsin and in most other states, current programs which already receive state funding traditionally have had a great advantage in the budgeting process. The question usually posed is what additional level of funding is needed for a program to continue and to improve. This is called incremental budgeting. Such a built-in advantage for current programs arises because the status quo is a result of continual evolution; most elected officials are reluctant to alter the current status. Programs have clients who vote and who want their programs maintained. Thus, campaign promises to eliminate or even to reduce the size of many state programs are more difficult to bring about than most campaigners will admit. Consequently, existing programs are difficult to eliminate while new initiatives are difficult to start. According to Loftus, a "smart" governor will have a budget which has three or more times what he really wants or expects in order to have "bargaining stock" available for negotiating with the legislature (Loftus, 1986). In recent years, however, Republican policy proposals have challenged this approach and initiated both funding and programmatic reductions.

When the budget bill has been introduced into the legislature, it is automatically referred to the Joint Finance Committee. During an extensive set of open hearings, the public, interested groups, and representatives of state agencies will be heard just like for all other bills. Hard questions will be asked by legislators of those choosing to testify at committee hearings. Lofty appeals to higher needs, as well as comments critical of the proposed expenditures and policies, will abound. Quietly, study groups of committee members also meet and review specific portions of the budget (e.g., higher education) in great detail with staff. These study groups have become major actors in the budget development for the various areas, even offering amendments during caucus deliberations. New ideas are proposed, often as "trial balloons" in the press. Eventually, a document is agreed to, and the stage is set for action.

Since the budget must be agreed to by a majority of members in each chamber, it becomes the task of the majority party caucuses, and especially their leaders, to "build a budget" which half of the members will support via their votes on the floor. Building a coalition sufficient to pass a budget is crucial, and sometimes takes the form of what one legislator labeled, "decorating the legislative Christmas tree." This imagery refers to the process sometimes used, whereby the majority leadership in open caucus and in private one-on-one sessions garners votes, typically within their party only, by providing specific benefits sought by individual members. These may take the form of appropriations for a legislator's favorite cause (usually something related to his/her district) or changes in policies and programs. Such provisions may have never received any committee review or comment. Regardless of the specifics, the majority caucus has sometimes "decorated" the state budget with dollars and programs sought by individual members in return for their votes on the budget and in an effort to assist them in their reelection efforts. Such help can be especially useful to freshmen legislators by demonstrating their abilities to bring concrete benefits to their districts. The 1987-89 budget had several examples of such "local pork" provisions:

> The budget authorized issuance of a liquor license to a motel in the legislative district of freshman Rep. Frank Boyle (D-Superior).

> It also provided a tax exemption for charter boats on Lake Superior, aimed at freshman Sen. Robert Jauch (D- Poplar).

> Other pet projects included a ban on locating two landfills in Dane County, permission for indoor horseshoe pitching arenas that sell alcoholic beverages to stay open all night [Note: this was a provision in the governor's original budget document], and construction of traffic islands and warning flashers at two school crossings in Whitefish Bay [the minority leader's district] (Schultze, 1987).

Another tactic has been to include provisions in the budget bill that were not a part of what was introduced and which have little relationship to the budget process. For example, a major revision of the Juvenile Code was included as part of the 1987-89 legislative budget.

The inclusion of such provisions in the budget bill seems to have declined slightly in recent sessions, according to most observers and has never reached the scale of New York where "member items reached a total of 2,744 projects in the last four years and cost $168 million" (Lynn, 1987). In Wisconsin, as noted above, this process is constrained by the possible action of the governor and the court in restricting private (locally oriented) provisions. In "building" this budget coalition, certain portions of the governor's proposed budget remain intact, other parts are changed, and still others are removed entirely. Legislators (especially the leaders) must constantly balance state needs with specialized needs of districts, interests and individuals, remembering that both chambers and the governor must concur on the product--a difficult task at best. A glimpse of the maneuvering can be seen in one newspaper account from the 1987-89 budget formation process:

> Madison, Wis. -- The clock was nearing 2 a.m. Wednesday in the hot, sweaty crowded Senate Parlor of the State Capitol as six lawmakers struck deals on the $20 billion state budget.

> It was a scene far from the pristine image of democratic government fostered by high school civics courses. It was, instead, a slice of real-world bargaining that plays a major role in shaping legislation.

> Assembly Speaker, Thomas Loftus, head of the three-man delegation to a budget conference committee, offered a deal to break two impasses between Senate and Assembly negotiators with one stroke.

> The deal would make an unlikely pair of the issues of additional University of Wisconsin faculty and increasing the auto registration fee, two of the more contested proposals now reduced to a few lines in the 900-plus page budget document.

> Loftus' proposal: The Assembly would back down from its insistence on 381 new UW faculty members if the Senate would back off on its insistence on a $10 increase in the auto registration fee.

After some ritual maneuvers--"the Senate is very serious about the $10 registration fee," intoned Senate Majority Leader Joseph Strohl--the deal was sealed.

The university would get 341 new positions--40 fewer than the Assembly had wanted, 40 more than the Senate had sought.

The auto registration fee increase, which the Senate wanted and the Assembly did not would not go into the budget (Schultze, 1987).

This process, repeated hundreds of times, illustrates how a Wisconsin budget bill is formed.

When the majority leadership believes they have sufficient votes for passage, they will bring the bill to the floor. If the governor is of the same party, extensive consultation between the leaders and governor will have taken place in order to maximize agreement. This was not the case when Republican Governor Dreyfus faced the Democratic majority between 1978 and 1982; however, in 1987, the Democratic legislative leaders met with Republican Governor Thompson during inter-chamber negotiations on the final legislative version to create a spending and taxing bill that was "acceptable" to him and to the Republican legislators. As a consequence, final passage of the 1987-89 budget was overwhelmingly bipartisan, 32-1 in the Senate (the lone dissent a Republican) and 78-19 in the Assembly (42 Democrats and 36 Republicans in favor, 13 Democrats and 6 Republicans against). This departure from past practice probably reflected Governor Thompson's prior legislative experience, his willingness to propose and support a budget embracing Democratic spending programs (originally proposed in defeated Democratic Governor Earl's budget), and the Democratic leadership's desire to "get along" this time with the governor and his party. This characterization, however, did not persist for subsequent sessions when conflict and vetoes by the Republican governor became commonplace.

Once both chambers agree on a budget bill, it is sent to the governor for his review and action. As noted above, however, the governor has the final say, since s/he can line item veto the budget bill, including the alteration of bill content, as described above. But, legislative leaders have been known to create opportunities for such veto action that may come back to haunt a governor seeking re-election.

Important Non-Legislative Organizations

Like any organization, the Wisconsin legislature cannot exist isolated from other political, social, and economic activities. The roles of two types of groups associated with these other activities and involved in bringing these activities into the legislative arena, however, deserve brief special attention--political parties and interest groups. While other chapters in this book discuss these topics, parties and interest groups have special roles related to the Wisconsin legislature, including selection of candidates for the legislature and the shaping of public policies.

Organizing the political party within the Wisconsin legislature has become increasingly important since the state became more competitive electorally in the late 1950s. As the "regular" party organizations in the state have focused more resources and attention on non-state legislative elections, and as a greater number of committed partisans have been elected to the legislative ranks, party leaders in the legislature have assumed more party maintenance and party building responsibilities (especially among Democrats). The increased level of partisanship in the legislature since the mid-1980s (with the election of a Republican governor) is evident to all observers. The basic unit for partisan organization in the legislature are the four caucuses--one for each party in the Senate and in the Assembly. Each caucus serves a party organizing function at the beginning of each two-year session when the members of each caucus nominate leaders and begin to plan for the upcoming session. The majority party caucus will initiate steps to organize formally the chamber for the upcoming session while the minority organizes in opposition to the majority party. During a session, the caucus also meets periodically to discuss issues of interest to members and specific bills. Many times, a party position on legislation will be formulated and members' support for a bill important to the party may be sought. The most extreme example of this takes place with regard to the budget bill, as noted above. In addition, each caucus will set about establishing its partisan posture on policy proposals and will initiate a plan for the recruitment and orientation of new candidates to run for "winnable seats. Each caucus has its own officers and staff to assist members in these tasks.

When the Republicans were in the minority, they opened their caucuses to the public. Beginning in 1977, caucuses of both parties in both chambers were generally open to the public, except during organizational meetings. Newspapers played a crucial role in insisting that caucuses be open and in arguing that it was not logical for the legislature to exempt itself from the open meeting laws which it had passed. It was claimed that these open caucuses were a nationwide "first;" nevertheless, numerous examples existed where a legislative caucus had gone into a closed session since 1977. Usually this happens on the budget and on important partisan issues. Members indicate that the only difference in a closed session is that a more candid exchange of views can take place without so much member "posturing" to private groups and narrow constituent interests. During the 1995-96 session, majority Republicans in the Assembly created much controversy when they re-instituted the practice of closed caucuses during the budget bill debate. Press reports indicated that this strategy was used to permit the Republicans "...to rework the budget in private" (Bice, 1995; see also Hildebrand, 1995).

Views differ on the effects open caucuses have had on public policy. An open caucus is assumed to assure public scrutiny for this important legislative activity and further removes decision making from "back rooms." At the same time, opening the caucuses has removed some of the "wiggle" room desired by policy makers for compromising differences. Some members charge that public policy suffers because lobbyists can now observe first-hand the deliberations and pressure members more effectively to comply with a pressure group's requests. At these caucuses, attempts may be made to work out a party position and to induce all members to support that position. Conflict between the major parties has been so intense in recent years that the caucuses have produced high party cohesion on an increasing number of roll calls. Those questions which affect the organizational interests of the parties themselves, for some of these proposals clearly help one party at the expense of the other, are most likely to produce roll calls on which all members of one party vote against all members of the other party.

In spite of this increase in legislative voting according to one's political party, it would be difficult to argue that the most important issues of recent years have been ultimately determined on a strict party basis. As noted above, the most important questions have been the budget-tax bills; and in most cases, after each party made its original policy clear, the ultimate decisions were compromises between what each party wanted. Similarly, many bills involving interest group advocacy split both parties so that members of each party sometimes voted against members of their own party based on the issues.

The other type of group important for understanding the Wisconsin legislature is the associations which work to influence policy decisions. Labeled both interest and pressure groups, these range from informal groups of people who come together to try to influence one policy, to large, well organized and highly financed groups seeking to have on-going impact on policy decisions.

Persons who actually represent these groups before government officials are labeled lobbyists. Sometimes lobbyists are permanent employees of the organizations they represent, sometimes they are volunteers in an organization who have a special interest in advocacy activity, and sometimes they are professionals (attorneys or public relations specialists or former legislators) who are retained by contract to represent the group during the legislative session. Regardless of their status, lobbyists are expected to represent the views of their organizations to legislators during informal meetings, committee hearings, and whenever possible. These organizational representatives appear and sometimes testify at hearings on bills, send information to legislators, introduce legislators to group members, and contribute campaign funds. They may also try to alert citizens in the legislators' districts to pending legislation, advising these constituents to make known their wishes to their legislator. More effective, even, is convincing members of the group to become involved, as have the chiropractors in various election campaigns, by getting to know legislators on a first name basis; however, this is standard advice to any citizen interested in affecting legislative policy making. Legislators have a long memory about who has supported and opposed them in their re-elections. While opinions differ greatly on how effective some of these tactics are in "obtaining" a legislator's vote, there is no question that these activities provide groups and individuals with better "access" to the legislative process. Legislators will listen to the group's views and many groups are willing to go to great lengths to get this access.

Since the number of lobbyists far outnumbers legislators and since lobbyists typically have impressive resources at their disposal, legislators have implemented several types of control over lobbying tactics and practices. Wisconsin lobby controls are stricter than those in most states. They are based on the recognition that lobbying is a legitimate means of petitioning legislators, but that it should be done with full publicity and in an open atmosphere without providing special advantages to one group over another and without giving groups special access over that of individual citizens. Thus, lobbyists must register and pay a fee. They must report on their activities and on the contributions of groups and individuals to campaigns, all of which become a matter of public record. In addition, lobbyists are prohibited from the extensive "wining and dining" of legislators sometimes found in other states; however, legislators and lobbyists both point to the important functions served by such interactions and to the degree to which they continue to exist. Lobbying activities by over 600 groups cost $35.4 million during the 1993-94 legislative session (Mayers, 1995b).

The use of wining and dining by lobbyists has, however, changed. On July 16, 1987, Governor Thompson and two cabinet secretaries (Administration Secretary James Klauser and Employment Relations Secretary John Tries) accepted a stipulated agreement in Dane County Circuit Court by which they forfeited $86.96 plus court costs for their acceptance of a free meal and beverages. (The group involved paid $700 plus court costs). During a routine audit of the Wisconsin Professional Police Association's lobbying expenditures, it was determined by the secretary of state's office that on December 22, 1986, this association entertained these three persons who were all state elected or appointed officials. While the nature of the stipulation and the participant comments referred to the violations as "inadvertent" and resulting because "...it (the entertaining expenses) had not been handled correctly...", notice was given by the secretary of state to public officials and lobbyists that these activities were being given closer scrutiny (Mell, 1987). Beginning in late 1988, a series of investigations found evidence of violations to several portions of state law, including campaign contributions and providing/accepting something of value for state officials. In 1990, some minor changes were made in the Wisconsin lobbying and ethics law; and there was a transfer of lobbying law monitoring/enforcement responsibility to the Ethics Board.

Conclusion

This chapter has provided an overview of what is considered by many to be one of the more professional and independent legislatures in the U.S.--the Wisconsin Senate and Assembly. The major themes have been that:

-the state constitution establishing the Wisconsin legislature provided more power to the Senate and Assembly than is true for many other U.S. state legislatures;
-restrictions on legislative powers that were imposed in the constitution have not become major drawbacks preventing legislative initiatives;
-in managing its work schedule, the Senate and Assembly have implemented alternating periods of committee review and floorperiods to integrate and facilitate consideration of legislation;
-leadership in each chamber, but especially the Speaker, is an important element in determining how

members will work as part of the organization and what will be accomplished of the legislative agenda;

-legislative committees in Wisconsin have become important and sometimes very independent centers of power over the fate of bills;

-extensive and highly qualified legislative staff are available to both senators and representatives in order to maintain legislative independence and competence in policy making;

-political parties play important roles in the legislative process and have different views on issues and policies in the state;

-the governor's power regarding legislation through the veto process is extensive, especially when compared with other states;

-elections and campaign finance has become a critical activity for legislators and leaders given the enormous increase in campaign costs;

-once elected to a legislative position, chances are good that one will be re-elected and continue to serve in the Senate or Assembly;

-since re-election of incumbents is the norm in Wisconsin, recent Republican governors have utilized effectively administrative appointments to bring about greater electoral uncertainty that Republicans have been able to use in capturing control of the Senate and Assembly;

-many legislators in Wisconsin fit the model of professional, full-time legislators rather than citizen legislators who maintain their occupational and professional standings once elected to the legislature;

-the budget process has become a means for legislators as well as the governor to obtain substantive policy changes as well as particularized as well as general benefits for specific interests and districts; and

-interaction by legislators with lobbyists and interest group representatives is extensive in the development of legislation which is passed and becomes law.

Understanding the Wisconsin legislature is an important component for understanding Wisconsin government and politics. The Senate and Assembly reflect well the values and orientations of the state. Considering all elements, the Wisconsin legislature is a strong and effective legislative body.

APPENDIX: GLOSSARY OF TERMS

Act
A law enacted by means of a bill that is approved by both houses of the legislature and signed by the governor. Bills passed by the legislature may also become law without the governor's signature if the governor fails to take action on them within set time limits or they are passed by the legislature over the governor's veto.

Adoption
Final action taken on all amendments and conference committee reports. Each house may "adopt" or "refuse to adopt" an amendment or report.

Amendment
A proposal to change a bill, joint resolution, or resolution by adding, deleting, or substituting language. (See also simple amendment and substitute amendment.)

Appropriations
The setting aside of public revenues for a specific use or program.

Author(s)
The legislator or legislative committee that introduces a bill or resolution. Additional members of the same house who sign the bill are referred to as "coauthors," while cosigners from the other house are called "cosponsors."

Bill
A proposal, drafted in legal language, to change current law by adding new language or deleting or amending existing language.

Bulletin of Proceedings
A legislative publication that contains: a numerical list of all bills and other measures introduced and the actions taken on them; indices by subject matter and author of all measures introduced; and, a numerical listing of existing statute sections and session laws affected by acts and enrolled bills of the current session and acts from previous sessions that have delayed effective dates.

Calendar
The daily schedule of business for each house that shows the order in which proposals and other business will be taken up on the floor.

Committee
A group of legislators appointed to review proposals and policies within a certain subject area. Committees typically hold public hearings on bills referred to them and report their recommendations for further consideration of the proposals on the floor of the house. (See also conference committee, special committee and standing committee.)

Concurrence
The action of the second house in agreeing to a measure that has passed the house of origin. The second house may "concur" or "nonconcur" in the measure.

Conference Committee
A committee whose members are appointed by both houses when the two have passed different versions of some proposal and cannot agree on identical wording.

141

Constituents
People who live in a given senate or assembly district.

Engross
A motion to incorporate all adopted amendments into a proposal in the house of origin and end the second reading. Occasionally, a proposal may be "printed engrossed." This requires printing a revised version of the proposal that incorporates all amendments and corrections before consideration in the second house.

Enroll
The action after a bill has passed both houses that consolidates its amendments and any chief clerk's corrections into one text to be presented to the governor for action.

Executive Session
A committee meeting in which committee members vote on the disposition of a bill or other proposal. Only committee members may speak in an executive session, but members of the public may attend and listen. "Executive" is often shortened to "exec" and used as an adjective or a verb; e.g. the committee may hold an *exec* session or decide to *exec* a bill immediately.

First Reading
The formal announcement on the floor of the legislature that a bill or other proposal is being offered for consideration.

Fiscal Estimate
An estimate of a bill's anticipated change in appropriation authority or the fiscal liability or revenues of the state or general local government.

Floor Debate
Discussion of a proposal in the senate or assembly chambers. A bill under debate is referred to as being "on the floor."

Floorperiods
Times set aside by the session schedule during which legislators consider and debate measures in the senate and assembly chambers.

Joint Resolution
A proposal acted upon by both houses that makes a request, affects operations of both house, pays tribute to public figures, or proposes a constitutional amendment. In Wisconsin, joint resolutions do not require approval by the governor.

Joint Standing Committee
A permanent committee, created by statute, that is composed of members from both houses of the legislature.

Journal
The official record of legislative business kept by each house of the legislature. Journals do not record floor debate.

Lobbyist
A person who is paid to represent an interest group before the legislature.

Override
The action of the legislature in passing a measure over the governor's veto by a vote of at least two-thirds of the

members present in both houses.

Parliamentary Procedure
The rules, rulings, and customs under which legislatures conduct their business.

Partial Veto
The action of the Wisconsin governor in disapproving a part of an appropriation bill. The "part" may be a single word and is thus smaller than the "item" that is susceptible to veto in some states.

Promulgation
The formal process by which state agencies officially create administrative rules.

Proposal
A resolution, joint resolution, or bill introduced in the legislature for consideration.

Public Hearing
A meeting held by a committee at which members of the public, lobbyists, legislators, and state agency representatives may speak or register their views about proposals or policies under committee consideration.

Relating Clause
The part of the title of a bill or other proposal that identifies the general subject matter of the proposal.

Resolution
A proposal that makes a request or affects the operations of one house, including amending its rules, and that requires no action by the other house or the governor.

Roll Call Vote
A vote in which members' votes on a particular question are recorded with their names. Every roll call is printed in the house journal.

Rules
The detailed code of parliamentary procedure officially adopted in each house. Rules prescribe the way in which the legislature does business and provides methods for settling disputes. In addition to the rules of each house, there are also joint rules which both houses agree to follow. In Wisconsin, rules carry over from one legislature to the next unless superseded by later action.

Second Reading
The stage at which amendments to proposals are considered on the floor.

Section
A part of a statue, a bill or an act. A section of the statutes is the primary division of a statue chapter, e.g. Section 13.10 is section 10 of statutory chapter 13. Bills and their resulting acts are also divided into numbered sections for easier reference.

Select Committee
See special committee definition.

Session
The entire two-year period that begins with the swearing in of a new legislature in January of the off-numbered year and ends with the swearing in of the next legislature.

Session Laws
The acts of the legislature compiled and published for every biennial session. The acts of the 1993 legislature will be known as the 1993 session laws, officially published as the *1993 Laws of Wisconsin*.

Session Schedule
A schedule adopted by the legislature through passage of a joint resolution at the beginning of each session, setting the dates of floorperiods and committee work periods.

Simple Amendment
A proposal to change some portion of a bill or other proposal by adding, deleting or substituting language.

Special Committee
A committee appointed to examine a particular topic. Sometimes called a "select committee," it automatically ceases to exist when its task is finished or when the session ends.

Standing Committee
A committee established by the rules of a house to examine legislation, hold hearings, and make recommendations on legislative measures. Standing committees may be abolished or created only by changing the rules.

Statutes
The general laws of the state the codify certain preceding legislative actions in numerically organized sections. The Wisconsin Statutes are printed every 2 years to incorporate the statutory changes made by the session laws enacted by the most recent legislature.

Substitute Amendment
A proposal to replace a bill or other proposal. A substitute amendment may be a complete revision of a proposal.

Sustain
Legislative action to uphold the governor's veto or partial veto of a bill through refusal by more than on-third of the members in one house to vote to override the veto.

Table
A motion to temporarily set aside a measure and attend to other business.

Third Reading
The stage at which bills and certain other proposals come up for final discussion and possible passage. No amendments may be offered at this point.

Veto
The action taken by the governor to reject an entire bill passed by the legislature. (See also partial veto.)

Veto Message
A constitutionally required explanation of the reasons for a veto or partial veto of a bill. The governor must submit the message in writing to the bill's house of origin.

Source: State of Wisconsin, *Blue Book* 1993 -94: 182-85.

CHAPTER VII

THE GOVERNOR
By Edward J. Miller[*]

Governors have been described as the chief executive officers of states, analogous to the heads of large corporations (Beyle, 1990: 201). The Wisconsin governor has a variety of powers and responsibilities, ranging from ceremonial rites as head of state to the management of an extensive state bureaucracy. Increasingly, the Wisconsin governor, like his counterparts in other states, spends time representing Wisconsin in intergovernmental organizations, such as the National Governors Association; in trade missions to other nations; and to in-state and out-of-state businesses, providing state resources to encourage their expansion in Wisconsin. Personal time and privacy are far more limited for the state's chief executive today than just two decades ago.

The contemporary governor is preeminent in formulating the issue agenda and in recommending policy action to the legislature. But these issues also are conflictual. Issues such as state taxes, commitment to economic development, Native American treaty rights, abortion, and the pressing demand for new or expanded state services often force a governor to make decisions which jeopardize his political future. Within recent history, acting Governor Schreiber was defeated in his bid for his own term, Governor Dreyfus decided against a second term, and Governor Earl was defeated in his attempt at a second four-year term. Governor Thompson, riding an economic boom period in Wisconsin in the context of a softer national economy, broke this streak, being elected to a third four-year term in 1994. This chapter examines the governor, charting the recruitment patterns for the office and his powers and roles in the governance of the state.

Legal Qualifications, Terms, and Succession

Legal requirements of eligibility for the office of governor are modest, specifying only that the candidate be a citizen of the United States and a qualified voter in Wisconsin. Most states set the minimum age for governor at 30, emulating the Constitutional requirement for president; but Wisconsin allows anyone reaching the 18 year old voting age to be governor. A prospective governor need not be born in the state nor even in the United States. In fact, five Wisconsin governors, one elected as recently as 1940, were foreign born, and many were born in other states.[1]

The governor is elected to a four-year term. However, before 1970, governors and other state-wide officers served for two-year terms. The change in Wisconsin mirrored term lengthening in most states and placed the gubernatorial election at the presidential mid-term. The four-year term gives the governor more time to accomplish the administration's goals and reduces the need to constantly campaign for reelection. By having the election in non-presidential election years, the election is insulated from presidential election politics and the potential influence of presidential coattails. Since 1970, the governor and lieutenant governor run together as a team in the November election, insuring that both are members of the same party.

Despite the existence of public funding, the campaign expenditures for this team have rapidly escalated, making it difficult for under-funded candidates to enter the race. A gubernatorial candidate must raise a significant

---

[*] Professor of Political Science, University of Wisconsin-Stevens Point.
[1] For other biographical information about Wisconsin governors, see the state of Wisconsin *Blue Book* published by the Wisconsin's Legislative Reference Bureau and especially the 1960 edition which contains brief biographical sketches of the governors who served from 1848 to 1960.

campaign chest, resulting in increased scrutiny of campaign contributions by opposing candidates, newspapers, and good government groups.

There are no limits on the number of terms a Wisconsin governor may serve, although prior to Governor Thompson a term limitation tradition was evident. Governor Walter J. Kohler, Jr. cited the unwritten "tradition" when he refused to run for a fourth, two-year term in 1956. However, Governor Philip La Follette made an unsuccessful attempt to win a fourth term in 1938. Even with the change to a four-year term, with no limit on the number of terms (unlike the two-term presidential limit), only one governor of Wisconsin, Tommy Thompson, has ever served for eight years or more. Governor Lucey, the first to be elected to a four-year term, came the closest, but resigned before completing his second term to become U.S. ambassador to Mexico.

In the event of the governor's death, resignation, disability, or removal from office, the lieutenant governor completes the governor's term as governor. Prior to the adoption of a constitutional amendment in 1979, the lieutenant governor was only an "acting governor" when succeeding the governor though this language had not materially affected the performance or powers of any of the six lieutenant governors who acted as governor. The 1979 amendment, in effect, brought the constitution into conformity with this custom by specifying that a lieutenant governor succeeding a governor becomes "governor," avoiding the ambiguity of the title of "acting governor," unless it is thought temporary as in the case of disability. In Wisconsin the lieutenant governor does not serve as governor when the governor leaves the state unless the governor is unable to carry out gubernatorial functions.

In an unusual incident in Wisconsin constitutional development, the state supreme court further clarified the issue of gubernatorial succession. In 1942 the governor-elect died in December, a month before the inauguration. The lame duck incumbent governor contended that he should remain in office until another election could be held. The lieutenant governor and the Secretary of State, both of whom had been re-elected in November, also claimed the office. The court decided that as of the start of the new term the office of governor would be held by the duly elected lieutenant governor (*State ex rel., Martin v. Heil*, 1942).

Another change made in 1979 specifies that if the office of lieutenant governor is vacant, the Secretary of State serves as acting governor in the absence of the governor. If the governor dies, resigns, or is removed from office under these circumstances, the Secretary of State serves for the balance of the unexpired term (Wisconsin Constitution, Art. V, Sec. 8). Vacancies in the office of Lieutenant Governor are now filled by gubernatorial nomination with Senate and Assembly confirmation as provided by Article XIII, Sec. 10 of the Constitution.

Since the removal of the constitutional specification of salary in 1925, compensation for Wisconsin Governors has steadily increased. The 1995-98 term has authorized a gubernatorial salary of $101,860 in addition to a state residence and further compensation for expenses. (Governor Thompson said that he would not take the salary increase from the salary of $86,148 received during his second term.) Wisconsin's governor's salary is greater than the average gubernatorial salary of $86,958 in 1994, but less than that paid the governors of neighboring states of Illinois, Michigan, and Minnesota. Iowa, though, pays its governor less.

Political Qualifications

In 1952 after a successful bid for re-election, Governor Walter Kohler, Jr. attended a meeting where he was asked by a fellow governor who his opponent had been. Kohler responded that he defeated a man who was born in Illinois, received degrees from Harvard and Yale Universities, married into the Rockefeller family, had worked for J.P. Morgan, and had lived in Wisconsin for a only a few years prior to the campaign. Upon hearing this description, the response was: "Gosh, Walter, did you choose him yourself?"

This suggests that in addition to the minimum standards of eligibility set forth in the state constitution, other characteristics impose practical qualifications on a prospective occupant of the governor's office. Such factors

146

as age, political experience, partisan affiliation, occupational background, race, and sex, among others, indicate what kind of person is most likely to become governor.[2] The political background of Wisconsin's 42 governors gives suggestions of practical eligibility. In analyzing these political backgrounds, state history is divided into four periods: 1) statehood through the Civil War (1848-1865), 2) the post-Civil War period to the end of the nineteenth century (1866-1900), 3) the La Follette era through World War II (1901-1946), and 4) the post-World War II period (1947 to the present).

Every Wisconsin governor and every major party nominee for the office has been a white male, clearly identified with a major political party, although degrees of partisan involvement varied considerably. Table VII-1 indicates the governors' places of birth, ages at becoming governor, and partisan affiliations.

Table VII-1

AVERAGE AGE, PLACE OF BIRTH AND PARTISANSHIP
OF WISCONSIN GOVERNORS, 1848 - 95

	1848-1865	1866-1900	1901-1946	1947-1995	Total
Average Age (Years)	38.2	51.6	52.4	47.7	
Place of Birth					
Wisconsin	0	0	10	10	20
Other State	7	9	0	1	17
Foreign Country	2	1	2	0	5
Partisan Affiliation					
Democrat	3	2	1	5	11
Progressive	0	0	2[a]	0	2
Republican	5	8	10	6	29
Whig	1	0	0	0	1

[a] Phillip La Follette served as a Republican, 1931-33, and as a Progressive, 1935-39.

The age at which governors have taken office averages slightly more than 48 years with the range being from 33 to 80. The earliest governors were generally much younger than those in subsequent periods. In the years from 1848 to 1865, the oldest of the nine governors was only 44 when he assumed the office, and the average age of the group was only slightly more than 38. In the other periods the average has been about 50.

---

[2]   These should not be accepted as unbreakable rules. Kohler's improbable opponent was William Proxmire, who after two more gubernatorial defeats, won a U.S. Senate seat in 1957. His opponent in that contest was again Kohler.

It is not surprising that the earliest governors were not born in Wisconsin. In fact, it was not until 1901 that a native son became governor. The places of origin of the non-Wisconsin born governors is consistent with the migratory patterns reflected in the state's population growth. Five were foreign-born, two in Germany, two in Scotland, and one in Norway. Of those from other parts of the United States, six were born in New England, seven in New York, two in Ohio, and one in Pennsylvania.[3] Since 1900, all but three of the 23 governors have been born within Wisconsin including all but one of those elected in the past forty years. This is not unusual given the typical characteristic of low geographic mobility of American elected officials, especially illustrated by the fact that about two-thirds of Wisconsin born governors were born in the county which became their political base.

The residence of Wisconsin governors indicates another significant characteristic of politics in the state. Virtually all of the governors advanced to the office from counties in the southern half of the state. In fact, nearly three-fourths of them came from the portion of the state included in the Milwaukee-Madison-Green Bay triangle, the area of the greatest population concentration. The two most populous counties, Milwaukee and Dane, have each contributed nine governors. No other county has supplied more than two.

Review of the party affiliation of the governors shows that 29 of the 42 governors were Republicans. This hegemony is even greater since one of the others was a Whig, a partisan ancestor of the Republicans, and two more were Progressives, a short-lived offshoot of the Wisconsin Republican party in the 1930s.

At statehood Wisconsin was predominantly Democratic, and three of the first four governors were Democrats. The Republicans won the state's highest office for the first time in 1856, and from then on Democratic victories were infrequent. Democrats held the governor's office for only eight years between 1856 and 1959. The Democratic party's fortunes have been rejuvenated in Wisconsin with Democratic governors serving 20 of the 35 years from 1959 to 1994. With victory leads being typically less than 55 percent in recent decades, one can conclude that Wisconsin is a two-party competitive state.

Wisconsin's governors have had a variety of educational and vocational backgrounds (Table VII-2). In terms of formal education, the most noticeable trend has been the increase in the number of college-educated governors.

Eighteen of the 23 governors in the twentieth century had at least some college training, with every governor since 1947 holding a college degree. The earliest governors generally had more impressive educational credentials than those who served from 1866 to 1900. Six of the first nine governors were attorneys who entered the legal profession by "reading for the bar" rather than attending a law school. The post-Civil War era through the end of the nineteenth century marked the nadir of formal education as a requisite for the state's highest office. The self-made man who enjoyed success in business was a likely prospect for political advancement.

Lawyers are the largest single occupational group represented among the governors, but Wisconsin has had a smaller percentage of lawyer-governors than most states. Slightly less than one-half (20 of 42) of Wisconsin's chief executives were lawyers. The business community has had considerable representation. Combining small business operators, industrialists, and publishers, a total of 17 governors have come from the business world. Farmers and laborers have had little representation as have members of professions other than the law. One governor was a college chancellor (University of Wisconsin-Stevens Point) prior to his election, a career route rare among governors in all states.

---

[3]   Of the New England states, Connecticut supplied four governors, Massachusetts and Maine, one each.

Table VII-2

EDUCATIONAL AND VOCATIONAL BACKGROUNDS
OF WISCONSIN GOVERNORS, 1848 - 95

	1848-65	1866-1900	1901-46	1947-95	Total
Education					
Less than High School Degree	2	7	4	0	13
High School Degree or Equivalent	3	1	1	0	5
Some College	3	1	2	0	6
College Degree	1	1	5	11	18
Occupation[a]					
Lawyer	6	2	5	7	20
Operated Large Business	0	2	3	2	7
Operated Small Business	3	2	1	1	7
Newspaper Publisher	0	2	1	0	3
Teacher	0	1	0	1	2
Farmer	0	1	0	0	1
Laborer	0	0	2	0	2

[a] In some cases, governors had more than one occupation. Their principal activity only is included.

Another approach to gubernatorial career patterns is through an examination of political offices used as stepping-stones to the state's highest office. Table VII-3 lists the cumulative political experience and the last public position held prior to becoming a governor. Other state-wide elective offices have clearly been an important route to the office of governor. Seventeen governors served in one of the state-wide offices as their last political position before becoming governor. Of these, eight were lieutenant governors, including six who advanced upon the death or resignation of a governor; five held the office of secretary of state; and four had been attorney general. The record of the secretaries of state and attorneys general who moved on to the highest office shows an interesting pattern. Secretaries of state, an important office for advancement to governor in the state's early history, has disappeared as an incubator for that office. On the other hand, each of the three attorneys general who directly advanced to the governor's office did so since 1920, but none since Governor John Reynolds in 1963.

Among the other career routes, service in the state senate has been the final stepping-stone for five governors (but only one in the twentieth century), municipal positions for six (none since 1933), county positions for three (none since 1931), and the U.S. House of Representatives for three (none since 1901). Only one, Governor Thompson, has jumped directly to that office from the state assembly.

In analyzing the career patterns leading toward the governor's office, another useful tool is the distinction between "career" and "amateur" politicians. The former are those who enter public service at a relatively young age and advance through a series of low-level offices to higher office, while the latter are those who cap a successful career in private enterprise or related endeavor with a tour of duty as governor. If these governors had any public service prior to achieving that office, it is likely to have been restricted to part-time elective or appointive positions in their home communities or appointive positions on prestigious state boards or commissions.

Table VII-3

PRIOR POLITICAL EXPERIENCE OF WISCONSIN GOVERNORS AND LAST
POLITICAL POSITION HELD BEFORE BECOMING GOVERNOR, 1848 - 95

	Cumulative Positions	Last Position Before Governor
Municipal	23	6
County	24	3
State		
Assembly	13	1
Senate1	4	5
State-wide Elective Office	20	17
Appointed Position	8	4
Federal		
House of Representatives	3	3
Appointed Position		
Local-Regional	6	1
National-International	2	0
Totals	113	40[a]

[a] Two held no political position prior to becoming a governor.

Wisconsin is somewhat unique among the states with respect to the number of amateurs who have won the state's highest office. Nine of them are among the 42 governors. Since most of these were prominent industrialists, they contributed to the previously noted high representation of businessmen among the governors.

The most obvious examples of this career pattern are Governor Walter J. Kohler, Sr. and Governor Julius Heil, both of whose surnames identify major Wisconsin industries. Neither held elective office prior to selection as governor. Kohler succinctly described his role in politics during his campaign for governor in 1928: "I do not claim to be a politician. I am running for office as a businessman on a business platform."[4] A general characteristic of the amateur governor is that he attains the office at an older age than the career politician. The nine amateurs averaged slightly more than 56 years of age upon assuming the office. The average of the remaining 32 governors is about 46 years.

Governor Dreyfus, formerly Chancellor of the University of Wisconsin - Stevens Point, is included within the amateur category since he too had not held elective office prior to becoming governor. However, his academic background and his state service as chief executive officer of a public university differentiate him from the previous amateurs drawn from the business community.

Typically, the career politician enters public service while relatively young and advances to the governorship through a series of political offices. These public figures have other occupations, but their time and

[4]   Quoted in Sorauf, 1953: 85.

energy are devoted primarily to the demands of various public offices. They begin with service in their local community or county. A jump to the state legislature follows with service for several terms. A successful race for one of the other state-wide offices places them on the threshold for contention for the state's highest office. Occasional electoral defeats mar the record, but victories far outnumber losses for the career politicians who ultimately become governor. They held an average of nearly three elective positions prior to their election as governor. The amateurs averaged less then one elective position prior to their gubernatorial victory, and five of them sought elective office for the first time when they competed for governor.

The tenure in the governor's office of the nine amateur governors is not markedly different from the record compiled by the career politicians (Table VII-4). A slightly higher percentage of amateurs was defeated after one term, but this is balanced by a higher percentage of three-term amateurs. Based on the past evidence, it is much more likely that an amateur will be a Republican rather than a Democrat. All nine of the amateurs were Republicans, a result shaped by the fact that all but one of them were drawn from the ranks of successful businessmen. Until Governor Dreyfus' election in 1978, none had been elected or received major party nominations for governor during the past 20 years.

Table VII-4

TENURE OF "AMATEUR" AND "CAREER POLITICIAN" GOVERNORS
(in percentages)

	Amateur N = 8		Career Politicians N = 33[a]	
One Term				
Did Not Run Again	1	13%	7	21%
Defeated	3	38	10	30
Two Terms				
Did Not Run Again	1	13	7	21
Defeated	1	13	4	12
Three Terms				
Did Not Run Again	2	25	5	15
Totals	8	102%	33	99%

[a] Governor Philip La Follette included twice because of his split service. Percentage Columns do not add to 100 because of rounding.

The political success and vulnerability of Wisconsin governors is charted in Table VII-5. Of interest is that every twentieth century governor but one who lived through his first term has sought a second term. Prior to 1900, four governors did not seek re-election after their first term. In part, this is a reflection of the impact of the primary as a substitute for the convention system of nomination. The latter's use in the nineteenth century gave party leaders the power to drop an incumbent governor. In several such instances, one-term governors indicated a desire to run again, but their inability to receive their party's nomination made it impossible. Four twentieth century governors were defeated in primary contests, but each of these occurred between 1916 and 1932, a period in which the principal state-wide political battle usually occurred in the Republican primary. The conservative and progressive factions of the Republican party competed in nearly every primary, even when it meant running a candidate against an incumbent Republican. The development of the progressive faction into a third party by 1934 largely removed the danger of a primary defeat for an incumbent. Since then no incumbent governor has been defeated in a primary, and few have had more than token opposition.

As the table also indicates, twentieth century lieutenant governors who have succeeded to the governor's office upon the death or resignation of the incumbent have carved out an impressive record of success in their own right in the governor's office. Two went on to win two terms on their own, and the third competed successfully once. Only one, Martin Schreiber, met electoral defeat.

Table VII-5

TENURE OF 19TH AND 20TH CENTURY WISCONSIN GOVERNORS, 1848 - 95

	1848-1900	1901-1995
One Term		
Did Not Run Again	4	1
Defeated		
Re-election	4	4
Renomination	1	3[a]
Died in Office	1	1
Two Terms		
Did Not Run Again	3	1
Defeated		
Re-election	1	2[a]
Renomination	1	1
Resigned from office	0	1
Three Terms		
Did Not Run Again	2	5
Succeeded to Office		
Did Not Run	2[b]	0
Elected		
One Term	0	1
Two Terms	0	2[c]
Defeated	0	1

[a] Includes Governor Philip La Follette in both categories.
[b] One temporary occupant.
[c] One successor died in office after winning two terms of his own.

Study of subsequent career patterns of the governors provides another source of insight into the nature of the office and the men who have held it. Five left the office voluntarily after at least two terms as governor to accept national Cabinet positions or seats in the United States Senate. Governor Nelson served 18 years in the U.S. Senate. Another, Governor Lucey, resigned to become Ambassador to Mexico. Five others were defeated in bids to attain U.S. Senate seats.[5] Governor Vernon Thomson, who was defeated after one term, subsequently won a seat in the House of Representatives, serving 14 years, and was later to serve on the Federal Elections Commission. Governor Fred Zimmerman, defeated for renomination after one term, was elected secretary of state ten years later, a position he then retained for 16 years. Several went into private business including recent Governors Schreiber and Dreyfus, both of whom joined Sentry Insurance in Stevens Point, but neither remained with the company very long. Governor Schrieber was unsuccessful in a second try for the governorship and in his quest to be mayor of Milwaukee. The most recent former governor, Anthony Earl, returned to the practice of law.

Powers and Responsibilities

The office of governor has a variety of powers and responsibilities which thrust its occupant into virtually every phase of state government. Holding the state's highest office, the governor is the personification of the state within and outside of its borders. Each chief executive, of course, has a primary responsibility as head of the executive branch of state government. In addition, the governor participates in the legislative process, has responsibilities which have an impact on the judiciary, and though not legally or formally specified, can play an important role within the governor's political party. Each of these roles is analyzed to demonstrate the nature and source of the governor's power as well as the limitations on the use of these powers. While each role is presented as a separate and distinct activity, during any governor's tenure the roles are constantly intermingled so that actions in one of the spheres may have a decisive impact on the exercise of power within one or more of the others.

In general, during the past twenty years the tendency has been to enhance the governor's power. Governors of both parties have urged that the office be strengthened, and in a variety of ways this has occurred. The executive reorganizations, reducing the number of agencies headed by boards, has expanded the governor's appointment power and strengthened his capacity to direct the executive branch. So too has the gradual increase in the governor's own staff. Throughout, the thrust is in the direction of the "strong executive" model in government. The 1995-1997 state budget further accelerated this trend by moving several state agencies directly under gubernatorial control.

Chief of State. Without question the governor is the chief ribbon cutter, crown bestower, and welcomer of visiting dignitaries. The governor frequently issues proclamations designating dairy month, United Nations Day, and a host of other enterprises in which the state takes pride. The governor has been described as "cheerleader" for the state at these events. These rites, innocuous and inconsequential as they may seem, are important for a governor, allowing public exposure which is neither partisan nor controversial. Thus, while it is occasionally argued that a governor should be spared some of this time-consuming activity, it is unlikely that any ambitious governor would agree to curtail this role, standing to lose too much favorable publicity. Moreover, someone must handle these ceremonial rites since citizens expect a state official at these events. If it is not the governor, it will be the lieutenant governor, another state-wide officer, or perhaps the legislative leaders. That a governor would willingly surrender opportunities for favorable publicity to possible competitors is extremely unlikely. Governor Thompson enjoys this role.

The press continuously turns to the governor for comments and analyses of policy proposals, legislative actions, and the state's economy. From press conferences to quick responses to questions to more detailed

---

[5]   Governor Randall became Postmaster General under President Andrew Johnson and Governor Rusk became the first Secretary of Agriculture in 1889. Governors Robert M. LaFollette, Sr., Blaine, and Nelson went on to the Senate. Governors Salomon, Fairchild, Washburn, McGovern, and the younger Kohler were unsuccessful in efforts to win Senate seats. To demonstrate the relative political prestige of the offices, no incumbent Senator has run for governor in Wisconsin .

interviews, the governor spends considerable time communicating to the public through the media. The ability to portray a strong positive image is a very big plus.

With increased emphasis on economic development, the governor increasingly has headed delegations of business executives to other nations aimed at expanding exports for Wisconsin firms. Governor Thompson has traveled to Asia and Europe on trade missions. Some legislators have questioned whether these trips' benefits exceed their costs. The governor meets with business leaders in Wisconsin and other states to encourage them to move to or expand in Wisconsin. Governor Thompson in particular has focused on being the "salesman of the state."

Chief Executive. The Wisconsin Constitution prescribes that the executive power of the state is vested in the governor. It further specifies that "he shall expedite all such measures as may be resolved upon by the legislature, and shall take care that the laws be faithfully executed." This broad language would seem to be a sufficient authorization of power. Yet there are several important restrictions on the governor's use of executive authority. The Constitution itself establishes four other administrative positions: the secretary of state, the state treasurer, the attorney general, and the superintendent of public instruction, each of whom is elected by popular vote in state-wide elections. Clearly, these separately elected officials are free from formal control by the governor. Governor Thompson, in the 1995-1997 budget bill eliminated the independent Department of Public Instruction and transferred authority to a Department of Education in his administration, leaving the independently elected superintendent of public instruction essentially with no department to manage. Some transfer of authority of each of the other independently elected offices to departments under the governor's control was also granted in the 1995-97 budget bill.

Of great significance as a potential impediment to the governor's executive responsibilities are the boards and commissions which have policy-making authority over a number of state administrative activities. Boards and commissions direct such important functions as the University of Wisconsin system, and the vocational educational system, among others. They consist of members appointed to overlapping terms which are usually as long or longer than the governor's term. Under normal circumstances it takes a governor more than one full term to appoint a majority of the members of these commissions. Democratic Governor Reynolds (1963-65) found his power of appointment restricted still further by a Republican-controlled senate which refused to confirm many of his appointments. In those cases, the incumbent board member or commissioner retained his position after the expiration of his term because of the absence of a successor.

The ability of the boards and commissions to inhibit gubernatorial executive control may take many forms. One illustration occurred during Governor Rennebohm's administration (1947-51) when the governor attempted to effect economies by the use of prison-made furniture in state agencies. The Conservation Commission (now the Natural Resources Board) flatly refused to cooperate, and there was no way that the governor could convince it otherwise.

The Commission for the Study of Administrative Value and Efficiency (SAVE) Report (1995) recommended that the state secretaries of Natural Resources, Agriculture, and Veterans affairs, now appointed by advisory boards, be appointed by the governor. The Commission further recommended that the independently elected superintendent of public instruction be appointed by the governor. The elected secretary of state and the state treasurer would be abolished. Additionally, the SAVE commission recommended that the lieutenant governor would be named by the governor. Underlying these recommendations is the executive leadership model of government. Under this viewpoint the governor should be given the power to appoint all policy officials and as a consequence could be held accountable by the people for their actions. Governor Thompson in his 1995-97 budget proposal advanced several of these initiatives. He was successful in winning the authority to appoint, beginning

July 26, 1995, the secretaries of the Agriculture, Education[6], and Natural Resources departments, subject to confirmation by the State Senate.

Opposition to enhanced gubernatorial control and the authority of his Department of Administration was strong. General opposition to a strong executive has been voiced with a preference for pluralistic power as a democratic safeguard. Special constituencies such as education and natural resources, who want to remain independent of the governor's administration, also opposed stronger executive power. Thus, efficiency and coordination values must be balanced with concern for appropriate concentrations of power.

A number of state agencies are headed by administrators appointed by the governor, but there is no assurance that the appointees will be particularly attentive to the wishes of the governor. Some of them have fixed terms which are longer than the governor's term. An incoming governor, therefore, may not have the opportunity to make his own selections for these posts. Recurring battles between the state auditor and Governors Nelson and Reynolds exemplified this gubernatorial difficulty. The auditor was reappointed in 1955 for a six-year term by Republican Governor Kohler. During subsequent Democratic administrations, at the height of election campaigns, the auditor ordered audits of the Department of Administration, which was established during the Nelson administration and is directly accountable to the governor. Democrats contended that the audits were politically inspired, and Governor Nelson appointed a new auditor in 1961. However, the senate refused to confirm this nomination or subsequent ones made by Governor Reynolds. The auditor remained in office without reappointment, survived a threat of having his paycheck withheld by the Department of Administration, and finally won reappointment by Governor Knowles, a Republican, in 1965. This partisan "civil service system" operated by the Republican-controlled senate clearly hampered gubernatorial efforts to control state administration.[7]

Gradually the governor has gained greater control through the appointment of department heads directly accountable to him. Several department secretaries previously appointed by boards were made gubernatorial appointments by Governor Thompson's 1995-1997 biennial budget. Now he is authorized to appoint most department heads who in turn name second line officials in the departments, including division heads who, prior to legislation approved at the recommendation of Governor Earl, were under civil service law, insulating them from the governor and department secretary. The change reflects the argument that these administrators, by controlling daily and long-term agency activity, should be responsive to the governor and his cabinet secretary.

In addition to appointments, the governor has other weapons to control state administration. Primary among these is his budget power. The power of budget formulation can be an effective club to force the governor's wishes upon agencies or administrators. With the assistance of the Department of Administration, governors have prepared biennial budgets for submission to the legislature at the start of its regular session (January of odd-numbered years). Some governors have submitted changes to the biennial budget in the second year of the biennium. This approach received statutory authorization in 1971. Although anticipated to be mere adjustments, these review bills vastly increased in size, reaching 458 pages in 1980, one of the largest bills submitted to the legislature. The legislature decided to end this procedure, repealing the budget review statute in the 1981-82 budget act. Nonetheless, even with the repeal the governor found it necessary to alter the budget to respond to changing economic conditions and several budget adjustment acts were submitted by the governor and approved by the legislature (Theobald, 1985:171-173).

---

[6] On March 29, 1996, The Wisconsin Supreme Court unanimously ruled in the action of *Thompson v. Craney* that provisions of the 1995 Wisconsin Act 27 (the 1995-97 state budget) related to restructuring the governance of the Department of Public Instruction are unconstitutional.

[7] The audit function has since been transferred to the legislative branch

In contrast to past governors, Governor Thompson wanted to put Wisconsin's budget on an annual basis to allow the formulation of the budget to take into consideration the latest information and not to have to make a two-year projection of needs and revenue. Opponents of his proposal argued that annual budgeting would result in the legislature spending too much time on the budget each year, in neglecting other policy concerns, and in having to battle interests wanting a larger share of the budget every year rather than every other year. The compromise reached between Governor Thompson and the legislature is that he will continue the practice of submitting budgets covering two years, but can submit a revision covering the second year. The second year budget must be acted upon by the legislature.

Agencies such as the Departments of Transportation and Natural Resources, which have extensive pools of earmarked funds, or those which are recipients of substantial amounts of federal funds, such as the Department of Health and Social Services, or the authorities, such as the Housing and Economic Development Authority, which raise much of their own funds, may feel a degree of immunity from gubernatorial control commensurate with the extent of earmarked or outside funds at their disposal. However, no state agency is completely independent of the need for support from the governor's budget. All federal funds expended must receive gubernatorial and legislative approval.

Other management controls handled by the Department of Administration, such as centralization of purchasing, record-keeping, engineering services, personnel administration, data processing and so on, give the governor additional leverage against state line agencies. The Secretary of the Department of Administration has been given a powerful role in some administrations to manage the executive branch as well as develop policy. James Klauser, Secretary in the Thompson Administration, has been a key official. Other governors have relied more on staff in the office of governor. Proposals adopted in the 1995-97 budget would expand these management controls by the Department of Administration to other agencies including the University of Wisconsin System.

Recent governors have made some use of the cabinet concept as a device to bring together the various department and agency heads. The cabinet does not have formal legal status, nor has it been convened on a regularly scheduled basis. At this point it appears to be primarily a communications device for the governor rather than a body actively involved in policy formulation. This body is likely to become more significant given the increase in the number of department heads subject to direct gubernatorial control. But if the Presidential model is any guide, the Cabinet will not become significant in policy development.

Increasingly, Wisconsin governors have exercised their executive power through the issuance of executive orders. Often the source of authority for these orders is unspecified. Some orders are issued to carry out a law, which stipulates the executive order as the means of statutory implementation (King, 1980:341). But many other orders have no authorization in law but are assumed to be legal by the implications of the general "executive power" provided the governor in the state's Constitution (Wisconsin Constitution, Art. V, Sec. 1).

Most conflict over executive orders has come when they resemble legislation, seemingly violating Wisconsin's Constitution (Art. IV, Sec. 17), which reads, "No law shall be enacted except by bill." This brings the governor into contention with the legislature. For example, Governor Dreyfus vetoed part of a nursing home bill because he disapproved of the administrative structure established by the bill. Subsequently, Governor Dreyfus issued an executive order, implementing an alternative program (King, 1980:354).

Similar conflicts have occurred when a more formal administrative action, called a rule, is issued. Governor Thompson had vetoed legislation raising the state's minimum wage. Through a rule, issued by the Department of Industry, Labor, and Human Relations, the minimum wage was raised but included a provision allowing employers to pay a lesser amount for the first 120 days of employment, known as a training wage, an approach that had been rejected by the legislature. The legislature, through its Joint Committee on Administrative Rules, voted to reduce the training wage for an inconsequential three days. The governor responded by directing his departments to ignore the legislative action and allow the full 120 day training wage. As can be seen, the executive power to issue orders and rules brings the governor into conflict with the legislature, often raising constitutional issues.

In general, although the power of the governor as "chief executive" would imply that the governor acts as "manager" of the state administration, reality in Wisconsin and other states challenges this. Governors sporadically become involved, but remain aloof on a daily basis, leaving the administrative tasks to department heads (Rosenthal, 1990: 170).

The Governor in the Legislative Process. Despite strictures of the separation of executive and legislative powers, chief executives in the twentieth century have come to be the single most important participants in the legislative process (Beyle and Dalton, 1983:125). Legislators in Wisconsin have come to expect that governors will present a policy agenda. This does not imply that legislators will enact the administration's proposals, but expect that governors will exercise policy leadership. In years in which the governor has failed to meet legislator expectations, the legislature has not done very well in establishing their own programmatic direction. The Senate majority leader at the time, William Bablitch, tried to do this during the Dreyfus administration but was not very successful.

Formally, the governor's entrance into the legislative process occurs through 1) messages to the legislature, 2) the executive budget, 3) vetoes of legislative enactments, 4) calling special sessions of the legislature, and 5) calling special elections to fill legislative vacancies. A constitutional directive requires that the governor "communicate to the legislature, at every session, the condition of the state, and recommend such matters to them for their consideration as he may deem expedient" (Wisconsin Constitution, Art. V, Sec. 4). Recommendations at this stage typically are non-specific exhortations to deal with expressed state problems. This "State of the State" address is customarily delivered by the governor before the legislature during the first week of its session in January. It is augmented by other messages, including the one accompanying the budget, given personally or sent by the governor. Typically these additional messages identify state problems and recommend specific solutions. The package of such recommendations makes up the basic outline of the governor's program. The messages receive a great deal of media coverage.

As part of the process of developing policy proposals, recent governors especially have made extensive use of task forces, blue ribbon panels, or other groups to study particular policy areas. The groups are usually created at the governor's discretion to explore and report on subjects that he considers important. Appointed by the governor, the members of such groups are typically prominent citizens, representatives of interested organizations, and appropriate state officials. The resulting reports, produced with the assistance of a hired staff, frequently form the basis of gubernatorial policy recommendations. Such groups have played important roles in executive reorganization (described more fully in the following chapter), judiciary reform, and more recently economic development, education reform, and administrative efficiency initiatives.

As previously noted, the governor's power to formulate the budget (executive budget) brings him into the legislative process when his proposed budget is submitted for legislative scrutiny. While the legislature can and does make changes in the governor's budget, the governor's prerogative of budget initiation gives him an advantage in legislative deliberation on the budget. Taking advantage of the budget initiative, governors frequently include substantive policies in the budget bill. As a consequence, the 1995-97 budget bill was 2,600 pages, including many substantive policy proposals.

Much debate has transpired over the appropriateness of this. Supporters claim that including policy in the budget is appropriate, given the close ties between policy and budgetary allocations. Others question the practice for it allows major policy changes to be buried in a large document, hindering public scrutiny (Rom and Witte,

1988: 17). In some years the legislature has extracted substantive policy from the budget to be considered separately.

The Veto and the Partial Veto. Following the passage of bills by the legislature, the governor has the opportunity to veto the entire bill, sending it back to the legislature which at its next session may override the veto by a two-thirds vote of both houses. A written message stating reasons for the veto is included. These messages are published in the Journal of the day and in a separate veto review bulletin. If the bill appropriates money, the governor has the additional power to veto parts of the bill, returning it to the legislature for possible override.

The partial veto, unique to Wisconsin, was added to the Wisconsin Constitution in 1930. The partial veto allows the governor a more selective veto, permitting him to negate "parts" of an appropriations bill while approving the remainder. The practice of the legislature to enact an omnibus appropriation bill rather than separate appropriation bills for different functions, begun in the 1911 legislative session and continued in the 1913 legislature, lead Governor Francis E. McGovern to recommend the adoption of a constitutional amendment permitting the governor to veto separate items in the appropriations bill. It wasn't until 1927 that the first of the two constitutionally required approvals of a constitutional amendment adding a more extensive veto power received its first legislative assent. At the same time as the creation of the veto power, the legislature adopted the executive budget system in Wisconsin, where the governor formulates the budget and then sends it to the legislature. The voters approved the partial veto power in the 1930 election, making it Article V, Section 10 of the Wisconsin Constitution. At the time of the referendum, Phillip LaFollette opposed the partial veto amendment in his 1930 campaign for governor, arguing that it "smacked of dictatorship," resulting in an excessive centralization of power in the hands of the governor (Legislative Reference Bureau, January, 1989:4).

Wisconsin's partial veto is unique. At the time of Wisconsin's adoption of the partial veto in 1930, 37 other states gave their governors the power of the "item" veto. Today, 43 states have this provision. For the item veto, a governor must restrict his disapproval to an entire item or section in a bill. As interpreted, the partial veto allows a governor to veto words, digits (such as changing an appropriation of $51 million to $1 million by vetoing the 5), or letters of words to form new words. The veto's more "creative" use developed slowly. In 1931 it was applied to a single paragraph, in 1935 to two sentences, in 1961 to a portion of a sentence, and in 1965 to a complete multi digit figure. Governor Lucey was the first to use the partial veto for single digits in 1971 and for words to change the meaning of a passage, known as the editing veto. Both Acting Governor Schreiber and Governor Dreyfus used the partial veto extensively to change legislative intent. But in 1983 Governor Earl further expanded its used by selectively vetoing letters to form a new word or digits to form a new number, referred to by legislators as the "Vanna White Veto" after the assistant, who turns letters on the game board, on the T.V. game show "Wheel of Fortune."

In 1991 Governor Thompson added another method of using the partial veto. The governor vetoed spending passed by the legislature as had been done in the past, but in this case wrote in his own lower numbers. He used this "write-in" veto 30 times in 1991 and nine times in 1993. Governor Thompson justified this partial veto use because he was vetoing "part" of the appropriated amount. Opposition Democrats charged that the write-in item reduction exceeded the constitutional authority given to the governor.

There is no indication in the historical record that there was an intention to give Wisconsin governors more power through the partial veto than other state governors had with the item veto. Nonetheless, the result certainly achieves this. Though restricted to appropriations bills, the partial veto has even a greater significance than changing funding would suggest. This is because governors and legislators have included major policy proposals in the budget. The purpose of legislative strategy is to ease the management of legislation since one bill is simpler than a multiple of separate authorizing legislation. Second, the single bill facilitates compromises among different substantive provisions (Gosling, 1985:459). Thus although technically the partial veto is restricted to appropriation

158

bills, its application is far greater. Most partial vetoes have been exercised for policy or partisan reasons rather than out of financial concerns (Burke, 1989: 142).

The Wisconsin Supreme Court through several cases affirmed the constitutionality of the partial veto's use. Ironically, the first test of the partial veto was a case brought against its use by Phillip LaFollette, who had originally opposed the partial veto (*State ex rel. Wisconsin Telephone Co. v. Henry*, 1935). In another test, the Court supported the controversial use of the veto by acting Governor Schreiber when through selectively vetoing words he was able to change the public financing of elections from individuals having to add a dollar to their taxes to be put into the campaign fund to allowing citizens to earmark a dollar from their taxes to go to the fund without increasing their taxes (*State ex rel. Kleczka v. Conta*, 1978). Governor Thompson's 290 partial vetoes of the 1987-89 Budget Bill, including digit, selective word, and selective letter vetoes brought him into confrontation with the legislature whose leaders challenged him in court arguing that this use of the partial veto violated separation of powers by allowing the governor to create law rather than review it for acceptability. In a 4-3 decision, the Wisconsin Supreme Court affirmed his use as constitutionally appropriate (*State ex rel., Wisconsin Senate, et al. v. Thompson*, 1988). The Court wrote that as long the resulting law after the vetoes was a complete and workable law and that what is left was germane to the subject matter of the vetoed provisions, the governor could selectively use the veto. The court was more divided on this decision than the previous five partial veto cases, all of which had no more than one justice in dissent. Justice Bablitch in dissent showed by way of example how the vetoing of letters in a criminal statute could enact the death penalty, a result never intended by the legislature (Loftus, 1994: 73). A further challenge to the partial veto, citing U.S. Constitutional grounds of due process (14th Amendment), has been rejected for hearing by the Wisconsin Supreme Court and denied by the Federal Court.

In 1988 the voters approved a constitutional amendment that disallows the governor from using the partial veto to reject individual letters in the words of a bill. More extensive limitations, such as a movement to a true item veto, recommended by some legislators, was rejected by the legislature in favor of this compromise limitation.

Based upon the Wisconsin court interpretations and the constitutional amendment to the partial veto provision of the state constitution, four conditions (Burke, 1989: 1427) must be met for a partial veto to be valid:

(1) The veto must be exercised on an appropriations bill.
(2) The text remaining must constitute a complete, entire, and workable law.
(3) The law remaining must be germane to the subject of the original bill.
(4) Single letters may not be vetoed.

Without further litigation or constitutional amendment, the legislature can eliminate the power of the Governor to change policy through the use of the partial veto by considering substantive policy in a bill that does not include appropriations. Since the partial veto can be exercised only on appropriation bills, the governor's power would be restricted to approving or negating the entire non-appropriation, policy bill (Burke, 1989: 1428). A tactic of legislators to allow a partial veto on a bill is to amend any bill to include a small appropriated sum. By doing this the bill becomes an "appropriations bill" subject to the governor's strong partial veto.

Table VII-6 records the use of vetoes by governors and the frequency of legislative overrides, requiring a two-thirds majority vote of each house of the state legislature. It is evident that the use of the total veto has not increased, showing a decline in the last decade. In contrast, the partial veto has been exercised more in recent times. Nonetheless, only a small percent of the bills enacted per session are negated in whole or in part by governors. Budget bills are most likely to be partially vetoed, with a large number of elements negated by the governor. For example, Governor Thompson exercised 112 partial vetoes in the 1995-1997 state budget. The actual exercise of the veto is only part of the story, however, as its availability can be used as leverage to get what the governor wants prior to the passage of legislation. As Table VII-6 indicates, few vetoed bills are overridden. Governors even with a legislative majority of the opposition party are able to sustain their veto, though more vetoes do often lead to more successful overrides. Nationally, there has been a mild trend of more successful legislative overrides of governor's vetoes (Beyle, 1990: 233). In Wisconsin under Governor Thompson, the veto has not been overridden. In a few instances, the legislature reenacted a vetoed bill rather than override Governor Thompson's action with the governor signing the new bill thus keeping his veto record perfect.

   <u>Governor's Other Legislative Powers</u>. The governor may call the legislature into special session. This power is enhanced by the constitutional provision that the resultant session is restricted to matters indicated by the governor in his call. It has been suggested that a shrewd chief executive can use this power for his own political gain, either to dramatize an issue in which he is especially interested and/or to embarrass the legislature into taking favorable action on those interests. To some degree the impact of this weapon is diminished by the increasingly longer legislative sessions and by the legislative tactic of recessing rather than adjourning.[8] Nonetheless since special sessions can be convened at anytime, even when the legislature is in regular session, governors still call the special session to highlight particular issues as evidenced by the frequent resort to special sessions in the 1980s. Though, as former Assembly Speaker Thomas Loftus stated, "It is the legislature's power to act or not act, to convene and then adjourn to a more convenient time, and if it acts, to arrive at any solution to the problems it wishes." (Rosenthal, 1990: 8). Finally, the governor has a formal impact on the legislature through his power to call special elections to fill vacancies in legislative seats. This has not been particularly significant, until recently, because of the few vacancies which develop in any given term, but it is a device that can be used, or in some cases not used, for partisan advantage. Delaying or refusing to call an election in a district dominated by partisan foes would be one manifestation of the entrance of political factors in this process. The closer the legislative partisan division, the more important this power is. In the most dramatic impact, Republican Governor Thompson, in early 1993, appointed a Democratic state senator to his administration resulting in a legislative vacancy in the district. After a special election was held in this and two other districts in which there were exceptionally large campaign expenditures, the Republicans by capturing two of the three seats were able to change the partisan majority in the state senate from Democratic to Republican.

Table VII-6

Gubernatorial Vetoes in Wisconsin, 1933 - 93

| | | | | Overrides of Bills Partially Vetoed | |
Year	Total Bill Vetoes	Total Bill Vetoes Overridden	Bills Partially Vetoed	Entire Veto	Part of Veto
1933-1943	91	0	11	0	0
1943-1952	115	28	6	3	0
1953-1962	209	10	11	0	0
1963-1971	180	9	29	0	0
1973-1982	101	15	79	1	12
1983-1988	48	0	30	0	1
1989-1993	76	0	65	0	0

---

  [8] Another reason for the use of recesses rather than adjournment was to keep the governor from making interim appointments.

Note: Partial Vetoes are the number of bills on which the governed negatived part of the bill. It does *not* refer to the number of partial vetoes exercised on each of these bills. For the biennial budget many partial vetoes are used.

Source: State of Wisconsin, *Blue Book*: 1993-94.

These formal powers, with the exception of the partial veto and budgetary initiation, have been held by Wisconsin governors since statehood. Yet the governor's legislative role has increased much more than the increase in formal powers would suggest. In essence, norms regarding the governor's role as policy leader have changed with an enhanced belief that the governor's program should set the framework of the legislative session. Thus, the largest blocks of time in legislative deliberations are typically given to the governor's proposed budget and policy recommendations.

Factors Related to the Governor's Legislative Success. Governors vary as to their legislative success. Several factors have been shown to relate to the receptivity of the legislature to the governor's proposals. Most significant is party balance in the legislature. Governors facing a legislative majority of the opposition party, a frequent occurrence in recent Wisconsin history, will have more difficulty. Additionally, governors winning by a large majority and those having favorable public support will have an easier time. Lastly, receptivity is enhanced if the governor is liked personally by legislators, a situation more likely, although not exclusively, to be the case with governors who were former legislators. These governor's have the best grasp of the pressures legislators are under and personally know a large number of legislators.

Receptivity to the governor's initiatives is important to a governor gaining success with the administration's program, but to have bills enacted over several sessions, additional factors need to be considered. Most notably, the governor must introduce bills that many legislators accept on their merits. If the governor's proposals are not widely accepted, some will pass through pressuring legislators to vote favorably, but success through this approach typically is limited. Further, successful governors have significant skills of negotiation and persuasion. Governors also use patronage, although Wisconsin less than many other states, and agree to legislator wishes to include funds for certain items in the executive budget. Without question, the governor spends considerable time in the legislative role. Evaluation of success of an administration is tied to the governor's ability to get his proposals enacted so much that it would be appropriate to characterize the contemporary chief executive as the "legislative governor."

Wisconsin governors have shown leadership in recommending innovative programs that other states have sought to follow. In the current era, the emphasis has been on economic development, tax reform, spending limitations, and business loans, among others have been intended to improve Wisconsin's "business climate." These measures have achieved some degree of success according to rankings by national business groups. Governor Thompson's welfare reform initiatives have also received national prominence.

Another factor of twentieth century state government is that major legislation increasingly emanates from executive agencies. Even though the governor may not have complete control over all the units within the executive establishment, the chief executive is partially judged by what they do. Further, agency recommendations of legislation may have fiscal implications for future budgets, a vital concern of the governor.

Judicial Responsibilities. Though much less extensive than either executive or legislative functions, the governor's responsibilities exert a direct impact on the state's judiciary and the governor himself plays a judicial role. The governor is solely responsible for filling interim vacancies on the state supreme court, the court of appeals, and the circuit courts. The combination of relatively long judicial terms--ten years for supreme court judges and six years for appeals and circuit court judges--and mandatory retirement at age 70 enhances the likelihood that vacancies will occur. At the present time, four of the seven supreme court justices were originally gubernatorial appointees. An appointee must then run for election at the next spring election at which no other

161

supreme court seat is contested, but appointment gives the advantage of incumbency. Only once in the past 30 years has an incumbent supreme court justice been defeated. Similarly, incumbency is of advantage to circuit court appointees although appointed circuit court judges have had a more difficult time winning election than those initially elected have had in being reelected.

On occasion the governor performs certain functions which are judicial in nature. County administrative officers may be removed by the governor after a hearing at which the accused officer has an opportunity to answer the charges brought. The governor is solely responsible for deciding if persons in Wisconsin are to be extradited to face criminal charges in other states. Additionally, the powers of executive clemency to grant pardons, reprieves, or commutation of sentences to persons convicted of criminal offenses are the governor's. A Pardon Advisory Board makes recommendations to the governor on executive clemency. Early parole is sometimes granted to free up space in the state's prisons. The governor is required to inform the legislature annually of details relating to each exercise of this power.

Commander in Chief. The governor is designated commander in chief of the military and naval forces of Wisconsin and exercises control over the Wisconsin National Guard through his appointee, the adjutant general. The Army and Air Guard of Wisconsin make up a security force available to the governor to deal with civil emergencies and disasters which exceed the capacities of county and municipal authorities. The guard may also be called into federal service to augment regular national armed forces during war or emergency. When so called, the guard is under the President's command. The political significance of this gubernatorial role is not generally very great, but there have been occasions when the use of the state's military forces has affected the political standing of the governors involved.

During the Civil War the governor's involvement in Wisconsin's contribution to the war was extensive. The governor was responsible for raising the state's quota of fighting men and equipping them with necessary supplies.[9] Governor Salomon (1862-64) also used the state's military forces to quell anti-war demonstrations in Ozaukee County and to meet the rumored threats of a massive Indian uprising in northwestern Wisconsin. Salomon's predecessor, Governor Harvey, was a Civil War casualty. He led an expedition to Tennessee to provide medical assistance for Wisconsin troops wounded at Shiloh. On the return trip, he fell from a steamboat and was drowned.

Since the Civil War, gubernatorial use of military force has been limited to meeting threats to domestic tranquility within the state. Governor Rusk (1882-89) sent the militia to Milwaukee to end a riot of workers who agitated for an eight-hour working day. During the Great Depression, Governor Schmedeman (1933-35) twice sent troops to quell disturbances caused by economic strife. The first occurred when farmers, incensed over low prices for dairy products, blockaded highways to prevent the distribution of milk. Similarly, troops were used during a particularly violent strike in 1934. No matter how objectively a governor weighs a decision to send troops in such instances, this action may be interpreted by one side or the other or both as unwarranted favoritism for employer or laborer, for farmer or consumer. Thus in Schmedeman's case, it is argued that he alienated substantial portions of the farm and labor vote, and these losses contributed to his defeat in 1934. Recent uses of the Guard occurred in connection with student demonstrations, the 1967 disturbance in Milwaukee's inner city, the Indian takeover at Gresham, the strike of state employees in 1977, and the Milwaukee firefighters strikes in 1981.

The Governor as Partisan. In addition to his formal roles in state government, the governor also has an important role as a leader of his party. Holding the state's highest office, the governor is automatically the titular head of his party in the state. Whether he can parlay this status into actual leadership of his party varies greatly from governor to governor. Some, like the elder La Follette, have been in firm command of their party. Others

---

[9]   Now the state's national guard is completely provisioned by the federal government.

have exerted much less influence because of competition from other powerful figures in the party or because of personal shortcomings in the art of wielding control over fellow partisans. The nadir of ineffectual gubernatorial control over his own party was reached by Governor Zimmerman (1927-29). At a time when the two factions of the Republican party competed fiercely for dominance, Zimmerman steered a middle course which alienated both factions. Seeking renomination in 1928, Zimmerman finished a distant third in the Republican primary.

Several characteristics of the office of governor in Wisconsin militate against efforts of governors to become strong party leaders. The sinews of party control are traditionally found in the power of patronage. The fact that the governor of Pennsylvania, for example, traditionally had some 50,000 appointments at his disposal did much to give him a preeminent role as his party's leader in that state. By comparison, the Wisconsin governor's appointment power is extremely limited. The governor does have a host of positions on state boards and commissions which he can fill, but as noted earlier these governing bodies are characterized by staggered terms which usually results in only a small number of appointments in any given year. Moreover, most of them pay little if any salary; thus, they are important as patronage plums only in an honorific sense. In addition, most of these positions require senatorial confirmation, and a governor may be reluctant to expose a zealous partisan to the cross-examination of unsympathetic senators. On the operating levels of state government, apart from department or agency heads and their deputies and his own staff, the opportunities for gubernatorial patronage are limited. The "civil service reform" act of 1977 increased the governor's appointment authority somewhat, but merit civil service provisions still cover most positions in state agencies. Nonetheless, criticism of increasing use of patronage in Wisconsin has been voiced though the number of patronage positions remains small in comparison to other states.

Many governors also face a major dilemma with respect to party involvement. Since the office does not contain the kind of power which automatically guarantees the incumbent the premier position within his party, it is necessary to work consciously at the task of being a party leader by use of persuasion and influence. To do this, however, is to risk alienating lukewarm members of the party, the uncommitted and those members of the opposition who contributed to the governor's electoral triumph and whose continued support may be essential in any bid for re-election. The dilemma produced by the often conflicting ingredients necessary to control partisan machinery as against those necessary to hold the support of a large numbers of voters, who are often openly suspicious of extensive party involvement, is especially pronounced in a state where the major parties are roughly equal in electoral strength. Basically, this was Governor Nelson's problem during his tenure in office from 1959 to 1963. The first Democratic governor in 24 years and the first Democrat to win re-election in the twentieth century, Nelson depended upon strong support from voters independent of the major parties as well as dissident Republicans who were attracted by Nelson's personality. The same characteristics which made him attractive to non-Democrats hampered him in his dealings with many Democratic party workers. When Nelson made an effort to wrest control of the party from a state party chairman, his effort was doomed to failure.

In another case, the career of Governor Robert M. La Follette, Sr. demonstrated how a magnetic personality could hold party or factional control as governor and also preclude subsequent governors from exercising the same power. La Follette, through his role as ideological spokesman for progressivism, bound his supporters closely to him; though he decried political bossism, he accomplished a degree of control over his adherents which would be the envy of many would-be bosses. When he went to Washington as U.S. Senator in 1906, he did not relinquish this hold. Thus, succeeding governors, drawn from the progressive wing of the Republican party, found their party leadership role curtailed by La Follette's continued domination.

Reducing the relationship between the governor and the party organization in the present era is the common practice of gubernatorial candidates maintaining a candidate centered campaign organization, independent of the party organization (Bibby, et al., 1990: 105). The actual relationship between the governor and the party organization has varied. For example, Governor Dreyfus kept the Republican party at arm's length while Governor Thompson, also a Republican, has maintained close ties with the party organization.

The Governor's Staff. At one time governors operated with very few staff members, relying almost exclusively on the departments. Although governors still depend heavily on the departments, especially the Department of Administration, whose secretary has on occasion been called "the second governor", the number of staff aids in the executive office has expanded. For example in 1975 there were approximately 26 employees of the executive staff and residence, increasing to 45 in 1993. Spending for the governor's office, like that of the legislature and the courts, may exceed budgeted amounts. These agencies can spend as much as they deem necessary to do the job, with the budgeted amount serving as a non-binding goal.

Most clearly defined positions are those concerned with press relations, those concerned with lobbying the legislature (typically called legislative affairs or liaison persons), and those involved with assisting the governor in making personnel appointments. Additionally, governors have a legal counsel as well as several staff individuals involved with policy analysis. Democratic Governor Earl supplemented the traditional staff with advisors on minority affairs (Women, Black, Hispanic, and Indian), an approach rejected by his Republican successor, Governor Thompson.

The Governor in National Politics. Activity of governors in national politics is usually a potential role flowing from gubernatorial service rather than one linked to his normal responsibilities as governor. These potential roles include subsequent careers in prestigious federal positions and an impact upon the process of presidential nomination and election. Overall the record made by Wisconsin governors in these endeavors has not been particularly impressive. As previously noted, only two went on to federal cabinet appointments, and both of these were nineteenth century governors. Failure to advance into presidential cabinets results from a variety of factors, basic among which is undoubtedly the personality and character of the governor concerned. In addition, politics in Wisconsin from 1900 to 1950 was out of step with national politics. While Democrats served in the White House for about one-half of the years, Wisconsin did not have a viable Democratic party. On the other hand the Progressives, either as a large faction of the Republican party or as a third party, were not likely to be rewarded by presidents of either party. By chance, every governor drawn from the conservative wing of the state's Republican party during this period was an industrialist capping a successful business career with public service in the governor's chair. They were not likely candidates for subsequent federal appointments.

On another level of involvement in national politics, no Wisconsin governor has ever won a major party nomination for president or vice president. Governor Rusk, later Secretary of Agriculture, purportedly was a strong contender for the Republican presidential nomination in 1888. Governor Robert M. La Follette sought the Progressive party nomination in 1912 and ran as an independent on a progressive platform in 1924.[10] Similarly, former Governor Lucey ran for vice president with John Anderson in 1980. Some of the reasons outlined above contribute to the absence of Wisconsinites on the national tickets of major parties. In addition, the state simply lacks the population base that would rank it with New York, California, Texas, Ohio, and other large states as an incubator for national candidates.

One area of active governor involvement has been in the national conferences of governors. Both the National Governors' Association and the party specific governor's conference have had strong participation by Wisconsin chief executives with Governor Thompson serving as chair of the National Governors' Association. The Association has developed recommendations for the states in several policy areas including education and welfare reform.

The increased importance of intergovernmental grants and the expansion of Federal legislation affecting states has led some to refer to a new role of governors as "intergovernmental middlemen" (Beyle, 1990: 235).

---

[10]   He carried Wisconsin and finished second in eleven states.

Governor Thompson has secured many waivers from federal rules, especially in the AFDC program, to allow Wisconsin flexibility in implementing intergovernmental programs. Thompson hopes that Wisconsin's "experiments" will serve as a model for the nation. With the election of a Republican U.S. Congress, legislation is anticipated to devolve many of these programs to the states, reducing federal requirements. To this end, Governor Thompson has testified at Congressional hearings pointing to the Wisconsin experience.

The Lieutenant Governor

Closely linked to the governor is the lieutenant governor, a position whose only constitutionally specified role is to succeed the governor in case of the governor's death, resignation, or disability and to serve as governor when the latter is not in the state. The authority to preside over the state senate was removed by constitutional amendment in 1979. Informally, he may be granted other responsibilities by the governor. As examples, Lieutenant Governor Schreiber was designated as ombudsman for nursing homes, while Russell Olson, a Racine County farmer, was named as liaison for urban affairs by Governor Dreyfus. Lieutenant Governor James Flynn was appointed by Governor Earl to serve simultaneously as Secretary of the Department of Development to emphasize economic development concerns of his administration.

With the reduced constitutionally designated function of the lieutenant governor, a reasonable case can be made for the elimination of the office with gubernatorial succession falling to either other state-wide elected officers or legislative leaders. With the occupants of these other offices frequently not being from the governor's party, it is doubtful that abolition of lieutenant governor's post will occur.

As previously mentioned, since 1970 the governor and lieutenant governor are elected on a single ticket. The change was made to offset the difficulties arising from the elections of a governor and lieutenant governor of opposite parties. This occurred three times during the 1960s, raising the possibility of a shift in partisan control of the governor's office in the event of the death or disability of the governor.[11] It also produced a minor vexation for governors who were reluctant to have lieutenant governors of the other party serving as governor even during the governor's brief absences from the state.

By tying the two offices together, the role of the lieutenant governor may be enhanced since a governor may be willing to delegate responsibilities to the person who has run with him on the same ticket. However, there will remain the possibility that the governor and his running mate do not represent the same faction of the party. Clearly the pattern of national ticket building points toward that result. In Wisconsin, moreover, the gubernatorial nominee does not select his running mate as is done at national conventions. Each is nominated in separate contests in the September primary. Under such circumstances it is even more likely that the governor and lieutenant governor will not be close political allies. Then if a succession occurs, it might produce a change in leadership as great as if partisan control had shifted.

Conclusion

The National Governor's Association has compared governors according to formal powers including how long a governor can serve (tenure potential), the power of appointment and removal, control over the budget formulation and execution, the power of the legislature to change the governor's recommended budget, the governor's veto power, and whether the governor's party controls the legislature. Based upon these formal powers,

---

[11] This occurred once in the six successions of a lieutenant governor. Lt. Governor Goodland, a Republican, took the office in 1943 upon the death of Governor-elect Loomis, a Progressive.

the Wisconsin Governor is placed in the high moderate category (receiving 22 of 29 points), but with 25 other states being considered as strong or very strong (Beyle, 1990:217-230). Formal powers though are only potential powers. Governors' abilities to convert formal to actual powers differs as do their abilities to lead and persuade.

Wisconsin's median formal powers status among states in 1990, though, represents an increased power position from the 1965 classification as weak gubernatorial powers. The reorganization of Wisconsin's executive branch, the lengthening the governor's term, the increased use of executive orders, and the increasingly creative use of the partial veto have strengthened the governor's power base. Counter to this trend has been the frequent differences in party control of the governorship and the legislature. The same party controlled both branches of government less than half the time in the last decade.

CHAPTER VIII

STATE ADMINISTRATION

By Donald B. Vogel[*]

Wisconsin state government is a huge enterprise. It is by far the largest employer within the state. Moreover, its operations are administered by a variety of agencies, ranging from relatively small offices to huge departments which annually expend billions of dollars of public funds. The enterprise is also characterized by geographic dispersal of its personnel and agencies. State offices and institutions are present in every corner of the state, from Kenosha to Superior, from Marinette to Platteville.

This chapter explores the administration of this extensive undertaking. It focuses on the various patterns of organization found in Wisconsin's state government, how the administrative process operates in the effort to achieve policy objectives, and how the process is controlled by the representatives of the people of the state. It places emphasis, therefore, on the roles played within the administrative establishment by the agencies themselves, the governor, and the legislature.

Throughout the twentieth century, Wisconsin government has continued to grow in the number and size of its operations. Traditional functions have expanded and new areas of activity have been entered into in response to recognized needs for services. For example, in 1900, the total work force of the state Railroad Commission consisted of the commissioner, a deputy commissioner, and a janitor.[1] As its name indicated, it was then responsible only for the regulation of railroads. Through the years it took on additional responsibilities, and in 1931 its name was changed to the Public Service Commission to reflect its broadened scope of activities. As the principal regulator of public utilities, it now exercises rate-making and other regulatory authority over the many electric, gas, telephone, and water utilities in the state. The Commission now employs over 180 persons. The state has entered other service and regulatory areas in response to technological developments as in its extensive activities related to highway, motor vehicles, and aeronautics -- while changes in social and economic outlook have prompted the state's entry into such areas as employment relations, problems of the aged and developmentally disabled, and the protection of human rights.

Civil Service

Table VIII-1 demonstrates the growth in the number of state employees since 1906. A small number of agencies employ the bulk of state personnel. At present the six largest units -- the University of Wisconsin System (30,750), the Department of Health and Social Services (7,654), the Department of Corrections (5,414), the Department of Transportation (4,052), the Department of Natural Resources (3,132), and the Department of Industry, Labor and Human Relations (2,198) -- account for over 70 percent of the state's employees.[2]

State employees are categorized as classified if they are covered by the provisions of the state's merit civil service system. At present, 54 percent (40,399) are included within the classified service.

The major exceptions to the classified service are elected officials, most gubernatorial appointees, and faculty members of the University of Wisconsin System. More than 95 percent of the unclassified employees are included within the last category in which a tenure system substitutes for the merit civil service. The extensive

---

[*] Professor of Governmental Affairs, University of Wisconsin-Milwaukee.

[1] State of Wisconsin, *Blue Book*, 1952:75.

[2] State of Wisconsin, *Blue Book*, 1995-1996:401, 428, 451, 478, 522, and 533.

application of merit system principles in Wisconsin state employment reflected efforts to reduce the impact of patronage and to limit the entry of politics into the operation of state government. This development has important effects upon executive or legislative efforts to exert control over state administration. As such, the classified civil service has a pervasive influence throughout the entire structure of administrative organization.

Table VIII-1

WISCONSIN STATE EMPLOYMENT, SELECTED YEARS, 1931 - 92

Year	Total
1931	10,287
1951	17,559
1961	27,995
1971	48,292
1983	57,551
1988	66,254
1992	74,017
1994	74,687

Sources: Wisconsin Legislative Reference Service, 1962:2; State of Wisconsin, *Blue Book*, 1979-80:792; State of Wisconsin, *Blue Book*, 1989-90:764; State of Wisconsin, *Blue Book*, 1993-94:333; State of Wisconsin, *Blue Book*, 1995-96:325; U.S. Bureau of the Census, 1984:Table 9.

Four developments in recent years have had significant impact on the merit system policies and procedures. These are: 1) the increase in unionization of state employees, 2) affirmative action policies, 3) the demand for greater accountability in the state bureaucracy, and 4) comparable worth. While current trends seem to indicate an erosion of support for affirmative action and comparable worth, their effect is still substantial.

Wisconsin state employees have long had the right to form or join organizations for the purpose of representing their interests before the legislature or agency management. In fact, one organization, the Wisconsin State Administrators' Association, created in 1932, later became the American Federation of State, County and Municipal Employees (AFSCME), which is now the largest public employee union in the nation. In 1965, employee organizations had their positions enhanced through the passage of legislation which authorized collective bargaining by state employees. It is estimated that nearly 85 percent of the merit employees are under contract. Contracts produced through collective bargaining cover salary scales, fringe benefits and conditions of employment. As such, they supersede or modify civil service rules and regulations. The impact of these unions was demonstrated in 1977 when the first general strike of state employees occurred. The strike lasted 15 days before a settlement was negotiated, and it affected virtually every state agency.

Affirmative action policies intended to increase the numbers of minorities and women in public as well as private employment, have a significant impact on civil service recruiting, hiring and promotion procedures. Congressional action in 1972 applied the affirmative action requirements of the Civil Rights Act of 1964 to state and local employment. This required state agencies to prepare affirmative action plans, extend the base of recruitment efforts, and remove or modify any job examinations which test for skills which are not related directly to the job under consideration.

Increasing concern about the growth of the state civil service and a feeling by elected officials that they had insufficient control over administrative programs and personnel led to the adoption of major changes in the organization and operation of civil service functions. The impetus for change was abetted by a lengthy controversy involving the effort of the State Personnel Board to identify candidates for the position of personnel director. The reform of the civil service law, passed during the 1977 special legislative session, created a new Department of Employment Relations headed by a secretary appointed by and serving at the pleasure of the Governor. The department is responsible for many personnel functions previously handled by the Bureau of Personnel of the Department of Administration. A separate three-member Personnel Commission was created to hear appeals and promotion decisions. The old Personnel Board was retained but its activities now are largely advisory in nature.

The most controversial part of the civil service reform effort was its removal of 37 positions from the merit system. Wisconsin's merit system was one of the most far-reaching in the nation. It included most heads of divisions and bureaus within departments. The 37 exemptions included such positions in various agencies, and they are now appointed by the respective department heads. Proponents of the change argued that it would increase the responsiveness of the state bureaucracy. Opponents charged that it would establish an undesirable patronage system in the state. As is usually the case in such matters, neither the hoped for responsiveness nor the feared corrupting patronage system have been realized since these changes were enacted. However, additional exemptions have continued on the basis that the initial 37 positions were insufficient to achieve the desired results of a more responsive state administration.

Recent attention has been given both nationally and within the state to marked disparities in the rate of compensation between those civil service classifications doing comparable work. Job categories where women and/or minorities comprise a majority of the work force were generally paid at a lower rate than other categories where white males were in the majority. After the passage of legislation in 1986, intended to rectify the inequities caused by a discriminatory civil service classification system, a special task force was created to establish the specific guidelines to determine which jobs were underpaid due to discrimination. Beginning in 1987, more than 4,000 state employees received raises as a result of the comparable worth guidelines. An additional 7,000 state workers received raises in 1988. A further increase was given to all 11,000 in 1989. The substantial costs of the program have raised considerable opposition to the program and it appears that the state's future commitment will at best be muted.

Administrative Organization and Reorganization

Continued growth in the number of state administrative agencies accompanied the expansion of state operations. "Let there be an agency" was the typical response as the state entered new areas of concern. By the mid 1960s there were more than 90 separate administrative offices which had a constitutional or statutory base. Other ad hoc committees further swelled the number of units involved with state functions.

In 1967, the legislature adopted a far-reaching reorganization proposal initiated by the Temporary Commission on Executive Branch Reorganization (the Kellett Commission). This action was consistent with the administrative reorganization movement in other states and the national government. First implemented in Illinois in 1916, it was then reflected in a bevy of state "little Hoover Commission's" patterned after the attempt to reorganize the national government. Wisconsin was a late arrival to the movement because of its weak chief executive system, its emphasis on direct popular control of state government, and the strength and extent of its merit civil service system. The guiding principles of reorganization, as specified in the Wisconsin act, were: 1) to provide the governor with "the administrative facilities and the authority to carry out the functions of his office efficiently and effectively," 2) to consolidate agencies into a reasonable number of departments, 3) to integrate departments on a functional basis, 4) to recognize the "conflicting goals of administrative integration and responsiveness to the legislature," and 5) to consider reorganization a continuing process.[3]

---

[3] *Wisconsin Statutes* (1979-80), 15.001.

Agencies were consolidated on functional lines, more department heads were made directly accountable to the governor, and certain policy-making boards and commissions were reconstituted as advisory only. The act also introduced standard nomenclature for administrative units. Previously, the same designation might refer to different kinds of units in different departments, or, conversely, similar units had different designations. It was a hodgepodge produced by the fact that the units had come into existence by separate actions of the legislature over time. In descending order, the terminology is: department, division, bureau, section, and unit. Corresponding titles are given to the head of each. Multi-member bodies, advisory to divisions or bureaus, are called councils, while boards refer to those operative at the departmental level. Commissions are independent regulatory agencies or those in charge of a department or division.

Those who welcomed reorganization as a device to pare budgets and reduce the number of state employees were disappointed by the initial results of Wisconsin's reorganization. Only three agencies were abolished outright: one was an advisory board, the other two were commissions which no longer had significant functions. These agencies had had no employees or budgets for a number of years preceding their elimination.

Moreover, while reorganization was a major innovation, it ignored certain areas of state administration altogether. For example, the whole tangled area of higher education was not touched by the Act. (In 1971, however, legislation was passed which merged the university systems.) Similarly, the independent regulatory agencies were largely unaffected by reorganization although the Commission recognized that there might be advantages in restructuring them.

Even in some cases where agencies were reorganized, the changes were often paper transactions rather than basic amalgamations or consolidations. The 1967 Reorganization Act defined a series of six types of transfers of agencies. At one extreme were transfers which placed existing agencies within a department without basically altering the composition, powers, or responsibilities of the transferred agency. They remained largely independent of the department head whose authority was restricted to "budgeting, program coordination and related management functions."[4] At the other extreme was the termination of a subunit as a distinct organization. Most of the transfers involving important state agencies were the first type. The same was true as the various examining and licensing boards were placed in the Department of Regulation and Licensing.

Furthermore, since the 1967 Reorganization Act was passed, new units have been created in moves that seem to conflict with the basic philosophy of the Act. In 1971, for example, the legislature established the office of the Commissioner of Credit Unions which separated control over that function from the banking commissioner. Legislation also elevated the Division of Business Development to departmental status. In so doing, it removed that unit from the Department of Local Affairs and Development. (In 1980 the two departments were merged into a new Department of Development.) There has also been continued agitation for the separation of certain functions brought together by reorganization -- most notably in natural resources and health and social services.

It is instructive at this point to examine the state organizational structure as set forth below in Figure VIII-1. Despite the noted revisions that occurred after the 1967 reorganization, this chart reflects the seminal change instituted in that year.

Given the changes adopted by Governor Thompson's 1995-97 budget, the revisions of this structure will be such as to render the current chart unusable in much the same way the 1967 reorganization altered the state administrative structure that preceded it. Reference to Figure VIII-1 will also be useful in the discussion of patterns of organization that follows this section.

---

[4] Ibid.

Figure VIII-1

WISCONSIN STATE GOVERNMENT ORGANIZATION
January 1995

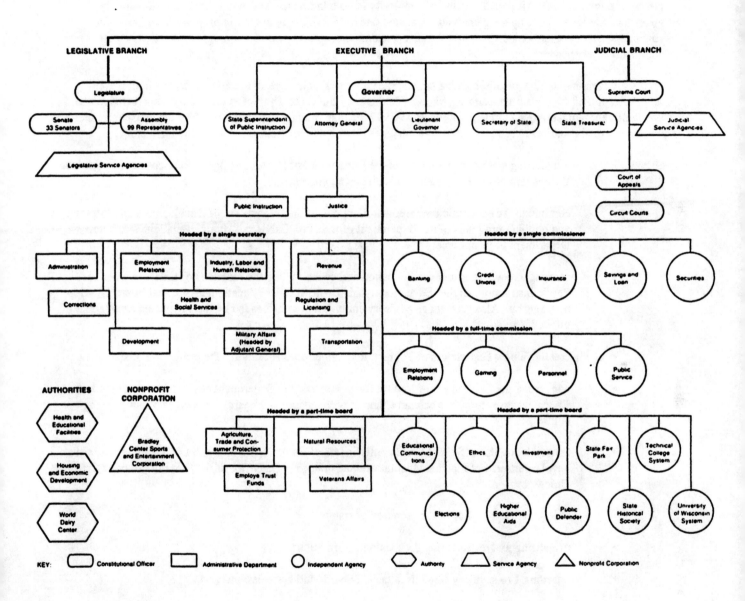

Source: State of Wisconsin, *Blue Book*, 1995-96:254-255.

At the present time, a number of events have occurred that have collectively focused attention on what promises to be a substantial alteration of state administration. Nationally, the great concern regarding the debt and deficits, coupled with the appeal of the "reinventing government" movement, has helped to focus on ways of reducing or eliminating governmental administrative activities. Sweeping electoral victories by republicans also have accelerated these efforts.

Wisconsin has been similarly affected with the unprecedented third term election of its most popular governor combined with his party's capture of a majority in both the Senate and Assembly. Additionally, the governor's pledge to make up a legislatively mandated one billion dollar reduction in property tax support for education without other tax increases has placed a premium on capturing savings through a reduction in state administrative expenses.

Given the confluence of the above factors, the current climate appears to strongly favor a major reorganization of Wisconsin state administration. To this end, Governor Thompson drafted a comprehensive and sweeping reorganization plan in his proposed 1995-1997 biennial budget. Largely passed by the legislature, the governor's plan promises to bring about historic changes in state administration. Major elements include:

- transferring welfare programs from the Department of Health and Social Services to a reorganized Department of Industry, Labor and Job Development;

- combining the economic development functions of the Department of Development and the safety and building programs of the Department of Industry, Labor and Human Relations into a new Department of Commerce;

- creating a new Department of Education and consolidating the functions of the Department of Public Instruction, Higher Educational Aids Board and the Educational Approval Board into this new agency. Also creating an advisory commission to be headed by the current superintendent of public instruction;[5]

- creating a new Department of Tourism to assume responsibility for the promotion of state parks;

- converting the Department of Natural Resources and the Department of Agriculture, Trade and Consumer Protection into cabinet agencies with the existing boards retained as policy-making entities;

- consolidating the Offices of the Commissioners of Banking, Savings and Loan, and Securities into a new Department of Financial Institutions and attaching the Office of the Commissioner of Credit Unions;

- reorganizing the office of the secretary of state;

- privatizing and restructuring the gaming commission;

- unsetting 170 statutory councils, attached boards and commissions; and,

- transferring responsibility for violent juvenile offenders to the Department of Corrections from the

---

[5] On March 29, 1996, The Wisconsin Supreme Court unanimously ruled in the action of *Thompson v. Craney* that provisions of 1995 Wisconsin Act 27 (the 1995-97 state budget) related to restructuring the governance of the Department of Public Instruction are unconstitutional. At the time of this writing and in light of the Court's decision, the legislature must further address the fate of the Higher Educational Aids Board and the Educational Approval Board.

Department of Health and Social Service while consolidating the administration of children's programs in this department and renaming it the Department of Health and Family Services.[6]

The net effect of these changes will be to complete the conversion of a weak gubernatorial system begun in earlier reorganizations; further, it will result in an unprecedented concentration of administrative control within the governor's office.

Patterns of Organization

Administrative agencies presently fit into four major organizational patterns: separate constitutional offices, administrative departments, independent agencies, and state authorities.

Separate Constitutional Offices. In addition to the governor and lieutenant governor, four state administrators are elected by state-wide ballot: the secretary of state, the state treasurer, the attorney general, and the superintendent of public instruction[7]. The latter is elected on a nonpartisan basis for a four-year term at the spring general election in the year following a presidential election. The others are elected in partisan elections in November when the governor is elected. The 1967 reorganization plan designated the attorney general and the superintendent as heads of major administrative departments which are discussed below

The Executive Office includes the governor's personal and administrative aides. Traditionally, Wisconsin's executive office was relatively small but has grown considerably in recent years. It now has more than forty employees including a professional staff headed by the governor's top aides. All positions in the executive office are filled by the governor without confirmation by the Senate, and the appointees serve at the pleasure of the governor.

The staff performs a variety of services for the governor including advice and assistance on the budget, gubernatorial appointments, and so on. Each governor organizes the executive office to suit his personality and political and administrative needs. Also attached to the executive office are a large number of boards, councils and special committees. Many of theses are ad hoc study groups created to investigate a particular problem area. Others have more permanent status and in some cases relatively large numbers of employees and budgets.

The offices of secretary of state and state treasurer are markedly similar in duties and political significance. Both offices have clerical responsibilities which are largely ministerial in nature. These functions generally do not allow the respective incumbents a great deal of discretionary authority. Thus, the office of the secretary of state is the depository for corporate records, municipal organization documents, lobbyist reports, bonds, and appointments and oaths of office of state officers. The state treasurer' s principal duties are to issue receipts for revenue received by the state, issue checks covering all payments made by the state, and have formal custody of state funds and securities.

While these offices had substantial prestige and influence during the nineteenth century, their importance and influence have greatly declined in recent decades. The general pattern has been for new activities to be assigned to new or existing agencies. In addition, functions previously held by the secretary of state or state treasurer have been transferred to other units. The 1967 Reorganization Act was consistent with this long-run development. It removed certain licensing and loan collection responsibilities from the secretary of state's office. Later the secretary's role in election administration was all but eliminated with the creation of the State Elections Board in 1973.

---

[6] State of Wisconsin, Department of Administration, Division of Executive Budget and Finance, *Budget in Brief 1995 - 1997*:2-3, 32-43.

[7] For a time, there were six elected administrators. In 1881, the offices of the Commissioner of Insurance and the Commissioner of Railroads were created as elective posts. From 1871 to 1876 there was also an elected Commissioner of Immigration. Raney, 1940:141, 410-411.

Occasionally, the secretary of state or the state treasurer have been embroiled in controversial policy matters. The most dramatic of these occurred in 1954 when the secretary of state refused to call elections under a reapportionment plan approved by the electorate in a constitutional amendment referendum. Legal steps were taken to force the secretary to act, but he was vindicated by the Wisconsin supreme court which declared invalid the constitutional amendment in question. The state treasurer entered the appointment fracas during the administration of Governor Reynolds. At one point she refused to issue payroll checks to two gubernatorial appointees. Subsequent court action overruled the state treasurer's decisions.[8]

The record of recent winners in races for these offices suggests that name identification has much more significance in deciding the outcome than it does in other election contests. This will likely result in campaigns for offices where the voter has few, if any, meaningful standards to judge the effectiveness of the officeholders.[9]

Because of the decline in importance of the offices and the potentially meddlesome role of independently elected officers, there have been frequent suggestions to eliminate the offices or make them appointive. The most recent action in this regard is included in Governor Thompson's reorganization plan, mentioned earlier, in which the office of secretary of state is virtually stripped of its functions.

<u>Administrative Departments</u>. There are fifteen administrative departments specified as follows:

<u>Headed by designated officers</u>
Justice (Attorney General)
Public Instruction (State Superintendent)
Military Affairs (Adjutant General)

<u>Headed by secretary</u>
Administration
Development
Employment Relations
Health and Social Services
Industry, Labor and Human Relations
Regulation and Licensing
Revenue
Transportation

<u>Headed by policy-making boards (number of members)</u>
Agriculture, Trade and Consumer Protection (7)
Employee Trust Funds (12)
Natural Resources (7)
Veterans Affairs (7)

Of the designated heads of departments, the attorney general and state superintendent of public instruction are elected. The adjutant general, the state's highest military officer, is appointed by the governor to a five-year term. Thus, these officials are completely or substantially beyond the governor's appointive powers.

---

[8] *State ex rel. Thompson v. Zimmerman*, 264 Wis. 644 (1954); *State ex rel. Reynolds et al. v. Smith*, 22 Wis. (2nd) 516 (1964).

[9] E.g., Fred Zimmerman was secretary of state from 1923 - 1927 and again from 1939 until his death in 1954. His son Bob, won the office in 1956 and held it until 1975 when he was succeeded by Douglas La Follette. Three Smiths held the office of treasurer for all but two years since 1948 until the 1990 election.

The superintendent of public instruction currently administers an extensive department which handles the state's responsibilities with regard to elementary and secondary education. While local school boards retain basic operating responsibility for most of the schools in the state, the department's administrative functions related to teacher certification, school district reorganization, and state financial aid for school districts give it an important voice in the state's educational system. It also directly operates some specialized schools for handicapped children. In addition to the administrative responsibilities within the department, the superintendent is also an ex officio member of the Board of Regents of the University of Wisconsin System and the Board of Vocational, Technical and Adult Education. The power of the superintendent would be severely proscribed under the governor's reorganization of the education department, which is under challenge in the state supreme court.

As the chief law officer of the state, the attorney general occupies a key position in state government. The reasons for the significance of this office are apparent from a brief description of the attorney general's most important responsibilities. First, he represents the state before the state supreme court in nearly all cases in which the state is party. Upon the request of the governor, either branch of the legislature, or by state department heads, he may appear for the state in other trial cases. This involvement in litigation ensures that he will receive a substantial amount of publicity.

A second way in which the attorney general is placed at center stage is by giving written legal opinions upon the request of the governor, either legislative chamber, state department heads, district attorneys, and county Corporation Counsels. These opinions do not have the force of law, but they have considerable influence on matters that have not been tested in the courts. Again, this function guarantees the attorney general the publicity accorded one at the forefront of legal controversy.

Third, either through opinions on local legal problems or through the obligation to consult with county legal officers on all matters concerning their duties, the attorney general is brought into contact with key county officials. These responsibilities may provide useful entree to the political grassroots.

Cultivation of these contacts may be invaluable in subsequent bids for reelection or for election to higher office. Past executive reorganization further augmented the attorney general's position. By heading the Department of Justice, his potential as an administrator, rather than merely as a legal officer, is underscored. And, in the process of creating the office, additional state functions and services, notably certain investigatory functions and the state crime laboratory, were transferred into the department.

Gubernatorial power with respect to the departments headed by secretaries is more direct. The governor appoints the secretaries, subject to senatorial confirmation, and with one exception, the appointees serve at his pleasure. The exception is the Secretary of Regulation and Licensing who is appointed to a six year fixed term. Having important department heads directly accountable to the governor has been a relatively recent development. Before 1959 the Wisconsin governor had no appointments of this nature. The number he is able to appoint is still considerably less than those appointed by the U.S. President or some other state governors, but the trend has been to increase the number of secretaries subject to gubernatorial appointment in Wisconsin.

Created in 1959, the Department of Administration is the most powerful administrative unit of the state. It provides important staff assistance to the governor and permits him an augmented degree of control over other elements of the administrative structure. The successive heads of this department have been persons closely associated with the governors who selected them. The department provides various staff services: budget, management, comprehensive planning, personnel, purchasing, data processing, and engineering services. Through these staff functions, the department seeks to coordinate management practices in state government and in general to serve as a watchdog over state administrative practices for the governor. In addition, a number of formerly independent agencies such as the Claims Board and the Tax Appeals Commission are attached to the department.

The Department of Administration works directly with the governor in the preparation of the all-important executive budget. To emphasize the importance of this agency in budget-making and other aspects of the governor's program, provision is made by law to allow a newly-elected governor to appoint the secretary of the department to begin working immediately with the outgoing head. This helps to make the gubernatorial transition as smooth and orderly as possible.

The Department of Revenue is another central agency tied closely to the governor. In addition to tax collection, the Revenue Department, through its estimates of prospective tax high level policy yields, can be an important adjunct to high-level policy determination. Prior to reorganization in 1967, the Commissioner of Taxation served a six-year term designed to isolate the office from political influence. However, even under that arrangement some commissioners became deeply involved in partisan infighting. For example, during the tax struggles of the Nelson and Reynolds administrations, John A. Gronouski, a Democratic ally, merged expertise in matters of tax administration with a keen interest in basic tax policy and direct involvement in politics. He clearly became a key figure as a political advisor to Governors Nelson and Reynolds on taxation issues. In this capacity his status in relation to them was similar to that of the secretary of administration.

The Department of Regulation and Licensing brought under one roof the host of state occupational licensing agencies, but as previously noted, the secretary has very little direct policy-making authority over them. The other agencies headed by secretaries are major functional departments described in more detail in the chapters on state functions.

Four administrative departments are headed by multi-member boards which operate on a part-time policy-making advisory basis. The Department of Veterans Affairs was not changed by reorganizations. An effort to include services to veterans in the Health and Social Services Department was abandoned in the face of vehement opposition from veterans' groups. They argued that such inclusion would treat veterans as welfare recipients. The Department of Agriculture, Trade and Consumer Protection (before 1977 the Agriculture Department) also was not changed by reorganizations. The subsequent change in the name of the department reflected the growing importance of its activities designed to protect consumer as well as producer interests in agricultural commodities. Most recently, the DATCP has been reorganized with the governor being given the authority to appoint the secretary of the department. The Department of Employee Trust Funds is an amalgam of previously separate agencies administering various retirement and insurance funds for specific groups of state and local personnel. The individual governing boards are retained, but there is an overall Employee Trust Funds Board composed of representatives of each board.

The creation of the Department of Natural Resources generated the most legislative controversy in the reorganization proposal of 1967. It merged the powerful Conservation Department with the department of Resource Development and a host of relatively minor administrative units. Intense pressure from conservation groups, sportsmen's associations, and resort interests threatened to defeat the proposed merger and possibly even the entire reorganization effort. One important compromise was the provision for guaranteed geographic representation on the Natural Resources Board. At least three of the seven board members must be from the northern half of the state and at least three from the southern half. All serve six-year staggered terms. Since the merger, there have been frequent proposals in the legislature and elsewhere to separate the two agencies.

Independent Agencies. Basically, regulatory and educational agencies comprise the so-called independent agencies listed below. Three patterns are represented in the leadership of these agencies: a single head, a full-time commission and a part-time board.

Headed by a Single Commissioner
Banking
Credit Union
Insurance
Savings and Loans
Securities

Headed by a Commission (three members each)
Employment Relations
Gaming
Personnel
Public Service

Headed by-Board (number of members)
Educational Communications (16)
Elections (8)
Ethics (6)
Higher Educational Aids (18)
Historical Society (36)
Investment (8)
Public Defender (9)
State Fair (7)
University of Wisconsin (17)
Vocational, Technical and Adult Education (13)

The five departments headed by a single executive are each regulatory agencies for specific financial institutions. Their directors are appointed usually for a six-year term by the governor with senatorial confirmation. (The Insurance Commissioner term is four years). They are subject to removal from office only for cause. The odds are that in any given year not more than one of these positions will be open for gubernatorial selection. Under normal circumstances, a governor would have to serve six years before he would have the opportunity to make appointment to all of these positions.

These are lucrative positions, eagerly sought after, which give the governor patronage opportunities. The affected institutions are also very much interested in who is appointed. They would certainly not wish to see an appointment go to someone not in sympathy with their general goals. If the regulated interests have competing factions, each will attempt to have an appointee selected who shares its viewpoint. When it was proposed prior to the current administration that the Banking, Savings and Loan, and Credit Union agencies be merged, predictably, representatives of each of the three regulated organizations voiced reservations about such a merger.

A full time board of three members heads the independent regulatory commissions. These members are appointed by the governor with senatorial confirmation for six-year terms and the appointments are staggered so that a term expires every two years (five-year terms for the Personnel Commissioners). In general, these positions carry salaries commensurate with those received by department heads. The major functions of these agencies are regulatory and organizational in nature. Thus, the public Service Commission regulates the rates and service of most public utilities in the state. The Employment Relations Board, a state version of the National Labor Relations Board, hears complaints of alleged unfair labor practices, decides which of competing claimants are rightful collective bargaining units, and provides mediation and arbitration services. The Gaming Commission is responsible for all lottery, racing and parimutuel wagering, bingo, raffles and crane games. It also oversees the Office of Indian Gaming. The Personnel Commission, with eleven employees, is by far the smallest of the commissions. It hears appeals from state employees regarding grievances on conditions of employment and equal rights complaints.

The regulatory and quasi-judicial functions of these agencies provided the rationale for the creation of a multi-member board rather than a single administrator. In rendering decisions on the appropriate rates of a bus line or on disputes involved in labor management relations, for example, it was felt that a collective judgement is superior to that of one person. Moreover, because of the volume of cases brought before these agencies, it is necessary that the members serve on a full time basis. To do otherwise would simply mean the delegation of decisional responsibility to the agency's administrators. There is a distinctive relationship between these agencies and the governor. First, the salaries attached to most of the positions make them attractive, and thus, they are useful patronage instruments. Second, the staggered, lengthy terms of the board members or commissioners means that the chief executive will be

177

unable to appoint more than one member of any of the boards during the first two years of his term. The result is that carry over members often retain policy control. In the case of Governor Thompson, there should be no such cases since he has been governor since 1987.

The pattern of appointment noted above was developed on the assumption that highly sensitive regulatory agencies should be insulated from direct political intervention, and that this could be accomplished by prohibiting any governor from immediately stacking the commissions with his partisan favorites. From the governor's perspective, however, it may mean that important state agencies are dominated by governing board members antithetical to his program and objectives. Further, the governing board has complete responsibility with respect to the personnel and internal administration of the agency, within the limitations of the merit civil service procedures. The commission, rather than the governor, is empowered to fill vacancies in administrative positions, pass on promotions and salary increases, and discipline employees. The possibility of gubernatorial influence through control of administrative staff is therefore reduced. Unless, of course, a governor is able to be elected for three terms as is the current case. Now Governor Thompson, because of his longevity, is able to overcome this pattern because all of commission members are now or will be his appointees.

The independent agencies headed by part-time boards include the state's institutions of higher education, related educational units and a miscellany of bodies ranging from the Public Defender Board to the Ethics Board. In general, the governor appoints the members of the respective governing bodies (except for the State Historical Society and the Elections Board). In some instances provision is also made for *ex officio* members.

Most of the appointments require senatorial confirmation. There are certain other restrictions on the governor's appointment power to the part-time boards. In many cases the legal authorization of the agency prescribes qualifications of board members. For example, the governor appoints nine of the twelve members of the State Board of Vocational and Adult Education, but his appointees must include three farmers, three employers, and three employees.

Remuneration for service on the various boards is never higher than a nominal salary, expenses and/or a per diem allowance. Clearly, financial gain is not an important incentive for service on these governing bodies. The power and prestige that accompany this service make them attractive to prospective appointees. The ability to shape the development and implementation of public policy in an area of interest to a board member often provides sufficient incentive to persons selected for appointment by the governor. Thus, these appointments give the governor additional patronage opportunities.

Along with his appointment powers, other aspects of the governor's relationship with the part-time boards are identical with his relationship with full-time commissions. The staggered terms of office restrict the power of a governor to achieve immediate control over the respective boards. The exception to this is the case of a newly created body where the Governor makes all the initial appointments.

State Authorities. Since 1971, five state authorities have been created by legislation. Each of the following is, or was, headed by a multi-member board (number of members):

- Community Development Finance Authority (13) (abolished in 1987 with functions transferred to the Department of Development)

- Health and Educational Facilities Authority (7)

- Housing and Economic Development Authority (12) (was the Housing Finance Authority - renamed in 1983)

- Solid Waste Recycling Authority (7) (abolished in 1983 with functions transferred to the Natural Resources Board)

- World Dairy Center Authority (23)

These are public corporate bodies designed to perform specified functions. They are authorized to issue bonds to raise the revenue necessary to support their activity. The Housing and Economic Development Authority provides funds to support various loan programs designed to alleviate the housing shortage for low and moderate income persons. In addition, this authority is charged with providing financing for business development loans and export sales of Wisconsin products. Similarly, the Health and Educational Facilities Authority may lend money to health institutions in order to improve medical care in the state. While it is not authorized to operate health facilities directly, it may acquire, construct or reconstruct Such facilities for lease or resale. The World Dairy Center Authority was established in 1991 to advance dairy development through data analysis, coordination of access to dairy information and the promotion of the dairy industry. The Authority works cooperatively with the Department of Agriculture, Trade and Consumer Protection.

Most of the members of the respective governing boards are appointed by the governor with the consent of the senate. However, there are additional restrictions on his appointment to each of the authorities. All of them serve for staggered terms of four or six years. No more than four of seven members of the Health and Educational Facilities Authority may be members of the same political party. In the case of the Housing and Economic Development Authority additional members beyond the six gubernatorial appointments include two senators and two members of the Assembly. It should be noted that none of the administrative staffs of the authorities are included in the state civil service system but are employed directly by their respective authorities instead.

Other Management Controls

One goal of both the 1967 Reorganization Act and the 1995 budget act was to strengthen the governor's administrative leadership role in order to provide more control over the functional units of state government. The hope was to render these agencies more responsive to those responsible for establishing policy. In certain respects, the 1967 reorganization had this effect, although it did not go as far in this direction as advocates of strong executive leadership would have preferred. However, the Wisconsin reorganization did not give the governor the authority to initiate subsequent alterations in the administrative structure. The legislature rejected a procedure which would have allowed the governor to make subsequent changes in administrative organization by executive order. The legislature could veto such orders, but if the legislature failed to act, the reorganization would take effect as promulgated. The U.S. President has such authority under the Federal Administrative Reorganization Act of 1949, and several state governors hold similar powers.

Apart from structural characteristics of state government, there are other central management tools which can be used as checks on administrative agencies, chief among these is the budget. The governor has effective budgetary control through the executive budget process which was adopted in Wisconsin in 1929. The essential features of executive budget procedures are establishing guidelines, review of agency budget requests by the governor, and his submission of a final budget to the legislature. Through the guideline and review processes, the governor can exert great influence on the direction and scope of agency activities. An example of this is the practice of requiring agencies to submit multiple preliminary budget requests based on no growth or percentage reductions in spending levels.

Basic organizational changes in agencies can also be accomplished through the budget as was demonstrated in 1975 when Governor Lucey affected a major reorganization of the Department of Health and Social Services. A major change was the designation of a secretary accountable directly to the governor to run the department rather than the preexisting board. Thus, through the budget process, the governor was able to exercise authority that had previously been denied to him. While the state operates on a biennial budget, the annual budget review process increases the governor's opportunity to influence agencies through their budgets.

Central purchasing, comprehensive state planning, central data processing as well as other functions handled by the Department of Administration, are other devices by which further centralization is achieved.

Conclusion

Administering the many state activities is a complex undertaking. Maintaining control over the agencies created to perform these tasks is difficult. There are several obvious administrative dilemmas. Agencies attempt to perform services in the best interest of Wisconsin's citizens. In order to do so they feel a high degree of autonomy is required; i.e., freedom from the outside pressures generated by the governor or legislature. At the same time the governor, as chief executive, has responsibility for all activities engaged in by state agencies. Finally, the legislature, collectively representing all of the people of the state, also lays claim to a predominant voice in the matter of deciding what and how state functions are to be performed. The legislative viewpoint may be antithetical to the quest for administrative autonomy of agencies and to the quest for far-reaching gubernatorial control over the agencies. Either prospect may appear to diminish effective legislative oversight of state administration.

Tensions between the legislature, governor, and agencies are therefore natural results of the conflicting values held by each. The strong, far-reaching state civil service system provides one frame of reference for the ongoing struggle. So, too, do the central management tools, especially budgetary control, available to the governor. Reorganization efforts represent another. No reorganization will create a pattern of absolute administrative accountability. This is understandable if viewed in relation to the pressures generated by the legislature and the agencies. Subsequent reorganization efforts may further enhance, or possibly diminish, the governor's administrative authority. They presumably will not eliminate the conflicting values held by the major participants.

CHAPTER IX

THE WISCONSIN JUDICIARY

By Melinda Gann Hall[*]

Courts are an integral part of the American system of governance. Charged with the fundamental function of resolving disputes in an orderly and authoritative manner, courts make some of the nation's most difficult and important political choices. In rendering these decisions, courts are guided by established rules, or law. But perhaps the most fundamental truth about these institutions is that the law simply is not, and cannot be, a vise that binds judges' decisions. Often laws are ambiguous or have no obvious application to particular factual situations. In every case, facts must be established and assessed, and laws must be interpreted to fit the dispute immediately before the court. Judges do not merely enforce existing laws in a mechanical fashion but rather contribute significantly to their meaning and development.

The simple notion, reinforced by traditional legal theory, that judges are completely neutral arbiters, yields to a much more complex reality. In practice, judges necessarily rely on, to varying degrees, their personal concepts of justice when making decisions. Moreover, patterns of interaction among members of a court, pressures from the external environment, and the operating rules particular to each institution all influence judicial choice. Quite simply, courts are inherently political, not only because of the importance of their decisions but also because of how these decisions are reached.

At the very core of the judicial enterprise are state courts, which have the awesome responsibility for resolving the vast majority of the nation's legal disputes. In fact, only about one percent of the litigation in the United States takes place in the federal system (Glick, 1993), and such important matters as the prosecution of criminal defendants and the resolution of family issues remain largely within the purview of the states. State courts resolve disputes that occur between private citizens in their daily interactions, between citizens and the government, and between the various branches and agencies of government. In the aggregate, these decisions have a profound impact on the overall distribution of wealth and power in the United States.

Even the most seemingly mundane state court case can have significant implications extending far beyond the litigants. Consider, for example, a divorce case. Divorce in the United States is quite common and, in most cases, is not very complex or contentious. Parties in a divorce seek simply to dissolve a contractual relationship, divide property accumulated during the marriage, and arrange for the custody and support of children. However, the manner in which property is divided between husband and wife, and the way in which issues of child support and custody are decided, have far-reaching consequences for the economic and political status of men and women. The extent to which women (and far less often, men) who forgo careers to be full-time care givers for their households will be compensated beyond the assets accrued during the marriage, and whether men will be considered equal partners in the care and custody of children, are among the fundamental judgements made daily in state courts.

Not so obviously, state courts play an important role in the interpretation of federal law, including constitutional law. In a state criminal prosecution, for instance, the defendant may raise issues about jury selection, access to legal counsel, or the propriety of a given sentence, matters governed by the United States Supreme Court's interpretations of the Constitution. While case law may exist to cover the subject being litigated, the actual application of these rules rests in the hands of state court judges who retain significant discretion. Especially when new fact patterns emerge or when Supreme Court rulings are not clear, state court judges necessarily must rely on their own interpretations of the Constitution to resolve the disputes immediately before their courts. Furthermore,

---

[*] Professor of Political Science, University of Wisconsin-Milwaukee.

In sum, perceptions that courts are not political, or that state courts are not important, are simply incorrect. Any understanding of state politics, or more generally American politics, demands an understanding of state courts - their organization, personnel, and procedures. The following sections describe the Wisconsin judiciary and its place among the American states. In many ways, Wisconsin's court system is quite similar to many other state systems. However, as the following discussion reveals, Wisconsin's courts are, to some extent, decidedly unique.

The Organization of American Courts

One of the most obvious features of state court systems is their complexity. There really are no two state court systems exactly alike. However, all courts in the United States, including federal courts, share common organizational features.

State and Federal Courts. First, all courts are either state or federal institutions. In the United States, state and federal courts operate simultaneously yet independently of each other. Rules governing the federal courts are found in the United States Constitution and statutes passed by Congress. Essentially, the jurisdiction of these courts extends to cases arising under federal law, any case to which the United States is a party, and diversity cases (i.e., conflicts between citizens of different states). In many situations, the jurisdiction of the federal court system is concurrent with the state courts; cases could be litigated in either. The most obvious exception is criminal prosecution under federal law, which must take place in the federal courts.

Each state court system is governed by the state constitution and other state law. In fact, it is important to recognize that the federal government has no control over state courts, except that the states are bound by the United States Constitution and other federal law. Within these parameters, states have complete discretion. Consequently, the fifty states have developed systems of courts reflective of their own unique political conflicts and culture. And like the relationship between state and federal systems, each state judiciary operates independently of all others.

Trial and Appellate Courts. Second, all courts are either trial or appellate. Trial courts are where cases begin in the judicial system. Trial courts resolve disputes over facts and then apply the appropriate law relevant to the case. In our adversarial system of justice, every lawsuit involves two parties pitted against each other in head-to-head competition. The party bringing the suit presents a particular view of the facts that casts the other party as guilty of some wrongdoing. Alternatively, the second party in the lawsuit refutes the accusations or levels countercharges against the first party. Trials are to determine which version of the facts is correct, or to establish what actually happened in any given situation.

To establish facts, trial courts utilize very detailed rules of procedure to collect information in a manner that does not favor one side over the other, or that does not bias the outcome of the case. In some situations, trial courts utilize juries, composed of citizens randomly selected from the community, to listen to the presentation of facts about the allegations in the lawsuit. In bench trials, judges make these decisions. And after reviewing evidence, trial courts then apply the law appropriate for the findings of fact. In some situations, this requires imposing sentences such as fines, incarceration, or death. In other cases, the remedy may be a court order requiring a specified action or the payment of a particular sum of money to the other litigant.

Appellate courts perform a fundamentally different function. Appellate courts review records of trials for errors of law and do not reconsider facts, except to determine whether the trial court reached any findings of fact completely contrary to the evidence. In other words, appellate courts do not second-guess trial courts about whether a criminal defendant actually is guilty or whether a civil litigant really behaved negligently. Appellate courts review records of trials to be sure that the trial court judge conducted the trial in accordance with the rules of procedure and interpreted the law governing the case correctly. In the United States, each case is entitled to one review.

To understand the function of appellate courts requires an appreciation of the importance of procedure, or due process. In the United States, one of the fundamental tenets of justice is that fair and neutral procedures are essential for reaching accurate judgements in disputes. Rules for conducting trials are designed to allow both parties equal opportunities to present evidence and to challenge the validity of the other side's evidence. Additionally, a certain order must be followed in the presentation of evidence, and comments that clearly are irrelevant or prejudicial are not permitted.

For example, the fact that a criminal defendant has received psychiatric care or has convictions on other charges generally is irrelevant to whether the defendant committed the particular crime being alleged. Introduction of this information by the state, however, may bias the jury's perception of the defendant and tip the balance toward conviction, apart from relevant evidence in the case.

Perhaps the best way to think about the judicial process and the role of appellate courts is to consider litigation as analogous to a game. In any game, there are rules for playing that are designed to make the game fair. Imagine any game where one team does not know the rules in advance or where the rules are enforced against one team but not the other. Without question, we would expect the team that knows the rules or receives favored treatment to win, irrespective of the merits of the players. We also would consider this situation fundamentally unfair. The judicial process is the same, where appellate courts have the responsibility for enforcing rules and keeping the process fair, hopefully facilitating correct conclusions about the facts.

In making decisions, appellate courts review records of trials for errors of law, based on written (and sometimes oral) arguments presented by attorneys. If the court fails to find an error, the court affirms the decision of the lower court, leaving the ruling in force. However, if the appellate court finds an error, the court then will order some kind of correction. The extent of the correction will depend upon the nature of the error. In some cases, errors can be corrected by modifying a defendant's sentence in a criminal case or by adjusting the monetary award granted in a civil case. Other errors necessitate completely new trials. Contrary to portrayals in the popular media, the reversal of a criminal defendant's conviction does not mean that the appellate court has decided that the defendant is innocent and must go free. Quite the contrary, it simply means that the appellate court found errors in the original trial that must be corrected.

Structurally, trial courts and appellate courts are quite distinct. Trial courts resolve disputes using one judge and sometimes juries. Individuals other than court personnel also participate in trials by offering testimony and other forms of evidence. On the other hand, appellate courts are composed of groups of judges and never use juries. The only participants in appellate proceedings are judges and attorneys.

In an appellate court, the number of judges reviewing a given case will depend upon the size of the court and the nature of the court's docket. Some appellate courts sit *en banc*, where all of the judges collectively review each case. Other appellate courts utilize panels, dividing the court membership into smaller subgroups and assigning different cases to each panel. Appellate courts reach decisions by majority vote; decisions in appellate courts do not have to be, and often are not, unanimous.

Additionally, some appellate courts have mandatory dockets while others have discretionary dockets. Courts with mandatory dockets must review the cases properly appealed from other courts. Courts with discretionary dockets choose which cases they wish to review from the cases brought to them from other courts, although there may be highly restricted categories of cases that courts with otherwise discretionary dockets are required by statute to review (e.g., cases in which defendants have been sentenced to death). Courts with mandatory dockets tend to sit in panels rather than *en banc*, and have lower dissent rates and reversal rates than appellate courts with discretionary dockets. Most basically, courts with mandatory dockets review large numbers of cases that are relatively routine, where few opportunities exist for finding error or for generating disagreement among the judges. Courts with discretionary dockets tend to select cases involving more important or controversial issues, and consequently manifest different decisional patterns.

<u>Geographic Jurisdiction.</u> Third, American courts are empowered to hear cases that arise within specific geographic jurisdictions. Courts can have a national, regional, state, county (or several county), or city jurisdiction. The geographic jurisdiction of each federal court is established by Congress. In the states, the geographic jurisdiction of each court is specified in the state's constitution or by the state legislature.

<u>Limited and General Jurisdiction.</u> Fourth, all courts have either limited or general jurisdiction. Courts with limited jurisdiction have authority over particular subsets of cases that arise within the geographic jurisdiction. General jurisdiction courts hear all matters within the designated geographic area, irrespective of subject.

These two types of courts typically utilize different procedures for resolving cases. Limited jurisdiction trial courts, often referred to as inferior courts, quite commonly use abbreviated procedures for conducting trials, sometimes exclude attorneys, and rarely utilize juries. Limited jurisdiction courts decide large volumes of cases on matters that are considered not very significant or complex relative to other disputes. Most courts in the United States fall into this category, and most cases are handled in these institutions.

General jurisdiction trial courts are much more formal in procedure, necessitating the expertise of attorneys. These courts are the major trial courts in the United States and hear the most significant disputes that arise within the jurisdiction.

<u>Original and Appellate Jurisdiction.</u> Fifth, all courts have original jurisdiction, appellate jurisdiction, or both. Original jurisdiction is the power to resolve cases on their facts, or to hear cases for the first time. Appellate jurisdiction is the power to review cases already decided for errors of law. At first glance, original and appellate jurisdiction seem indistinguishable from trial and appellate courts. Trial courts, after all, exercise original jurisdiction while appellate courts exercise appellate jurisdiction. However, many appellate courts in the United States also have original jurisdiction over a limited range of subjects. A more precise definition of a trial court, therefore, is a court that primarily exercises original jurisdiction, and an appellate court is one that primarily exercises appellate jurisdiction.

<u>Civil and Criminal Proceedings.</u> Finally, all courts are designed to hear criminal cases, civil cases, or both. These areas of law are quite distinct and necessitate different rules of procedure. Criminal law involves disputes where a government (national, state, or local), on behalf of the society, accuses an individual of performing an action prohibited by written law. In a criminal case, a government seeks to punish an individual for harming the public through these deviant actions.

Civil law, on the other hand, involves everything else. Civil disputes are those that are private in nature, or that do not implicate the broader society. Every possible type of human interaction can give rise to a civil suit, from contract disputes, to family law (divorce, adoption, paternity, child custody, probate), to environmental protection, to labor-management conflicts, to automobile crashes, to product liability, to neighborhood preservation.

Courts utilize different rules of procedure for these two types of cases. Criminal cases require a higher standard of proof and involve many protections, constitutional and otherwise, to insure that defendants' rights are not violated in the process of adjudication. In Wisconsin, for example, juries in criminal cases typically have 12 members and are required to reach unanimous decisions. Moreover, the defendant has the right to legal counsel if indigent and is not required to talk with the police or prosecution at all, unless the defendant wishes to do so.

On the other hand, juries in civil cases commonly are composed of six members, and verdicts from a majority of five are permitted. The right to counsel does not apply in civil cases; individuals wishing to obtain legal advice must pay for it themselves, even when indigent, except under very limited circumstances. Additionally, in a civil case, each side has access to the other side's witnesses, including the litigants themselves, before trial.

The Structure of the Wisconsin Judiciary

Wisconsin's judiciary is a reformer's dream. In the 1970s, the system was restructured to fit the prototype advocated by the court reform movement. Efforts to reorganize the system actually began in the 1950s, were taken up again in the 1970s, and were finalized in 1978. The current structure essentially reflects the organization adopted in 1978.

What is so impressive about the Wisconsin courts from a structural perspective? The Wisconsin judiciary is streamlined to eliminate the confusing mess of concurrent jurisdictions characteristic of many state systems. Further, the management of the court system is centralized under the authority of the Wisconsin Supreme Court, which establishes procedural rules for the entire system and exercises supervisory jurisdiction. Other states continue to operate systems where multiple courts have jurisdiction to hear a particular case, where rules of procedure are promulgated by each institution, and where no methods are provided for supervising the lower courts. These kinds of institutional arrangements result in confusing and complicated litigation procedures, provide strategic opportunities for attorneys to engage in court or judge-shopping, and allow lower court judges to operate with relatively little supervision and, consequently, little accountability.

With the goal of eliminating these problems, Wisconsin's courts are structured in the following manner. At the lowest level of the judicial hierarchy are limited jurisdiction trial courts, called Municipal Courts. The decision to have such a court is left to each city, village, or town in the state. Municipal Courts have original jurisdiction to hear cases arising under the laws of the municipality where the court is located. There is no requirement in state law that Municipal Court judges be attorneys. However, such standards have been set by local law. In Wisconsin, 203 cities, villages, and towns have established Municipal Courts. These courts are not courts of record, which means that *verbatim* transcripts are not kept of the proceedings. If an appeal is taken from Municipal Court, the case becomes an appeal *de novo* to the Circuit Courts, the general jurisdiction trial courts. An appeal *de novo* simply means that the case is re-litigated as though the case had not been decided. Municipal Courts do not hear civil cases and do not use juries.

Next in the organizational structure are general jurisdiction trial courts, the Circuit Courts. These courts in other states have a variety of names, including, most commonly, Superior or District Courts. These courts also have names like Chancery Courts (Mississippi, Tennessee) and Courts of Common Pleas (Ohio, Pennsylvania). In Wisconsin, Circuit Court boundaries generally conform to county boundaries, for a total of 69 circuits in the state. More populous counties have several branches, with one judge assigned to each branch. As of August 1, 1993, there was a combined total of 223 circuits or circuit branches with the same number of judges operating throughout the state. Circuit Courts have original jurisdiction over all matters arising under state law within their respective geographic jurisdictions. Circuit Court judges are elected for six-year terms and must reside in the circuit in which they serve. In larger jurisdictions, the Circuit Court is organized into separate civil and criminal divisions, to maximize efficiency in processing heavy caseloads. Milwaukee, for instance, has separate civil and criminal divisions in its Circuit Court.

Wisconsin does not have limited jurisdiction trial courts to hear small claims cases, or civil cases involving relatively small sums of money. Instead, Small Claims divisions are located in the Circuit Courts, where civil cases involving a maximum dollar amount of $4,000 are litigated using summary procedures. Jurisdictional limits in the other states for similar types of cases range from $1000 (Kansas) to $10,000 (Tennessee).

Wisconsin is one of the thirty-eight states in the United States having an intermediate appellate court.[1] This institution in Wisconsin is called the Court of Appeals, created in 1978. Actually, the other states utilize a variety of labels for these courts. For instance, some states have labeled these courts the Appeals Court or Appellate Court (Connecticut, Illinois, Massachusetts), District Courts of Appeals (Florida), Intermediate Court of Appeals (Hawaii), and Superior Court (Pennsylvania).

Organizationally, Wisconsin is divided into four appellate districts, with principal offices in Madison, Milwaukee, Waukesha, and Wausau. Four judges serve in each district (which are combinations of circuits) except in Wausau, which has only three judges, for a statewide total of 15. These courts have mandatory appellate dockets, with jurisdiction to review cases from the Circuit Courts. Judges in the Court of Appeals are elected to six-year terms and must reside in the district in which they serve.

At the top of the judicial hierarchy is Wisconsin's court of last resort, the Wisconsin Supreme Court.[2] This court has statewide jurisdiction and is composed of seven members known as justices, who are elected statewide for ten-year terms. The Chief Justice is the court's most senior member. However, the most senior justice may chose to decline the position yet continue to serve on the Court. The Chief Justice has administrative responsibilities and is paid a slightly higher salary than the other justices.

Like other state courts of last resort, the Wisconsin Supreme Court has both original and appellate jurisdiction. The Court has original jurisdiction over matters pertaining to members of the bar and a variety of other matters crucial to state government. The Court actually decides relatively few of these cases annually. On the appellate side, the Court has a completely discretionary docket; no appeals can be taken to the Supreme Court as a matter of right. Generally, cases are brought to the Supreme Court from the Court of Appeals. In order for these cases to be granted review, three of seven justices must agree to take the case. However, with the approval of four justices, cases can bypass the Court of Appeals and go directly to the Supreme Court.

Table IX-1 presents caseload data for all states combined and for the Wisconsin judiciary separately. To some extent, the figures are misleading, because many states fail to report caseload data for their trial courts of limited jurisdiction.[3]

Table IX-1

TOTAL FILINGS IN STATE COURTS, 1993

	All States	Wisconsin
Courts of Last Resort	75,953	1,156
Intermediate Appellate Courts	179,050	3,290

---

[1] States not having intermediate appellate courts are the following: Delaware, Maine, Mississippi, Montana, Nevada, New Hampshire, North Dakota, Rhode Island, South Dakota, Vermont, West Virginia and Wyoming.

[2] Other names for state courts of last resort include the Supreme Court of Appeals (West Virginia), the Supreme Judicial Court (Maine, Massachusetts) and the Court of Appeals (Maryland, New York).

[3] *USA Today* reported on April 16, 1992 that sixty-seven million traffic and other minor cases were filed in the state courts in 1990.

General Jurisdiction Trial Courts		
Civil	9,514,882	339,291
Criminal	3,974,371	92,647
Limited Jurisdiction Trial Courts		
Civil	9,569,440	----
Criminal	8,503,233	13,859

Source: National Center for State Courts, 1995.

As Table IX-1 indicates, the total filings in all state courts reached almost 32,000,000 cases in 1993. Most of these cases were civil rather than criminal disputes. Also, the caseloads for trial courts greatly exceeded those of the appellate courts. Wisconsin courts manifest these same patterns, handling far more civil cases than criminal and having far fewer cases filed at the appellate than trial court level. In 1993, the Wisconsin judiciary received a total of 450,243 filings, or 1.4 percent of the nation's litigation. Excluding limited jurisdiction trial courts (which are not used as extensively in Wisconsin as in other states), Wisconsin courts handled 436,384 filings, or 3.2 percent of the nation's legal business in 1993.

Table IX-2 presents filing trends in Wisconsin appellate courts from 1984 through 1993. Overall, the volume of litigation in both the Court of Appeals and Supreme Court has increased. The Court of Appeals processed about 3,300 filings in 1993 while the Supreme Court handled over 1,150. Although most cases taken to the Wisconsin Supreme Court are denied review, the Court still must decide whether to grant or deny review in each case, an increasingly burdensome task.

Table IX-2

TEN YEAR FILING TREND, WISCONSIN APPELLATE COURTS, 1984 - 93

year	Supreme Court	Court of Appeals	year	Supreme Court	Court of Appeals
1984	718	2239	1989	896	2355
1985	761	2358	1990	842	2853
1986	836	2053	1991	992	2972
1987	869	2185	1992	972	3187
1988	915	2147	1993	1156	3290

Source: National Center for State Courts, 1995.

Table IX-3 lists the total number of judges serving in each state's court of last resort, intermediate appellate court, and general jurisdiction trial courts. As the data indicate, the states vary significantly in the number of judges staffing the bench at all levels of the judiciary. General jurisdiction trial courts range in size from 16 (Maine) to 820 judges (Illinois). Wisconsin ranks 13th among the states in the size of the trial court bench. It is important to note, however, that the figures reported in Table IX-3 for the trial courts do not include commissioners or magistrates, who often serve in these courts to assist the regular judges with their routine duties.

Table IX-3

THE NUMBER OF JUDGES SERVING IN STATE COURTS, 1993

State	Court of Last Resort	Intermediate Appellate Court	General Jurisdiction Trial Courts
Alabama	9	5	127
Alaska	5	3	30
Arizona	5	21	125
Arkansas	7	6	99
California	7	88	789
Colorado	7	16	114
Connecticut	7	9	150
Delaware	5	-----	20
Florida	7	57	421
Georgia	7	9	159
Hawaii	5	3	25
Idaho	5	3	34
Illinois	7	40	820
Indiana	5	15	242
Iowa	9	6	183
Kansas	7	10	149
Kentucky	7	14	91
Louisiana	7	54	207
Maine	7	-----	16
Maryland	7	13	123
Massachusetts	7	14	320
Michigan	7	24	206
Minnesota	7	16	242
Mississippi	9	-----	79
Missouri	7	32	134

State	Court of Last Resort	Intermediate Appellate Court	General Jurisdiction Trial Courts
Montana	7	-----	37
Nebraska	7	6	50
Nevada	5	-----	38
New Hampshire	5	-----	29
New Jersey	7	28	374
New Mexico	5	10	61
New York	7	48	597
North Carolina	7	12	77
North Dakota	5	-----	24
Ohio	7	65	355
Oklahoma	9*	12	71
Oregon	7	10	92
Pennsylvania	7	15	366
Rhode Island	5	-----	22
South Carolina	5	6	40
South Dakota	5	-----	36
Tennessee	5	12	494
Texas	9**	80	386
Utah	5	7	35
Vermont	5	-----	31
Virginia	7	10	135
Washington	9	17	153
West Virginia	5	-----	60
Wisconsin	7	13	223
Wyoming	5	-----	17

* Statistics reported for the Supreme Court. Five judges sit on the Court of Criminal Appeals.

** 9 Judges sit on both the Supreme Court and Court of Criminal Appeals.

Source: Council of State Governments, 1994.

As Table IX-3 also reveals, intermediate appellate courts range in size from three to 88. Wisconsin ranks 19th among the states in the size of its intermediate appellate bench. As noted earlier, these courts usually decide cases using three-judge panels.

Courts of last resort in the American states are composed of five to nine members. In most states (26, including Wisconsin) courts of last resort consist of seven members. These courts sit *en banc*. Also note that Oklahoma and Texas each have two courts of last resort; these states divide the civil and criminal jurisdiction into separate institutions. Oklahoma and Texas have courts called Supreme Courts, which have final review of civil matters, and Courts of Criminal Appeals, which have final authority over criminal cases.

Table IX-4 reports salary information for state court judges. As the table reveals, substantial variations exist among the states in the compensation of judges. Moreover, salaries are higher for judges in appellate courts than in trial courts; movement up the judicial hierarchy results in increased compensation.

In 1993, salaries for justices in state courts of last resort ranged from $64,452 (Maine) to $127,267 (California) annually. Although not included in the table, additional salaries are paid by most states to the Chief Justice because of the additional administrative responsibilities associated with the position. Compensation for judges in the intermediate appellate courts ranged from $73,388 (New Mexico) to $119,314 (California). Finally, salaries in the general jurisdiction trial courts ranged from $61,565 (Michigan) to $113,000 (New York) annually. Interestingly, Wisconsin ranks 21st among the states in judicial salaries for each of the three types of courts.

Table IX-4

ANNUAL SALARIES (IN DOLLARS) FOR STATE COURT JUDGES, 1993

State	Court of Last Resort	Intermediate Appellate Court	General Jurisdiction Trial Courts
Alabama	107,125	106,125	72,500
Alaska	104,472*	98,688*	96,600*
Arizona	91,728	89,544	87,360
Arkansas	93,349	90,379	87,439
California	127,267	119,314	104,262
Colorado	84,000	79,500	75,000
Connecticut	106,553	99,077	94,647
Delaware	105,100	-----	99,900
Florida	103,457	98,284	93,111
Georgia	96,118	95,509	73,344
Hawaii	93,780	89,780	86,780

State	Court of Last Resort	Intermediate Appellate Court	General Jurisdiction Trial Courts
Idaho	79,183	78,183	74,214
Illinois	103,097	97,032	82,977
Indiana	81,000	76,500	61,740
Iowa	90,300	86,800	82,500
Kansas	84,465	81,451	73,430
Kentucky	78,273	75,078	71,883
Louisiana	94,000	89,000	84,000
Maine	83,616	-----	79,073
Maryland	99,000	92,500	89,000
Massachusetts	90,450	83,708	80,360
Michigan	111,941	107,463	61,565*
Minnesota	94,395	88,945	83,494
Mississippi	90,800	-----	81,200
Missouri	92,910	86,755	70,810
Montana	64,452	-----	63,178
Nebraska	88,157	83,749	81,546
Nevada	85,000	-----	79,000
New Hampshire	95,623	-----	89,628
New Jersey	115,000	108,000	100,000
New Mexico	77,250	73,388	69,719
New York	125,000	115,000	113,000
North Carolina	91,855	86,996	77,289
North Dakota	71,555	-----	65,970
Ohio	101,150	94,200	72,650
Oklahoma	83,871	78,660	71,330
Oregon	83,700	81,700	76,200
Pennsylvania	108,045	104,444	92,610
Rhode Island	99,431	-----	89,521
South Carolina	92,986	88,338	88,338

State	Court of Last Resort	Intermediate Appellate Court	General Jurisdiction Trial Courts
South Dakota	72,079	-----	67,314
Tennessee	96,348	91,860	87,900
Texas	94,685	89,952	85,217
Utah	89,300	85,250	81,200
Vermont	73,890	-----	70,188
Virginia	102,700	97,565	95,340
Washington	107,200	101,900	96,600
West Virginia	72,000	-----	65,000
Wisconsin	94,906	89,358	83,773
Wyoming	85,000	-----	77,000

* Location and cost of living differences; lowest listed

Source: Council of State Governments, 1994.

Needless to say, the job of state court judge is an attractive one. Apart from the power and prestige accorded the position, the salaries are quite high for state political office. While some have argued that the most qualified attorneys do not seek judgeships because of the low salaries relative to private practice, there is little evidence that qualified attorneys fail to seek state judicial office.

The Selection and Retention of State Court Judges

Every American state has the difficult task of deciding how the judges of the state judiciary will be chosen. In addressing this extremely important and complex issue, the states have attempted to design selection mechanisms that balance the principles of judicial independence and electoral accountability, two principles clearly at odds. Judicial independence rests on the assumption that judges should be insulated, to the greatest extent possible, from external political pressures. The principle of electoral accountability, however, asserts that public officials are representatives who must justify their decisions to the voters or face removal from office.

While some states have opted for the federal model which maximizes the degree of judicial independence by eliminating the electoral process, the large majority of states have struck the balance more in favor of accountability by choosing to utilize elections, a device to promote popular control. As a result, judges in thirty-eight states must seek voter approval regularly, either in partisan elections, nonpartisan elections, or retention elections.

More precisely, the states have developed five basic methods for recruiting and retaining judges, which emphasize, to varying degrees, the principles of independence and accountability. First, a number of states utilize partisan elections to staff the bench. In partisan election systems, candidates seek judicial office in elections where the candidates' partisan affiliations are listed on the ballot. Additionally, candidates in general elections typically are nominated in partisan primaries.

Second, some states use nonpartisan elections to select their judges. In nonpartisan elections, candidates appear on the ballot in general elections without political party designations. Nonpartisan elections were designed as a reform, where voters are expected to substitute assessments of the candidates' qualifications for the candidates' partisan affiliations as the primary basis for casting ballots. Also, nonpartisan elections were designed to reduce political party control over the judicial selection process.

Third, the largest proportion of states currently use the Missouri Plan, or the "Merit" Plan, to staff the state bench. The Missouri Plan is an interesting combination of appointment and election and was designed to capture the best features of both. While there are significant variations from state to state in the way the Missouri Plan actually operates, the basic process is this. To begin, the governor appoints a judicial nominating commission, which has the responsibility for recommending candidates for each vacancy. As vacancies occur, the commission screens potential nominees, evaluating their suitability for the judgeship. The commission then presents a list of three candidates to the governor, who must appoint one of the three to fill the vacancy. Upon appointment, the nominee immediately assumes office. Shortly thereafter, usually in the next general election, the candidate must win voter approval in a retention election. Retention elections ask voters to decide whether a current officeholder should continue in office; opposing candidates do not appear on the ballot nor is the partisan affiliation of the candidate listed on the ballot. If voters approve, the judge begins a regular term of office, facing subsequent retention elections at the end of every term. If voters disapprove, the process begins anew.

Fourth, some states allow their governors to appoint judges, usually with the approval of the state senate. Some of these states restrict the governor's choices to nominees approved by a judicial nominating commission. Other states allow the governor complete discretion in nominating candidates. This process most closely parallels the system used in the federal courts.

Finally, three states empower their legislatures to select judges. Each chamber of the legislature has a committee to handle judicial appointments, and nominees are approved or rejected through the normal legislative process. Choices are not subject to veto by the governor.

A number of states actually use several methods of selection, depending upon the type of court being staffed. For instance, some states utilize partisan or nonpartisan elections for choosing trial court judges and the Missouri Plan for the court of last resort. Table IX-5 provides information about the method utilized by each state for selecting justices for the court of last resort. As the table reveals, ten states utilize partisan elections, 12 states (including Wisconsin) use nonpartisan elections, 16 states employ the Missouri Plan, nine states utilize gubernatorial appointment, and three states use legislative election.

Table IX-5

METHODS FOR SELECTING STATE COURT JUDGES: COURTS OF LAST RESORT

Partisan Elections	Nonpartisan Elections	Missouri Plan	Gubernatorial Appointment	Legislative Election
Alabama	Georgia	Alaska	Connecticut	Rhode Island
Arkansas	Idaho	Arizona	Delaware***	South Carolina
Illinois*	Kentucky	California	Hawaii***	Virginia
Louisiana	Michigan	Colorado	Maine	
Mississippi	Minnesota	Florida	Massachusetts***	
North Carolina	Montana	Indiana	New Hampshire	
Pennsylvania*	Nevada	Iowa	New Jersey	
Tennessee	North Dakota	Kansas	New York	
Texas	Ohio**	Maryland	Vermont***	

193

West Virginia	Oregon	Missouri
	Washington	Nebraska
	Wisconsin	New Mexico*
		Oklahoma
		South Dakota
		Utah
		Wyoming

* Retention after initial election
** Partisan primaries
*** Governor's choices limited to list provided by Judicial Nominating Commission

Source: Council of State Governments, 1994.

The preceding discussion necessarily simplifies the politics of judicial selection in the states. In practice, selection systems are much more complex and varied than just described. For example, judges in some states are elected from districts (Illinois, Louisiana, Mississippi, Kentucky, Maryland, Nebraska, Oklahoma, South Dakota) while judges in other states are elected statewide. Also, there often are substantial differences between formal selection mechanisms and informal practice. For instance, every state has a procedure for filling vacancies that occur during a term, usually by allowing the governor to appoint someone to fill the vacancy until the expiration of the term. Because judges often resign or retire from the bench during a term if their political party controls the governorship, many judges in elective systems actually get their jobs initially through appointment rather than winning an election. Through strategic retirements and *ad interim* appointments, the political party retains control of the office and the appointee gains the advantage of running as an incumbent in the next regular election. In short, gubernatorial appointment is much more widely used than formal descriptions indicate, and seemingly straightforward selection procedures often are manipulated to achieve critical political goals.

Table IX-6 lists terms of office for each state's court of last resort, intermediate appellate court, and general jurisdiction trial courts. The states differ substantially in the length of time judges serve at all levels of the judiciary, although appellate court judges generally enjoy longer terms than trial court judges. Also note that terms for judicial office at all levels tend to be longer than terms for most other state and federal political offices.

Table IX-6

TERMS OF OFFICE (IN YEARS) FOR STATE COURT JUDGES

State	Court of Last Resort	Intermediate Appellate Court	General Jurisdiction Trial Courts
Alabama	6	6	6
Alaska	10	8	6
Arizona	6	6	4
Arkansas	8	8	4*
California	12	12	6

State	Court of Last Resort	Intermediate Appellate Court	General Jurisdiction Trial Courts
Colorado	10	8	6
Connecticut	8	8	8
Delaware	12	-----	12
Florida	6	6	6
Georgia	6	6	4
Hawaii	10	10	10
Idaho	6	6	4
Illinois	10	10	6
Indiana	10	10	6
Iowa	8	6	6
Kansas	6	4	4
Kentucky	8	8	8
Louisiana	10	10	6
Maine	7	-----	7
Maryland	10	10	15
Massachusetts	Life	Life	Life
Michigan	8	6	6
Minnesota	6	6	6
Mississippi	8	-----	4
Missouri	12	12	6
Montana	8	-----	6
Nebraska	6	6	6
Nevada	6	-----	6
New Hampshire	Life	-----	Life
New Jersey	7**	7**	7**
New Mexico	8	8	6
New York	14	8	14
North Carolina	8	8	8

State	Court of Last Resort	Intermediate Appellate Court	General Jurisdiction Trial Courts
North Dakota	10	-----	6
Ohio	6	6	6
Oklahoma	6***	6	4
Oregon	6	6	6
Pennsylvania	10	10	10
Rhode Island	Life	-----	Life
South Carolina	10	6	6
South Dakota	8	-----	8
Tennessee	8	8	8
Texas	6***	6	4
Utah	10	10	6
Vermont	6	-----	6
Virginia	12	8	8
Washington	6	6	4
West Virginia	12	-----	8
Wisconsin	10	6	6
Wyoming	8	-----	6

* Chancery probate court judges serve 6 year terms
** Tenure granted upon reappointment after initial term
*** Terms of office are the same for the Supreme Court and Court of Criminal Appeals

Source: Council of State Governments, 1994.

Across the fifty states, terms in courts of last resort range from six years to life. Terms for intermediate appellate courts and general jurisdiction trial courts range from four years to life. However, only non-elective states grant judges lifetime tenure.[4]

Looking only at the thirty-eight states that utilize elections, the range of terms in the courts of last resort is six to 12 years. Most commonly, justices in these courts serve six-year terms, although a substantial number of states provide eight-year or ten-year terms for these offices. Wisconsin is one of the ten states where supreme court

---

[4] Even in appointive states that do not formally provide lifetime tenure, the expectation is reappointment.

justices serve ten-year terms. Only three elective states (California, Missouri, West Virginia) elect justices for 12-year terms.

In elective states having intermediate appellate courts, almost half (15 of 31, including Wisconsin) designate six-year terms for these courts. Only one state (Kansas) uses a four-year term. The remaining 15 states utilize eight-year, ten-year, or twelve-year terms.

Finally, the most common term for judges in general jurisdiction trial courts in elective states is six years. Twenty-two states (including Wisconsin) use six-year terms for their major trial courts. The remaining states use terms ranging from four to 15 years for these courts.

Judicial Selection in Wisconsin

Wisconsin, like every other state, has established qualifications for serving on the state bench. The primary formal requirement for holding judicial office in Wisconsin is being an attorney licensed to practice law in the state for five years immediately prior to selection. Most other states have similar requirements, where candidates for judgeships must be members of the state bar, usually for some specified minimum period. Only a handful of states fail to require state bar membership as a qualification for judicial office.

Like most other states, Wisconsin does not have a minimum age requirement for serving on the state bench. However, 20 states do have such requirements, even if the age is set at a relatively low minimum. For instance, several states specify that judges must be at least 21 years of age (North Carolina, Rhode Island), 25 (Alabama, Louisiana, Nevada), 26 (South Carolina), 30 (Arizona, Arkansas, Idaho, Kansas, Maryland, Mississippi, Nebraska, Oklahoma, Utah, West Virginia, Wyoming), or 35 years of age (New Mexico, South Dakota, Texas). Unlike most states, however, Wisconsin has a mandatory retirement age of 70. Only Massachusetts, New Hampshire, and New Jersey have similar provisions.

Judges in Wisconsin are elected on nonpartisan ballots in April. When three or more candidates file for the same office, a nonpartisan primary is held before the April election. As mentioned, justices are elected to the Supreme Court in statewide elections for ten-year terms. Judges are elected to the Court of Appeal and Circuit Courts from their respective districts or circuits for six-year terms.

Two of the most prominent features of judicial elections in the American states are the incumbency advantage and low levels of electoral competition. In a study of elections to state supreme courts in 23 non-Southern states (including Wisconsin) from 1948 through 1972, Dubois (1980) reported that incumbents tend to win, often without ever being challenged by opposing candidates. Moreover, candidates for judgeships tend to win with large proportions of the vote. Dubois determined that the incumbency advantage is highest in retention races, less so in nonpartisan elections, and lowest in partisan elections. Additionally, competition is greater in partisan than nonpartisan elections and also for open seats.

Dubois also noted, however, that of the 23 states in his study, five (approximately 22 percent) could be classified as competitive. Although Wisconsin was not one of these five, Wisconsin did emerge as the most competitive of the 14 nonpartisan election states. During the 1948-1972 period, seven of Wisconsin's 22 supreme court elections (31.8 percent) were competitive, or won by 55 percent of the vote or less.

Are statewide judicial elections in Wisconsin competitive into the 1980s and 1990s? The pattern is somewhat mixed. An examination of elections to the Supreme Court from 1980 through 1995 reveals a very striking, yet not surprising, pattern - incumbents win. No incumbents were defeated during this period, nor have any been defeated since 1967 when then Chief Justice Curric was defeated by Robert W. Hanson. However, while some incumbents are reelected without being challenged, others face very stiff electoral competition.

In 1984, 1985, 1986, 1987, and then again in 1993, incumbents seeking reelection to the Supreme Court were not challenged by opposing candidates. However, in 1989, 1990, and 1994, incumbents were challenged by opponents. Although each incumbent won reelection, the races for two of these three seats were quite competitive, where the sitting justices succeeded in retaining office by very narrow vote margins. In 1989, Shirley Abrahamson was challenged and managed to win reelection by only 55.0 percent of the vote. In 1990, Donald Steinmetz was challenged and won by only 51.9 percent of the vote. On the other hand, Janine Geske was challenged in 1994 and won reelection by a strong 77.2 percent of the vote. In short, judicial incumbents in Wisconsin safely can assume that they will retain their positions. However, incumbents are incorrect to believe that they will necessarily remain insulated from stiff electoral competition.

Additionally, competition for open seats is quite vigorous in Wisconsin, especially when activity in the primaries is considered. In 1980, 1983, and 1995, elections were held for open seats, or elections that did not involve incumbents seeking reelection. Three candidates entered the primary in 1980, and in the general election Donald Steinmetz won by 50.2 percent of the vote. In the 1983 race, three candidates entered the primary, and in the general election William Bablitch won by 58.9 percent of the vote. In the 1995 contest, five candidates ran in the primary, and in the general election Ann Bradley won by 54.8 percent of the vote.

Dubois described another interesting pattern in his study of judicial elections - slightly more than half of all justices serving in state supreme courts from 1948 through 1972 initially obtained their positions through gubernatorial appointment rather than election. The Wisconsin Supreme Court is very much in line with the nation on this dimension. Of the justices serving from 1848 through 1995, 42 of 75 initially were appointed rather than elected.

Several important background characteristics of the twelve justices serving on the Wisconsin Supreme Court from 1980 through 1995 are described in Table IX-7. Until very recently, the composition of the Wisconsin Supreme Court was almost exclusively male. Until 1993, only one female had ever served on the state's highest court, reflecting an extraordinary under-representation of women. However, with the appointment of Janine Geske in 1993 and her reelection to the court in 1994, and the election of Ann Bradley in 1995, three female members now sit on the Wisconsin Supreme Court. As Table IX-7 also reveals, justices are closely tied to the state by birth or education, and are initially appointed about as often as initially elected. The average age at accession to office for these justices was 50.1 years. Of the 41 justices completing their service on the Wisconsin Supreme Court in the 20th century, the average length of service was 11.8 years. Service ranged from a mere 15 days to 34 years.

Table IX-7

JUSTICES OF THE WISCONSIN SUPREME COURT, 1980 - 96

Justice	Place of Birth	Legal Education: J.D.	Initial Method of Accession	Age at Time of Accession
Beilfuss	Wisconsin	UW-Madison	Elected	48
Heffernan	Wisconsin	UW-Madison	Appointed	44
Day	Wisconsin	UW-Madison	Appointed	55
Abrahamson	New York	Indiana*	Appointed	43
Callow	Wisconsin	UW-Madison	Elected	56
Coffey	Wisconsin	Marquette	Elected	56

Justice	Place of Birth	Legal Education: J.D.	Initial Method of Accession	Age at Time of Accession
Steinmetz	Wisconsin	UW-Madison	Elected	56
Ceci	New York	Marquette	Appointed	55
Bablitch	Wisconsin	UW-Madison	Elected	42
Wilcox	Wisconsin	UW-Madison	Appointed	56
Geske	Wisconsin	Marquette	Appointed	45
Bradley	Wisconsin	UW-Madison	Elected	45
Crooks	Wisconsin	Notre Dame	Elected	57

* Graduate work at UW-Madison, SJD

Source: State of Wisconsin, *Blue Book*, 1995-96.

These characteristics are quite typical of supreme court justices in other states. A study recently conducted by Dudley (1994) revealed that, of the supreme court justices completing their careers from 1960 through 1992 in 42 states (672 justices), the overwhelming majority were male. Moreover, in terms of age, justices in the Midwest on average were 53.9 years of age at the time of accession to office and tended to serve an average of 12.9 years on the bench. And as Glick and Emmert (1987) noted, most supreme court justices are connected to the states in which they serve by birth or education.

Given the variations in selection systems among the states and the increasing interest in adopting the Missouri Plan, do these recruitment processes actually shape the quality of the bench? In other words, do certain selection systems result in the recruitment of more qualified justices? Based on the evidence accumulated to date, the answer seems to be an unqualified no.

In a comprehensive study of the background characteristics of justices in state supreme courts, Glick and Emmert (1987) examined the question of whether different recruitment systems result in the selection of different types of people for the bench. They concluded that the credentials and backgrounds of those selected for judgeships are quite similar, regardless of the method of selection. However, they also noted that the Missouri Plan tends to disfavor, to some extent, the appointment of Jews and Catholics to state supreme courts.

Much more importantly, is there evidence that the process of having to seek reelection affects justices' decisions? The answer to this question is a highly qualified yes. There is some evidence that, at least on the issue of the death penalty, justices facing competitive electoral conditions are much more likely to uphold death sentences, all other factors taken into account (Hall, 1992, 1995). However, the extent to which elected justices respond to their constituencies on all other matters of public policy, especially issues not very salient to voters, remains unknown.

Methods for Removing Judges

Wisconsin judges face a high degree of formal accountability. Since judges in Wisconsin are elected, all are subject to removal simply by being voted out of office at the completion of their terms. However, judges also can be removed by a wide variety of other methods, either by voters, the Wisconsin Legislature, or Wisconsin

Supreme Court. In fact, Wisconsin is one of but a handful of states providing four separate formal mechanisms for ousting sitting judges. Table IX-8 lists the various methods currently operative in the states for removing judges and the states that utilize each method.

Table IX-8

METHODS FOR REMOVING STATE COURT JUDGES

State	Impeachment	Recall	Supreme Court	Legislative Address
Alabama			X	
Alaska	X		X	
Arizona	X	X	X	
Arkansas	X		X	X
California	X	X	X	
Colorado	X		X	
Connecticut	X		X	X
Delaware	X		X	
Florida	X		X	
Georgia	X		X	
Hawaii			X	
Idaho	X		X	
Illinois	X		X	
Indiana			X	
Iowa	X		X	
Kansas	X		X	
Kentucky	X		X	
Louisiana	X		X	
Maine	X		X	X
Maryland	X		X	
Massachusetts	X		X	X
Michigan	X		X	X
Minnesota	X		X	

State	Impeachment	Recall	Supreme Court	Legislative Address
Mississippi	X		X	X
Missouri			X	
Montana	X		X	
Nebraska	X		X	
Nevada	X	X	X	X
New Hampshire	X			X
New Jersey	X		X	
New Mexico	X		X	
New York	X		X	X
North Carolina			X	
North Dakota	X	X	X	
Ohio	X	X	X	X
Oklahoma	X		X	
Oregon			X	
Pennsylvania	X		X	
Rhode Island	X		X	
South Carolina	X		X	X
South Dakota	X		X	
Tennessee	X			X
Texas	X		X	X
Utah	X		X	
Vermont	X		X	
Virginia	X		X	
Washington	X		X	
West Virginia	X		X	
Wisconsin	X	X	X	X
Wyoming	X		X	

Source: Council of State Governments, 1994.

As Table IX-8 demonstrates, state court judges across the nation are subject to impeachment, legislative address, recall, and removal by the state supreme court. Impeachment is a process conducted by the legislature, only for actions described in the state constitution. Wisconsin judges are subject to impeachment "for corrupt conduct in office, or for crimes and misdemeanors." Simply disagreeing with a judge's rulings is not grounds for impeachment. In Wisconsin, impeachment trials are conducted in the state senate, and a two-thirds vote of members present is required to convict. Forty-three other states provide for the impeachment of their judges.

Like 13 other state legislatures, the Wisconsin Legislature has the power to remove judges through the process of legislative address. Grounds for removal through legislative address are broader than the grounds for impeachment. However, the result is more difficult to achieve, requiring a two-thirds vote of the membership of both houses of the legislature.

In addition to voting judges out of office at the completion of their terms, Wisconsin voters can remove sitting judges during their terms through recall. Generally, recall is a citizen-initiated process where petitions are collected requesting a special election. If the required number of signatures is gathered, an election is scheduled where voters are asked on the ballot whether the judge in question should continue in office. If a majority of those voting cast ballots against retention, the judge immediately is removed. If the majority of those voting indicate that the judge should be retained, the judge simply continues to serve the remainder of the term. Only five other states allow their judges to be recalled.

Finally, the Wisconsin Supreme Court, like virtually every other state court of last resort, has the authority to remove judges. In Wisconsin, the Supreme Court can remove any judge upon conviction of a felony, recommendation of the Disciplinary Committee, or retirement for a disability. The Wisconsin Constitution specifies that judges are "subject to reprimand, censure, suspension, removal for cause or for disability, by the supreme court pursuant to procedures established by the legislature by law." A committee called the Wisconsin Judicial Commission has been established to receive complaints against sitting judges and make recommendations to the Supreme Court for further action.

The Annual Report of the Wisconsin Judicial Commission for Calendar Year 1994 indicates that from 1990 through 1994, the Commission received 1,986 complaints. After screening, the Commission filed 297 requests for investigation, 223 of which were dismissed on preliminary evaluation. The Commission then authorized 74 investigations. In these 74 cases, 53 complaints were dismissed with no action, 20 complaints were dismissed with letters of concern, and 5 complaints were filed with Supreme Court (several cases contained more than one complaint). Of these five complaints, none resulted in removal.

Overall, in the disciplinary cases sent to the Supreme Court from 1978 through 1994, two judges were removed from office, eight judges were suspended, two judges were reprimanded, and three complaints were dismissed. In the cases where judges actually were removed from the bench, the first (in 1981) involved a sitting judge who had been convicted of a felony. In the second case (in 1985), a judge was found guilty before the Supreme Court of falsifying court records and using judicial power in a retaliatory manner.

Despite the formal methods for removing judges, the fact remains that the tenure of a judge in Wisconsin, and in all states, is very secure. Even with the Wisconsin Legislature, Supreme Court, and voters having power to oust sitting judges, the likelihood of a judge being removed from office is quite remote.

Decision-making in State Supreme Courts

Discussing the decision-making propensities of state courts is surprisingly difficult. While the statistics already reported in this chapter are collected regularly and systematically for all states, information about the decisions actually rendered by state judicial institutions are gathered only infrequently, usually by political scientists conducting case studies of a single state or handful of states. Therefore, it is not possible at this point to compare state courts comprehensively along the lines of who wins and loses the cases, what kinds of sentences or monetary awards.are being handed down, how often trial courts are overturned by appellate courts, or how individual judges decide cases.

Nonetheless, some data have been gathered that allow comparisons on several interesting dimensions related to decision-making in these courts. These data have been collected for state supreme courts rather than other types of state courts, largely because political scientists have used state supreme courts to test the generalizability of studies of the United States Supreme Court. To date, state supreme courts have been compared in terms of their dissent rates, levels of judicial activism, and internal operating procedures.

Dissent rates measure the proportion of cases decided by an appellate court in which at least one member openly expressed disagreement with the decision of the court. One might expect dissent to result simply from ideological disagreement; a justice dissents because (s)he does not agree with the majority's decision about the proper outcome of the case. However, dissent rates are determined by a variety of complex factors, including the court's docket type, the internal operating rules used by the court, and conditions in the external environment (Peterson, 1981; Brace and Hall, 1990, 1993).

The most recent data on dissent rates in state supreme courts indicate that the Wisconsin Supreme Court ranked 28th among the states in 1980-81 (Glick and Pruet, 1986). For that period, 15.1 percent of the decisions handed down by the court invoked disagreement among the justices. During the same period, California ranked highest, with a dissent rate of 54.8 percent, while Hawaii ranked lowest with a dissent rate of 2.4 percent.

State supreme courts also vary in how frequently they overturn acts of state legislatures, an action generally defined as judicial activism. A study of all fifty states (Emmert, 1988) noted that from 1981 through 1985, 2,660 state laws in 3,248 court cases were challenged as unconstitutional in state supreme courts. While there were significant variations among the states in the number of laws challenged and the percent actually invalidated, state supreme courts, on average, invalidated about 2.4 laws per year per court, or about one-quarter of the statutes challenged. In the aggregate, state courts are active in checking the power of state legislatures.

Among the states, Wisconsin ranked 42nd in the number of laws challenged as unconstitutional. During the 1981-1985 period, 31 laws were challenged in the Wisconsin Supreme Court, compared to the national average of 53.2 laws. However, and more importantly, when the states are ranked by the percentage of laws challenged being declared unconstitutional, Wisconsin ranked 11th among the states. In Wisconsin, 32.3 percent of the laws challenged were invalidated by the Supreme Court, a statistic well above the national average of 22.7 percent. In short, the Wisconsin Supreme Court is an active player in state politics and by no means manifests deference to the state legislature. When statutes are challenged, the Wisconsin Supreme Court subjects the legislature to a high degree of constitutional scrutiny.

Finally, as mentioned, state courts utilize detailed rules for resolving disputes, and state supreme courts are no exception. Among the most interesting rules are those that establish patterns of interaction among appellate court justices. How justices interact within a court can affect the level of dissent and, in some situations, the outcomes of cases, quite apart from the facts of the cases.

Table IX-9 describes conference practices in state supreme courts.[5] As the table reveals, the states utilize an interesting variety of procedures for allocating opinion assignments among the justices and for conducting business in conference. And, quite clearly, the states do not follow the example of the United States Supreme Court, where opinion assignments are made by the Chief Justice when in the majority and where voting and discussion take place in order of seniority. Only three states emulate the nation's highest court.

---

[5] This discussion is based upon information reported by Hall (1990).

Table IX-9

CONFERENCE PRACTICES IN STATE SUPREME COURTS

State	Opinion Assignment	Discussion Order	Voting Order
Alabama	Rotation	No formal order	Reverse seniority
Alaska	Rotation	Reverse seniority	Reverse seniority
Arizona	Chief Justice if in majority	No formal order	No formal order
Arkansas	Rotation	Reverse seniority from reporting justice	Reverse seniority from reporting justice
California	Chief Justice	Seniority, Chief Justice last	Seniority, Chief Justice last
Colorado	Chief Justice	Reverse seniority	Reverse seniority
Connecticut	Chief Justice	Most junior justice first, then no formal order	Most junior justice first, then no formal order
Delaware	Chief Justice	Reverse seniority	Reverse seniority
Florida	Rotation	Seniority, Chief Justice last	Seniority, Chief Justice last
Georgia	Rotation	No formal order	No formal order
Hawaii	Chief Justice	No formal order	No formal order
Idaho	Random	Reverse seniority	Reverse seniority
Illinois	Rotation	No formal order	No formal order
Indiana	Consensus of the majority	Reverse seniority	Reverse seniority
Iowa	Rotation	No formal order	No formal order
Kansas	Chief Justice	No formal order	No formal order
Kentucky	Chief Justice	No formal order	No formal order
Louisiana	Random	No formal order	No formal order
Maine	Rotation	Reverse seniority	Reverse seniority
Maryland	Chief Justice if in the majority	Reverse seniority	Reverse seniority
Massachusetts	Chief Justice	Seniority, Chief Justice last	Seniority, Chief Justice last
Michigan	Random	Rotation	Rotation

State	Opinion Assignment	Discussion Order	Voting Order
Minnesota	Rotation	Seniority, Chief Justice last	Seniority, Chief Justice last
Mississippi	Random	Alternating seniority and reverse seniority	Alternating seniority and reverse seniority
Missouri	Rotation	Reverse seniority	Reverse seniority
Montana	Rotation	No formal order	No formal order
Nebraska	Rotation	No formal order	Seniority
Nevada	Rotation	No formal order	No formal order
New Hampshire	Random	No formal order	No formal order
New Jersey	Chief Justice if in the majority	Rotation	Seniority
New Mexico	Rotation	No formal order	No formal order
New York	Random	Reverse seniority	Reverse seniority
North Carolina	Rotation	Reverse seniority	Reverse seniority
North Dakota	Rotation	Reverse seniority	No formal order
Ohio	Random	Seniority	Reverse seniority
Oklahoma Court of Criminal Appeals	Rotation	Seniority	Seniority
Oklahoma Supreme Court	Rotation	Reverse seniority	Reverse seniority
Oregon	Chief Justice	Rotation	Rotation
Pennsylvania	Chief Justice	Seniority	Seniority
Rhode Island	Rotation	Reverse seniority	Reverse seniority
South Carolina	Rotation	Seniority	Seniority
South Dakota	Random	Seniority	Seniority
Tennessee	Random	No formal order	No formal order
Texas Court of Criminal Appeals	Random	Seniority	Seniority
Texas Supreme Court	Rotation	No formal order	No formal order
Utah	Rotation	No formal order	No formal order
Vermont	Rotation	Reverse seniority	Reverse seniority

State	Opinion Assignment	Discussion Order	Voting Order
Virginia	Random	No formal order	No formal order
Washington	Random	No formal order	No formal order
West Virginia	Rotation	Reverse seniority	Reverse seniority
Wisconsin	Random	Seniority	Seniority
Wyoming	Chief Justice	Rotation	Rotation

Source: Hall, 1990.

Opinion assignments are very important in appellate courts. The majority opinion, or opinion of the court, explains the court's decision on the merits (i.e., whether the court is affirming or reversing the lower court) and presents the authoritative interpretation of law relevant to the case. Additionally, the method for assigning opinions may create important strategic opportunities for certain members, as will be described in greater detail below.

When making opinion assignments, the states have a pronounced tendency to assign cases randomly or by rotation, removing any likely strategic advantage for particular members of the court. Thirty-seven of the fifty-two state courts of last resort assign majority opinions randomly or by rotation. Generally, with rotation, the clerk of court or central staff maintains a roster of justices, usually listed in order of seniority. The clerk simply takes a list of docketed cases and assigns the next case to the justice next on the list from the previous assignment. In states making opinion assignments randomly, the clerk or other court personnel (or sometimes the justices) draw docket numbers or conduct some similar lottery-type procedure to allocate assignments among the justices.

In states using rotating or random opinion assignments, if opinion assignment takes place before oral argument or discussion of the case merits, there always is the chance that the justice assigned the opinion will not be in the decision majority. Consequently, the 29 courts assigning opinions before conference have developed procedures to reassign opinions if the justice initially assigned the case ends up on the losing side. These rules are quite informal and include such methods as volunteering or trading cases. Eight states (Michigan, Mississippi, New Hampshire, New York, North Carolina, Ohio, Tennessee, Wisconsin), however, assign opinions through rotation or randomly after consideration of the case merits, thereby avoiding the problem of reassignment.

Ten states permit the chief justice always to make opinion assignments, whether in the majority or not. Only Arizona, Maryland, and New Jersey follow the practice of the United States Supreme Court, granting assignment power to the Chief Justice if in the majority or otherwise to the most senior justice in the majority for each case. Finally, in only one state (Indiana), opinions are assigned by consensus of the majority. Justices in the majority either volunteer for assignments or nominate others in the majority.

The states also vary significantly in the rules governing discussion and voting in conference. It should be noted, however, that these rules are not rigidly adhered to in many courts. Informality and collegiality dominate the operating environments of state supreme courts. Also, opinion assignment methods influence the process of discussion and voting.

As mentioned, the clear majority of states utilize rotating or random opinion assignments. In these states, the justice receiving the assignment is referred to as the reporting or assignment justice. Irrespective of discussion or voting rules, the reporting justice speaks first and often votes first. Thereafter, order for discussing cases varies. Overall, the states are about evenly divided between discussion in reverse seniority and having no preordained sequence among the justices. Twenty supreme courts do have a designated order among the justices for discussion, while 16 follow the order of reverse seniority. In 11 supreme courts, the justices speak in order of seniority, and in five the order for discussion is based on rotation.

The Wisconsin Supreme Court is quite typical in the manner in which opinions are assigned. As Table IX-9 indicates, opinions in the Court are assigned randomly. More specifically, opinion assignments are made in conference after oral argument, by random draw. If the justice drawing the opinion is not in the majority, the case simply is returned for redrawing. Justices in Wisconsin follow a seniority rule for discussion and voting, making the state somewhat less typical on this dimension.

Each of the methods just described for opinion assignments and conference participation has potentially important ramifications for the operating environment and the distribution of power within the institution. Opinion assignments made at the discretion of particular members facilitate the development of substantive specializations among the justices. With the acquiescence of the assigner, justices can volunteer for cases in their particular areas of interest and can serve as experts for the court on those subjects. Discretionary assignments also present strategic opportunities. Justices with opinion assignment responsibilities can use assignments as rewards or sanctions to encourage consensus or support for the assigner's position. Interesting or politically important cases can be used as incentives while uninteresting or routine cases can be used as punishments. Additionally, assigners can use opinion assignments to increase the chances of holding together tenuous majorities. By assigning the majority opinion to the most marginal member of a decision coalition, the assigner may be able to prevent vote defection, or a justice changing sides before the decision is announced. Finally, justices with assignment responsibilities can maximize their power by taking assignments for themselves in areas most politically salient to them or by assigning the opinion to the justice closest ideologically, guaranteeing greater control over the wording of the opinion in areas especially significant to the assigner.

Rotating or random assignments have important consequences as well. These methods disperse power among the members of a court rather than concentrating power in the hands of a few court members. By precluding an effective system of rewards and sanctions, rotating or random assignments actually facilitate the expression of disagreement among members of the court. Moreover, such methods insure that each justice writes on a wide array of legal issues, mitigating against the development of specialists with the court.

Regarding discussion and voting rules, rotating or randomizing the sequence in which justices are allowed to raise issues or express preferences in conference minimizes the likelihood that dominant personalities or more senior members will control the court's agenda or be in a preferred position to influence other members. Conversely, conference practices that grant either the most senior or most junior justice the opportunity always to speak first or vote first create important advantages. When discussion and voting occur in order of seniority, the most senior members potentially can maximize their influence over more junior colleagues, especially if the court utilizes discretionary opinion assignments. When justices speak and vote in reverse order of seniority, the least senior members are more quickly socialized into the job of supreme court justice.

Research on the consequences of alternative rule structures on the politics of courts is in its infancy. However, evidence clearly suggests that these rules affect the manner in which individual justices are willing to express disagreement within the court and, to a lesser extent, cast votes in the cases.

Conclusion

As the preceding discussion reveals, Wisconsin courts are important, and sometimes aggressive, players in state politics. The Wisconsin judiciary handles a large and diverse caseload, processing nearly 500,000 disputes a year. The judges who decide these cases are closely connected to the political culture of the state through their upbringing and educational experiences, and are linked directly to the voters through the electoral process. Wisconsin courts also have frequent opportunities to interact with the other branches of state government and do so in a highly independent manner. In short, the Wisconsin judiciary and all other courts in the American states are fascinating political institutions that have a profound impact on the landscape of American politics.

Part IV: Public Policy in Wisconsin

CHAPTER X

BUDGET AND FINANCE

By Mort Sipress*

State government budgeting and finance is dynamically changing with revisions in relationships among the different levels of government in the American system of federalism. Local governments are subject to state government controls, but state government also serves in an intermediary position between the national and local levels. Thus, we cannot look simply at what the state derives from its own taxation and spends on its own operations. We must also examine what the state receives from the national government and other sources as well as what the state provides to local units of government.

There are several fiscal consequences to the intermixing of federal, state and local roles in the federal system. One consequence is complexity. It is difficult to unscramble which expenditures and programs are to be attributed to each level of government. For example, a cognitively disabled person may receive both financial aid and special services from each level of government. Table X-1 identifies many of the programs, funding sources and benefits typical for such a person. One can see in this table a complex of programs and funding sources for a cognitively disabled person who cannot care for himself or herself. State budgeting and finance, as well as other state policies, are central to determining the levels of benefits and the mix of programs for the support of disabled persons.

Another consequence of the state's role in the system of federalism is that many funds, including those derived from the national government, are tied together in complex formulas which govern their distribution to local units of government. Shared taxes, for example, involve the state returning certain percentages of money to the local unit of government. Proposed changes in formula-driven state expenditure policies are among the more contentious controversies in Wisconsin politics. But once a formula is established there is little discretion over total expenditures for local aid. As a result, other discretionary items in the state budget attract considerable attention but constitute a relatively smaller percentage of total spending.

It is also important to understand that the portion of the state budget that attracts the most attention, the general purpose revenue (GPR) portion, is NOT the total budget. The total budget includes federal aid, segregated funds (separate funds which are earmarked for particular programs), program revenue (earmarked for particular programs, but with the revenues deposited in the general fund), borrowed money and GPR. The total budget is much higher than general purpose revenue spending and taxing, but the GPR portion is popularly referred to as "the budget." The non-GPR portion tends to receive less attention in budget deliberations and reporting because less discretion is exercised over important parts of it and because special taxes and fees are less controversial, or at least less noticeable, than general tax sources such as income and sales taxes. Notable exceptions to this general point exist, however. For example, during the last budget deliberations, Joint Finance Committee members spent many hours debating an increase in hunting and fishing licenses. Moreover, almost the entire transportation budget is funded by segregated funds and federal money, not through general taxes. However, the legislature was unable to resolve funding issues for this portion of the budget and therefore put off making any decisions on transportation funding until later in 1995 for the 1995-97 biennium.

State budgeting and finance will be discussed in four sections: 1) budgeting approaches, conflicts and processes; 2) expenditures; 3) shared revenues, taxes, and credits; and 4) internal sources of revenue.

---

* Professor of Political Science, University of Wisconsin-Eau Claire.

Table X-1

FUNDING AND TYPES OF BENEFITS IN SELECTED PROGRAMS FOR THE COGNITIVELY DISABLED

Program	Source of Funds	Type of Benefits
Supplemental Security Income (SSI)	Federal	Cash
State Supplement to SSI	State	Cash
Medical Assistance (Medicaid)	Federal and State	Services
Supplement for supervision if care-taker is employed outside the home	Federal	Cash
Supportive Employment (for community based jobs)	State, Federal and Personal	Salary and Services
Community Aids (supplement to other services)	State and County	Services
Community Integration Program (CIP)	Federal, State and County	Services
Community Options Program (COP - keeping disabled and elderly in own community)	State	Services
Respite Care (to relieve caretakers)	CIP	Services
Day Services (independent living skills and pre-vocational training)	State and Federal	Services
Work Services (e.g., sheltered workshops, supportive employment)	Community Aids	Services and Salary
Special Transportation	CIP, COP, Community Aids	Services

Sources: Interviews in June 1995, with Kevin Mannel, Supervisor, Adult Services, Eau Claire County Department of Health and Human Services and Sylvia R. Sipress, member, Eau Claire County Long Term Support Committee.

Budget Making: Approaches, Conflicts and Processes

Government budgeting is more than a mechanical exercise. It is no less than the distribution of the resources that the government is prepared to allocate for a variety of purposes. Indeed, the budget is a significant policy statement in that it constitutes much of a government's policy priorities. At the same time, the budget-making process is rarely marked by a thorough evaluation of many programs in any given year.

In past years, political scientists found that decision makers tended toward what is called *incrementalism* in developing budgets. Robert A. Dahl and Charles E. Lindblom defined it as "a method of social action that takes existing reality as one alternative and compares the probable gains and losses of closely related alternatives by making relatively small adjustments in existing reality" (Dahl and Lindblom, 1963: 82). In budgetary practice, this is a process through which spending for most programs in a budget are adjusted upward, usually modestly, from the previous year's allocation without any real examination of the existing base. It is also possible for there to be small spending reductions which is called *decrementalism*. The degree of change is often all that is examined. As Aaron Wildavsky, one of the leading analysts of the politics of budgeting at the federal level, has said, "the largest determining factor of the size and content of this year's budget is last year's budget. Most of the budget is a product of previous decisions" (Wildavsky, 1984: 13).

It is clear today, though, that incrementalism was more a product of earlier decades. Donald Axelrod points out that in "the relatively affluent 1960s and 1970s . . . fair shares of increments and ploys to protect the base budget appeared to be realistic expectations." However, Axelrod maintains that in the more recent "era of austerity, large deficits, expenditure ceilings, cutbacks in base budgets and changes in fiscal policy," incrementalism has become less relevant (Axelrod, 1988: 306-307). This certainly is true for the 1990s as well.

In Wisconsin, the previous budget combined with incremental adjustments determined many of the initial budgetary requests in earlier decades. As a Legislative Fiscal Bureau report pointed out, "agency budget requests... use as a starting point the existing budget level." There may be required technical adjustments to this base, but the budget instructions from the State Budget Office in the Department of Administration tended to "direct an agency to 'build' its budget request by identifying the budget changes (either increases, decreases or reallocations) that are needed or that it would like from its current base budget level. Most of the budget 'decision items' identified in agency requests and the Governor's Budget Books represent, then, increments of change over the existing or continuation level of spending" (Rhodes, 1987: 17).

In 1994, however, Governor Tommy Thompson and the Department of Administration asked all state agencies to develop budgets which would produce five percent and ten percent reductions in their base budgets. Only the University of Wisconsin System was spared this exercise. The cuts were a product of legislation passed earlier in 1994 which committed the state to funding two-thirds of the costs of elementary and secondary education instead of the current approximately 40 percent state support as a way of producing substantial local property tax reductions. Indeed, the perceived pressure to cut property taxes drove much of the fiscal decision making in the development of the 1995-1997 budget. Thompson's directive portended significant spending reductions for many state agencies and programs in exchange for property tax relief through school aids to local districts.

Budgetary demands tend to determine the initial expectation of revenue needs. Even when governors attempt to have the legislature first revise the state's tax structure so as to establish the amount available for expenditures, lawmakers have generally rejected the approach, preferring first to react to the governor's budget. In the 1970s and 1980s, both Governors Lee Dreyfus and Tommy Thompson experienced legislative rejection of proposals to adopt revenue bills before adopting a budget. Legislators appear to prefer first getting a picture of what they believe are the state's programmatic needs, then examining how they might adjust the governor's budgetary and revenue recommendations. By the 1990s, however, Governor Thompson directed that budgets be developed without any general increase in income or sales taxes. This sharply restricts expenditures largely to what the existing tax structure can support along with selective fee increases, such as university tuition.

Some of the legislature's leadership had also attempted to establish a process by which revenue sources would be examined somewhat separately from expenditure considerations. In 1985 the Assembly Ways and Means Committee was created for this purpose. However, that committee has not had the intended impact of developing tax policy independently of spending policy because of both tradition and the interdependence of spending and taxing.

Nevertheless, this does not mean that budgetary considerations are unrelated to revenue expectations.

213

Varying projections of the amount that the tax system and federal aids will produce, changing economic conditions in the state, and periodic perceptions of public disapproval of tax levels do initiate consideration of both budgetary and tax revisions throughout the budget-making process.

Programs can be substantially increased, reduced, or even eliminated while new ones may be created. Moreover, policy changes proposed by the governor or legislature are a common feature in the budget bill that is ultimately passed. H. Rupert Theobold, as former head of the Legislative Reference Bureau, observed that as much as one-third of all new law created during a two-year legislative session is passed as part of the budget (Hurley, 1987: 10).

James J. Gosling found that agencies, the governor, his chief budgetary lieutenants, and key elements of the legislature do promote significant spending, taxing, and other policy changes in the budget. He points out that the State Budget Office director "stresses policy development over budget operations. Responsibility for budget operations and control is relegated to the team leader for budget operations" (Gosling, 1987:62). Indeed, as a key aid to the governor, the budget director works to incorporate important policy initiatives into the budget.

The 1995-1997 budget as proposed by Governor Thompson was over 2500 pages long with large numbers of policy initiatives included. Especially notable was the reorganization of important parts of state government to give the governor the power to put most state agencies under his control.

The state of Wisconsin uses what is called *program budgeting*. The state budget is made up of the "appropriations allocated for each program carried on by a department or other state agency," including the amounts for shared revenue and other aids to local units of government, instead of itemizing specific amounts for things like supplies, equipment, and personnel (State of Wisconsin, *Blue Book*, 1985-86: 272).

The state also uses an omnibus budget bill approach. Unlike the federal and many other state governments, which use separate appropriations bills for different programs and agencies as well as separate revenue bills, Wisconsin places most of its spending and revenue law into a comprehensive budget bill. Governor Tommy Thompson attempted to revise this approach in 1987 by introducing five bills with one each for revenue, general spending, natural resources, transportation and capital construction. However, in that year the Joint Committee on Finance consolidated its considerations into an omnibus approach with the traditional exception of capital construction.

By 1995, Thompson succeeded in getting the transportation budget considered separately. However, the legislature attempted to blend the transportation budget back into the general budget. Only the inability of Republican legislative majorities to agree on tax and other financing means for highways led to separating transportation out of the budget and putting off new funding decisions of those programs to the fall of 1995.

The process of developing and adopting a budget is much more than simply adopting principles of accounting. It takes place in a charged and partisan political atmosphere precisely because political priorities are at stake. There are numerous conflicts that must be resolved through the various steps of the budget making process. The major conflicts revolve around several elements:

1. Revenue projections by the executive branch's Department of Revenue and the Legislative Fiscal Bureau, a specialized service staff in the legislative branch, frequently differ. Each tailor their projections to economic expectations which can range from a worst-case possible to a best-case possible set of assumptions. In turn, what various policy makers think can be budgeted is constantly caught up in these differences over revenue projections.

2. The share of state funds to be transferred to local units of government and school districts is a perpetual point of controversy. More than half of state funds are passed on to local areas. The formulas for distribution, along with the degree to which the state might transfer direct property tax relief to local

residents, are regular bases for dispute among legislators and between the legislature and the governor.

3. State mandates to local governments and school districts concerning programs to be run at the local level are usually not completely funded through state grants. This has usually forced municipalities, counties, and school districts to boost the increasingly controversial level of property taxes. The local units, in turn, constantly press for either more funds or reduced mandates.

4. The likelihood of conflict increases still further when the governorship and legislature are controlled by different political parties. Given the usually competitive nature of gubernatorial and several legislative elections, the possibilities of party division in Wisconsin government are increased.

5. Rural-urban divisions also are an important source of conflict, even in years when the governorship and the legislature are controlled by the same party. Financial strains in both the rural and urban areas exacerbate conflicts over formulas for distribution of shared revenues, over state programmatic mandates, and over the very level of shared revenues that will be provided by the state.

6. The distribution of funds to state agencies and the state employee salary structure are also constant areas of conflict. Agencies, of course, prefer at least incremental increases even in times of fiscal stress. They may be forced, however, to emphasize minimization of funding cuts during such periods. They press their demands on the Department of Administration, the governor, the Joint Committee on Finance, and the legislature as a whole. Meanwhile, state employee unions press their demands in collective bargaining negotiations with the Department of Employment Relations. Any agreements are submitted to the legislature's Joint Committee on Employment Relations as are salary recommendations for those employees who do not possess the right to bargain collectively (mainly University of Wisconsin faculty and management level officials).

These kinds of conflicts were certainly on display during the 1995 budget deliberations. In appearances before hearings by the Joint Committee on Finance during the spring, thousands of citizens signed up to testify on various parts of the governor's proposed budget. At the hearing in River Falls on March 30, 1995, so many hundreds sought to testify that the committee members indicated a willingness to sit into the evening, but also wound up restricting most who testified to two or three minutes each (Direct observation, March 30, 1995).

Large numbers of elderly and disabled people sought to reverse proposals to eliminate a home care program designed to help people avoid going into nursing homes. University personnel opposed a proposal which would have required the University of Wisconsin to place a significant portion of its computing activities under the control of the Department of Administration. Law enforcement personnel opposed a proposal which would have put a key computer data base which they access 24 hours a day onto a Department of Administration centralized mainframe computer. School board members and teachers strenuously opposed efforts to put control of elementary and secondary education under an appointee of the governor instead of under the superintendent of public instruction. Many school districts opposed revisions in the school aid formula which would give wealthier districts greater gains than less well off districts. Others supported the massive shift in funding of public schools from property taxes to state coffers to the tune of two-thirds of school costs (estimated to be a $1.2 billion shift). Environmental organizations testified against eliminating the Public Intervenors office. Indeed, in these hearings relatively few rallied around the governor's proposals. Most sought to avoid what they perceived as disadvantageous policies and funding arrangements concerning programs from which most present benefitted. It became clear, however, that the majority on the committee and in the legislature as a whole were strongly inclined to support much of what the governor submitted. This was partially out of political party loyalty and partially out of a primary focus on property tax relief via a shift in school funding. Some of the governor's proposals would be modified or eliminated, such as eliminating one to cut the highest income tax bracket but reduce a property tax credit which would raise income taxes for many middle income people. Most of his policy and funding priorities, though, were supported by the Republican majority throughout the process.

Wisconsin uses a biennial budgeting approach. Governors usually submit recommended budgets for a two-year period and the legislature operates from that perspective. However, changing economic conditions, including changes in projected state revenues, usually necessitate budget review and special legislative sessions during the fiscal year in order to make adjustments in the two-year budget. The biennial budget initially adopted by the legislature and governor rarely winds up being the final budget by the time the end of the biennium is reached. Biennial budgets are not significantly different from annual budgets when the former are regularly adjusted through budget review bills and special legislative sessions. In practice, the executive and legislative branches have been in a posture of almost continual budget review for a number of years.

The budget process begins some 18 months in advance of the start of the fiscal year. In January of even numbered years, about a year before a governor's proposed budget is submitted to the legislature, budget analysts in the State Budget Office of the Department of Administration are asked to "identify issues that might become the subject of policy analysis." The state budget director then meets with the secretary of the Department of Administration, the governor and the governor's policy director to identify topics which the budget analysts should develop more fully. The governor may also solicit input from key cabinet agency heads, key legislators from his own party, and other important political advisors (Gosling, 1987: 56).

By May the analysts and state budget director review the status of this policy development stage. Some studies may have been done in consultation with relevant cabinet departments, but noncabinet agencies and those likely to oppose the polices are unlikely to be involved. The review, some four months before the autumn submissions of proposed budgets by the agencies, produces briefing sessions with the governor, the secretary of the Department of Administration, the state budget director, budget team leaders and analysts, some of the executive office staff, and selected cabinet agency heads.

This part of the process tends to put noncabinet agencies at a disadvantage. It is the State Budget Office which establishes the review session agenda and these agencies are not usually represented at the briefings (Gosling, 1987: 56-57). Moreover, the subsequent briefings help produce gubernatorial budget guidelines which the Department of Administration (DOA) issues to the various state agencies when asking them to develop their spending requests.

Agency officials build their requests around a combination of the guidelines and their concern for sufficient funds to continue their operations, in the past often at an incrementally higher level of expenditure. In some instances, the agencies may propose expansions in response to the governor's priorities, changing conditions and agency goals. They may also make some strategic decisions to pad their requests in anticipation of cuts so as to try to avoid reductions below a program maintenance level. At the same time, and periodically throughout the year, revenue officials develop projections for what the tax structure could be expected to produce.

In 1994 Governor Thompson forced what can be called "reduced base budgeting." It involved asking all agencies to submit significant reductions in base budgets: a five percent reduction in the first year of the biennium and ten percent in the second. Given that the rate of inflation was expect to increase by more than 3 percent each year of the biennium, the reductions would be closer to a 16 percent cut from base budgets by the end of the second year of the two-year budget cycle. As mentioned earlier, this was driven by the overriding desire by the governor and the legislative majority to significantly reduce property taxes by having the state fund two-thirds of elementary and secondary education. The major exceptions were the Department of Corrections, which would have to oversee a substantial increase in prison construction and populations, and the University of Wisconsin system. The UW system would be cut to a lesser extent in part because tuition increases would replace some of the state funds (Department of Administration, 1995c: 15-18, 85).

In a fast-changing economy it is quite difficult to predict accurately for a fiscal year which will conclude some 24 to 40 months after different parts of the process begins. Even when considering that the legislature may complete its role about 12 months before the end of the first fiscal year in a biennium, projections remain very much subject to the vagaries of the economy. Previous attempts to budget for a biennium are subject to even more

216

difficulty because of the likelihood of unexpected events and circumstances. And the state statutorily must keep 1 percent of all state funds in reserve for cases of emergency. Thus, periodically the media report that the state is on the verge of a deficit or has a surplus. Some 1995 reports, based on Legislative Reference Bureau scenarios, even predicted a $585 million shortfall in the 1997-99 biennium because of commitments to be made in the 1995-97 period (Walters, 1995). Politicians from the party out of power often react to these reports with allegations of mis-management, over taxation or deceitfulness. But students of budgeting are quite aware of the difficulty of predicting accurately two or more years in advance.

The deadline for agency requests to be submitted to DOA is usually in early fall. Once agency requests are developed, there tends to be bargaining with DOA and the governor, both through public hearings that the governor often conducts and in direct contacts with the chief executive. Interest groups are also likely to seek opportunity to have input with the governor on budgetary matters of direct concern to them.

The governor has the assistance of the Department of Administration and its State Budget Office in analyzing agency requests, in conducting the hearings, and in preparing the final budget recommendations. The deadline for the governor to submit his recommendations to the legislature is at the end of January, although that is often extended into February, especially just after a gubernatorial election. Just as the agencies face strategy decisions on their requests, so the governor also makes strategy decisions. For example, if the governor has reason to believe that the legislature may add to the budget of some agencies, he may recommend less than he believes the final amount should be.

DOA reviews the agency requests, sorts them on the basis of fiscal and policy effect, and holds final briefings with the governor in November and December. These briefings especially deal with major policy issues for which agreements have not yet been made.

Since most major policy issues are in some way related to the budget, it is not difficult to include many policy proposals in the budget. The advantage from the governor's point of view is that some items which might be defeated if they were analyzed separately might be approved if held "hostage" in the budget bill. It certainly can also be argued that many policies have important fiscal implications thus justifying their inclusion in the budget bill.

There is often controversy when major policy initiatives are included in the budget bill. Opponents of gubernatorial policy proposals in the budget bill usually claim that such policies should be considered separately on their own merits. However, given that the budget itself is a statement of policy priorities in terms of the state's distribution of resources, it is more a matter of strategy and degree of change that would promote such opposition. Critics also can contend that policy in the budget adds incentives for logrolling and other increases in spending. Governors of both parties, though, have persistently included significant new policy choices in their budgets. The legislature usually accepts some, deletes others, and adds some of its own.

Under Governor Anthony Earl, items such as statewide high school graduation requirements, expanded county administrative home rule, and a toxic waste prevention program with authority to set toxic standards where no federal standards exist were among the more important policy initiatives included in the budget in 1985 (Department of Administration, 1987a: 4-13). Governor Tommy Thompson, in his first budget recommendations to the legislature, listed in excess of 112 of what he called "major policy changes" as part of the budget bill (Department of Administration, 1987c: 22-46). In 1995 Thompson proposed a major restructuring of state government to centralize more authority in the office of the governor. While indirectly related to budgeting, this was one of the most extensive sets of reorganization policies to be considered by the governor and the legislature in recent years. Table X-2 identifies his major initiatives and the legislature's disposition of them in the 1995-1997 budget bill.

217

Table X-2

GOVERNOR'S MAJOR STATE GOVERNMENT REORGANIZATION PROPOSALS IN HIS BUDGET
PROPOSALS, 1995 - 97

Governor's Proposals	Legislative Action
Create Department of Industry, Labor and Job Development (combines old Dept. of Industry, Labor and Human Relations with welfare programs).	Approved.
Create Department of Commerce (to administer economic development programs spread among the Departments of Development, Industry, Labor and Human Relations, Administration, Agriculture, Trade and Consumer Protection, and Natural Resources.	Approved.
Create Department of Tourism and Parks.	Approved Tourism Department, including promotion of state parks, but left care and protection of parks with the Department of Natural Resources.
Move Justice Department's consumer protection functions to the Department of Agriculture, Trade and Consumer Protection.	Approved.
Create Department of Education and shift most of the Department of Public Instruction's functions to it.	Approved department, but created an advisory commission to be headed by the Superintendent of Public Instruction.[a]
Create University of Wisconsin Hospital Authority.	Approved, but kept many state unionized employees as state employees.
Convert Departments of Natural Resources and Agriculture, Trade and Consumer Protection to Cabinet Departments with secretaries appointed by the Governor. The Natural Resources and Agriculture boards would become advisory councils.	Approved the conversion and gubernatorial appointment power, but retained the boards as policy makers.
Transfer most functions from the Secretary of State's office to other departments.	Approved.
Transfer most functions from the State Treasurer's office to other departments.	Rejected.
Eliminate both Public Intervenors for environmental protection (located in the Attorney General's office).	Retained one Public Intervenor, placed in the Department of Natural Resources, but eliminated litigation authority.

[a] On March 29, 1996, the Wisconsin Supreme Court unanimously ruled in the action of *Thompson v. Craney* that provisions of the 1995 Wisconsin Act 27 (the 1995-97 state budget) related to restructuring the governance of the

Department of Public Instruction are unconstitutional.

Sources: Department of Administration, 1995c; *On Wisconsin*, 1995.

As is common in most of the United States, the governor's budget proposals constitute the initial budgetary agenda for the legislature. The formal legislative process begins with a gubernatorial budget address to a joint session of the legislature and the introduction of the governor's budget bill which is then referred to the Joint Committee on Finance.

The use of a joint committee to deal with the budget is one of the unique features of the process in Wisconsin. The more common practice in other states is for each chamber to handle its own deliberations and to go to a joint process only when a conference committee is needed to reconcile differences between the houses. That a single joint committee initially considers and revises the governor's budget makes that committee particularly influential.

Because of the great amount of time needed to analyze the budget, the legislature provides for a recess from regular sessions so that the members of the Joint Committee on Finance can concentrate on the budget. Typically, the recess lasts six weeks to the beginning of April. The committee spends a great deal of time conducting hearings and meetings on various parts of the budget. Typically, the Committee also divides itself into a number of specialized working groups, each dealing with different parts of the budget. The actual process is up to each set of co-chairmen. During the 95-97 budget process, issue groups were not used. Instead, the co-chairs worked with individual legislators on specific issues.

A 1980s development, reflecting resentment that the other standing committees may be bypassed when the budget contains many policy issues, is that these other committees also consider aspects of the budget recommendations. They may hold hearings and deliberate on those issues within their subject matter jurisdiction and thus try to influence the Joint Finance Committee. However, the decisive committee decisions are made by Joint Finance.

When the Joint Committee on Finance has completed its work, it prepares a substitute amendment which is, in effect, a new omnibus budget bill, incorporating its modifications to the governor's proposals. The bill is then sent to the chamber whose turn it is for first floor consideration. That chamber can, of course, consider additional amendments. When it is passed, it is sent to the other chamber which may also consider amendments.

Once reported out by the Joint Committee on Finance, the crucial decision making is normally carried out in the majority party's caucus. Floor action may be an important part of the formal process, but the real bargaining and compromising goes on in both caucuses. It is here that legislators attempt to add, delete or modify the budget provisions with which they are especially concerned. A good deal of informal trading goes on in a process of coalition building designed to assure passage of a budget bill. Within the majority party caucuses, there is usually agreement that whatever provisions receive majority support will go into the budget bill. Thus, fewer than fifty percent of a chamber can secure provisions in the budget if they constitute a majority of the controlling party.

In 1995, an added controversy involved the majority Assembly Republicans deciding to hold their budget caucuses in closed session. Although Assembly Democrats had considered budgets in closed caucuses in previous biennia, the media suggested that Assembly Republicans should operate openly on budget issues. The Republican leadership justified the secrecy as needed because of the inexperience of many new members as well as "to keep lobbyists out of the deliberations." Former Democratic State Senate majority leader Joseph Strohl, who is now a lobbyist, also defended the closed caucuses. He saw them as necessary "if the parties hold only slim majorities and have no hope of luring opposition votes. Secret caucuses are sometimes used to 'beat up members and hammer out a compromise' if a proposal favored by legislative leaders lacks a few votes." In the 1995 Assembly Republican caucus, some 180 proposals were considered with about 30 of them adopted. A comprehensive "super amendment" was drafted incorporating all of the caucus changes from the Joint Committee on Finance proposals (Bice, 1995).

Several political scientists in the state also defended the use of closed caucuses. Peter Eisenger, director of the La Follete Institute of Public Affairs at UW-Madison, called them "a way of maintaining party discipline and party control." Dennis Dresang, another UW-Madison political scientist, called the caucuses "a reasonable way of taking a number of interests and getting them to agree on a complicated piece of legislation. If we didn't have caucuses, we wouldn't have a bill," Dresang concluded. John Johannes, a Marquette University political scientist, said that they are needed as planning tools and to plan strategy (AP dispatch, 1995c). The Senate Republicans, however, held their caucuses in open session. However, some of the deals were cut behind closed doors by the Senate leadership in private meetings with individual legislators.

The majority party legislative leadership does play a key role in the caucus. The leadership attempts a good deal of brokering in order to produce the majority coalition needed for passage. In some years, though, the leadership has bypassed the caucus if agreement on a budget appears deadlocked. For example, in 1987 the Assembly Democratic leadership moved the budget process to an informal conference committee among key legislators in the majority party before the caucus completed action so as to bypass what appeared to be hopeless wrangling within the party. In 1989 and 1990, Assembly Speaker Tom Loftus especially asserted controls over the budget process in order to try to mold budgetary proposals which would aid his expected gubernatorial campaign against Governor Tommy Thompson. In 1995, Speaker David Prosser and Senate Majority Leader Michael Ellis were able to secure passage of most of the budget through the caucus process. However, the transportation portion of the budget wound up getting stripped out by the Assembly Republicans because 10 of them would not support the increased gasoline tax that was supported by the party leadership. The transportation budget would not be considered until the fall 1995 legislative session (Jones, 1995).

When the majority party has sufficient support to pass a budget, an amended budget bill will be brought to the floor for formal action. Many amendments may be offered, usually by members of the minority party, but they are generally defeated as the leadership strives to maintain the majority coalition among the party's members, and perhaps with a few minority party members, in order to produce an appearance of bipartisanship. The minority often complains about a "tyranny of the caucus," but a change in party control has done little to modify the basic process as the new Republican majorities in both houses of the legislature proved. In the end, the final vote for passage of the budget in each chamber is largely along party lines.

In years when party control in the two houses was divided, each chamber was more likely to differ on the budget, thus necessitating a conference committee to iron out the differences. However, single party control of both chambers does not eliminate inter-chamber differences over the budget. Nor have differences been eliminated when the same party controls the governorship and legislature. The legislature continues to rely on either a conference committee or informal negotiations among chamber leaders from the majority party to work out a final budget to be submitted to the governor. Nineteen ninety-five saw a modification of this. The Assembly Republicans accepted all of the changes put forth by the Senate Republicans with the exception of the transportation package. Thus, a conference committee was not used for passage of the 1995-1997 budget in June 1995.

When a formal conference committee is convened, it is typically composed of three members of each house and actually makes the final decisions because the conference report is not subject to floor amendment. Their recommendations may or may not reflect all the previous deliberations which consumed months of time and may even include some major departures from what passed each chamber. For example, at Governor Patrick Lucey's urging in 1973, a budget conference committee "pulled a rabbit out of the hat" by including an exemption from local property taxes for manufacturers' machinery and equipment in the final compromise. That issue had not been considered or approved by either house during the earlier deliberations and, over the years, represented a major loss of revenue for local governments.

The budget is supposed to be passed by June 30, but the legislature and governor have not always been able to meet this deadline. When that occurs, Wisconsin state government does continue to operate. The previous budget remains in force until the new one is adopted. This arrangement permits the state to avoid the prospect of the government having to shut down for lack of appropriations. In 1995, the legislature completed its work on all but the transportation portion of the budget by June 30. However, the governor would need until later in the summer to complete his consideration of the budget bill.

When the June 30 deadline is not met, pressures mount for the passage of a budget, any budget. The strongest pressures of this nature come from local and school officials who are thrown into confusion about what to expect from the state as they develop their own budgets. Similarly, state agencies face problems because of uncertainty. This pressure to pass a budget is one reason why some measures which might not have passed if considered separately are passed in the budget bill.

Of course, the budget that is eventually submitted to the governor can be substantially revised through the use of the *partial veto,* which differs from a line-item veto. Any part of any bill involving appropriations is subject to this kind of veto. As James Gosling has pointed out, the partial veto is "an effective tool of gubernatorial policy making. In addition to striking appropriations, it can be used to eliminate legislative statutory initiatives or, short of elimination, to change legislative intent" (Gosling, 1986: 294). Governors have vetoed individual words, letters and digits as well as specific spending items. With such a power, governors can, and do, completely change the thrust of a policy that has been included in the legislature's budget bill. Governor Patrick Lucey, in 1971, changed a $25 million item to a $5 million appropriation by vetoing a digit. In 1978, acting Governor Schreiber used the partial veto to change a campaign finance bill from one where the taxpayer could add a dollar to his or her tax bill for state election campaigns to one where the dollar would come out of the state treasury. Governor Tommy Thompson has carried the power to its greatest extent. He has vetoed words, letters, and punctuation marks to create entirely new sentences and policies. He has also vetoed whole amounts and substituted lower amounts.

Between 1931, after the partial veto authority was added to the state constitution, and 1985 there were 698 partial vetoes (Legislative Reference Bureau, 1989: 2). Rarely were any overridden. Although many of the vetoes did reduce spending, "policy considerations, colored by partisanship, appear largely to guide gubernatorial item-veto choice." For example, 72 percent of the partial vetoes between 1975 and 1985 had no fiscal impact at all and only 14 percent directly affected appropriations. About one-third were designed to restore proposals originally made by the governor and another one-fifth to the Joint Committee on Finance version. When the legislature was controlled by the governor's party, 24 percent of the vetoes restored the committee's recommendation, but when the opposition party to the governor controlled, less than 15 percent were restored to the Joint Committee on Finance's version (Gosling, 1986: 294- 297).

Governor Tommy Thompson has used the partial veto far more than any governor (see Table X-3). He exercised the power a record 290 times in 1987 and, through the end of his first full term as governor, exercised it some 616 times. In 1991 he set another record with 457 partial vetoes, then added a comparatively modest 78 in 1994. Thompson accounted for nearly 64 percent of all item vetoes since 1931. Indeed, his average for his first two terms is some five times the biennial average since the partial veto power was established (Legislative Reference Bureau, 1989: 2; Mayers 1991, 1). For the 1995-97 budget, Governor Thompson recorded 112 vetoes.

Thompson's actions were designed primarily to bring the budget bill passed by the legislature much closer to the one he had submitted early in each year. The partial veto power was challenged in the Wisconsin Supreme Court, but the governor's extensive powers were upheld. In *State ex rel. Wisconsin Senate v. Thompson* (144 Wis. 2d 429), decided by a 4-3 vote in 1988, the court stated that the partial veto power gives the governor broad veto authority. "The court stated that this authority can be used to create new words and sentences by striking letters and punctuation, and to reduce dollar amounts in an appropriations bill." The only limit the court appeared to place on the governor was that what remained after the veto be a "'complete, entire and workable law'" as well as be "'germane to the topic or subject matter of the vetoed provisions'" (Legislative Reference Bureau, 1989: 10).

Table X-3

PARTIAL VETOES BY WISCONSIN GOVERNORS

Governor	Years	Number of Vetoes	Average per Biennium	Percent of Total
All for period	1931 - 64	37	2.2	1.9
Warren Knowles	1965 - 70	28	9.3	1.5
Patrick Lucey	1971 - 77	217	72.3	11.3
Martin Schreiber	1977 - 78	44	44.0	2.3
Lee S. Dreyfus	1979 - 82	224	112.0	11.7
Anthony Earl	1983 - 86	148	74.0	7.7
Tommy Thompson	1987 - 94	1224	306.0	63.7
TOTALS	**1931 - 94**	**1922**	**60.1**	**100.0**

Sources: Legislative Reference Bureau, 1989: 2; Mayers 1991: 1; Daley 1993.

Unable to override any of Governor Thompson's vetoes, the legislature proposed an amendment to the state constitution which provided that "the governor's power to veto appropriation bills in part does not permit the creation of a new word formed by rejecting individual letters in the words of the bill passed by the legislature." In effect, "the striking of letters to form new words would be prohibited" (Legislative Reference Bureau, 1990: 2). This was approved by the voters in 1990, but the partial veto power has become even more extensive since then. In 39 instances in 1991 and 1993, Governor Thompson actually wrote in a dollar figure that was lower than the one approved by the legislature. The Citizens Utility Board and two legislators challenged such a use of the partial veto power in the courts. In a 4-3 decision on June 30, 1995, the Wisconsin Supreme Court upheld the power of the Governor to "write-down" or "write-in" a lower figure. Justice Jon Wilcox, writing for the majority, said that the state constitution's grant of power to veto budget bills "in part" allows governors "to strike a numerical sum appropriated in the bill and to insert a different, smaller number. The governor has the power to approve part of an appropriation bill by reducing the amount of money appropriated, so long as the number is part of the original appropriation. It is readily apparent that $250,000 is 'part' of $350,000." In effect, the court approved expansive use of the partial veto and leaves to the Legislature mainly the power to place a cap on funding or to deny funding to programs altogether (Mayers 1991; Walters 1995).

This type of veto authority makes available "a powerful aggressive weapon" whereby "a governor can actually write new law with his veto pen" (Friederich, 1987: 13A). Clearly, the partial veto power is used "more as a tool of policy than as one of fiscal restraint" (Gosling, 1986: 296).

The legislature will usually schedule a floor session in the fall, following adoption of the budget, to consider overriding some of the vetoes. However, rarely are any overridden. Indeed, under Tommy Thompson, none through the end of 1994 had been overridden. The required two-thirds vote in each chamber is a formidable obstacle, thus frequently giving the governor the final word on budgeting and much of state public policy.

Expenditures

Describing state expenditures is less straightforward than one might think. Portions of the budget depend on state income, sales, inheritance, gift, and utility taxes for continuing and new programs. These make up the *general purpose revenue* (GPR) portion of the budget. But many programs are in part, or even entirely, dependent on other sources of revenue such as federal funds, segregated fees, bonding and program revenue. Funds from these latter sources generally are earmarked for particular programs and are not considered a part of the general purpose revenue budget. The GPR budget usually is the most visible and controversial portion of state spending. However, sometimes a non-GPR portion of the budget will stir up controversy as did transportation funding in 1995.

As in most states, expenditures in the state of Wisconsin have been increasing on a continual basis, often at a rate of increase exceeding that of the national government. Part of this has been due to inflation, but some has been due to nationally sponsored programs that states might otherwise have not adopted on their own. Some is also due to public and interest group demands on state government and, in the past decade, lower levels of federal aid. Part of the Reagan and Bush administration agendas was to transfer to state government greater programmatic and fiscal responsibilities. The new Republican majority in Congress is interested in continuing the same trend.

In Wisconsin, the general purpose budget alone has gone from approximately $300 million in the fiscal year ending June 30, 1964, to over $9 billion in the 1996-97 fiscal year. Additional revenue from the national government, segregated funds, and fees enables total spending now to exceed $15 billion, an increase from slightly over $1 billion in the 1963-64 fiscal year.

These figures indicate that state spending increases have been substantial and dramatic both for general purpose revenue expenditures and the total of all expenditures for many of the years between 1970 and 1993. (See Table X-4.) Moreover, when the GPR increases are adjusted for inflation, the year-to-year change for a majority of the years varies upward between incremental and substantial, but in seven of the years there were actual decreases in spending with some decreases quite substantial.

Table X-4

WISCONSIN BUDGET EXPENDITURES
(Billions of Dollars)

Fiscal Year	All Funds Amount	Percent Change	General Purpose Revenue Amount	Percent Change	GPR Inflation Adjustment Constant Dollars	Percent Change
1970 - 71	2.507	10.0	1.226	8.0	1.226	2.0
1971 - 72	2.729	8.9	1.347	9.9	1.275	4.0
1972 - 73	3.088	13.2	1.566	16.2	1.427	11.9
1973 - 74	3.596	16.5	1.934	23.5	1.715	20.2
1974 - 75	4.073	13.3	2.168	12.1	1.816	5.9
1975 - 76	4.723	16.0	2.299	6.0	1.725	-5.0

1976 - 77	5.089	7.7	2.463	7.1	1.691	-2.0
1977 - 78	5.440	6.9	2.634	6.9	1.710	1.1
1978 - 79	6.317	16.1	3.149	19.6	1.934	13.1
1979 - 80	6.837	8.2	3.278	4.1	1.864	- 3.6
1980 - 81	7.375	7.9	3.447	5.1	1.748	- 6.2
1981 - 82	7.542	2.3	3.451	0.0	1.514	- 13.4
1982 - 83	8.591	13.9	4.078	18.2	1.632	7.8
1983 - 84	8.889	3.5	3.978	- 2.5	1.492	- 8.6
1984 - 85	9.981	12.3	4.588	15.3	1.673	12.1
1985 - 86	10.532	5.5	4.868	6.1	1.703	1.8
1986 - 87	10.899	3.5	5.054	3.8	1.706	0.2
1987 - 88	11.217	2.9	5.300	4.9	1.757	3.0
1988 - 89	11.903	6.1	5.608	5.8	1.794	2.1
1989 - 90	12.752	7.1	5.812	3.6	1.790	- 0.2
1990 - 91	14.057	10.2	6.327	8.9	1.874	4.7
1991 - 92	15.301	8.8	6.664	5.3	1.917	2.3
1992 - 93	NA	NA	6.963	4.5	1.946	1.5

Sources: State of Wisconsin, *Blue Book*, 1989-1996; Department of Administration, 1989b and 1981-1995c; Rhodes, 1987: 37-38, 50-51; Cranford, 1989: 52.

Another important characteristic of state expenditures is that a sizeable portion is not spent for the state's own operations. Table X-5 shows that much more of the money collected by the state goes to aid for local areas and individuals than to state government operations. In fact, less than one-fourth of general purpose revenues goes to state operations while more than half goes to local units of government and school districts. The distribution for local assistance especially goes up in fiscal years 1996 and 1997, to nearly 58 percent in the first year of that biennium and to over 61 percent in the second year. This is a product of the decision to increase school aids to two-thirds of public school costs. By 1997, the drive for property tax relief is reducing the share of GPR funds for state operations to under 22 percent and, even more significantly, the share for aids to individuals to barely 17 percent. Of the share of GPR funds for state operations, a good deal of that too, goes for education. Nearly half of the state funds in 1997, 9.1 percent, will go to the University of Wisconsin system, though it is important to point out that the UW's share of state GPR funds has been declining for some twenty years. The system's share of state funds in 1975 was 13.7 percent (Department of Administration, 1981-95c; University of Wisconsin System, 1994).

Table X-5

GOVERNORS' PROPOSED GENERAL REVENUE BUDGET BY PURPOSE
PERCENTAGES: 1981 - 97

Biennium	State Operations	Local Assistance	Aids to Individuals
1981 - 83	26.6	54.6	18.8
1983 - 85	23.9	56.7	19.4
1985 - 87	22.9	57.0	20.1
1987 - 89	23.1	57.4	19.6
1989 - 91	23.2	57.0	19.8
1991 - 93	23.1	56.6	20.3
1993 - 95	23.8	54.7	21.5
1995 - 97[a]	22.4	59.5	18.1

[a] Estimates

Sources: Department of Administration, 1981-95c; State of Wisconsin, *Blue Books*, 1991-92, 1993-94, 1994-95.

When examining the major programs for which state government spends its GPR funds, it is clear that education commands the largest amount. Both Governors Earl and Thompson, through 1994, proposed that more than 38 percent of such state expenditures go to elementary, secondary, and higher education. With the property tax relief effort, that percentage will exceed 46 percent of all GPR fund for education. (See Table X-6.)

Table X-6

TOP NINE GENERAL PURPOSE REVENUE PROGRAMS
AS PROPOSED BY THE GOVERNOR
BY PERCENTAGE, 1985 - 97

Program	1985 - 87	1989 - 90	1994 - 95	1996 - 97
School Aids[a]	27.7	27.7	28.4	38.4
Shared Revenues	15.2	13.8	12.3	10.9
UW System (excluding debt)	10.5	10.6	10.1	8.3
Medical Assistance	9.2	9.9	12.7	9.9
State Property Tax Credits[b]	9.1	5.5	4.1	3.5

Community Social Services Aids	6.0	5.6	4.6	4.1
Income Maintenance Payments (AFDC)	5.0	3.1	2.1	1.5
Debt Retirement	3.5	2.9	3.8	3.2
Correctional Services (excluding debt)	2.4	2.5	3.6	4.2
All Other GPR Funded Programs	16.2	18.4	18.1	15.9
Total Amount ($ millions)	**10,104.3**	**5,840.9**	**7,703.3**	**9,122.0**

[a] Includes general and categorical school aids as well as state property tax credits that are supposed to be for the purpose of reducing the school property tax levy.

[b] Does not include the portion designed to reduce the school levy; that portion is included under school aids.

***The 1988-89 budget proposals incorporated debt retirement into the agency budgets. Aids to the Vocational, Technical, and Adult Education system would be the tenth largest item with 1.5 percent of GPR funds.

Sources: Department of Administration, 1985-1995c.

Within the area of state operations, the largest single expenditure is for education. Slightly less than 50 percent of both Governor Earl and Thompson's GPR budgets for state operations (but less than nine percent of the total GPR budget in 1997) was for the University of Wisconsin system, with spending approaching $700 million per year. When adding GPR funds, tuition and fees, federal funds, and grants, spending for the University system is beginning to approach $2 billion a year. As sizeable as this is, by far the largest amount of state GPR money still goes to local governments and school districts with school districts slated to get the lion's share.

Two other "specialized" areas of expenditure involve aids to individuals and transportation. Neither derives most of its funds through the general purpose revenue budget. For example, while aid to individuals constitutes around 17 percent of the GPR budget, the federal government provides funds sufficient to more than double the amount that is spent in the state. These are generally entitlement programs whereby the level of benefits is determined by a formula built into the law. Aid to Families With Dependent Children, the major welfare program in the state and nation, is typical of this approach. The formula tends to drive the level of expenditures thus making it more difficult for public officials to control the level of spending, although Governor Thompson has limited increases in the levels of such benefits through the partial veto. As of this writing, the national government is considering a block grant approach to welfare funding. If that occurs, levels of spending and the rules that drive that spending may be sharply reduced.

The transportation portion of the budget comes almost entirely from segregated funds and federal grants-in-aid, with the total exceeding a billion dollars a year in 1990, but slated to exceed as much as $1.5 billion for each year of the 1995-1997 biennium. However, the 1995 budget deliberation involved a great deal of division among the majority Republicans. Governor Thompson had proposed using an oil company franchise fee to pay for a sharply increased highway building budget. The legislature considered converting that at least in part to an increase in the gasoline tax, but ten Republicans in the Assembly refused to support any transportation package which included a tax increase. Given the partisan nature of budget voting in the legislature, all Democrats jointed the ten Republicans to defeat the transportation package in June 1995 (Walters and Jones, 1995). In the end, the legislature could not pass a transportation budget as part of the total budget or separately by the end of fiscal 1995. No action on transportation would come from the legislature until the fall of 1995, several months into the new fiscal year.

Wisconsin governors do tend to find most of their budgetary proposals incorporated into the final budget bill, especially after the exercise of the partial veto. The power of the veto helps assure that the legislature will either reach advance agreement with the governor on much of the spending that goes beyond his proposals, or, as indicated earlier, the governor will impose his will.

James Gosling found, in the late 1970s, that about 73 percent of the budgetary decision items emanating from the State Budget Office on behalf of the governor became law. He also found that an even larger percentage, approaching 90 percent, of the decision items proposed by the Joint Committee on Finance and the legislature as a whole became law. The state operating agencies had the least success in getting their decision items enacted, although over half of their proposals also were enacted (Gosling, 1985: 468). In a later period, gubernatorial success remained high. Using the 1985-87 biennium as an example, Table X-7 shows that Governor Anthony Earl attained most of his goals. Then, in 1995, with a Republican majority in both chambers, Thompson secured most of his initiatives and funding levels. As he put it, "it's pretty much what I asked for" (AP dispatch, 1995e). That the governor and both houses of the legislature were from the same party helped.

Table X-7

GUBERNATORIAL BUDGET PROPOSALS AND LEGISLATIVE ACTION
1985-87 BIENNIUM

(Millions of Dollars)

Program	Proposed	Appropriated	Change
School Aids[a]	$ 2,307.0	$ 2,288.4	- $ 18.6
Shared Revenues	1,538.8	1,538.7	- 0.1
UW System[b]	1,062.0	1,018.6	- 43.4
Medical Assistance	932.1	919.1	- 13.0
State Property Tax Credits[a]	918.7	968.8	+ 50.1
Community Social Service Aids	603.2	604.9	+ 1.7
Income Maintenance Payments	508.9	495.4	- 13.5
Debt Retirement	354.4	204.7	- 149.7
Correctional Services[b]	238.8	231.1	- 7.7
Homestead Tax Credit	197.0	235.4	+ 38.4
Other Local Assistance	NA	442.0	+ 442.0
All Other GPR Funded Programs	1,443.4	1,384.4	+ 59.0
TOTAL GPR BUDGET	**10,104.3**	**10,331.5**	**+ 227.2**

[a] School aids in the form of property tax credits to individual property tax payers are included with the state property tax credit item in this table.

Sources: Department of Administration, 1985c:9 and 1987a:8.

Data in Gosling's work also shows that the largest number of decision items come from the executive branch. The largest number naturally come from the operating agencies as can be seen in Table X-8. The data also show that relatively few proposals come out of Joint Committee on Finance and the legislature. However, legislative initiatives can and often do involve important policy positions, such as the Assembly Democratic proposal in 1994 to sharply increase state support of elementary and secondary education.

Table X-8

BUDGET DECISION ITEMS PROPOSED BY BUDGET PARTICIPANTS

Budget Participant	Percent of Decision Items Proposed	Percent in Final Approved Budget
Operating Agencies	56.0 %	46.6 %
State Budget Office	26.7 %	29.9 %
Joint Finance Committee	13.4 %	18.5 %
Legislature	3.9 %	5.0 %
TOTAL NUMBER	671	438

Source: Developed from data in Gosling, 1985:468.

Capital Construction Budget. The state's capital construction budget is treated separately and is funded primarily through bonding. Agencies submit their building requests to the State Building Commission which, in turn, submits its recommendations to the legislature. The commission was originally established in 1949, but became especially important in 1969 when the state could begin to borrow directly. Today, the commission is the only state agency that can authorize debt. The commission's budget consists of spending for capital construction and debt service payments.

The State Building Commission is chaired by the governor and includes three legislators from each chamber and a citizen member. Three administrators, including the Secretary of the Department of Administration and two subordinates, serve as advisory members. In submitting requests to the legislature, the commission sets priorities as to which projects it wishes to emphasize as more important for the biennium.

Needless to say, agency requests tend to far exceed what the governor, commission, and legislature are likely to accept. Table X-9 shows that governors and the State Building Commission tend to cut from a third to nearly half of the building funds requested by the various agencies. For example, in 1991 the governor and State Building Commission approved authorizing $330 million for construction in response to nearly $630 million requested by the agencies. The legislature, in turn, does make additional adjustments both in terms of what projects will be authorized and in the total dollars to be authorized. With occasional exceptions, however, the total capital construction spending passed by the legislature is usually closer to the governor's proposals thus solidifying the sharp reductions in the agency wish lists. Consequently, the agencies tend toward persistent resubmissions in hopes that previously rejected requests will eventually be a high enough priority to be funded.

Table X-9

CAPITAL CONSTRUCTION REQUESTS AND LEGISLATIVE ACTION, 1985 - 91

Biennium	Amount Requested by Agencies	Amount Proposed by Building Commission and Governor	Percent Reduced	Amount Authorized by Legislature
1985 - 87	$ 321,310,300	$ 167,925,900	47.7 %	$ 185,122,200
1987 - 89	$ 370,293,400	$ 232,273,700	37.3 %	$ 275,073,700
1989 - 91	$ 516,400,000	$ 291,962,400	43.5 %	$ 312,356,900
1991- 93	$ 629,542,100	$ 330,022,700	47.6 %	$ 544,578,400

Sources: State Building Commission, Capital Budget Recommendations, 1985-1990; Legislative Fiscal Bureau, Wisconsin State Budgets 1985, 1987, 1989; Legislative Reference Bureau Summary of 1992 Legislative Session.

In 1995, there was a sharp increase in agency capital requests and gubernatorial support. For the 1995-1997 biennium, agencies asked for $954,206,300 and the Governor and Building Commission in turn recommended $668,685,000 to the Legislature. An expanded prison building program accounted for a good share of the increase. Democrats charged that the increase was due to Republican insertion of "pork barrel" projects in Republican districts, including prisons. Typical of the partisan bantering is this exchange:

- Republican Senate Majority Leader Michael Ellis - "How can prisons be pork? A prison serves a statewide constituency."

- Democratic Assembly Minority Leader Walter Kunicki - "Of course prisons are pork. It used to be that people voted against a budget if there was a prison anywhere near their district. Now people kill for them."

- Democratic State Senator Joseph Wineke, with a bit of candor - "They are as bad or worse at it than the Democrats were." (Eggleston, 1995a)

Wineke admits that both political parties engage in pork barrel politics.

The Governor and Building Commission may actually add building projects not asked for by the involved agency. For example, an $8 million building renovation was added into the budget despite its having a lower priority in the UW system. Some suggested that the active pushing for the project by three majority party legislators around Platteville had more to do with the project's approval than anything else (AP dispatch, 1995b).

Whatever the motivation for approving particular building projects, one net result is usually higher debt for the state. By May 1995, the state budget already included $258 million annually for the principal and interest on existing loan debts for building projects. The governor's $669 million capital budget proposal would add another $36 million to the annual payments over the 1995-1997 biennium because $437 million in bonding was included. The Joint Committee on Finance did reduce that to $375 million in bonding (AP dispatches, 1995a and 1995b).

Shared Revenues, Taxes and Credits

Wisconsin is similar to most states in the complex financial relationship it has with the national government and with localities. The relationship between state and locality is different from the relationship between state and national government. Beyond general provisions of the U.S. Constitution, the states are not required to enter into fiscal relations with the national government. The national government has little legal power to limit taxing sources or spending patterns of the state. Limitations are usually put into effect through such policies as grant-in-aid programs whereby the national government sets conditions that the states must accept in order to receive federal funds.

On the other hand, local governments are created by the states. As a result, states frequently use their legal powers to limit the taxing and borrowing powers of localities so that sources of money remain available to the state. As described in the chapter on the state constitution, in 1924 localities were given home rule, which is the ability to decide how to spend money, but little freedom was granted in terms of raising money. Bonding (the ability to borrow) and taxing limits on localities continue to be maintained by the state through its constitution and statutes.

The national government has provided monies in three forms: categorical grants in aid, block grants, and revenue sharing. Categorical grants provide monies from higher levels of government to lower ones for particular purposes, but with specific strings attached. Such grants usually include matching requirements, so that if Wisconsin accepts the grant, it must pledge a portion of its own money to the project. Block grants provide monies from higher levels of government to lower ones in general areas of expenditure with some strings attached. Revenue sharing, now discontinued, provided monies from higher to lower levels of government with few strings attached. The differences therefore are over how much discretion the sending government retains and how much is granted the receiving government.

Federal funds account for slightly over one-fifth of Wisconsin's revenue, although that percentage steadily declined in the 1980's because the Reagan and Bush Administrations attempted to reduce national domestic expenditures and leave states and localities to provide a greater part of them (see Table X-10). This, for example, is evidenced by the elimination of federal revenue sharing to the states. Moreover, these administrations reduced aid which went directly to local governments, including direct federal to local government revenue sharing. The latter part of the Bush administration and the Clinton administration did produce a reversal of this trend with federal revenue to Wisconsin moving toward 23 percent of the state's revenue.

Table X-10

SOURCES OF REVENUE
SELECTED BUDGETS, 1975 - 91

Source of Funds	1975 - 77	1981 - 83	1985 - 87	1989 - 91	1995 - 97*
General Purpose Revenue	51.8 %	54.4 %	53.9 %	51.1 %	57.3 %
Federal Revenue	27.3 %	23.8 %	22.4 %	21.1 %	23.3 %
Program Revenue	10.6 %	10.0 %	11.7 %	12.8 %	13.7 %
Segregated Revenue	10.3 %	10.6 %	9.6 %	11.1 %	5.0 %
Bond Revenue	--	1.1 %	3.9 %	3.8 %	0.7 %

* Estimates.

Source: Wisconsin Department of Administration, 1975-89c; *Wisconsin State Budget: Governor's Recommendations*, 1995.

Washington has also sought to reduce its regulatory role over state and local governments. Thus, a number of programs have been shifted from categorical to block grant formulas of distribution. This has been true particularly in the areas of housing assistance and environmental control, areas where the funds to the state are usually passed on to the local governments. There is a great deal of consideration being given to expand this trend toward block grants into other policy areas, including welfare.

The state provides other financial assistance to local units of government through shared taxes and individual property tax credits in addition to state aids for specific functions (similar to categorical grants from the national government to the states). Shared taxes are a percentage of taxes that the state collects from its own taxing process but which is returned to the locality in which the taxpayer resides. Shared taxes can be spent in any way the receiving government wishes. Individual tax credits go directly to taxpayers and therefore would have to be recovered through additional taxes should local governments want to use this money. A principal reason for tax credits has been to use state taxes to relieve local property taxes. As a result, property tax related credits and shared revenue are interrelated. Both are often designed to reduce the role of property taxes in funding local activities. In effect, the state can give more aid to the locality through shared taxes, thus giving the local unit the political benefits of lowering property taxes, or the state can give the money to individuals through a credit and thereby keep the political benefits of lowering taxes to itself. When credits are used, the local government loses the discretion to keep the money and also the discretion to decide who receives the money. On the other hand, if the criteria used to distribute tax credits are similar to those used to distribute shared revenue, the net financial benefits may be the same to the taxpayer. In the 1980s, Wisconsin relied more on credits, including a directly mailed rebate in 1990, to reduce a state budget surplus. In the 1995-1997 biennium, however, the state is moving strongly to more direct aids to school districts to cover two-thirds of the costs of education. But, this increased aid will come with tight restrictions on how much local school districts can raise and spend.

There is also a homestead tax credit which is designed to relieve property tax burdens for low income people even if they have no income tax liability. Moreover, there are other tax credits which are applied on income tax returns but which are unrelated to property taxes. Many income tax return credits, then, are separate from the shared revenue system.

Until the early 1970s, the most important single source of state derived revenue for general municipal purposes was the shared income tax. Wisconsin has always relied more heavily on the income tax than most other states. In 1911, Wisconsin was the first state to adopt an income tax. Between 1911 and the early 1970s, income tax credits were part of a basic formula for these shared taxes whereby the state retained 40 percent of the income taxes, returned ten percent to the county and returned 50 percent to the city in which the taxpayers resided. Under this formula the municipalities in which there were many poor persons became poorer and those in which there were many rich taxpayers became richer. There were, in fact, "tax islands" in which local governments did not have to levy any property taxes because they derived so much money from the state income tax. This could be defended in that the income tax was argued to be a better tax than the property tax. Nevertheless, it seemed to many unfair that only richer areas received such a benefit.

Under Governor Patrick Lucey (1971-1977), the system of shared taxes was changed by devising a new formula for the distribution to municipalities. At first the distribution was based mainly on population along with some additional relief to areas of high property taxes. This led to such reliance on the census that in 1975, fearing reduced shared tax revenue, Milwaukee paid to have a new census conducted. Further controversy arose from the practice of increased annexation and consolidation of municipal areas based on the likelihood of greater state revenue.

The system has subsequently changed from one which follows a simple formula designed to benefit a single group to a changing formula in each budget which reflects the interest group relationships in the legislature at the time of passage. Claims to "tax neutrality" have been greatly exaggerated since every formula benefits some municipalities tot the disadvantage of other municipalities. Several different factors come into play.

For example, population and need are two considerations. Suburban legislators have generally favored a formula based on population because their numbers have swelled. The bigger cities and rural areas, which have poorer populations, generally favor some recognition of need in the formula in order to gain a higher percentage of the available funds.

Some legislators and administrators have argued that a simple need-based formula will give incentive to areas to greatly reduce property taxes with the expectation that such reduction will generate greater financial need and, therefore, generate greater aid from the state. On the other hand, simply basing the formula on levels of income tax payments creates the "tax island" problem noted above. In 1977 and 1978 further modifications were made in recognition of this. The formula gave more money to communities with a low tax base and high tax effort than to communities with a high property tax base. Thus, property tax effort has become a component in the formula.

Partisan politics, of course, is another component. Will the monies go to predominantly Republican or Democratic areas of the state? However, conflict between rural and urban areas has increasingly divided legislators in recent years thus intensifying differences over various state aid formulas. Finally, a more indirect factor involves whether the combined shared tax, state aid, and tax credit system should go principally to help schools or municipalities. School districts have traditionally received funds through aids rather than shared taxes, but increasingly school levies have entered into the formula for distributing shared revenue to municipalities and determining tax credits. Each budget resolves this point a bit differently with school districts most recently gaining more attention, especially with the state commitment to fund a much higher share of school taxes.

The state has usually reserved the general sales tax for the state and viewed the property tax as something to be reduced rather than widened through shared practice. Nevertheless, sales taxes can end up affecting local government resources. For example, in 1982 when the sales tax was "temporarily" raised from 4 percent to 5 percent, the increase was earmarked for property tax relief based on school tax levies. In 1983 the increase was made permanent and was separated from property taxes. When in 1987 the national government discontinued general revenue sharing for localities, Wisconsin allowed its counties to impose a local sales tax of 0.5 percent. A substantial majority of counties are using this resource as a way to accommodate the loss of federal aid as well as to reduce some of the reliance on property taxes. However, the restriction of a local sales tax to counties and to such a low rate makes the tax of marginal importance, thus forcing localities to continue to rely on shared revenue and property taxes.

Internal Sources of Revenue

Within the state, Wisconsin uses four money sources: 1) general purpose revenue, raised principally through income and user taxes; 2) program revenues, essentially fees which partially pay the cost of certain services; 3) segregated revenue, raised by a variety of sources but earmarked to be spent on a special program; and 4) borrowing through the sale of bonds.

General Purpose Revenue is now more than one-half the total revenue of the state. GPR is derived from individual and corporate income taxes, general sales taxes and a variety of other "user" taxes, such as excise taxes on particular items or services. Because general purpose revenue is spent on various services provided through statute, it is usually the revenue most focused upon in the legislative process. This is so much the case that mention of the budget in the press or in common discussion often treats GPR as the only source of state revenue.

Historically, Wisconsin has treated the mix of taxes used to create the GPR, or general, fund differently from the mix in other states. Table X-11 shows the tax sources for the general fund. Most states rely more heavily on sales and other user taxes than on the income tax. In most states income taxes have been of lesser importance and have been increased slowly throughout the century mainly to supplement user taxes. Wisconsin has relied more heavily on the income tax in this century and is one of a handful of states to do so. User taxes, particularly the general sales tax, have been seen in Wisconsin as supplementary to the income tax rather than as the principal source of general purpose revenue. Thus, the general sales tax was not adopted until the early 1960s. It has remained at a relatively low rate and has contained more exceptions than in most states. The sales tax is expected to generate about $2.9 billion in the 1995-97 biennium, but could generate about $1.2 billion more if all services were included and $1.6 billion more if all goods were included (Legislative Fiscal Bureau report, quoted in University of Wisconsin System, 1994).

Wisconsin's income tax rates are graduated or progressive. That means that a slight increase in per capita income produces a sizeable increase in state revenue; conversely a slight dip in per capita income causes a significant drop in state revenue. At times it is used to try to achieve more than revenue producing objectives. As a result, a complicated system of deductions, partially based on the national government's model, spreads benefits unevenly and may make the tax less progressive than a system without deductions. Wisconsin has generally resisted regressive deductions. For example, the child care deduction in Wisconsin is based on income unlike the national child care deduction which is given to rich as well as poor. However, in the 1980s the state reduced capital gains taxation in an effort to attract business investment to the state, and also reduced income tax rates primarily for upper income individuals, thus benefitting more so those at higher income levels than lower income levels. Later, the estate tax was sharply reduced to produce the same kind of result.

Table X-11

GENERAL PURPOSE TAXES PERCENTAGES, 1983 - 95

Tax Source	1983 - 84	1987 - 88	1995 - 97
Individual Income	48.2 %	44.8 %	51.2 %
General Sales and Use	30.4 %	34.2 %	33.4 %
Corporate Income and Franchise	8.7 %	8.9 %	7.4 %
Public Utility	6.0 %	4.7 %	3.2 %
Excise			
Cigarette	2.7 %	2.8 %	2.0 %
Liquor and Wine	0.8 %	0.6 %	0.4 %
Beer	0.2 %	0.2 %	0.1 %
Tobacco Products	0.1 %	0.1 %	0.1 %
Inheritance and Gift	1.6 %	1.9 %	0.6 %
Insurance Company	1.0 %	1.4 %	1.3 %

Pari-Mutual	---	---	0.1 %
Miscellaneous	0.4 %	0.5 %	0.5 %
Total Amount (% millions)	**$ 4,529.0**	**$ 5,173.7**	**$ 8,643.0**

*Estimate.

Source: Data computed from Department of Administration, 1983-1995c.

A problem with the income tax is that it can be less stable in terms of the amount of income it produces for the state. When Wisconsin's economy fluctuates between boom and recession, the income tax generates, first, budget surpluses and then budget deficits. There are two principal ways to insulate the income tax from creating such instability: by establishing so-called "rainy day" funds to bank money during economically good times for use when the tax is bringing in less money; or use of another tax, such as a sales tax, which yields steadier amounts of revenue.

Rainy day funds have not proven popular. When the budget generates a surplus, particularly in an election year, the temptation is to return the surplus to the taxpayer in the form of a rebate as was done twice in the 1980s and again in 1990.

Reliance on the general sales tax is a partial protector against instability. But the sales tax protects against instability by being regressive; i.e., it places a higher burden on people as their ability to pay goes down. Actually the most recession-proof tax would be on necessities, because people must eat while they can defer luxuries. Accordingly, the Wisconsin 5 percent sales tax is less stable than in those states which tax food. Therefore, the increases in the sales tax have come mainly in periods when the instability of the income tax is most apparent, rather than because the sales tax itself is seen as a better tax.

More recent debate has been over whether the sales tax should be used more extensively to provide property tax relief. The removal of a number of exemptions was seriously considered in order to provide some of the funding for the sharply increased school aids. However, in his 1995-1997 proposed budget, Governor Thompson relied much more on increases in user fees, economic growth and budget cuts rather than attempting to raise sales or income taxes to any significant extent. The 1995 legislature even removed the increase in some income taxes for middle income people and substituted a five-cent increase in the cigarette tax to make up the lost income (*On Wisconsin*, 1995).

Rural-urban divisions also surfaced during the 1995 budget and tax debates in the legislature. Republican rural and suburban legislators succeeded in incorporating policy in the budget bill that would tax agricultural property according to use instead of potential for development. This would mean significant reductions in property taxes for farmland located near urban areas, but it also would mean the citizens in the nearby urban areas would see an increase in property taxes in order to maintain local government and school district revenues. The more urban oriented Democrats opposed the change, but did not have the votes to stop it.

As states in the Midwest suffer from the movement of some industry to the Sunbelt, their businesses have claimed that corporate income taxes are a driving force. Wisconsin has relatively high corporate income tax rates because it has generally relied so heavily on income taxes. Actually, few corporations, usually only specialized ones which are heavily regulated, move out of one state and to another based principally on tax climate. The availability of cheap natural resources, labor costs, labor supply, perception of quality of life, and even the weather prove to be more important reasons.

Nevertheless, the balance between corporate and individual income taxes is often discussed in the context of whether the corporate rates will produce job losses. This kind of argument led Governor Lucey to eliminate the merchandise and equipment property tax in the early 1970s, the legislature to repeal a surtax on corporations in 1984, a year ahead of schedule, and the legislature and Governor Anthony Earl to lower the top brackets on the income tax. Under Governor Thompson, capital gains and estate taxes were also sharply reduced as an incentive to the business community. Moreover, Governor Thompson has strongly resisted any attempts to increase taxes that would appear to be costly to business.

Special item excise taxes are a fourth source of general purpose revenue. Taxes on cigarettes and liquor are the most obvious examples. Despite the increased evidence of the danger of smoking and periodic increases in the price of cigarettes, the cigarette tax is the largest excise tax source and is quite stable. The legislature was more willing to raise that tax, by five cents a pack in 1995, than it was the gasoline tax. The beer tax is stable but the popularity of beer drinking in Wisconsin has made it a particularly controversial tax. There is rarely any strong sentiment among policy makers to raise it.

Another source of general purpose revenue is the public utility tax, the largest of which is on electric utilities. This tax is collected by the state and shared with local units of government based on complex formulas. As the state has increased its percentage of the total with the influx of new power plants, once again controversy arises about the use of state power over localities in a political system which values localism.

Segregated revenue is "sacred" money which must be spent for a specific purpose and is subjected to less gubernatorial and legislative discretion. The largest segregated fund is derived from the gasoline tax and is used for transportation purposes. The second largest segregated fund is derived from hunting and fishing licenses, which are allocated to the Department of Natural Resources (DNR). This had contributed to the DNR's independence from the governor, but the 1995 budget bill grant of authority for him to appoint the DNR secretary may significantly change that situation despite the Natural Resources Board continuing as a policy making body.

Program revenue is money collected by the state for specific goods and services. This money is earmarked for these goods and services although it is paid into the general fund. Fees and tuition paid by University of Wisconsin students are an example of program revenue although some fees are often mislabeled as segregated fees.

The state may also borrow money. The original Wisconsin Constitution prohibited debt exceeding $100,000 except to repel invasion or to put down domestic insurrection. For all practical purposes, that was a flat prohibition of direct state debt which would pledge the state's full faith and credit. Because such a prohibition came to be viewed as unrealistic, especially for capital improvements, these constitutional provisions were frequently circumvented.

One means of circumvention was to use the counties to borrow the money for U.S. and state highways. One result of this strategy was to give county boards a veto over state highway construction. Another means of circumvention was to establish "dummy" building corporations, controlled by state officials, to borrow money indirectly. The Wisconsin Supreme Court held that such borrowing was not pledging the full faith and credit of the state, although the major source of money to pay interest and to pay off the debt was derived from the state (*State ex rel Thompson v. Giessel*, 1954). The result of this strategy was to increase the interest rates on the borrowed money above what they would have been had the state borrowed money directly.

A constitutional amendment, approved in a referendum in 1969, allowed for direct state debt (Wisconsin Constitution, Art. VIII, Sec. 7). One section of this amendment allowed borrowing for capital improvements and another allowed borrowing for emergencies. Under the first section, a state bond board was authorized to borrow money for public purposes such as land acquisition and the construction of buildings and highways. To avoid being straight-jacketed again by setting a limit which would be meaningless in the face of continuing inflation, the constitutional amendment set a limit based on percentages of the aggregate value of all taxable property in the state. But the second section allowing for emergency borrowing requires a vote of the people. Such a constitutional restriction leads to infrequent use and restrains the state legislature from borrowing far more so than is the case in some other states. Nevertheless, Wisconsin does rank tenth in per capita long term debt (*City and State*, 1990:12).

Finally, Wisconsin has established a new source of income in the form of revenue from gambling. The state constitution was amended to permit gambling through a state run lottery and through state supervised pari-mutual betting. In addition, the Wisconsin Supreme Court has interpreted the constitutional amendment as permitting Native American-sponsored casinos. Lottery revenues are supposed to go toward property tax relief, but the amount has not been particularly significant in the form of a lottery tax credit.

In general, Wisconsin produces more per capita spending than most other states by diversifying its tax sources and through extensive aids to local governments. Table X-12 shows the ranking of Wisconsin in the United States for a variety of taxes. The state ranks fifth in the percentage of personal income which goes to taxes. This translates to a ranking of twelfth in terms of per capita tax load. Also, the tax structure is less progressive than the state's reputation suggests. A study by the Citizens for Tax Justice, a Washington-based group which advocates taxation on the basis of ability to pay, found that both upper and lower income Wisconsinites have a lower tax burden than middle income residents. The overall tax load for low income people was slightly above 12 percent in 1991 and below ten percent for high income people. Middle income tax payers had a load of 13-14 percent (Srb, 1991). Time will tell whether the developing changes in property taxes will change this kind of balance.

Table X-12

WISCONSIN TAX RANKINGS IN THE U.S.

Type of Tax	As Percent of Personal Income	As Per Capita Tax Load
Income Tax	6	7
Corporate Income Tax	16	13
Sales Tax	31	30
Property Tax	11	12
Total Taxes	5	12

Source: U.S. Census Bureau, "*State and Local Government Finances, 1990-91.* Reprinted in Office of University Relations, University of Wisconsin System, "Wisconsin's Property Tax, Budget Debate." July 1994.

Conclusion: Continuing Controversies

Every budget cycle ends with significant controversies still percolating throughout the state's political system. The 1995 budget decisions for the 1995-97 biennium are no different. Three major controversies are especially likely to persist throughout the biennium and into the next. All three involve the education policies adopted in the 1995 budget bill.

First is the debate over whether the state should provide funding to make it possible for K-12 students to attend parochial schools. This is the so-called "choice" policy. At the governor's request, the state extended a "voucher" program whereby children could use state vouchers towards the costs of attending private, nonsectarian schools. The new policy as passed by the legislature would permit up to 7000 low income pupils in the Milwaukee

Public School System to also attend parochial schools in 1995-96. That would be possible for up to 15,000 low income pupils in the second year of the biennium. A major point of contention is over whether the U.S. Constitution's First Amendment prohibition of the establishment of religion would bar such vouchers. A lawsuit and national attention are likely to sustain this controversy (*On Wisconsin,* July 6, 1995). If the choice plan is upheld, there would likely be pressure to extend it to higher income pupils thus further igniting controversy.

Second is the debate over whether the revised formula for the distribution of school aids is fair to all parts of the state as well as whether the degree of property tax relief is significant. The Legislative Fiscal Bureau estimates that the average home in the state will see an increase in property taxes of about $50 in 1996 and a decline of about $243 in 1997, for an average cut of $193 (Eggleston, 1995b). Partisans and others will undoubtedly argue over whether this is sufficient tax relief, especially in the face of many fee increases. On whether the funding shift is equitable across the state, the Wisconsin Taxpayers Alliance says that based on school district rankings by property value per pupil, "the top 20 percent of the school districts will receive 29.3 percent of the $1.2 billion in new state funding, while the bottom 20 percent receive only 8.4 percent of the increase" (AP dispatch, 1995d). A lawsuit may very well be filed challenging the distribution as violating the state constitution's call for equitable finances behind every public school pupil. Regardless of how the courts might rule on this controversy, levels of state aid for public schools and the distribution formulas for that aid are likely to be major points of contention in the future as they have been for many years in the past.

Third is the controversy over the creation of a Department of Education headed by a gubernatorially appointed secretary while severely diminishing the authority of the elected nonpartisan superintendent of public instruction. The state constitution gives both the superintendent and the legislature the authority to set policy concerning K-12 education in the state. The courts are likely to be engaged in resolving the controversy over who should control education.

All three of these controversies appear to be on their way to a litigious future. But whatever the court decisions, the legislature, the governor, interest groups, teachers, school administrators and many others are likely to continue to battle over these kinds of policies. Moreover, a future change in political party control of the legislature and/or the governorship could rekindle many of this year's other controversies. Would Democrats try to reverse some of the diminishing of environmental and consumer regulation? Would Democrats try to reverse some of the power that has been centered in the governorship with this budget? Even without split party control, differences in estimates concerning the economy and how much the tax structure will likely continue to generate conflicts between the executive and legislative branches of state government. In short, budgetary politics sees policies settled only for the short run - no more than two years at a time - the length of the budget biennium.

237

CHAPTER XI

EDUCATION

By David M. Jones[*]

Introduction

In Wisconsin, as in all other states, education is one of the most important functions of state and local governments. Measured by expenditures and by numbers of persons involved, education exceeds any other single function of government at this level. Indeed, in the school year 1993-1994, total expenditures for public education in Wisconsin amounted to approximately $8.4 billion (State of Wisconsin, *Blue Book*, 1995-96:641).

Furthermore, education at the elementary, secondary, and higher levels is primarily a state and local function. The role of the national government in education is minimal as contrasted with its role in many other areas of domestic public policy. Although various presidents have held widely publicized meetings to set national goals for education, federal financial support for elementary and secondary education has traditionally been less than ten percent of its total cost, an average that declined during the Reagan years. In 1993-94 only 4.4 percent of Wisconsin's expenditures at this level came from the Federal Government (State of Wisconsin, *Blue Book*, 1995-96:641). National contributions for the cost of instruction in higher education are minor; the most significant federal funds are for research.

Because education is seen as a very important function of state and local government, and because it is expensive, it inevitably becomes an issue in the political arena. Although, much of the governance of education in the state is *nonpartisan*, it does not necessarily follow that it will be *nonpolitical*. If one accepts the definition of politics as the study of "who gets what, when, and how" (Lasswell, 1938) or the "authoritative allocation of values" (Easton, 1965), then education in Wisconsin (and in other states) is an intensely political concern. Many of the controversies surrounding the subject that have arisen in recent years have dealt with resources. How much money should be spent on education? How should it be allocated? Who should pay? These are, by the above definitions, political questions.

Indeed, education has become a major political issue throughout the nation. Many in the U.S. are concerned about this country's competitive position in the world economy and many feel that a strong educational system is necessary if the U.S. is to continue as a world leader. Yet, there is widespread concern about the quality of education here. Virtually everybody believes that improvement is necessary. Where the consensus breaks down is over how this improvement is to come about. Is a large infusion of funds necessary? Some would argue yes; others do not consider this to be the case. In many school districts curricular issues (I. e., what should be taught and how should it be taught) are also topics of contention. The political actors in the state of Wisconsin are by no means immune from these controversies.

Elementary and Secondary Education

Historically, elementary and secondary education has been a function of local school districts. There were, in 1995, 427 such districts in the state. This is a dramatic decrease from the 7,424 districts that existed in 1940. It is likely that the number of school districts will continue to decrease somewhat because the ultimate goal of state policy is to have districts which operate schools from kindergarten through twelfth grade (K-12 districts).

---

[*] Associate Professor of Public Affairs, University of Wisconsin - Oshkosh. The author would like to thank Dr. James Cibulka of the University of Wisconsin-Milwaukee for his comments on an earlier draft of this chapter.

Moreover, a commission established by Governor Thompson in 1994, the Study of Administrative Value and Efficiency (SAVE) Commission, has advocated a further reduction in the number of school districts as a cost cutting measure.

In Wisconsin school districts are independent of other local governmental units. This independence increases the complexity of local government in the state, for school district boundaries may or may not be coterminous with those of municipalities. In Milwaukee and other large cities the school district boundaries are the boundaries of the municipality. In most of the state, however, school districts do not have the same boundaries as do municipalities. Typically, a small city is the center of a district which includes all or parts of adjacent towns and villages. When districts are not coterminous with municipalities, many complex problems (e.g., taxation) may arise. In addition, certain issues (e.g., the behavior of juveniles) may be of concern to both educators and other governmental officials. When separate jurisdictions deal with a particular problem, complications may arise.

Currently, there is some variance in school district governance throughout the state. Over 85 percent of the school districts are "Common School Districts," while most of the rest are "Unified School Districts." There are also a small number of "Union High School Districts" in operation. Finally, the Milwaukee school system is governed by a separate set of statutes.

There are both similarities and differences in the governance of these different types of districts. The basic governing body of all school districts is the school board, which consists of an odd number of members. The size of the board may vary somewhat from district to district. School board members are elected in the April nonpartisan elections for three year terms. In common and union high school districts, the role of the school board is supplemented by the "annual school meeting." This gives the voters the opportunity to express their views concerning school policy and, most importantly, to approve the school budget prepared by the school board. In unified school districts, on the other hand, final approval of the district's budget lies with the school board.

The other source of variation is in the number of grades the district operates. While most unified and common school districts maintain kindergarten through twelfth grade schools, union high school districts, as the name implies, contain only high schools. Whatever their type, school districts maintain "fiscal independence." This means that budget and tax decisions concerning the schools are made independently of other local governing bodies, a fact that at times gives rise to some tensions among local governments. The problem is exacerbated because all local units of government in Wisconsin have traditionally depended heavily on the property tax as a significant source of income. That tax is unpopular with the voters. Consequently, if one unit, (e.g., the school district) raises property tax levies to meet its needs, other units (e.g., counties) may face increased taxpayer resistance to their doing the same thing. Thus, there is competition among local units of government over this scarce resource.

Although schools are local government activities, and there appears to be strong support in Wisconsin for local control over schools, the state also plays an important role by setting general policies and minimum standards, and by providing state aids to enable poor school districts to meet these standards. The state agency which currently has jurisdiction over elementary and secondary education is the State Department of Public Instruction. It is headed by the state superintendent, a constitutional officer elected for a four-year term in the April non-partisan election. Wisconsin is currently one of fifteen states which has an independently elected superintendent. At various times the desirability of a separately elected official has been debated. For instance, one of the SAVE Commission's recommendations was that this elective office, as well as several others, be abolished. Those in favor of the current organizational arrangement argue that it provides a buffer between educational policy and partisan politics. Proponents of an appointive superintendent, on the other hand, contend that the change would enhance organizational responsiveness and efficiency. In any case, unlike a number of other states, the elections for state superintendent have been separated from the usual patterns of Wisconsin politics.

The current arrangement was set to change, however, because the 1995-97 budget act, effective July 1, 1996, abolishes the Department of Public Instruction and replaces it with a Department of Education. Under the budget act, the Department of Education will be under the direction and supervision of a Secretary of Education nominated by the governor with the advise and consent of the Senate. The Secretary of Education will be assigned all statutory duties and powers currently authorized to the state superintendent of public instruction and the Department of Public Instruction. However, a lawsuit was filed in the Dane County Circuit Court alleging that the abolition of the Department of Public Instruction and the replacement of the powers of the elected superintendent of public instruction by a gubernatorially appointed Secretary of Education violates the provisions of the Wisconsin Constitution which call for an independently elected superintendent to supervise education. These cases were accepted by the state Supreme Court which issued a decision on March 29, 1996. The Court unanimously ruled in the action of *Thompson v. Craney* that provisions of 1995 Wisconsin Act 27 (the 1995-97 state budget) related to restructuring the governance of the Department of Public Instruction are unconstitutional. In essence, the Court's decision voided 148 sections of act 27 relating to the creation of the Education Commission, the creation of the position of Secretary of Education, the creation of the Office of the State Superintendent of Public Instruction, and the renaming of the Department of Public Instruction, and the transferring of powers and duties of the State Superintendent of Public Instruction.

The state Department of Public Instruction: 1) certifies teachers; 2) enforces standards of school construction, program, and transportation; and, 3) administers state aids. It also is involved with the regional Cooperative Education Service Agencies (CESA) which provide information and cooperative assistance to local school districts. Assistance is provided primarily through shared teachers and shared services. The regional agencies have replaced the county superintendents of schools, and thus the county is no longer directly involved in elementary and secondary education.

State aids administered by the state Department of Public Instruction once played a critical role in forcing school consolidation and in achieving minimum standards. Consolidation was achieved by state policies which involved both a "carrot" and a "stick." The carrot involved additional state money for schools which consolidated; the stick involved subsequent policies for school districts which resisted consolidation. Since 1971, however, state aids have not been used for this purpose.

However, these aids still constitute an important and controversial element of Madison's involvement in the politics of education. State aid has two major goals: to reduce the reliance upon the local property tax as a major source of revenue for K-12 education, and to guarantee that a basic educational opportunity is available to all students no matter what the wealth of the district in which they reside. How large these aids should be and how they should be distributed is a matter of significant political contention.

There are a number of different programs through which the cost of K-12 education is supported by the state. The most important of these, general education programs, are funded by means of a formula that distributes state aid on the basis of the "relative fiscal capacity" (Clancy, 1987: 1) of each school district. This is measured by the district's per pupil value of taxable property, and is designed to give relatively more state aid to those districts most in need. The formula has been known as the "general school aid" or "equalization" formula. State funds have been primarily distributed in two different ways: direct payments to school districts and as property tax credits. In addition to these, the state has established a number of other aid programs which also are related to the equalization formula.

In the state's 1995-97 biennial budget, the governor and legislature have agreed to modify this current equalization aid formula beginning with the 1996-97 aid distribution. Now, instead of the formula described above, equalization aids will be distributed using a three-tiered formula. This new calculation of aids is designed to allow wealthier school districts a small slice of the state aid to public education pie in order to permit all school districts to benefit from the states' commitment to fund a larger portion of public education in Wisconsin. This, too, is likely to be challenged in the courts.

Another type of state grant is given in the form of "categorical aids" which help to fund such specific program costs as handicapped education and pupil transportation. These are not directly related to the equalization formula. Finally, the state also subsidizes education by means of general government and school levy property tax

241

credits.

State aids to local districts add up to a good deal of money. In a recent school year (1993-1994), state expenditures on elementary and secondary schools (not including aid packaged in the form of property tax credits) totaled $2.189 billion. This accounted for almost 30 percent of all general purpose spending in the state budget ("The Coming Change . . . ," 1994: 5; Shively, 1994). Beginning in 1997, two-thirds of the cost of public education, or 67.7 percent, will be funded through state aid.

In spite of these large expenditures aimed in part at equalizing educational funding throughout the state there still remain considerable differences among school districts in the amount they are willing and able to spend on their students' education. While the school tax rates in most districts approximate the state average ("1993-1994 School Tax Levies . . . ," 1994: 4), equal rates do not necessarily lead to equal expenditures. For instance, while the three year average expenditures in the Elroy-Kendall-Wilton School District in central Wisconsin was $4,273, the average expenditures for the same period of time in the Nicolet School District in suburban Milwaukee was $11,916 ("Election 1994 . . . , 1994: 11). Such differentials in funding raise, in the view of some observers, questions about the equality of educational opportunity found in this state. Indeed, in many states (e.g., Alabama, California, and Kentucky) large disparities in school district finance have been challenged on state constitutional grounds.

One of the reasons for these disparities is that Wisconsin has had a tradition of relatively high reliance on local rather than state revenue sources in primary and secondary school funding. Indeed the issue of the state's role in the financial support of K-12 education has been one confronted by many recent governors. Although former Governor Dreyfus was committed to a goal of raising state aids to 49 percent of the local school costs, he did not achieve this goal. In fact, even under his successor's administration, state aid to local schools remained at the level of slightly less than 45 percent of total school costs. This was in contrast to a national average at the time of approximately 55 percent (Cibulka, 1984).

The problem of state aid to local school districts became a partisan political issue in the 1986 gubernatorial contest when Republican candidate Thompson promised that, if elected, he would seek to increase the level of state funding to local districts while at the same time working to contain rising district costs. He was generally unsuccessful in his efforts at that time. In the school year 1987-88, the state proportion of total K-12 expenditures remained at approximately 45 percent of total school expenditures (DPI, 1989). This fact was raised as an issue by Democratic candidate Tom Loftus in his unsuccessful attempt to defeat Governor Thompson in the 1990 election.

Educational finance has remained a hot political issue in Wisconsin. More than half of the property taxes levied in 1993 were by school districts. Moreover, these taxes have increased at a rate exceeding inflation. ("The Coming Change . . . ," 1994). In 1993, for instance, school taxes rose almost 11 percent over the previous year ("1993-1994 School Tax Levies . . .," 1994). Since the property tax is perceived as being a highly unpopular one, political leaders have grappled with mechanisms for relieving reliance on the property tax as a mechanism for funding education. For instance, in the 1989-90 legislative session a constitutional amendment that would have totally eliminated the property tax as a source of public school financing was unsuccessfully proposed. This proposal received support from spokes people for some interest groups (e.g., the Farm Bureau) while at the same time causing apprehension among others. A problem the idea faced stems from the unanswered question of what tax (or taxes) would replace the one on property. For instance, a greater reliance on the sales tax as a basis for educational finance would be likely to shift the burden of payment from property owners to consumers. As a result, the costs of K-12 education would be transferred to some degree from one group of voters to another. If this were to happen, some people would receive more of a value (in the form of lower taxes) while others would receive less.

At the beginning of the 1994 legislative session, Governor Thompson proposed a significant increase-- $200,000,000--in state aid to school districts. His proposal was countered by one from the Democratic leaders in the state legislature, which proposed total state funding of K-12 education. The result was a compromise between the republican governor and the democratically controlled legislature which called for the assumption by the school year 1996-1997 by the state of two-thirds of the funding for K-12 education in the state. This means that state expenditures for school aids will rise by over $1 billion.

However, the compromise did not settle some important political issues. For instance, the concern that sank the proposed constitutional amendment--how is the increase in state aid to be paid for--was not addressed. Subsequently, Governor Thompson has taken the position that this substantial increase in state funding can take place without any general increase in state taxes. In fact, in his 1995 budget message, Governor Thompson did propose the state assumption of $1 billion worth of local school finance while at the same time arguing there were no new taxes in his budget. Indeed a number of educational policy proposals were contained in the enacted budget. These included a continuation of state controls on local spending, the transfer of most of the functions currently undertaken by the Department of Public Instruction to a new Department of Education to be headed by a Secretary appointed by the governor, and greater decision-making autonomy for many local school districts. Many of these proposals were attacked by various political actors in the state, especially the current state superintendent of public instruction, James Benson, who is involved in the lawsuit mentioned earlier.

Related to the issue of who pays for education is that of how much money should be allocated to support this function. Currently, although Wisconsin ranks 23rd among the states in terms of per capita income, it ranks sixth in the percentage of its income spent on education (Wisconsin Legislative Reference Bureau, 1993). At the same time, by many measures (relatively low drop out rates and relatively high scores on national standardized tests), Wisconsin students perform very well. Many would argue that there is a relationship between these two facts.

By extension, a number of people assert that if the state wants to enhance the educational attainments of its citizenry, it should be willing to spend even more. In particular, spokespersons for the Wisconsin Educational Association Council (WEAC) have asserted that public schools would perform more effectively if teachers' salaries were substantially increased. On the other hand, representatives of taxpayers' groups have argued that pay for teachers in this state has risen appreciably in recent years and that higher expenditures in this area should not have a great impact on student performance. A number of political actors have advocated a stronger state role in controlling school costs. For instance, for some time the state has been involved in local school district labor negotiations. In 1985 the legislature made permanent a law mandating that, in the event they were unable to reach agreement on contract negotiations, local school boards and teachers' unions would submit to binding arbitration proceedings. Many representatives of school boards have contended that the existing arbitration law encourages wage settlements which have been, in their view, excessive. In his 1986 campaign for governor, Mr. Thompson stated his agreement with their position and advocated changes in the law that would require arbitrators to keep their recommended settlements within close range to changes in the cost of living. Such changes, however, were not enacted into law.

Governor Thompson's failure to achieve this goal at that time may be attributed in part to the political clout of the state's largest teacher's union, the Wisconsin Education Association Council (WEAC). WEAC's strength is due in large part to the fact that its members are located throughout the state. Moreover, every one of them is expected to perform a minimum of two hours of election work every two years. Thus, the union's leadership is in a position to mobilize workers in election campaigns. Furthermore, members of this organization are expected to contribute at least $10 per year to WEAC's Political Action Committee. Because it has many members, WEAC is able to raise a significant amount of money. These funds are used, among other things, to support candidates considered to be favorably disposed to WEAC's position on important issues. For instance, the education union's PAC was one of Democrat Tom Loftus' largest political contributors in his unsuccessful 1990 gubernatorial race. It also spent about $100,000 of its own on political advertisements independently supporting Loftus and attacking Governor Thompson. The union's PAC also has contributed significant amounts of aid to candidates (most of them Democrats) in state legislative races. The total sum of money spent by this organization is significant--in 1991-92 it added up to more than $900,000 (Milwaukee *Journal*, October 26, 1990, p. A7).

In addition, the organization has been blessed with effective leadership. Indeed, according to journalistic observers, WEAC's executive director was widely viewed as one of the state's most effective political operators. In short, WEAC is well-organized and well-led. It also controls a substantial amount of money which can be used in political campaigns. These factors, added together, make WEAC a power to be reckoned within the educational politics of in the state of Wisconsin. In part, perhaps, because of WEAC's political power, while the state ranks twenty-second in the nation in personal income, it ranked 14th in average salaries of public school teachers in the 1993-1994 school year (State of Wisconsin, *Blue Book*, 1995-96:641, 669).

However, WEAC has not won all of its legislative battles. In 1993 the legislature passed a bill limiting increases in local school revenues to an inflation-adjusted $190 per student, or the increase in the Consumer Price Index, whichever is higher. Increases greater than these would have to be approved by a voter referendum in the school district. Current indications are that the Republican controlled state legislature will vote to continue these restraints. Such constraints are likely to put a damper on increases in faculty salaries, a major concern of WEAC. In short, many of the financial issues involving education affect the distribution of important costs and benefits within the state. Because of this, educational finance will remain an important political issue in Wisconsin.

The state has also become involved in local school issues in other ways, particularly in Milwaukee, the state's largest school district. Concern has been expressed because Milwaukee's school drop out rate has remained at about nine to ten percent annually, the highest in the state, and well above the state average of about three percent (State of Wisconsin, *Blue Book*, 1995-96:648). One of the solutions proposed to deal with this problem that has been tried on an experimental basis is "school choice." Under this program, which has the strong support of such diverse political actors as Republican Governor Thompson, Milwaukee Mayor John Norquist, and Polly Williams a Democratic Assembly member from Milwaukee, but generally opposed by WEAC, a limited number of students from lower income families in the city may receive financial subsidies from the state in order to attend private, non-sectarian schools. Subsidies are paid for by a reduction in state aid to the Milwaukee public school system.

Evaluations of the program have been somewhat mixed. While students enrolled in the program do neither better nor worse in standardized reading and math tests than do their peers in Milwaukee's public schools, the parents of children in "choice" schools prefer the private to the public schools. In spite of, or because of, these findings many political actors are advocating, and gaining through the budget act, an expansion of the choice program, an expansion that includes Milwaukee's religiously affiliated parochial schools. Opponents of this expansion have argued this could violate constitutional provisions mandating the separation of church and state. The courts have issue a temporary injunction against students using the choice program to attend parochial schools in 1995-1996 while it reviews the constitutionality of this issue.

For his part, the current state superintendent of Public Instruction, John Benson, has proposed an "Urban Initiative" which would, among other things, provide greater resources to public schools in low income areas in order to reduce class sizes in the lower grades. The budget act provides for some of "Urban Initiative" to be implemented in the upcoming biennium. In contrast to Governor Thompson and his allies, Superintendent Benson would like to attack low school performance by means of a greater infusion of resources into the public sector.

There is also a movement to more fully involve the private sector in public education in the problem of dealing with "at-risk" students. Since 1986, Wisconsin law has allowed school districts to contract with private agencies to work with students who are considered at risk of dropping out of the formal educational process before they graduate from high school (Quick, 1993). Power to do this was expanded in the 1994 legislative session.

The greater use of the private sector in the provision of public education raises significant issues, both practical and ideological. The practical issue is that, if limited resources exist, public money provided to the private sector for educational purposes is a resource the public sector loses. The ideological issue involves the relative size of the public and private sectors in American society, a topic of hot debate for many decades. Both of these issues have obvious political overtones.

State government has an impact upon local school district governance in other ways, too. For instance, in its 1983-84 session the legislature passed a bill mandating stricter high school graduation requirements throughout the state. It has also required that local school districts develop programs to identify at an early age those students most likely to drop out before graduating and provide appropriate assistance. In the 1995-97 budget, Governor Thompson proposed to allow 17 year olds to drop out of school. This proposal was modified by Joint Finance to allow 16 year olds to drop out of school with a parent's permission and proof of being either enrolled in an alternative school or having a job. However, this modification was vetoed by Governor Thompson and current law prevails.

The state has also become involved in the school segregation problems afflicting the Milwaukee metropolitan area. For instance, the legislature in 1976 appropriated extra financial aid as an incentive to increase racial integration. This program, known as "Chapter 220," provides additional aids for school districts which accept minority pupils while continuing to pay the usual aids to the districts from which they transferred. The state also pays the transportation costs. Although the bill would apply to the whole state, its most important impact has been in the Milwaukee area.

The problem of racial segregation is still festering in the area. In 1986 the Milwaukee school district sued 24 suburbs and the state of Wisconsin for pursuing policies that would racially isolate Milwaukee school children. The settlement that grew out of this lawsuit preserved, and even strengthened, the provisions of Chapter 220. However, the program is still under attack as being relatively ineffective (a Legislative Audit Bureau study indicated the program had little impact on the academic performance of the students being bussed) and too expensive (it costs $64 million per year.) It is, indeed possible that extensive changes in the current desegregation program will be considered in an upcoming legislative session.

In short, while the tradition of local control of elementary and secondary education in Wisconsin remains powerful, state government and state politics also plays a very important role in this critical arena of public policy.

Vocational Education

Vocational schools were established at the beginning of the century, when high schools were placing emphasis on preparing students for college. Vocational schools were perceived as an alternative to high schools. In most states, these schools were administered by the boards which also had control over the elementary and secondary schools. In Wisconsin, a pioneer in vocational education, a separate vocational system was established in 1907.

The legislature authorized municipalities to establish vocational schools with the right to receive a specified percent of the cities' assessed valuation for their operations. City councils could provide more money than this formula mandated if they wished. These schools were administered by special boards composed of representatives of employers, employees, and farmers. A state board, appointed by the governor, had some authority over these schools. In 1914 federal aids for vocational education became available, and the state passed along these funds to the local schools. However, the state itself contributed very little to this educational system.

By the time Warren Knowles became governor in 1965, it had become apparent that vocational education in Wisconsin was woefully inadequate. It also had become clear that vocational education was increasingly post-high school education rather than an alternative to high school. Except for Milwaukee and Madison, whose city councils had regularly appropriated more than the minimum levy to their vocational schools, most of the Wisconsin vocational schools could not provide the expensive hardware for the technology of the modern era. Moreover, persons living in communities with no vocational school could attend another district's school only on a tuition basis and at the option of the vocational schools concerned.

Accordingly, in 1965, Governor Knowles initiated a fundamental reform in vocational education. Subsequently, reform was implemented by 1970. The state policy board was renamed the Board of Vocational, Technical, and Adult Education (VTAE). It is composed of nine members appointed by the governor (three employers, three employees, three farmers) for six-year terms plus, three ex-officio members (superintendent of public instruction, President of the Board of Regents of the University of Wisconsin, and a commissioner of the Department of Industry, Labor and Human Relations). This has made Wisconsin unique in that it is the only state to have a completely separate board to oversee vocational and technical education. Far more important, the state was to be divided into operating districts--first 18, now 16--so that each district would have the tax base to provide quality technical training for such skills as electronics, computer science, and the like. Each district has a seven-member board which is composed of two employers, two employees, two members at-large (each of whom are selected for a six-year term) and a district superintendent of schools, who serves a two-year term. In three of the 16 districts, including Milwaukee, the board members are appointed by a committee of school board presidents. In the other 13 districts they are appointed by a committee of county board chairpersons.

The local board selects the district administrator and controls the district's programs. Through its extensive use of advisory committees, each board seeks to tailor its programs to meet the needs of its labor market and its students.

As was true in elementary and high school district consolidation, there was much controversy and agony over this reorganization. Cities wished to retain their own local schools, and there were many arguments about how the boundaries should be drawn. Eventually, however, this political issue was settled.

The funding of VTAE districts has also become another political issue. Because vocational education is now primarily post-high school training, and because the state bears the primary cost of parallel higher education, the question arises whether the state should provide funding for vocational schools proportionate to what it provides for the University of Wisconsin system. A proposal embodying that idea was defeated in a referendum, but the question persists, especially in view of the increasing inability of local property taxes to adequately fund such educational expenditures. This is particularly a problem for the VTAE system because, by law, such districts are limited to a levy of no more than 1.5 mills of the district's equalized property value for operational purposes. For this reason, Governor Lucey followed Governor Knowles in putting greater emphasis on state aids and relatively less on local property taxes for the vocational system. In 1967 the state spent $6 million on vocational education. The 1974-75 appropriation was $41 million, an increase of nearly 700 percent in eight years. In 1977-79 an additional $20 million was added for state aids, bringing the state share to a level of 36 percent of costs. Proportionate increases have been made in recent years. Currently, state aids add up to more than $110 million. However, local VTAE districts still provide the bulk of the funding for their programs. Increased spending has come about in part because of the recognition that workers must be continuously retrained to meet the demands of an ever-changing labor market. Wisconsin remains in the forefront of vocational and technical training among the states, and enrollment of students over 18 in such programs is well above that of the national average.

In spite of its success the VTAE system is not without its problems and controversies. As is the case with K-12 education, local funding means reliance on the local property tax. This has led to questions about the adequacy of support and to continued calls for greater state financial involvement. This, in turn, has raised questions of control--who should have primary influence over local technical colleges, local VTAE boards or the state?

A second set of issues has arisen concerning relationships among units of the VTAE system and between the system itself and other institutions of learning in the state. The concern in the first instance relates to students from one district taking courses, tuition-free, in another. Because of the tradition of local control and local funding this was not allowed in this state. While some favored a change, others, concerned about incurring extra costs from an influx of students, opposed such an idea. Closure was brought to this dispute in 1990 when legislation was passed providing for such inter-district movement.

Relations between the two post-secondary systems in the state have also become a matter of discussion. Currently, very few courses from a limited number of VTAE institutions are automatically accepted in transfer by member institutions of the university system. Some legislators, and others, have asserted that this situation is wasteful of resources and have pushed for a change, while others, especially in the university system, have been somewhat resistant to these proposals. Negotiations are currently taking place over this contentious issue.

In short, the political concerns surrounding the distribution of resources and influence have affected the governance of the VTAE system as they have other elements of education in the state of Wisconsin.

Higher Education

In July 1974, Governor Lucey signed a university merger implementation bill which completed action initiated in 1971 to create a new University of Wisconsin system. The merger of the University of Wisconsin with the Wisconsin State University System created the third largest university system in the nation. Whether bigger is better is debatable, but, as political scientists, our interest is in observing the extent to which university policies are involved in politics. Thus, we shall trace the history of higher education in Wisconsin to indicate how merger came about.

University of Wisconsin. The state constitution of 1848 provided that there should be a university at or near the seat of state government. The institution at Madison got off to a slow start, but its status was assured with its designation as the state's land grant college after congressional passage of the Morrill Act of 1862.

The establishment of the Agricultural College as an integral part of the university in Madison is probably the most important political explanation as to how a state with merely average income could develop an institution with high ranking among the universities of the nation and of the world. Many states, such as Wisconsin's neighbors, Iowa and Michigan, established separate institutions at different locations for their land grant universities. Wisconsin, with only one institution, was not faced with the rivalries found in other states. Moreover, the land grant college, with its agricultural agents distributed throughout the counties of the state, developed considerable support from Wisconsin citizens. This service concept was later to be developed at the turn of the century into "the Wisconsin idea," with the slogan, "the boundaries of the campus are the boundaries of the state." Popular support for the university induced succeeding Wisconsin legislatures to treat the university more generously than did legislatures in most other states.

Although proposals for reorganization of higher education in Wisconsin had been made before, the first real threat to the preferred status of the University of Wisconsin at Madison came during the administration of Governor Walter Kohler, Jr. (1951-57). Governor Kohler proposed that the University of Wisconsin, which by then had established two-year branches or centers throughout the state--most notably in Milwaukee--be merged with the nine state colleges. University of Wisconsin administrators, faculty, and alumni strenuously opposed this proposal, and it was defeated. In 1955 two major compromises emerged from Kohler's proposal. The most obvious argument for merger was found in Milwaukee, where both a University of Wisconsin branch and a state college existed. One compromise merged these institutions to create the University of Wisconsin-Milwaukee under the jurisdiction of the Regents of the University of Wisconsin. The other compromise was the creation of a Coordinating Committee of Higher Education to coordinate planning by the two systems of higher education.

Wisconsin State University System. Seven of the nine institutions which were ultimately to be the Wisconsin State University system were initially two-year teacher training institutions. (Stout and Platteville had somewhat different backgrounds.) Founded near the turn of the century, they were originally called normal schools. Over time these institutions were changed to state teachers colleges, to state colleges, and to state universities.

Initially the teacher training function of these institutions was so clearly differentiated from the functions of the University of Wisconsin that there was little rivalry or competition for funds. However, as these institutions began offering degrees and then expanded beyond teacher education, and as the university expanded its School of Education, rivalry between the two systems developed. The competition became more serious as the state universities began offering graduate work and as both systems established additional two-year branches.

247

<u>Coordinating Committee of Higher Education</u>. The Coordinating Committee of Higher Education (CCHE) was supposed to provide comprehensive planning for higher education in the state, but this mechanism did not succeed. In a period of rapid growth in higher education, more and more communities in the state sought institutions in their areas. The two university systems competed with one another for these new sites. The University of Wisconsin, under the aggressive leadership of Fred Harvey Harrington (1962-1970), was probably more successful in this competition. For instance, the University of Wisconsin obtained authorization to open four-year degree-granting institutions at Green Bay and at Parkside (between Racine and Kenosha). Each of the systems obtained authorization for new two-year centers.

The reason usually cited for the failure of the CCHE is that it was composed of too many members from the boards of regents of the competing systems. Moreover, the committee did not have an independent staff director; rather, each of the two systems designated a co-director of the CCHE staff. Thus, the committee operated more as a conference of ambassadors from competing powers rather than as a policy-making body with the interests of the entire state at heart. Inevitably, there was considerable log rolling on the committee.

Governor Knowles became so dissatisfied with these arrangements that he brought about some institutional changes in what was renamed the Coordinating Council of Higher Education. The new council had a majority of public members (i.e., not regents of either system) and an independent staff director and staff. This tinkering with the coordinating mechanism apparently did not satisfy Governor Lucey, who, upon taking office in 1971, urged the merger of the university systems.

Governor Lucey put a very high premium on achieving passage of merger legislation. Initially, he attempted to include this change in the budget and insisted he would not sign a budget bill unless the university systems were merged. Subsequently, after a series of compromises with Republicans in the state senate, merger was passed as a separate bill in the fall of 1971. The creation of the new system was, in short, a highly politicized process.

<u>The University of Wisconsin System.</u> The 1971 legislation provided for a merged board of regents and took some steps toward creating a central administration of the university system. The details of the merger were to be worked out by a merger implementation study committee composed of regents, faculty, students, and legislators.

The board of regents of the system is composed of fourteen regents appointed by the governor (with the consent of the state senate) for seven-year staggered terms, plus two ex-officio members: the state superintendent of public instruction and the president of the Board of Vocational, Adult, and Technical Education. In 1985 provision was also made for the appointment of a student regent to a two-year term. Who serves on the board of regents has at times become a political issue, for, in recent years some candidates nominated by Governor Thompson have been criticized by his political opponents for being too conservative and too business-oriented. The regents appoint the president of the system, who, in turn, plays a key role in the selection of the other central administration officials, the chancellors of the thirteen degree-granting institutions, and the administrators of the center system and extension. In the main, each university campus has greater autonomy than it had in the past. Other provisions of the merger implementation bill, an elaborate set of compromises worked out by the affected parties, generally allow institutions to continue their past practices.

Many of the proponents of merger sought, and many of the opponents feared, the equalization of the two systems, especially in funding. When one considers that the cost of instruction per student at Madison and Milwaukee was almost twice as much as the cost of instruction at some former state universities, one can see how important this issue would be. However, since 1973 the budget has preserved funding differentials between different types of universities. Using a cluster concept, Madison and Milwaukee are designated the doctoral cluster and are funded at a higher level than the other degree-granting institutions. Green Bay and Parkside, created as part of the old University of Wisconsin system and originally anticipating quality at a Madison standard, probably were the chief losers, since they are now designated as part of the university cluster along with the former state universities.

While all the universities--including the two-year "centers" located throughout the state--are governed by a single board of regents, strains still exist within the system. This became most evident in the furor that arose over the issue of "catch up" pay for faculty at the different institutions. Studies conducted in the early 1980s concluded that teachers in the various institution of higher learning in the state were being paid substantially less than were their colleagues at comparable institutions elsewhere. To remedy this problem, the board of regents recommended that the 1985-87 biennial budget contain provisions for a rather large "catchup" increase in faculty pay. The regents' recommendation (that Madison faculty average a 15 percent increase, those at Milwaukee receive 11 percent, and those at the other institutions get 9 percent) touched off a controversy among representatives of the different campuses. While partisans of the differential increase argued that these were necessary in order that Madison retain its status as one of the premier institutions of higher learning in the country, opponents contended that it would give the status of "second class citizens" to the faculty and students of the university cluster campuses. After a good deal of rancorous debate, both within and outside the legislature, the final decision was that while "catch up" at Madison would remain at 15 percent, those at Milwaukee and the other campuses be raised to 12 percent and ten percent respectively. Thus, this important debate was over "who gets what" was resolved by compromise. A second "catch up" proposal passed by the legislature in 1989, on the other hand, was not as controversial as the first.

A continuing controversy surrounding higher education in Wisconsin has revolved around the problem of how it is to be financed. There is a growing concern among many influential actors in the state political system that its tax and expenditure levels are such that a poor "business climate" has been created. As a result, pressures have been growing to limit the growth of state spending. Since higher education expenditures constitute a significant proportion of the state's budget, they are an obvious target for those concerned about limiting spending. This is especially true since Wisconsin rates rather high in terms of expenditures per $1000 of personal income for higher education. This issue is likely to be exacerbated by the state assumption of greater funding of local school financing discussed earlier in this chapter. Indeed, already in December 1994, the University of Wisconsin system was required by the governor to return $8.7 million to state coffers in order to soften the budgetary pinch expected to be produced by this program. It is highly likely that budgetary pressures will not decrease in coming years. Consequently, budgetary battles among the different levels of education are likely to increase in the future.

To deal with financial concerns the Wisconsin Expenditure Commission recommended that enrollment in the state's universities be limited more stringently and that students attending school in the system bear a greater proportion of instructional costs through tuition increase (Wisconsin Expenditure Commission, 1986). While there was some resistance to these recommendations (especially on the part of students) they were, to a great extent, put into practice.

For one thing, enrollment caps were established for institutions in the system. Under the rubric of "enrollment management," most four year institutions have been expected to decrease the size of their student population over time. This has meant that some of the students who formerly would have started their academic careers at these universities are now enrolling at the two-year centers for their first years of higher education. The implementation of enrollment caps was made easier by the decline in the number of students graduating from Wisconsin high schools during the decade of the 1980s. However, this trend has reversed, and the increase in the number of those students who have traditionally sought admission to the University of Wisconsin system is likely to lead to pressures for increasing enrollments. How the political system will respond to these pressures remains to be seen.

Second, students attending institutions in the University of Wisconsin System are now being expected to pay a larger proportion of the total cost of their education. For a long time, the expectation was that undergraduate student tuition should pay for approximately one-fourth of the system's instructional costs. In recent years this proportion has risen to about 32 percent. Tuition for nonresident students has increased proportionately. Consequently, there has been something of a shift in the cost of higher education from the general taxpayer to the consumers of the service, the students. An important value (money) thus has been allocated in a different fashion by the political system. It should be noted, however, that higher education in Wisconsin is still a "good deal" for the students, since tuition at both of the types of clusters in this state is still well below the average tuition paid at comparable institutions elsewhere (Suchman, 1987).

Another element that continues to be an important function of the University of Wisconsin system is its Extension system. Initiated primarily as a service to farmers, this tradition of service is continued through a state wide enterprise which provides services to many other persons in the state: workers, business-persons, government officials, and the general public. A continuing issue concerning instruction is whether it should be directed from a state headquarters or based on each campus. The issue was not dealt with in merger legislation.

Thus, education at all levels is an important public policy issue in this state. The citizens of Wisconsin are committed to a sound educational system. However, they are also concerned about how the costs and benefits of education are distributed. Such issues inevitably become fodder for the political system.

CHAPTER XII

HEALTH AND SOCIAL SERVICES
By Julie M Knier*

Introduction

The 1995-97 budget act (1995 Wisconsin Act 27) allocates approximately 33% of the total 1995-97 state budget to human relations and resources programs, which include programs administered by the Department of Health and Social Services (DHSS), the Department of Corrections, the Department of Industry, Labor, and Human Relations, and several smaller agencies. Act 27 provides DHSS approximately $8.4 billion (all funds) for the 1995-97 biennium, which represents approximately 25.4% of total funds budgeted for this two-year period (Legislative Fiscal Bureau Act 27 Summary 1995, 35).

According to the Executive Budget Book, the mission of the department is

to work in partnership with local governments, human service agencies, private providers and concerned and affected citizens to develop and support availability of the care, treatment or assistance people need to cope with illness, injury, impairment, economic reversal, family disintegration, delinquent behavior and inappropriate dependency. This includes attempting to prevent or minimize conditions that limit well-being and independence in their physical, mental, social and economic lives (1995, 227).

If you are a Wisconsin resident, the department's programs quite possibly affected you directly within the last year -- and they almost certainly affected a member of your family, a neighbor, a friend, or a relative. Figure XII-1 shows the department's current organizational structure as of July 1, 1996, reflecting transfers authorized in Act 27 .

The department literally takes note of your birth and death in its Vital Records and Health Statistics unit. In between those points, department programs address the citizenry's health, safety, financial solvency, family well-being, and overall quality of life.

The wide-ranging responsibilities of the department and the impact of its programs can be seen in the array of issues considered by public policy-makers in recent years.

- Should Wisconsin regulate medical pricing and health facility expansion in an effort to make health care more affordable for its citizens? And how can reasonable access to health care be assured for all citizens, particularly those without insurance or located in rural areas far from medical centers?

- What should the state do to help care for the increasing number of elderly who need long-term care? How can elderly individuals be supported so they can remain in their homes and communities? What level of nursing home care should be made available? At what cost? Who should pay?

---

*   Research assistant to Dr. Ronald Weber at the University of Wisconsin, Milwaukee. The author is profoundly grateful to Charles Morgan and Pris Boroniec of Wisconsin's Legislative Fiscal Bureau for their expert advice and thoughtful contributions toward updating this chapter.

251

Figure XII-1

DEPARTMENT OF HEALTH AND SOCIAL SERVICES ORGANIZATION

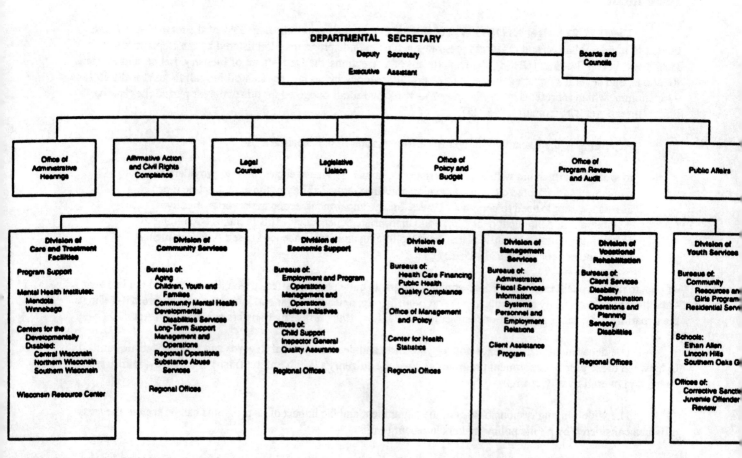

Source: State of Wisconsin, *Blue Book*, 1995-96:432-433.

- Do "welfare" programs encourage dependency by the poor -- fostering a continued culture of poverty? Are Wisconsin welfare payments too high, creating a "welfare magnet" or are payments just the minimum needed for the financially needy to survive?

- What are the best ways to prepare the disadvantaged --welfare recipients and others -- for jobs?

- Alcohol and other drug abuse are pervasive social problems. What is the best strategy to reduce these problems? What mix of law enforcement or treatment is likely to work?

- The percentage of mothers with preschool children who work outside the home is ever increasing, and finding affordable, quality child care is a difficult problem for many of these families. What should the state do to help?

These, and a lengthy list of other social issues and human services needs, face the state while simultaneously the federal government is reducing its investment in social programs. Meanwhile, elected state officials are also seeking to keep increases in state spending and taxing below the rate of inflation. The challenge of meeting increased needs with reduced funding focuses attention on the need to set priorities, and on cost-effectiveness and accountability for service delivery and budget use.

One human services issue, welfare reform, is discussed in more detail following an overview of the state's health and social service programs.

Overview of Health and Social Services Programs

State Department Organization. The Department of Health and Social Services (DHSS) is the largest state agency in terms of its budget based on Act 27 total funding amounts (Legislative Fiscal Bureau Act 27 Summary 1995, 33). With respect to program diversity, however, this department is the largest. The department was created in 1967 in a government wide reorganization (resulting from the "Kellett Commission"). The agency's scope and mission were fundamentally changed in 1989 when its Corrections Division was made a separate agency. Its internal structure is constantly changing. The most significant change was in 1975, when the department became a cabinet agency with a secretary appointed by the governor, rather than an agency governed by a board with members appointed for staggered terms by the governor with the consent of the senate. The intent of the change was to create an agency leadership more responsive to policy direction from the governor. The department will undergo more changes as a result of recent legislation. Under the 1995-97 biennial budget act , the scope and activities of the department have again been dramatically altered. Beginning July 1, 1996, the department will be renamed the department of Health and Family Services. In addition, several programs will be shifted out of this department and into other state agencies. The department of Industry, Labor and Human Relations (DILHR) will take over the administration of several programs including AFDC and other income maintenance programs, employment training programs, refugee assistance programs, the employment opportunity program, vocational education responsibilities, and a new division of children's services and economic support. In addition, this department will be renamed the Department of Workforce Development effective July 1, 1996. The low-income energy assistance program will be moved to the Department of Administration (DOA). All juvenile correctional services and youth services will be moved to the Department of Corrections (DOC). The new department of Health and Family Services will pick up health care facilities plan review functions from DILHR.

Medical Assistance. The agency's largest program is the Medical Assistance (MA) program, with funds budgeted totaling approximately $900 million state general funds (GPR) and $1.5 billion in 1995-96 and $940 million (GPR) and $1.56 billion in 1996-97 (Legislative Fiscal Bureau Summary of Act 27, 399). MA pays for medical services provided to eligible low-income persons. The program supports the costs of providing acute and long-term care to certain groups of persons including those who are aged, blind, disabled, members of families with dependent children and certain other pregnant women and children who meet specified financial and nonfinancial criteria. According to the department, in November of 1994, 487,475 persons living in 303,883 households were eligible for MA. As of December 1994, about 214,000 individuals were receiving Aid to Families with Dependent Children (AFDC) or a related benefit. One hundred six thousand people were receiving Supplemental Security Income (the aged, blind, and disabled) and 324,000 individuals were receiving Food Stamps. In some instances, individuals qualify for more than one MA program. Some who receive MA are "medically needy" -- that is, they are individuals who would qualify for MA except that they have excess income. They become eligible for MA by incurring medical expenses such that they "spend down" this excess income to the maximum income level.

Medical Assistance alone is approximately 58.1 percent of the DHSS budget in the 1995-1997 biennium. Using a combination of federal and state funds, MA pays for care in hospitals, nursing homes, clinics, and other health care settings and sometimes in people's own homes. It pays doctor, dentists, nurses, pharmacies, psychiatric social workers, chiropractors, and many others. In fiscal year 1993-94, $757, representing 37.9 percent of total MA expenditures, was expended for services to persons who were disabled or blind, $723.4 million (36.3 percent) was expended for services to aged individuals, $376.2 (18.9 percent) was expended for services to persons who qualified for MA benefits as a result of their eligibility for aid to families with dependent children (AFDC) benefits, and $138.5 (6.9 percent) was expended for services to other individuals (primarily low-income pregnant women and children who do not qualify for AFDC). As a very large buyer of health care services in the state, the department can and does have an extensive impact on the organization and financing of health care. Issues such as the rate of reimbursement paid for nursing home care are heavily lobbied concerns in the State Capitol because of the significant financial role the state plays in funding those institutions.

Other Health Programs. The department has many other roles in the health care of Wisconsin people. In the calendar year 1995, an average of 109,400 individuals received WIC benefits, another important federal-state health program. Other special programs target the medically unserved, or those with certain chronic diseases requiring special care (such as chronic renal disease). Vaccines are provided for immunization clinics. Working with local public health agencies and others, the department promotes good health and wellness, and seeks to prevent and control communicable and preventable diseases and injuries such as AIDS, high blood pressure, Lyme disease, sexually transmitted diseases, and lead poisoning.

In a variety of ways, the department has attempted to control costs experienced in both the publicly and privately funded health care systems. In the 1970s through the early 1980s, "health planning" functions were federally authorized and funded. Wisconsin, along with many other states, attempted to regulate the growth of facilities and expensive equipment through prior public approval requirements, to control rate increases by public rate regulation, and to otherwise control health care costs through regulatory strategies. To facilitate this regulation, the Cost Containment Commission was created. In the 1980s, both the federal and state governments phased-out or phased-down regulatory controls on health care costs. A significant exception has been the state's "cap" on nursing home beds, which has been intended to match an emphasis on supporting certain elderly and disabled individuals in community and home care programs, as well as to control the public (especially Medical Assistance) costs of nursing home care. However, even this area is no longer immune from the cost-reduction ax wielded by governments. Now, where the costs of community care exceed the costs of nursing home care, benefits are limited and caps on spending have been imposed. Along with this limit, however, Wisconsin state government officials seem interested in helping individuals stay in a community setting rather than forcing institutionalization. Community Options Program (COP) funding, which provides community-based services for eligible individuals as an alternative to institutionalized care, has been increased by approximately $18 million in this fiscal budget period to fully fund existing slots.

Recently, cost-containment regulations have been reduced, and the Cost Containment Commission was eliminated as of July 1, 1995. In addition, the state has stepped up alternative methods of cost containment authorized by the federal government through waivers granted from traditional methods of delivering health care services. Waivers have been approved to enable the state to deliver services to certain MA populations through managed care (health maintenance organizations, primary provider and targeted managed care systems) and to provide home- and community-based services, including community integration program (CIP) and the previously mentioned COP program, as an alternative to institutionalized care. Health maintenance organizations (HMOs) are health care plans which provide comprehensive health services to enrolled members for a fixed, period payment. The delivery of services through HMOs provides an alternative to the fee-for-service method, since in most instances, the HMO rather than the state, assumes the risks associated with utilization of most MA services by the covered population. Exceptions to this would be services for persons with HIV or AIDS and neonatal intensive care treatment where the state and the HMO would share costs. In 1994, the HMO enrollment was 40 percent of the total AFDC or related MA eligible recipients. Under the primary care provider program, the department requires certain AFDC, SSI and healthy start-related MA recipients to select a primary care provider and receive most nonemergency medical services from the assigned provider or though referrals made by the provider. This initiative was implemented in order to improve preventative care and produce cost savings for the MA program by reducing the provision of inappropriate care, such as emergency room hospital services in nonemergency situations. For targeted case management, the department assigned SSI-related MA clients to a case manager to coordinate medical care and monitor services to high-cost MA recipients to ensure the most efficient and cost effective treatment alternatives are utilized.

While cost-containment regulations have been reduced, the department has maintained its long-standing responsibilities to regulate various businesses to promote public health and assure adequate medical care. This includes inspecting and licensing or certifying hospitals and other health care providers and places such as restaurants, public swimming pools, and campgrounds.

Community Social Services. The department funds a wide variety of community services providing help to the mentally ill, developmentally disabled, physically and sensory disabled, alcohol and other drug abusers, juvenile delinquents, abused and neglected children, and families in need of social services. Generally, these services are available free to those who cannot afford to pay for them, and available with some fee payments to others. In calendar year 1994, over 387,000 people were served in DHSS-funded community programs. Of these, 98,750 were served in mental health programs, 62,000 were in alcohol and other drug abuse programs, and 85,000 received general children and family services, while smaller numbers fell into other categories.

Typically the community services programs are funded by the state through county governments, although some programs are funded by the state directly through private agencies or carried out by state employees. State laws define health and social services responsibilities of county and local governments, and require these governments to establish local agencies to deliver specified services. Counties are required to establish comprehensive "human service departments," or else to maintain separate social services departments and "Chapter 51 agencies" to provide services to the mentally ill, developmentally disabled, and alcohol and other drug abusers. These county agencies must provide certain services directly, and may contract to private organizations other responsibilities.

The basic arrangement is that the state provides policy and program direction and funding for community services; county agencies set priorities within state policy parameters and available state funding (often supplemented by county tax dollars), design the program delivery system, and oversee actual service delivery.

The state-local relationship in carrying out human services is mutually dependent but not always supportive. Local agencies are consistently concerned about "mandates without money" -- state prescriptions and requirements for services which are not fully financed in the state budget.

Income Maintenance Programs. This function will be transferred to the Department of Workforce Development as of July 1, 1996. Some income maintenance, or economic support programs, are administered in a state-county partnership. County workers -- whose position costs are reimbursed by the state -- take AFDC, food stamps, and medical assistance applications. Eligibility determination and administrative systems for these three programs are uniform statewide, in contrast to community services programs where each county designs the mix of services within some state-allowed flexibility.

Supplemental Security Income (for certain persons who are aged, blind, and disabled) is directly provided by a bureau of DHSS, operating within federal guidelines. Several program changes have been made to control the state costs of this program. First, the state will now administer state payments under this program rather than the state paying the federal government to administer the program and distribute funds to recipients. In addition, beginning January 1, 1996, no person can receive the state SSI supplement without qualifying for federal SSI benefits, unless they were receiving state-only SSI benefits as of December 1, 1995.

The department helps prepare people on income maintenance programs for employment -- such as AFDC recipients who have been targeted for job training and placement services as part of a "welfare reform" initiative. DHSS funds these job programs through counties and other community service providers.

Vocational Rehabilitation. This function, too, is scheduled to be transferred to the Department of Workforce Development as of July 1, 1996. However, currently, department employees directly provide job preparation and rehabilitation for the disabled, with some 42,000 persons served in federal fiscal year 1995. The Division of Vocational Rehabilitation (DVR) is a federal-state program in which individualized evaluation and assistance is given to disabled persons so they can function as independently as possible, securing and/or maintaining suitable employment consistent with their potential. The DVR program provides a full range of services including medical and vocational evaluations, counseling, job seeking assistance, training, job site modifications, physical restorations, and more.

Aging. A variety of special programs -- from meals on wheels to in-home care -- are provided to the elderly. In addition to regulating and funding nursing homes and other health care as previously described, the department has placed increasing emphasis on encouraging community care and support so the elderly can live as independently as possible. Over 97,000 elderly persons received community services, not including meals, in federal fiscal year 1994. Moreover, almost 89,000 elderly persons received nutrition assistance and over 23,000 received home meals, although some of these individuals were served through community services as well. Local area agencies on aging and county aging units are supported by the department.

The increasing number and share of older people in the state's demographic profile have in effect dictated a policy emphasis on providing a continuum and increasing array of services for long-term support of this group. The basic policy thrust was emphasized in the late 1970s and since then has been continued through changing gubernatorial administrations and legislatures.

State Institutions for Mentally Ill and Developmentally Disabled. A smaller number of people receive direct care in the department's mental health institutes and centers for the developmentally disabled. These institutions are intended to provide services to those people who cannot obtain appropriate services in the community at a given point in time.

Two mental health institutes offer specialized in-patient clinical services for the acutely mentally ill and substance abusers, and evaluations and treatment of forensic (criminal justice system) patients. The department has placed emphasis on community care for persons with mental illness, and the number of patients in the institutions has declined dramatically over the past 20 years. One policy tool used by the department to foster community instead of institutional placements was to provide the funding for care to counties, and not directly to the institutions. This has meant counties are charged for placement in the institutions, providing counties an incentive to pursue less expensive community care where it is feasible.

The institutes are dealing with some increasingly difficult patients. Corrections-type clientele have generated a need for increased physical security, and challenged the institute staff to provide effective rehabilitation and treatment.

Three centers for the developmentally disabled provide treatment, placement planning, education, training and rehabilitation to persons with development disabilities. They are considered a specialized type of nursing home, and much of their funding comes from the MA program. Due to Wisconsin's long-term efforts to move people with developmental disabilities into the community, the state had begun efforts to phase out residential services at one of the three cites, the Southern Wisconsin Center, over the next three years with a target closure date of July 1, 1998. However, this effort has recently been suspended due to the unpopularity of this proposal.

Like the mental health institutes, these three centers have experienced dramatic reductions in patient populations as a result of an emphasis by the department on community placements rather than institutional placements. In 1971, average daily populations were 3,722; in 1989 they were 1,674; and as of April 1, 1996, 1,208 persons resided in the centers. However, even with reduced populations, the centers are expensive to operate with more than $119 million budgeted for 1994-95. Until the 1970s, even people who were only moderately retarded might be placed at one of the centers for a lifetime. Currently, the policy of the department has favored creating the most normal life possible for disabled people. An active "community integration program" has sought community placements for many long-time center residents including some severely disabled individuals.

The population which remains in the centers is severely disabled individuals. The goal of the centers' programming is to help each individual achieve the highest level of functioning.

Department Budget. Income maintenance and human services are paid for by a mix of federal, state, county, local, and user fee funds. For state fiscal year 1995, over half is federally funded (approximately 60 percent), and about 33 percent is state general funds with the remainder being funded locally. Each of the widely varying programs has its own funding arrangements. The largest programs are Medical Assistance and Aid to Families with Dependent Children, which are about 60 percent federal and 40 percent state funding. The basic vocational rehabilitation program is about 80 percent federal and 20 percent state, although, as with other programs in the department, there is currently a waiting list under the vocational rehabilitation program. Other programs of the department are more dependent upon state funds, proportionately, and less on federal funds. Services for the mentally ill, developmentally disabled, and alcohol and drug abusers are provided with a mix of federal, state and local property tax funds -- with some fees for services for clients that are able to pay.

A Brief History

This complex and extensive system of state-administered financial aids and human services has developed largely since the 1930s. Earlier, "public welfare" programs were a function of families, private charity, local government, and to a limited extent state government. In general, state participation in welfare was limited, and national participation was non-existent, before the depression.

Wisconsin was somewhat unusual among the states in its involvement in public welfare concerns in the late 19th century and early 20th century. Laws were passed during Wisconsin's early years of statehood to address problems relating to public care and rehabilitation of the mentally ill, law violators and delinquents, the handicapped, the neglected and dependents. In 1871, there were six separate institutions responsible for such programs. Public health legislation was enacted first by the territorial Legislature in 1839, with an emphasis on communicable disease control. In some respects, Wisconsin laws were forerunners of federal-state categorical aids for dependent children, the blind, the deaf, and elderly individuals.

In the 1930s, the federal government initiated a national role in public welfare programs and funding. The social security program was established as a direct federal program (contributions, i.e., taxes, are paid by employers and employees to the federal government, and payments are made by the federal government directly to eligible persons). Other federal welfare and income maintenance programs, however, generally provided financial assistance to state governments to operate programs. These included, among others, income support for the elderly, the blind, families with dependent children, and the disabled. Thus the national legislation, patterned on the Wisconsin laws, induced states which had previously left public assistance exclusively to local governments, to become active partners in these programs.

Some states administer these programs directly with state employees. Wisconsin has chosen to maintain its county-based system of services and income supports. Wisconsin has supplemented the federal funds with state funds, and passed the funds to the counties for use within federal and state requirements.

Some needy persons are not eligible for the federal and state programs. In order to provide for the needs of this population, "general relief" programs are typically in place at the local/county level, although providing this type of support is not mandatory pursuant to 1995 Wisconsin Act 27. These programs tend to support working age adults without dependent children or physical disabilities, who are nonetheless in financial need.

During the 1970s, changes were made in income maintenance programs at both the federal and state levels. Following changes in the seventies, state and federal funds support all the costs of income maintenance assistance for the elderly, blind, disabled, and families with dependent children. Elimination of local funding provisions was done partly to provide uniformity or equality of treatment, and also to provide property tax relief by substituting (theoretically more progressive) state funding for local funding. The majority of other human services costs are also supported by state and federal funds, rather than local funds.

During the 1960s and 1970s, human services programs expanded greatly at all levels of government. There was a "war on poverty," a "war on drugs" (declared by every President since Nixon), and a host of other initiatives by a "Great Society" intending to solve problems of public health and welfare.

In the 1980s, the federal government's budget deficit led to restraint and in some cases actual reductions of funding for many human services programs administered through states, county and local governments, and private agencies. This shifted the leadership and financial responsibility for human services increasingly to states and local governments. Despite the efforts of the sixties and seventies, the numbers of people in need of services continued to grow and to some extent the severity of the problems seemed to increase. To budget managers, the needs seemed insatiable.

In the 1980s, the number of people living in poverty in the country and in the state grew. This seems to be due to a mix of factors -- structural changes in the economy, demographic patterns, societal changes, and federal government tax and spending policies. Women and children account for a disproportionate share of people living in poverty, as do ethnic minorities.

For the 1990s, the impetus of the department is to rationalize and control expenditures. Oftentimes, expenditures are controlled by initiating programs which insist upon recipients taking personal responsibility and becoming actively involved in correcting the problems which led to a dependence upon government assistance. The legislature has implemented many programs with such names as "bridefare" which ties increased benefits with two parent families, and "learnfare" which reduces a family's benefit if a child is habitually truant. In addition, the federal government appears committed to giving states more control and flexibility over entitlement programs. To this end, more block grants are being given so states can make individual decisions about how the funds can best be spent to serve needy populations in each state.

Welfare Reform

During the 1980s, there was a growing bipartisan consensus among elected officials in favor of welfare reform. Conservatives and liberals have both questioned the effectiveness of public assistance programs in helping recipients achieve self-sufficiency and a reasonable standard of living.

Typically, conservatives have argued that the benefits available in welfare programs were too high and fostered dependency, i.e., created incentives to stay on welfare and not to move into unsubsidized employment. Typically, liberals have argued that the benefits available were inadequate to keep children and their mothers from living below the poverty level, and that although clients wanted a better life they did not receive enough positive help to achieve independence. Regardless of which perspective one might choose, the debate seems to have reached a reasonable agreement that welfare programs needed to be reformed to emphasize self-support and parental responsibility (for child support).

These discussions have focused especially on the Aid to Families with Dependent Children (AFDC) program. AFDC was created by Congress in 1935 to help children in need due to the death of their fathers. Now, AFDC provides cash payments for needy children and their mothers or other caretaker relatives who have been deprived of support due to the absence or incapacitation of the primary wage earner. In Wisconsin in early 1994, about 1.3 percent of the caseload was due to death of the primary wage earner parent. AFDC now serves mostly children whose parents never married, were divorced, or separated. The program also serves needy families with two parents who are unemployed. The total caseload for AFDC as of January 1994 is 70,918.

Wisconsin, like other states, establishes "need" or eligibility requirements for the program, sets benefit amounts, and administers the program, within a basic federal framework. Financial eligibility criteria include tight limitations on the assets and income available to a family. The income criteria used in Wisconsin are based on an historical definition of a "lower living standard" for a family, published by the U.S. Bureau of Labor Statistics. This standard was intended to provide a minimally adequate amount for a family's income (with the specific amount varying with family size). However, the standard which is used in 1990 is based on 1977 BLS figures, adjusted by only part of the inflation rate that has occurred since that time. Actual payments are then made at 80 percent of the standard, and other benefits such as food stamps, Medical Assistance, etc. are available to supplement the AFDC grant.

Wisconsin's AFDC program was among the most generous in the nation in 1986, ranking third among states. Currently, however, Wisconsin's AFDC program benefit level is ranked 12th among the states as of July 1994, providing a maximum monthly AFDC benefit for a family of three of $517. Much of this difference can be explained by the change in policy focus of the current administration.

The 1987 budget introduced by Governor Thompson highlighted a welfare reform initiative that included a six percent benefit reduction which was reinvested in increased programming to help AFDC recipients move into the work force. Other elements of the initiative included expanded job training and employment assistance programs, added transitional services such as child care and medical support after AFDC recipients leave the program due to earned income, financial incentives for children to remain in school, and increased emphasis on collecting child support from noncustodial parents.

In proposing the initiative, the governor's 1987 Budget Policy Papers noted that the growth in the number of people relying on AFDC was substantial between the mid-1970s and the mid-1980s. The monthly caseload grew and average of nearly nine percent a year from 1974 to 1985, far faster than the state's population. In 1970, the percentage of the state population receiving AFDC payments was 2.2 percent of the population, and by 1986 nearly 6.3 percent of the population received AFDC.

In his 1989 budget, the governor continued an emphasis on welfare reform, and cited progress in reducing the AFDC rolls. The administration projected that the percentage of the Wisconsin population receiving AFDC would be reduced to 5.5 percent in 1989-90. It can be noted that the AFDC caseload had actually peaked in 1984-85, and its reduction correlates to a period of sustained economic strength and relatively low unemployment in the state.

In proposing added changes for 1989, the governor noted that Wisconsin benefits remained relatively high -- at that point, eighth highest in the nation; and expressed the view that high benefits remain a "magnet" for poor people from neighboring states. The governor proposed creation of a two-tier payment system, with lower rates for recent "immigrants" to the state, on a pilot basis in a limited number of counties. The "welfare magnet" theory has been disputed by academicians as well as politicians. Even so, as of July 1994, the two-tier benefit structure is operating as a pilot program in Kenosha, Milwaukee, Racine and Rock counties and applies to all new recipients/arrivals in those counties.

The relative success or lack of success of the 1987 employment and education initiatives was also debated in 1989. Most observers perceived that it was simply "too soon to tell" the relative success of the new and expanded programs.

Perhaps most controversial was the 1987 "learnfare initiative." "Learnfare" required children between the ages of 13 and 19 to attend school or possess a high school diploma as a condition of receiving AFDC benefits. When adolescents were truant or dropped out, the payment to the AFDC family would be reduced as though that child were not an eligible member of the family. A total of 2,285 teens were sanctioned in January 1989 as a result of "learnfare."

Opponents of learnfare argued this amounts to an unfair and punitive reduction in the already inadequate income support for poor families. Proponents argued that financial incentives for teens to complete their high school education can be effective and thereby enhance the employability of those young people. The Governor and his appointees at the department tout the success of the program, while a number of other observers are critical of the claims for the program's effectiveness.

While the relative success of learnfare is still being debated, the state received a waiver from the federal government allowing an expansion of the learnfare program. Under the expansion waiver, if a child age six through 12 is determined to have violated the attendance requirement without good cause, the state is required to provide case management services prior to imposing a learnfare sanction. The child's family must fully comply with case management activities in order to avoid a sanction. In September 1994, the expansion of the learnfare program was implemented in four pilot counties: Brown, Fond du Lac, Kenosha and Rock.

The general philosophy that parents should be responsible for their children, and that families should be encouraged to achieve financial independence, is well accepted by state policy-makers. However, specific program approaches to achieve these results are still being tested.

The state is moving toward eliminating the entitlement nature of programs. To this end, it is moving toward a more work-driven benefit. Under 1993 Wisconsin Act 99, the department was required to request a federal waiver to allow implementation of a work-not-welfare pilot program which limits the length of time a recipient may receive AFDC benefits to 24 months. As a condition of receiving cash benefits, every person over 16 years of age must comply with certain employment and training requirements. In addition to providing sanctions for non-compliance, the program offers transitional child care, medical benefits and shelter payments. As of July 1994, the pilot is operating in Fond du Lac and Pierce counties and applies to all AFDC recipients in these counties.

The most recent and most ambitious initiative toward the work-driven benefit goal was passed by both houses of the state legislature and signed by Governor Thompson in April of 1996. The purpose 1995 Wisconsin Act 289, creating the Wisconsin Works program (W-2), is to eliminate the cash and health care benefits provided under the current AFDC and medical assistance programs. Instead, recipients of public assistance would be required to work in unsubsidized employment or in government-subsidized trial jobs and community service jobs. For incapacitated individuals, special job placements with limited work requirements are available. The program also establishes time limits for the receipt of benefits. For example, participation in trial jobs and transitional placements would generally be limited to 24 months each. Overall participation in W-2 would be limited to two consecutive years and five years total participation.

There are several additional and substantial components of the W-2 program. The Employment Skills Advancement Program would provide up to $500 of educational assistance for low-income parents who are working. Also, Job Access Loans would be available to address immediate financial crises of W-2 participants. To assist participants with young children, child care would be provided in part by modifying current low-income and at-risk Child care currently funded under community aids. W-2 would require co-payments for child care and provide additional funding to qualified working parents for eligible types of child care and other expenses. In addition to allowing participants to utilize state-licenced child care providers, the program covers kinship care. In this case, a relative is providing care and maintenance for a child and these expenses are partially reimbursable. Also incorporated into the W-2 plan is a health plan called "Wisconsin Works health plan". Under the act, coverage for all AFDC-related and healthy start groups under the MA program are eliminated. Instead, the plan establishes eligibility for health care coverage under the Wisconsin Works heath plan for members of certain families with dependent children, pregnant women with no depended children and minor custodial parents with specific eligibility requirements.

As one might imagine from reading a summary of W-2, this plan is very expensive. The major expenditure categories under the program include wage subsidies for participation in employment positions, health care coverage, child care and local agency office expenses. In addition, costs would be incurred for cash assistance and health care for children whose parents receive disability assessments for transition placements, foster care an kinship care, foregone child support revenues, job access loans, emergency assistance, employment skill advancement grants, state administration, burial costs and expansion of the children first program. The cost of the program is expected to be over $48 million in 1997-98 and over $73 million in 1998-99. While expensive, the program was designed to move people from public assistance and dependency into the job market and toward more independence from government assistance. An evaluation of the plan is due by July 1, 2000 at which time policy-makers and citizens alike will learn whether this revolutionary and controversial plan is destined for success.

One program area that is showing signs of improvement is child support collections. Improved collection of adequate amounts of child support from noncustodial parents can, potentially, offset public welfare payments. More importantly, an improved child support system could improve the standard of living for many children and their custodial parents.

According to Nichols-Casebolt et al. (1988), one of five Wisconsin children was potentially eligible for child support -- that is, they have a living parent not residing with them who could be contributing to their financial support. In 1994, a total of 68,265 babies were born to women who were Wisconsin residents. Of these babies, 18,523 were born to unmarried mothers. The proportion of out of wedlock births in Wisconsin has increased from approximately 14 percent in 1980 to 27.1 percent in 1994.

The family court system establishes parents' obligations to provide child support. Until fairly recently, amounts were determined essentially on a case-by-case basis, and were highly inadequate when compared to the costs of the child's care. The majority of noncustodial parents pay no child support. Actual amounts of child support ordered seemed inequitable as well as uneven. Also, about half of the court-ordered payments are never made and not enforced.

In 1980, DHSS contracted with the University of Wisconsin to study the child support system in Wisconsin. The UW report recommended a new system of "child support assurance" in which all parents living apart from their children would be obligated to share income with them. The law would determine the amounts and these amounts would be deducted from the parent's earnings, automatically as social security and income taxes are.

The state has progressed towards implementing this type of system. The first emphasis was improving collections. Automatic wage assignment (i.e., withholding child support from paychecks of responsible parents), transfers from a deposit account (i.e., requiring a payer of child support to establish an account from which funds may be transferred for the payment of support), "intercepts" of tax refunds, and other active governmental assistance did improve collections substantially. Between federal fiscal years 1983 and 1992, total child support collections per dollar of total administrative expenditures more than doubled.

Whenever a court enters a judgement of annulment, divorce or legal separation, approves a stipulation for child support or makes a determination of paternity, the court must direct either one or both parents to pay an amount reasonable or necessary to fulfil the parental responsibility to provide for their minor children. The court is required to determine the child support amount by using the percentage standard established by administrative rule (HSS 80).

Child support reform, improved incentives for public assistance recipients to work, affordable and available child care, and health insurance seem to be a combination of elements that can help many poor families achieve improved financial well-being and "get off the welfare rolls." The state seems to be moving in this direction with some success, although the ultimate outcome is yet to be seen.

Conclusion

State government officials are continually faced with the challenge of making tough fiscal and policy decisions in every aspect of state government. These decisions become even tougher in an atmosphere of more demands for services and limited resources. For example, Wisconsin faces skyrocketing juvenile costs and state prison costs due to a "get tough on crime" focus of government officials and state residents. In addition, legislators and the governor made a commitment to contribute more from the state coffers to fund public education in an effort to lighten the load on property tax payers. To this end, the 1995-1997 biennial budget provided an increase of more than $1.2 billion for public schools. Along with Governor Thompson's pledge of no general tax increase, these policy demands and financial commitments necessarily reduces funds available for other state programs. Since public health and welfare programs gobble a large portion of state revenues, this is one area lawmakers will turn to in order to tighten up the state's fiscal waistline. However, lawmakers are cognizant of the importance of these programs in the human services area to the public and the widespread needs that they serve, and this explains why these decisions are so difficult and time-consuming.

Welfare reform is only one of many complex public policy issues in the human services arena. While operating with tighter state and federal funding, the state is being challenged to provide more and better services in several areas. To cite a few examples, the public is concerned that there is quality long term care for an increasing number of frail, elderly people; that medical care is accessible, affordable, and good quality for everyone in the state; that pervasive problems of alcohol and drug abuse are confronted effectively; and that quality child care is available to meet increasing demands from working parents of modest means. These demands for increased or improved services are accompanied by an expectation that the state will also continue to support the wide array of services described throughout this chapter. The recent reorganization of the department is an attempt to streamline the process of providing services through the most efficient mechanisms available. The reorganization, however, is not an end in itself. It is a step in the process of providing a menu of human services in the year 2000 and beyond. As a whole, this situation continues to require public and policy-makers to consider priorities carefully, and to make difficult decisions about increased funding or lesser services.

CHAPTER XIII

NATURAL RESOURCES AND ENVIRONMENTAL QUALITY

By Richard D. Christofferson, Sr.[*]

Introduction

Wisconsin is proud of its natural resources and the careful management devoted to them. On the other hand, Wisconsin also takes pride in lumbering, paper making, industry, agriculture and other economic activities that impose heavy burdens on land, water, and air. Not surprisingly, conflicts over public policies for resources and the environment are sharp and frequent.

Before Europeans arrived in the land that would become Wisconsin, the native peoples competed for its abundant game, fish, wild rice, and other natural resources. At first the Europeans were inclined only to explore, evangelize to and trade with the Indians. Around 1820, however, the pace of settlement accelerated as lead miners followed the ore bodies from Illinois into southwest Wisconsin. To this day at Mineral Point you can see the scars of their mining as well as some of the stone structures they left to us. In significant numbers, other settlers came to the Lake Michigan shores and gradually spread from there to settle all of the state.

Evidence of the environmental costs of development and growth soon appeared in lakes and streams. Describing conditions around 1850 when Wisconsin's 300,000 settlers used Wisconsin's waters ". . . as a sort of natural self-cleansing waste-disposal system . . . ," Parker recounts,

> Raw sewage washed into the streams; cities discarded ashes, rubbish and excavated dirt; slaughterhouses retained only the edible meat and flushed the bones, blood and viscera into the water; fishermen dumped fish offal overboard; sawmills deposited sawdust, bark and shavings. In just a few years the careless outpour . . . began to obstruct navigable channels, fish kills developed, disease was transmitted by water. The need for laws to control water pollution became obvious (1973:116).

In 1862 the legislature produced Wisconsin's first environmental law, the Slaughterhouse Offal Act, fixing administrative responsibility in the State Board of Health. Nevertheless, neither this nor later laws intended to deal with wastes from sawmills and fish processors significantly slowed the pace of resource exploitation. In but a few years, timber companies had converted the virgin white pine covering much of the state to farm lands. Wisconsin was on its way to becoming one of the greatest agricultural states in the Union. Of the state's 35.9 million acres, 17.1 million remain "agricultural" (State of Wisconsin, *Blue Book*, 1995-96:605).

The rapid exploitation of the state's natural resources likely helped to stimulate the progressive movement (1890-1920), which was particularly strong in Wisconsin. Conservation of resources was one of the many planks in the progressive platform. Progressive conservationists advocated "wise use" without waste, multiple use, sustained-yield management, and other scientific, rational, and utilitarian principles. Theirs was a movement and a management policy concerned more with the quantity rather than quality of natural resources. Leaders like Theodore Roosevelt and Gifford Pinchot, for example, led the way in establishing and expanding national forests and parks (Udall, 1963; Hays, 1972).

---

[*]   Professor of Political Science, University of Wisconsin - Stevens Point. Thanks to Tammy Castonia, student researcher, for her assistance in revising and updating this chapter.

The roster of distinguished Wisconsin conservationists, preservationists, and environmentalists is a lengthy list starting with John Muir and including the likes of Aldo Leopold, Gaylord Nelson, and many others of national renown. The state of Wisconsin has always been a leader in resource management and preservation. Even after the "golden age" of progressivism, particularly during the 1930s, new national programs and agencies appeared. For example, the Civilian Conservation Corps set young men to work improving the national forests and parks. The Soil Conservation Service assisted and educated farmers in better stewardship of the land. Other New Deal programs engaged contractors and the unemployed in building various public works, including sewage systems.

Meanwhile, Wisconsin refined and augmented its natural resources laws, culminating in the 1960s with what Parker concluded were ". . . some of the most advanced laws in the nation" (1973:120-121). He characterized Wisconsin's 1965 Water Resources Act as ". . . the most significant water protection law in Wisconsin history." Parker called Wisconsin's Outdoor Resources Action Plan of 1969 (ORAP-200) "a major financial breakthrough" because one feature of ORAP-200 provided state funding for local sewage treatment facilities, years before most other states or the national government began to do so.

The Environmental Movement

By the 1960s, lay persons could see, smell or otherwise sense that the environment had deteriorated; one did not have to be a scientist to know that. Nevertheless, it was biologist Dr. Rachel Carson who revealed in *Silent Spring* how pesticides like DDT persist in the environment, accumulate in the food chain, and eventually exterminate non-targeted organisms and even entire species. This was the germinal event of the Environmental Movement. Opinion leaders in government and the media, e.g., President Kennedy and Walter Cronkite of CBS News, legitimized environmental concerns and added them to the national agenda. Wisconsin banned DDT, the first state to do so, and national policy makers followed Wisconsin's lead a few years later.

On April 22, 1970, Earth Day I, millions of Americans attended "teach-ins," protest demonstrations or other events. The environmental movement was underway. Environmentalism was not conservation warmed over. While environmentalists have retained the concerns of the conservationists, they emphasize environmental quality, particularly by controlling, reducing, and eliminating pollution. The philosophical basis of environmentalism is holism, drawn from the science of ecology, the central principle of which is: everything is related to everything else.

Extended to the political realm, this philosophy obviously points toward national and global approaches to environmental problem solving. Before 1970 the national government had limited its environmental protection role to research or planning grants, technical assistance, or mediator services in interstate conflicts over pollution abatement. The accelerating deterioration of the environment drove home the point that national and international governments must share or even dominate environmental problem-solving.

During the 1970s, the "Environmental Decade," the Congress and the presidents of the decade agreed that the national government should take the lead in conservation efforts. They enacted a flood of new laws; they reorganized existing agencies and created new ones. On New Years Day of 1970, President Nixon signed the National Environmental Policy Act (NEPA) which seeks a "harmonious man-nature relationship" and obliges the government to guarantee it. NEPA, and its counterpart WEPA (Wisconsin Environmental Policy Act), provide for Environmental Impact Statements for actions that will have major or significant environmental effects. The Clean Air Act of 1970 "nationalized" ambient air through uniform air quality goals and standards. The 1972 Federal Water Quality Act did much the same for lakes and streams. Throughout the decade, Congress added laws to deal with solid wastes, hazardous wastes, toxic substances, drinking water, and wetlands, for example, and to strengthen existing policies.

The National/State Partnership

In economic and other human endeavors natural resources will be consumed or degraded. If all were consumed or badly damaged, the foundations of the economy and society would have been destroyed. However well the market serves us in many respects, in general the motives and the methods of the market will tend to degrade "The Commons" (Hardin, 1968). What institution but government can protect the commonwealth of soil, water, and air?

The evolution of the concurrent powers, i.e., those functions shared by national, state, and even local governments, is the most significant development in American federalism. The Constitution delegates certain powers to the central government and reserves the others to the states. What Congress cannot constitutionally compel states to do, it often can accomplish by other means, especially through funding grants. Congress and federal agencies often depend on state and local governments to administer national policies. This is particularly the case for programs for clean air, clean water, and hazardous wastes. Federal officials set national environmental goals and standards, but generally it is the states that must plan and implement the programs to attain the goals.

Like most states Wisconsin has replicated a great deal of federal environmental policies, laws, rules and agencies. As a result, national and state governments work together within a double set of complicated statutes, rules, and court opinions. We rely heavily on the Wisconsin Department of Natural Resources (DNR) to administer the programs although the federal Environmental Protection Agency can take control when a state fails to perform adequately. Obviously, a state agency will likely be more "understanding" of interests within that state than a more remote federal agency. Consequently, there are times when it is to the DNR's advantage to threaten to "sic the feds on" a recalcitrant player (Segerson and Bromley, 1988:251-252). Environmentalists have also invoked EPA actions against the DNR.

The Department of Natural Resources

In 1967 the legislature reshaped the executive branch " . . . to integrate agencies on a functional basis and make them responsive to the elected chief executive" (State of Wisconsin, *Blue Book*, 1995-96:322). Merging the Department of Resource Development with the Conservation Department, the legislature created a Department of Natural Resources and a Natural Resources Board to govern it. Seven citizens appointed by the governor and confirmed by the state senate for staggered six-year terms comprise the board. Most members are drawn from the elite of Wisconsin (Thomas, 1989) and favored by the governor who appoints them. They serve without pay.

Within the boundaries of legislative mandates, the board makes natural resources and environmental policies, which the DNR implements. The board also appoints and may dismiss the secretary and other agency administrators. All recent governors have advocated giving the state's chief executive the power to appoint and dismiss the DNR secretary. This power was given to the governor in the 1995-1997 budget which took effect on July 26, 1995.

The agency's mission is " . . . implementing state and federal laws that protect and enhance Wisconsin's natural resources--its air, land, water, wildlife, fish, and plants; [coordinating] the many state-administered programs that protect the environment; and [providing] a full range of outdoor recreational opportunities for Wisconsin residents and visitors" (State of Wisconsin, *Blue Book*, 1995-96:478). The index of the "Natural Resources Department" in the Wisconsin Statutes stretches to 105 inches of closely-spaced tiny type. Natural resources and environmental laws are fleshed out in five volumes of agency rules in the Wisconsin Administrative Code.

Because natural resources and environmental issues are conflict-laden and complicated, the Department of Natural Resources arguably is the most controversial agency in Wisconsin. As Bromley and Irvin (1991) observe, "Whether one hunts, fishes, or relies on a private well or septic tank, the DNR is involved. It is inevitable that such pervasive interaction with the citizens of Wisconsin brings both praise and scorn." In addition to legal limits on the agency, there are many political and economic constraints. Some private interests resent and resist the DNR's expansion of state holdings that remove real estate from the property tax base of local governments and from land available for development. A business leader equating environmental protection programs with a "hostile business climate" may threaten to move to a friendlier regulatory climate.

The NRB and DNR must be responsive to or interact with many other officials, including the legislature and its committees; particularly the Assembly's committees on Natural Resources, Tourism and Recreation, and Environment and Utilities and the Senate's Environment and Energy Committee and the Human Resources, Labor, Tourism, Veterans and Military Affairs Committee. The DNR must interact with other state executive-branch agencies and with national policies and agencies as well as local governments and neighboring states. Politics compel the board and the DNR to relate effectively to the desires and communications of the private sector, including conservation and environmental organizations, business, industry and trade associations, and individual citizens.

It is easy to think that the DNR relies mainly upon its clout as a regulatory agency to "lay down the law." While the DNR at times does, indeed, flex its muscles, usually the agency relies on persuasion, not raw power. The DNR is sensitive to contradictory charges that either it is abusive of citizens and hostile to business and economic development or it is too lenient with violators of laws and rules. The agency hopes to take the middle ground.

Sometimes little is known for certain about a problem--if it is a problem--like chemicals in Great Lakes fish. In such circumstances the DNR might issue advisories, which merely recommend avoiding certain fish completely or eating others only in limited quantities. The DNR might promulgate guidelines for action on groundwater contaminants rather than impose strict rules.

Organization of the DNR

With responsibilities for both resource management and environmental protection functions, the DNR has been called an "umbrella" or "super" agency. Approximately 3,132 employees in the DNR's four divisions within the six field districts around Wisconsin carry out its mission. The current *Blue Book* describes the divisions and their functions.

The Division for Environmental Quality plans and supervises development of water quality standards, as well as programs for water supply, groundwater, toxics management, air pollution control, and solid and hazardous waste management. It emphasizes prevention, rather than treatment, as the preferred way to protect public health and the environment from toxic and hazardous substances. The division helps implement several grant programs for solid waste planning, recycling, sewage treatment, and nonpoint source water pollution control.

The Division of Resource Management has major responsibility for conserving, protecting and managing . . . resources [and] works closely with the Wisconsin Conservation Congress and many other citizen groups. [M]anagers coordinate the maintenance and improvement of fish and wildlife populations and habitats on public and private lands. Foresters emphasize the multiple uses of state and municipal forest lands, assist private woodlot owners and the state's wood-using industries, and work with local fire departments to prevent and control forest fires. DNR personnel coordinate the acquisition, development, and operation of the state parks and trails systems. [Managers] protect . . . endangered and threatened native plants and wildlife. It . . . coordinates the department's land acquisition and land management programs.

The Division of Enforcement directs coordinated law enforcement programs . . . , including environmental actions, fish and wildlife violations, water management, air and water pollution control, and waste water and solid waste management. It coordinates compliance with the Wisconsin Environmental Policy Act; recruits the department's law enforcement personnel; develops hunter, boating, snowmobile, and all-terrain vehicle safety training classes; designs and maintains dams and other structures in state waters; plans and supervises shoreland zoning and floodplain regulation; and helps local governmental units protect lives and property through floodplain management and dam safety inspections.

The Division of Management Services provides [staff support] services for the department. . . . The Field Districts enable the department to make its programs accessible to the . . . public [and] this decentralization . . . localizes environmental protection and resource management. (State of Wisconsin, *Blue Book*, 1995-96:78-79)

Figure XIII-1

THE DEPARTMENT OF NATURAL RESOURCES

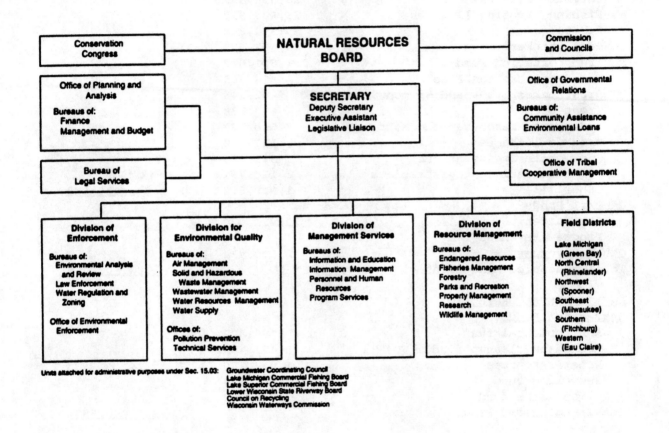

Source: State of Wisconsin, *Blue Book*, 1995-96:480.

DNR Budget

DNR's share of the state's budget is modest, not among the top 10 programs. The agency collects substantial amounts of ear-marked (segregated) funds from hunting and fishing licenses, fees, permits, federal grants, checkoffs on personal income tax returns, and other segregated revenue sources. (See Table XIII-1.) On the one hand, this system enables the DNR to emphasize how little resource management programs cost "the taxpayers." On the other hand, those who pay hunting and fishing license fees claim special rights to access and influence that nonconsumptive users, who pay little or nothing in licenses and fees, do not.

Table XIII-1

DEPARTMENT OF NATURAL RESOURCES FUNDING
Funding, Resources and Environment, FY1993-94

RESOURCE MANAGEMENT
Segregated Funds:

Forestry mill tax	$ 28,836,983	
Fishing, hunting licenses	25,807,918	
Federal aids	13,374,812	
Park stickers	5,652,426	
Transportation Fund	1,651,017	
Boat Registration Fees	856,762	
Great Lakes Trout and Salmon Stamp	801,248	
Trout stamps	670,238	
Endangered resources checkoff	600,607	
Waterfowl stamps	327,542	
Snowmobile registrations	311,373	
Off-road vehicle registrations	115,791	
Other	1,019,862	$80,026,579

General Funds:

GPR (taxes)	$ 20,911,070	
Program revenues	372	
Other Revenues	$ 2,170,734	
Total, Resource Management		$103,108,755

ENVIRONMENTAL PROTECTION
Segregated Funds:

Environmental fund	$ 10,187,822	
Petroleum cleanup fund	3,481,703	
Water resources	1,048,100	
Recycling fund	201,846	
Clean water fund	930,500	
Total Segregated Funds		$17,040,687

General Funds:

GPR (taxes)	$ 18,690,494	
Program revenues	13,200,865	
Federal aids	13,078,337	
Other	380,153	
Total General Funds		$45,349,849
Total, Environmental Protection		$62,390,536

SOURCE: State of Wisconsin, *Blue Book*, 1995-96:636-37.

Although the DNR may not be as dependent on general tax funds as other agencies, it is dependent on tax payers for many of its environmental protection functions, and appropriations by the legislature or federal grants provide the bulk of these funds. Environmental protection consumes slightly more than half of the amount spent for natural resource management. (See Table XIII-2.) Forestry, fish and wildlife management, solid waste management, and land acquisitions are the most expensive DNR activities.

Who pays for cleaner air when the policy instrument is regulation? Auto makers and public utilities shift the costs to the consumer in higher car prices and electric rates. Although these costs are substantial, they are not easily measured.

Evaluations of the DNR

What states do in managing their resources and administering programs under federal standards is critical, especially in light of federal devolution of authority and responsibility to them. As Lester notes, the states are no longer the weak link in environmental protection, but they vary a good deal in capacity and commitment (1994:52).

Using various methods, environmental organizations compare state natural resources and environmental agencies. Generally, the Wisconsin DNR has fared very well. Ranking the states separately on (1) natural resources/environmental quality and (2) strength of economies, The Institute for Southern Studies' 1994 Green Index placed Wisconsin in the top 12 on both lists. Wisconsin is one of nine states that prove that environmental quality and vigorous economies are not mutually exclusive (Smothers, 1994). Wisconsin was in the top 10 in the Institute's 1991-92 Green Index as well, which took particular note of Wisconsin's stationary air pollution sources program.

Table XIII-2

DEPARTMENT OF NATURAL RESOURCES EXPENDITURES
Expenditures, Resources and Environment, FY 1993 - 94

Resource Management:

Forestry	$ 25,058,000	
Land acquisition and development	19,090,000	
Fish management	17,608,000	
Wildlife management	11,460,000	
Parks	10,745,000	
Research	5,950,000	
Property management	5,071,000	
License administration	2,203,000	
Southern forests	2,945,000	
Other	2,979,000	
Total, Resource Management		$103,109,000

Environmental Quality:

Solid waste	$ 21,545,000
Water resources	13,305,000
Air management	11,914,000
Wastewater management	7,837,000
Water supply	6,050,000
Other	1,739,000

<u>Total, Environmental Quality</u>   <u>$62,391,000</u>

<u>Total Expenditures</u>   <u>$165,500,000</u>

Source: State of Wisconsin, *Blue Book*, 1995-96:638.

  The Institute for Southern Studies and the Council of State Governments' comparisons of states on fiscal measurements of environmental effort, i.e., total spending, per capita spending, and percent of state budgets, placed Wisconsin 12th, 16th, and 22nd, respectively. The Fund for Renewable Energy and the Environment (FREE) evaluates and compares states on non-fiscal factors, i.e., policies and rules, placed Wisconsin among the "good" states for the quality and comprehensiveness of its laws and rules. Lester classifies states as (1) progressives, with both commitment and capacity; (2) strugglers, with commitment but not capacity; (3) delayers, with capacity but not commitment; and (4) regressives, with neither commitment nor capacity. He places Wisconsin in the progressives together with California, Florida, Maryland, Massachusetts, Michigan, New Jersey, New York, Oregon, Virginia, and Washington, states in which " . . . conditions will likely get better, not worse" (1994:63-65).

Wisconsin's Natural Resources and Their Management

  Wisconsin and its local governments provide a wonderful range of recreational amenities: parks, bicycling, hiking, skiing, snowmobiling trails, fishing, hunting, and many other outdoor activities. These give Badger State citizens great pleasure at reasonable cost, and they are absolutely vital to the tourism and recreation industry. As "Manager of Natural Resources," the DNR is an active presence in all parts of this state with more than 14,000 lakes, 2,000 trout streams, 45 parks, nine state forests, 12 state trails, and four recreation areas. (See Figure XIII-2.) About 68 million fish and three million game animals are harvested each year. These are but a few examples of the state's outdoor assets and the DNR's management responsibilities.

  Forests are a good example of a renewable resource that can contribute to Wisconsin's economy indefinitely if government and the private sector cooperate. Nearly 45 percent of the state is covered by forests. The national government holds two forests; the state has nine; and counties and school districts own many others. Yet nearly 60 percent of Wisconsin's woodlands are in the hands of private owners, most of them in units of under 100 acres. On the other hand, Georgia Pacific, a paper company, owns more than 400,000 acres of forests.

  Because forests are so vital to the state's ecology and economy, there are many public policies for managing governments' forests and other policies to control or to bias the decisions of private-sector forest owners. Nevertheless, only a fraction of the productive potential of Wisconsin's forests is being realized (Segerson and Bromley, 1988:272 ff.).

  Wisconsin has regularly expanded its land holdings and owns or controls more than six million acres of publicly owned or controlled land. In 1989 the legislature established a $250 million "Stewardship Fund," enabling the DNR to expend $25 million each year to expand state land holdings.

  For many state citizens the DNR is most significant to them as manager of game and fish, especially whitetail deer, about 270,000 of which were "harvested" in 1993. Of the approximately 65 million fish harvested annually in Wisconsin's waters from 1990-1993, an average of 64 million were bass, perch, or other panfish and about 1 million were northern pike (State of Wisconsin, *Blue Book* 1995-96: 633).

Figure XIII-2

WISCONSIN PARKS, FORESTS AND TRAILS

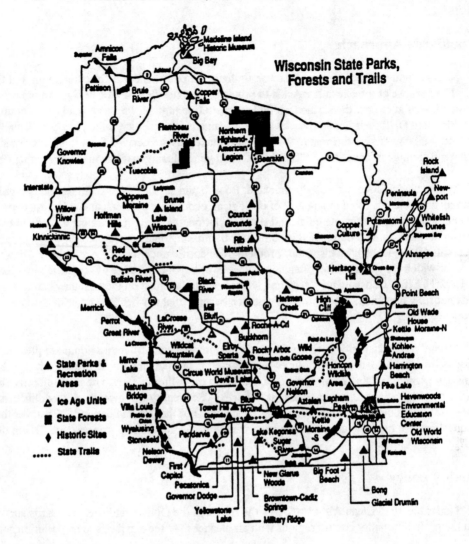

Source: State of Wisconsin, *Blue Book*, 1995-96:638.

Protecting Environmental Quality in Wisconsin

The second role of the DNR is "Manager of Environmental Quality." Although controversies over natural resource management in Wisconsin are not unusual, policies and practices for resolving or containing the conflicts have been in place for many years and are well-worked out. This is not the case for environmental protection, where the work of government is not so far advanced and new problems seem to appear as fast as old ones are solved.

As a partner of the national government, Wisconsin has enacted laws for clean air, clean water, hazardous waste management, and other laws similar to the federal statutes (Wisconsin Statutes, Chapter 144). Often supported by federal grants, the DNR has drafted State Implementation Plans and received the federal Environmental Protection Agency's (EPA) authorization to administer environmental quality programs in Wisconsin.

The Standards Approach

National and state policies are based on uniform national standards for ambient air and for lakes and streams. The purpose of the Clean Air Act is to protect public health and well-being, and the program emphasis has been on conditions at or near the surface within administrative regions where air quality is not up to standards. The basis for EPA and DNR jurisdiction over lakes and streams is navigability, which has been broadly construed by national and state courts over the years. Water quality standards are derived from the Congress's goals of supporting a full range of aquatic life ("fishability") and guaranteeing safe whole-body contact ("swimmability").

Many standards are not well documented. Rosenbaum says, "In short, almost every significant environmental problem is fixed in a matrix of ecological, economic, political, and scientific causes and consequences that usually frustrate quick and simple solutions . . . [and that] almost all current evaluations of environmental quality are compromised in some way by missing data, constricted time frames, and incompatible measurements (1995:46, 75)." This is the "problem of scientific uncertainty," particularly when toxic substances are the issue, for which " . . . regulation often takes place at or beyond the edge of scientific knowledge" (Findley and Farber, 1992:167 ff.). Consequently, state and federal regulators must do the best they can to set and to stand by standards not fully documented by scientific research because that is what the law or due care for the public's well-being requires.

Promulgating standards is easier than gaining compliance. Polluters seldom are pleased by regulations and restrictive permits while distributive policies like tax credits or matching grants are eagerly sought. Although many economists are convinced that effluent charges, i.e., taxes on pollution, would be more effective and efficient than regulations or distributions, this approach is still untried. The reality is, however, that administrators regularly grant variances and stretch out compliance timetables to the limits of the law and beyond. Whatever the instruments, the critical questions are two: (1) are standards consistent with the goals and purposes? and (2) are the standards attained?

Air quality policy

Under the 1970 Clean Air Act (CAA), the EPA and the DNR established standards and devised instruments to attain them. In air quality control regions with air cleaner than the standards, new pollution sources are permitted if
"Reasonably Available Control Technology" is used. But if the region is a "nonattainment area," polluters should be held to the "Lowest Achievable Emissions Rate" and no significant new sources should be permitted. (See Figure XIII-3.)

Convinced that a substantial fraction of air pollution in the southeastern part of the state originates in Illinois which the EPA had failed to regulate, Wisconsin sued the EPA. The EPA agreed to impose stricter controls in the Chicago region, but no significant reductions are yet apparent.

Wisconsin Act 302 is particularly significant for southeastern Wisconsin, where occasionally ozone levels exceed the standard. In regions not meeting standards, employers must plan programs to reduce employee travel, e.g., by car pooling. The law provides for reformulated gasoline designed to reduce emissions of volatile organic compounds and toxic air pollutants. Owners of vehicles failing emissions tests may be required to spend up to $450 to bring their vehicle into compliance.

Figure XIII-3

AIR STANDARDS VIOLATIONS

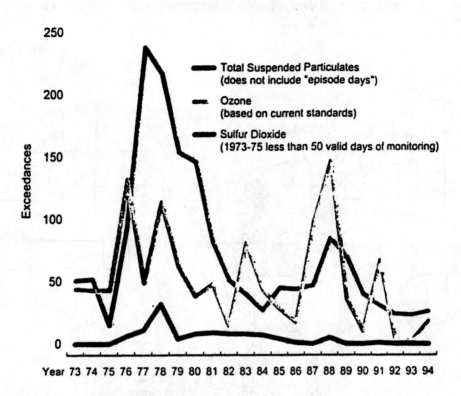

Total Suspended Particulates
(does not include "episode days")

Ozone
(based on current standards)

Sulfur Dioxide
(1973-75 less than 50 valid days of monitoring)

based on standards at the time of measurement

Source: Wisconsin Department of Natural Resources, 1995b:3.

Discharges by the largest stationary source, coal-burning electric generating plants, are controlled by DNR permits limiting various pollutants or stipulating certain technologies to control them. Emissions from stacks and stationary sources require other sets of rules, each appropriate to a particular industry. In the 1990 Clean Air Act Amendments, Congress added 189 hazardous or toxic air pollutants to the list of regulated substances and mandated a 50 percent reduction in sulfur oxide discharges. Concerned about acidification of its lakes, Wisconsin had taken that step several years earlier with Wisconsin Act 414. Consequently, sulfur dioxide discharges by Wisconsin industries have dropped by about 40 percent from their 1980 levels. Some of these industries have marketed their unused discharge allowances to utilities in other parts of the United States. Figure XV-4 shows substantial progress over two decades in controlling three major air pollutants

Figure XV-4

AIR STANDARDS VIOLATIONS IN WISCONSIN COUNTIES, 1970 AND 1990

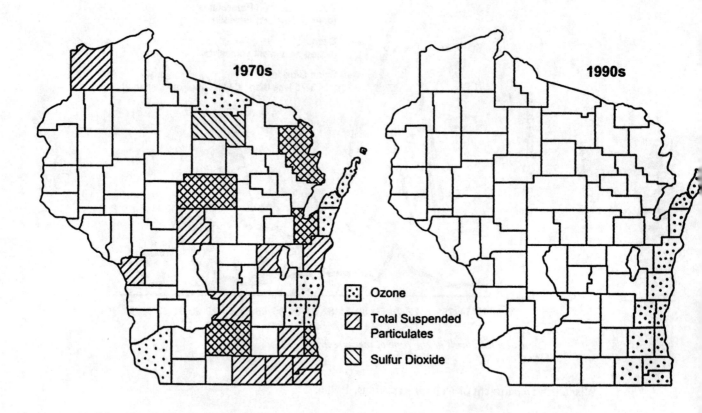

Source: Wisconsin Department of Natural Resources, 1995b:4.

Water quality policy

Like the national standards for ambient air, water quality standards are uniform throughout the United States. Water polluters are classified as point or nonpoint sources. The two major point sources, municipal and industrial, typically discharge wastes in fixed locales from single pipes. But non-point pollution by agriculture, mining, construction activities, and runoff from streets and parking lots as well as air-transported pollutants is generalized and not as easy to control as point sources.

Point Sources. Point sources are governed by the National Pollution Discharge Elimination System (NPDES). The EPA and the DNR make rules appropriate to each major group, e.g., paper, food processing, petroleum refining, etc., and extend the rules to point sources by permits. A typical NPDES permit is valid for five years, sets limits on various conventional, toxic, and nonconventional pollutants, and requires the polluter to report regularly to the DNR/EPA. As a permit's expiration approaches, the regulators may use the occasion to tighten the controls by reducing the allowable amounts or by adding additional substances to the list to be limited.

Wisconsin's quest for cleaner water by regulating private sector point sources has been costly, especially for paper makers; but the industry has continued to prosper--and the Wisconsin and Fox Rivers, still far from pristine, nevertheless flow much cleaner than 20 years ago (Wisconsin Department of Natural Resources 1995b:7) However, for all the progress in reducing "conventional" pollutants, the effort to control toxic substance discharges is just beginning. The sheer number of toxic substances, uncertainties about risks, and the methods and costs to control them present extraordinary regulatory difficulties. The state has only just begun to deal with them. When federal authorities added more than 100 "toxics" to the list of air and water pollutants that must be controlled, the DNR's regulative workload increased sharply. Eventually, the list will likely include hundreds of substances.

To control pollution from municipal sewage treatment systems under the Clean Water Act, Congress has sent more than $100 billion in grants to state and local governments. The DNR set the priorities for the distribution of federal dollars in this state. A large share of federal grants has funded a costly project to separate storm and sanitary sewer systems in Milwaukee and its suburbs and reduce pollution of Lake Michigan.

Responding to the phase-out of federal grants, the Wisconsin legislature established a Clean Water Fund raised by selling state bonds. The Fund issues low-interest loans to local governments building or upgrading their sewer systems.

In the DNR's 1994 Water Quality Report to Congress, the agency estimated that 4,466 miles of Wisconsin's 21,246 miles of streams evaluated do not meet national standards for "fishability" and "swimability." According to DNR, "Polluted runoff also has impaired 90 percent of Wisconsin's 15,000 lakes and major portions of Great Lakes harbors and coastal waters." Of 1,860 lakes, 508 (27 percent) meet none of the goals. Another 200 (10.8 percent) meet only part of the goals (Wisconsin Department of Natural Resources, 1995a:3). The DNR is giving lake improvement high priority, offering grants to local governments, lake associations, and lake districts. The grants are funded by motorboat fuel taxes. (See Figure XIII-6.)

Figure XIII-5

METALS (cadmium, chromium, copper, lead, nickel and zinc) DISCHARGED INTO MUNICIPAL WASTEWATER TREATMENT FACILITIES

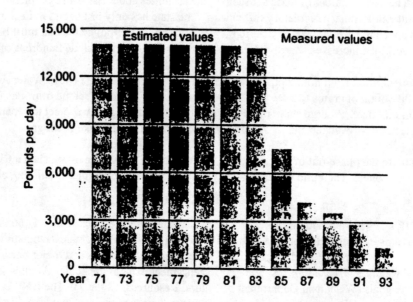

Source: Wisconsin Department of Natural Resources, 1995b:9.

Non-Point Sources. Non-point sources, e.g., cattle operations, crop-growing, forestry practices, and storm water runoff, are the most common causes of water quality standards violations. Nonpoint polluters are difficult to deal with, and examples of agency non-point enforcement actions are rare. However, in late 1994 the DNR began to administer new rules that will subject industries, municipalities, and construction companies to limits stipulated in permits issued under the Wisconsin Pollutant Discharge Elimination System (WPDES). While construction activity is a major source of non-point pollutants, agriculture is the greatest threat to Wisconsin's waters. Contamination of lakes, streams and groundwater is inherent in today's conventional farming practices, which make heavy use of chemicals and often exacerbate soil erosion by water and wind.

On occasion Wisconsin has effectively regulated large feedlot operations and curtailed or banned application of certain agricultural chemicals, notably aldicarb and atrazine. The state offers financial incentives and subsidies for animal waste holding facilities and soil conservation, yet few farmers participate. At the same time, certain federal farm policies work to reward the very practices that must be curtailed (Behm, 1989). Protection of the quality of Wisconsin's lakes and of wells public and private will not be accomplished until non-point sources are broadly and effectively governed. Secretary George E. Meyer says, "We . . . see good land use decisions as those which enable the department to carry out its mission. . . . Good land use decisions are essential for our state's

276

economic viability and our quality of life" (Wisconsin Department of Natural Resources, 1995a:5).

Groundwater. Groundwater is the source of most domestic water supplies for municipal systems as well as private dwellings. The federal Safe Drinking Water Act protects public water supplies. Threats to groundwater, whether for private wells or municipal supplies, come from agricultural chemicals, defective underground storage tanks, landfills, or septic systems. In 1936 Wisconsin became the first state to legislate a well-water code. Wisconsin also was the first state with comprehensive legislation to protect groundwater from certain contaminants once they have been measured at "action levels" indicated by state or federal standards or guidelines [1983 Wisconsin Act 410, Sec. 15.347 (13) Wis. Stats.]. This has resulted in regional or state-wide bans on certain pollutants. An eight-member Groundwater Coordinating Council advises state agencies on groundwater management and each year reports on the status of Wisconsin groundwater (State of Wisconsin, *Blue Book* 1995-96:484).

These are not Wisconsin's only water-policy problems. Rivers and lakes belong to the people, held in trust by the state to be managed in the public's interest. In some cases the public is denied access or has only limited access to "public" waters by shoreline landowners or restrictive local ordinances. In other cases, when the public uses lakes or streams encircled by private property, disputes over who should pay the costs of management (e.g., weed control) are common. Such conflicts are not readily resolved locally. Federal permits authorize paper and power companies to operate systems of dams and reservoirs on public waterways, and lake levels and stream-flow volumes generate controversies. Yet another challenge to Wisconsin water-quality management is the conservation of remaining wetlands (i.e., marshes and bogs), rich in wildlife but attractive to agriculture and developers.

Solid wastes. Open-dump trash burning was once the standard method of garbage disposal in Wisconsin. Today, we bury most solid wastes in landfills. Although building and operating landfills are responsibilities of local governments, the EPA and DNR set specifications for siting, building and maintaining them. Landfills must be located where they are geologically acceptable, properly lined with clay, and underlain with tile, sumps and pumps to collect and recover the liquid (leachate) oozing from the garbage to be processed by sewage treatment plants. It is difficult to find sites that are politically as well as geologically feasible.

Meanwhile, trash production per capita rises steadily. Wisconsin buries or burns more than six million tons of trash per year (Wisconsin Department of Natural Resources, 1995b:11). However, this trend can be reversed. Possibilities include: (1) removing certain materials from the market or waste stream, e.g., plastic milk containers and Styrofoam fast-food containers; (2) reusing materials, e.g., beverage containers, accomplishable by mandating deposits and refunds; and (3) recycling some materials, e.g., aluminum. Composting organic materials like lawn clippings and yard wastes produces useful fertilizer and soil conditioner. Burning trash to produce electricity or steam is an alternative to landfills. (See Figure XIII-7.)

Wisconsin's 1990 Recycling Law (Wisconsin Act 335) bans burying or burning major appliances, used motor oil, vehicle batteries, yard waste, newspapers, office paper, magazines, corrugated cardboard, aluminum, steel, bi-metal or glass containers, number 1 and 2 plastic containers, and tires that, altogether, comprise about 60 percent of the waste stream. Of course, this presents powerful incentives to local governments to recycle what they may no longer bury or burn; but whether there will be steady market demand for these materials remains to be seen. The Council on Recycling " . . . promotes a regional and interstate marketing system for recycled materials and . . . works with the packaging industry on standards for recyclable packaging . . . " (State of Wisconsin, *Blue Book* 1995-96:486).

State grants to local governments enable them to develop, implement and enforce programs to separate the components of the waste stream, and most have begun to do so. Nevertheless, the DNR estimates that 200 communities have yet to enact recycling ordinances in compliance with the law (Wisconsin Department of Natural Resources, 1995a:9).

Figure XIII-6

WISCONSIN SOLID WASTE DISPOSITION

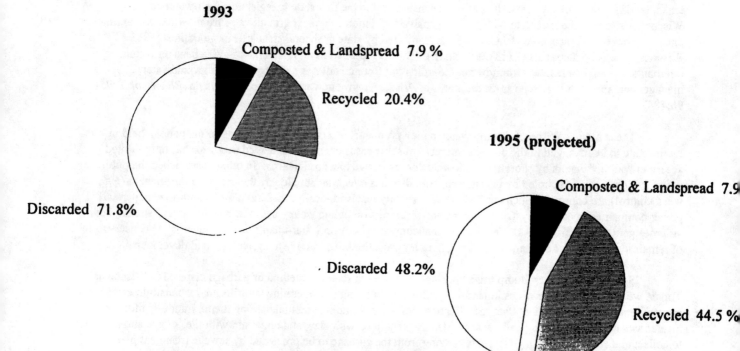

Source: UW - Madison Recylcing Economics Group in association with RecylceWorlds Consulting Corp.

Hazardous wastes. Hazardous wastes are substances that are toxic, ignitable, corrosive, or reactive. Federal and state laws and rules governing hazardous wastes are massive and complex. In separate statutes, each fleshed out with voluminous administrative rules, the national and state governments regulate pesticides, hazardous wastes, toxic substances, and abandoned landfills containing hazardous wastes.

In the Resource Conservation and Recovery Act of 1976, Congress contemplated controlling hazardous wastes "cradle to grave;" i.e., by regulating them from their origins in raw materials and feed stocks, through their transportation, use, and final disposal. Under Wisconsin's counterpart law, the Hazardous Waste Management Act, the DNR administers the RCRA program. The Hazardous Pollution Prevention Board awards grants, monitors and reviews prevention programs, and submits reports to the legislature and the governor.

The Federal Insecticide, Fungicide and Rodenticide Act of 1972 regulates pesticides. This law requires balancing the hazards of pesticides against the need to sustain food production. Under FIFRA some "old" chemicals have been banned and new ones are more closely scrutinized than before. Some particularly potent pesticides are legally available only to professionals trained in handling them. The Wisconsin Department of Agriculture, Trade and Consumer Protection (DATCP), not the DNR, holds the rule-making authority for pesticides and shares pesticide regulation with federal agencies. The Pesticide Review Board recommends rules to DATCP, and a

Pesticide Advisory Council assists the Pesticide Review Board with scientific and technical information (State of Wisconsin, *Blue Book* 1993-94:446).

Since DDT and other "hard" pesticides were banned, some endangered raptor birds have made impressive comebacks. (See Figure XIII-8.)

Figure XIII-7

ACTIVE TERRITORIES IN WISCONSIN: BALD EAGLES AND OSPREYS

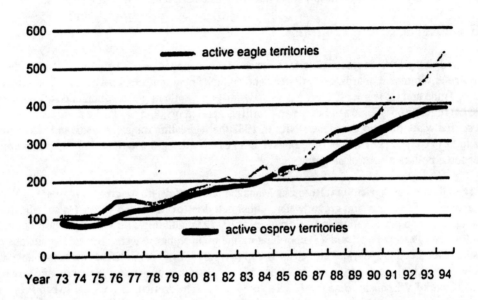

Source: Wisconsin Department of Natural Resources, 1995b:15.

The need for policies to remediate abandoned hazardous waste dumps and leaking underground storage tanks (LUSTs) became apparent in the 1970s. The legislative result was the Comprehensive Environmental Response and Liability Act of 1980; i.e., the "Superfund" law and the Superfund Amendment and Reauthorization Act of 1986.

As with other federally-driven policies, Wisconsin has legislated in tandem with the federal laws to qualify the DNR to identify and remediate the hazardous dumps and leaking underground LUSTs within the state. The Wisconsin Environmental Repair Fund is used to deal with hazardous waste emergencies. The Waste Management Fund covers state liability for costs after a site has been closed. The DNR has located and prioritized many waste-disposal sites and identified responsible parties. The list of sites and potential sites is long--though no longer, it seems, than the process used to determine which will be cleaned and who will do it.

The central concept of CERCLA (Superfund) seemed simple enough: (1) When parties responsible for a hazardous waste dump can be readily identified and can clean it up, then they must. But (2) if they cannot be identified or cannot correct the problem, EPA will use a "Superfund" generated by a tax on chemical and petroleum companies and supplemented by general appropriations to do so. And, (3) issues like responsibility, liability and compensation awards can be answered after the hazard is controlled. For a variety of reasons Superfund has not worked, and after 15 years only a small percentage of sites has been remediated.

The federal government is responsible for high-level radioactive wastes from nuclear power generation and weapons production, with no permanent storage site or disposal process in sight. Meanwhile, high-level wastes are stored "on site;" e.g., at the Point Beach nuclear power plants on Lake Michigan. Congress has made each state responsible for the safe disposition of low-level nuclear wastes originating within its borders.

Other State Agencies and Programs

Although the DNR is responsible for most resource management and environmental protection functions, other resource/environment boards, commissions and councils play important parts. The Department of Agriculture, Trade and Consumer Protection: (1) administers farmland preservation and soil conservation programs, (2) regulates pesticides and trains and certifies applicators, and (3) shares administration of agricultural nonpoint source water pollution with the DNR. In 1982 the legislature transferred soil and water conservation programs to DATCP. In 1987 the legislature gave DATCP control of the agricultural component of the state's nonpoint source pollution control program.

The Division of Agricultural Resource Management administers programs to govern agricultural contaminants of surface water and groundwater. Other activities of DATCP include: (1) coordinating state-county programs for farmland preservation and land conservation; (2) regulating sale and use of pesticides; (3) conducting programs for plant pests control; and (4) coordinating the toxic response team. Recent expansions of DATCP programs have included the "agricultural clean sweep program, lawn care notification, sustainable agriculture and gypsy moth control [as] the department addresses changing issues in agriculture, forestry, and environmental protection" (State of Wisconsin, *Blue Book* 1995-96:393-94). The Agricultural Clean Sweep Program provides grants to counties to carry out collection and proper disposal of unwanted pesticides and other agrochemicals from farmers, paid for by fees assessed on the sale of pesticide products.

The regulatory authority and activities of the Department of Industry, Labor and Human Relations (DIHLR) and the Department of Transportation (DOT) must also be taken into account. For example, DIHLR sets standards for home construction to control soil erosion, and DOT's decisions on highway siting and design are of great environmental significance.

In the State Justice Department are two assistant attorneys general whose duties as "public intervenors" are " . . . to protect public rights in water and other natural resources [with] authority to initiate actions and proceedings before any agency or court" (Wisconsin Statutes 165.07). Most commonly the intervenors' opponents are other state agencies. An advisory committee of seven to nine members conducts meetings to generate public participation and comments. One of the Public Intervenors was eliminated in the 1995-1997 biennial budget.

The Wisconsin Conservation Corps "provides work experience and personal development opportunities for underemployed and unemployed men and women ages 18-25 each year by implementing conservation and human services projects for federal and state agencies, local units of government and non-profit organizations" (State of Wisconsin, *Blue Book* 1995-96:389). The Wisconsin Conservation Corps Board, attached to the Department of Administration, is the policy-making board for the Conservation Corps. When a member of the corps has served a year, he or she receives a cash bonus or a tuition voucher.

The Particular Place of the Conservation Congress

The directory of conservation and environmental interest groups in Wisconsin is also lengthy. Some of them are old-line conservation groups; e.g., the Isaac Walton League, which dates back to 1922, and the Wisconsin Wildlife Federation, founded in 1936. Environmentalism generated a host of new groups while stimulating the older conservation organizations to broaden both the scope of their concerns and their membership bases. Some are affiliates of national organizations. Others, the Environmental Decade, for example, have organized and operated only within Wisconsin. Some specialize, concentrating on water quality, endangered species, or land conservancy, for example. Some lobby the Congress and legislatures, others work with particular administrative agencies, still others litigate. Many educate the public.

Wisconsin law accords the Conservation Congress a special relationship with the DNR (Wisconsin Statutes 15.348). Originated in 1934, organized in 12 districts, and comprised of two delegates elected from each county, the Congress advises the natural resources board on all matters under the board's jurisdiction. Dominated by hunters and fishers, the Congress is preoccupied almost exclusively with game and fish questions. Following annual public hearings around the state, the Congress develops its policy positions on definitions of what animals are fair game, lawful means for taking game, dates and lengths of seasons, bag limits, etc. Its leaders present the recommendations to the DNR/NRB, which must take them into account. Heberlein and Beckley (1991) observe that the Conservation Congress " . . . acts as a state-funded lobbying group in the legislature either to support or to oppose DNR requests." They also conclude that "proposals to support non-game species and species diversity usually receive much less support in the DNR and the legislature when compared to game species programs." Although there are advisory councils with statutory mandates to advise the DNR, no other group is as influential as the Conservation Congress.

Conclusion

Wisconsin has been a leader in managing and preserving natural resources and controlling environmental degradation. From the 1970s on, by adding environmental quality to the national agenda, the Congress and presidents have given the states a long list of new tasks. Wisconsin has generally been in the first rank of states trying to achieve the goals.

Wisconsin citizens, proud of the Badger state's natural resources and quality of life, depend on lumbering, paper making, heavy industry, agriculture, tourism, and other economic activities that consume resources and degrade the quality of the environment. We cannot always have all we would like of both environmental quality and economic goods; but we can strike a reasonable balance. Finding that balance, however, often is a difficult and at times thankless task.

Some policy issues are perennials of intense interest to some segments of the public, especially game and fish management and how to fund them. Who will control the DNR is another contentious question. Policies for acquiring and developing state lands stimulate conflicts.

The DNR focus in the 1990s is on land use, lake quality, lake and riverbed rehabilitation, groundwater, nonpoint water pollution, wetland preservation, hazardous waste management, government/private sector cooperation, and incentives-based compliance policies. Wisconsin has an enormous stake in the quality of Lakes Superior and Michigan, water treasures that can be cleansed and protected only if the United States, Canadian, state and provincial governments act in concert.

The new global agenda includes acid depositions, ozone depletion, global warming, biodiversity, deforestation, and other grand challenges. Wisconsin must manage and protect that part of nature's legacy entrusted to it while national and international efforts address earth's largest problems.

CHAPTER XIV

WISCONSIN AMONG THE STATES

By Thomas M. Holbrook and Craig J. Svoboda*

The preceding chapters have described the nature of politics and government in Wisconsin. As is appropriate in a book on Wisconsin politics, the focus in these chapters has been on Wisconsin itself, without considering other states. However, in order to gain a better understanding of the politics of a single state, it is sometimes useful to look to other states for comparison. For instance, to say that Wisconsin is a progressive state begs the question, "Compared to what?" In response to this question we could compare the public policies of Wisconsin with other states and see how much more progressive Wisconsin is than some states as well as how much more progressive some states are than Wisconsin. In this chapter Wisconsin is placed in a national setting. In doing this, the institutions, policies, and electoral politics of Wisconsin are compared to the remaining forty-nine states.

Political Culture

One conceptual framework that is sometimes useful for making comparisons among the states is that of political culture. A state's political culture defines the role of the individual in politics and the role of government within the state, and is thought to be the result of early migration patterns and historical developments within the states. Elazar (1984) distinguishes between three broad political subcultures among the states: individualistic, moralistic, and traditionalistic. According to Elazar, Wisconsin is best described as having a moralistic political culture. The moralistic political culture is characterized as placing confidence in government to act in the public interest, favoring a strong government, and encouraging participation in government by all citizens, not just the elite or the power hungry (Elazar, 1984).

Given this theoretical classification, what can be expected when the political structures and policies of Wisconsin are compared to those of other states? As a moralistic state, it can be expected that Wisconsin's institutions are more professional than most states, its policies are more redistributive and interventionist than most states, and that its political system exhibits characteristics of competition and openness. In the remainder of this chapter, Wisconsin is compared to the rest of the states on a number of different dimensions of political culture.

Governors

Although the charisma and political savvy of any governor can have a strong impact on the power of the governorship, the institutional power of the office is largely determined by constitutional provisions or by statutory law. Some examples of such provisions are found in Table XIV-1: tenure potential, budget control of the governor, the governor's veto power, the size of the governor's personal staff, and the number of other statewide elected officials. Each of these aspects of the governor's office has significant influence on the ability of the governor to exercise control over state government. Table XIV-1 ranks the states on each of these sources of gubernatorial strength according to a scale developed by Thad Beyle (1990): 1=very weak, 2=weak, 3=moderate, 4=strong, 5=very strong.

---

* Associate professor of Political Science, University of Wisconsin - Milwaukee and Research Associate, Public Expenditure Research Foundation.

Table XIV-1

GUBERNATORIAL POWER

State	Others Elected	Tenure Potential	Budget Authority	Veto Power	Staff Size	Power Index
Alabama	2	4	5	4	1	16
Alaska	4	4	5	5	4	22
Arizona	2	4	5	5	2	18
Arkansas	3	4	5	4	3	19
California	3	4	5	5	4	21
Colorado	3	4	4	5	2	18
Connecticut	3	5	5	5	2	20
Delaware	4	4	5	5	2	20
Florida	3	4	4	5	5	21
Georgia	1	4	5	5	2	17
Hawaii	4	4	5	5	2	20
Idaho	3	5	5	5	2	20
Illinois	1	5	5	5	5	21
Indiana	3	4	5	1	2	15
Iowa	3	5	5	5	1	19
Kansas	3	4	5	5	2	19
Kentucky	3	4	4	4	2	17
Louisiana	3	4	4	5	3	19
Maine	5	4	5	2	2	18
Maryland	4	4	5	5	4	22
Massachusetts	3	5	5	5	4	22
Michigan	1	4	5	5	4	19
Minnesota	3	5	5	5	2	20
Mississippi	3	4	4	5	2	18
Missouri	3	4	5	5	2	19
Montana	3	5	5	5	2	20
Nebraska	3	4	5	5	1	18

284

State	Others Elected	Tenure Potential	Budget Authority	Veto Power	Staff Size	Power Index
Nevada	3	4	5	2	1	15
New Hampshire	5	2	5	2	2	16
New Jersey	5	4	5	5	5	24
New Mexico	2	4	5	5	3	19
New York	4	5	5	5	5	24
North Carolina	2	4	4	0	4	14
North Dakota	1	5	5	5	1	17
Ohio	3	4	5	5	4	21
Oklahoma	2	4	5	5	2	18
Oregon	3	4	5	5	2	19
Pennsylvania	3	4	4	5	4	20
Rhode Island	3	2	5	2	2	14
South Carolina	2	4	4	5	2	17
South Dakota	2	4	5	5	1	17
Tennessee	4	4	5	4	2	19
Texas	2	5	4	5	5	21
Utah	3	5	5	5	1	19
Vermont	3	2	5	2	1	13
Virginia	4	3	5	5	2	19
Washington	2	5	5	5	2	19
West Virginia	3	4	4	5	3	19
Wisconsin	3	5	5	5	2	20
Wyoming	3	5	5	5	1	19
Mean	2.9	4.1	4.8	4.4	2.5	18.8

Source: Council of State Governments (1994).

Other Elected Officials. Although the governor is elected as the chief executive of the state, there are many other officials in the executive branch of state government who are also elected on a statewide basis. In Wisconsin, these officials include the Attorney General, the State Treasurer, the Secretary of State, and the Superintendent of Public Instruction. To the extent that there are others elected to the executive branch of state government, it is more difficult for the governor to control the activities of the executive branch. This is because, if the heads of executive agencies are not elected, the governor usually has the power to appoint individuals to these positions, thus giving the governor leverage over these agencies. If the heads of executive agencies are elected, however, the governor has very little control over who gets elected or what they do after they are elected. It is entirely possible that not only could someone with different policy preferences than the governor get elected to these offices but also that future political opponents could get elected.

According to the data in the first column in Table XIV-1, the governor of Wisconsin has a moderate level of power in this area, which makes the Wisconsin governorship slightly stronger in this area than the average.

Tenure Potential. Another important source of power for governors is how long they can serve in office. Some states have two year terms while others have four year terms with limits on running for reelection, and still others have four year terms with no limits on reelection. Governors with long tenure potential have a greater opportunity to make appointments and build up a bank of favors owed by others in state government. Also, others in state government may be more likely to oppose a governor's program if they know the governor cannot run for reelection.

The Wisconsin governor, with a four year term and no limit on reelection attempts, has a very strong tenure potential, while the average governor has only strong tenure potential. An illustration of the strength of tenure potential can be found in the current Wisconsin's current governor, Tommy Thompson. Thompson was elected to his third four-year term in 1994, making him one of the longest serving governors in the country. This strength in tenure potential may be useful in redressing any weaknesses the governor may have in other areas (Beyle, 1990).

Control Over The Budget. Control of the budget can also help redress inadequacies in other gubernatorial powers (Beyle, 1990). Most governors have full responsibility for putting together the state's budget. In some states, however, this power is shared with the legislature or some other actor in state government. In Wisconsin, the governor has full responsibility for drafting the budget. This gives the governor a very strong budget-making power. It should be noted, however, that 39 other governors also have very strong budget making powers.

One aspect of the budget process that detracts somewhat from the governor's power is the role of the legislature. In all but a few states, the state legislature can make virtually any change in the governor's budget as it makes its way through the legislative labyrinth. In Wisconsin, like most other states, the legislature can make unlimited changes in the governor's budget. Still, it is the governor's budget that establishes what the legislature has to work with.

Veto Power. Perhaps one of the most potent weapons in a governor's political arsenal is the veto power. With the veto power, the governor can effectively cancel legislation unless there is enough support for the legislation to override the veto. In addition to vetoing entire bills, some governors have a line-item veto, which gives them the power to cancel parts of bills. This power is usually reserved for spending provisions. In Wisconsin, the governor has been able to use the line-item veto to erase words, letters, or decimal points in spending proposals--as well as spending amounts--until a constitutional amendment was passed in April, 1990 that was intended to weaken the governor's veto power. Even with the passage of this constitutional amendment, however, the governor is still able to exercise considerable control of legislation with the creative use of the line-item veto.

According to the data in the fourth column of in Table XIV-1, even with the new constitutional amendment, the Wisconsin governor has a very strong veto power. Again it should be noted that the average governor has at least a strong veto power.

Staff Size. One aspect of power that exhibits a lot of variation across the states is personal staff for the governor. These staff people may include the governor's legal counsel, appointment secretary, press secretary, policy advisors, legislative liaison officer, or any number of other important individuals (Dresang and Gosling, 1989: 74-75). What the staff provides the governor is time, energy, and ideas (Dresang and Gosling, 1989:74). The more staff a governor has, the better able he or she is to give matters of state government the attention they deserve.

As Table XIV-1 reveals, the governor of Wisconsin has relatively weak (2) staff resources. The average governor has moderate to weak (2.5) staff powers. In fact only five governors have very strong staff resources.

Power Index. Is the Wisconsin governorship institutionally strong or weak? One way of gauging this is to take an average of all of the individual indicators and create a single index of gubernatorial power. One serious drawback with an index such as this is that it assigns equal weight to each aspect of gubernatorial power. Nevertheless, a simple additive index provides a fairly good picture of the relative strength of American governors.

According to the power index presented in the last column of Table XIV-1, Wisconsin's governorship is institutionally strong (4), according to the 1 to 5 scale, and is slightly stronger than the average governorship (3.8).

Legislatures

State legislatures, like governorships, vary a great deal in terms of structure and capacity. Some legislatures meet only every other year, some hardly pay their members at all, some provide their members with personal staff, and some have taken full advantage of the computer and information technology revolution. Table XIV-2 provides comparative data on these aspects of state legislatures, data that can be used to assess the relative strength of the Wisconsin legislature.

Table XIV-2

LEGISLATIVE PROFESSIONALISM

State	Session	Salary	Bills	Staff	Computers	Power Index
Alabama	1	1050	3.1	1	17	3
Alaska	1	24012	1.4	2	19	4
Arizona	1	15000	2.9	0	18	1
Arkansas	0	12500	9.8	0	10	1
California	1	52500	10.9	2	22	5
Colorado	1	17500	3.4	0	17	2
Connecticut	1	16760	2.6	1	19	1
Delaware	1	24900	1.6	2	16	3
Florida	1	22560	2.5	2	17	3
Georgia	1	10641	2.7	0	18	2
Hawaii	1	32000	4.8	2	14	4
Idaho	1	12000	4.0	0	17	2
Illinois	1	38420	3.0	2	19	4
Indiana	1	11600	1.8	0	19	2
Iowa	1	18100	1.2	2	16	2
Kansas	1	5704	1.8	1	12	1
Kentucky	0	5800	3.1	0	18	1

State	Session	Salary	Bills	Staff	Computers	Power Index
Louisiana	1	16800	7.2	0	11	2
Maine	1	9975	3.1	1	15	1
Maryland	1	28000	3.4	2	18	4
Massachusetts	1	30000	2.5	2	19	4
Michigan	1	47723	2.4	2	19	4
Minnesota	1	27979	1.7	1	18	3
Mississippi	1	10000	2.3	0	16	1
Missouri	1	22863	1.0	2	17	4
Montana	0	5136	4.7	0	20	2
Nebraska	1	12000	7.0	2	17	4
Nevada	0	7800	10.6	2	14	2
New Hampshire	1	100	0.9	0	17	2
New Jersey	1	35000	3.2	2	20	4
New Mexico	1	4500	4.1	2	13	3
New York	1	57500	3.4	2	20	4
North Carolina	1	13026	2.1	2	17	3
North Dakota	0	9090	4.4	0	16	1
Ohio	1	42427	0.6	2	19	4
Oklahoma	1	32000	2.5	2	20	4
Oregon	0	13104	9.1	2	18	3
Pennsylvania	1	47000	0.5	2	19	4
Rhode Island	1	300	3.5	0	16	2
South Carolina	1	10400	1.3	2	15	2
South Dakota	1	4000	3.6	0	14	2
Tennessee	1	16500	4.8	2	12	3
Texas	0	7200	5.9	2	19	3
Utah	1	3825	3.0	0	19	3
Vermont	1	8160	0.6	0	11	1
Virginia	1	17820	7.1	2	16	3
Washington	1	25900	3.6	2	21	5
West Virginia	1	6500	1.3	1	15	1
Wisconsin	1	35070	0.9	2	16	3

Wyoming	1	2925	2.6	0	14	1
Mean	0.86	18633	3.5	1.2	16.8	3

Source: All legislative data except that for staff are taken from Council of State Governments (1994). Data for legislative staff are taken from Council of State Governments (1992).

Legislative Sessions. Most legislatures convene every year for a fixed period of time. A number of legislatures, however, meet only once every other year. The frequency with which the legislature convenes is important because the business of state government has become so complex and the states have been given so many new responsibilities in the past ten years (Nathan, 1989) that legislatures are required to spend more and more time taking care of the business of state government. In the first column of data in Table XIV-2, those states that meet every year are given a score of 1 and those that meet every two years are given a score of 0. The overwhelming majority of states (43) now convene their legislatures at least once a year. Wisconsin is with the majority of states that meet every year.

Salary. Another important variable to consider when comparing legislatures is how much they pay their members. Legislator salary is important because, as the complexity of governing has increased, the job of state legislator has become more of a full-time job in many states. In order to entice well-qualified individuals into serving in the legislature, a state has to be willing to provide adequate compensation.

The salary figures in the second column of data in Table XIV-2 are calculated by taking the base salary for state legislators and adding the per diem allowance times the maximum session length allowed by state law. In some states (AL, ID, KS, KY, MT, NV, NM, ND, RI, VT) there is no base salary--legislators are only paid a per diem living allowance. The range in salaries is quite vast. The average salary for state legislators across all 50 states is only $18,633. Legislators in states such as New York ($57,500) and Michigan ($47,723) are paid much more than average, while legislators in New Hampshire ($100-- that's right, $100) and Rhode Island ($300) are paid much below average. State legislators in Wisconsin earn $35,070, almost twice the national average.

Legislative Activity. One measure of the capacity of state legislatures is the pace of legislation, or the amount of work completed. One way of judging this is presented in the third column of Table XIV-2. The data presented here represent the number of bills per member per year passed by the legislature in a two year period. Although this is a rough measure of output, it should provide us with insights into the capacity of the state legislatures.

The average number of bills passed per member per year is 3.5. If we look at states above the average we see that some are truly extreme cases: California (10.9) and Nevada (10.6) are far above average. The state with the lowest level of output is Pennsylvania (.5), though Ohio (.5) and Vermont (.5) are almost as low. The Wisconsin legislature had one of the lowest levels of output per member (.9) for the two years analyzed here.

Staff. Legislators, like governors, can benefit from personal staff. Staff members in the legislature can help control the flow of information between the legislator and the constituency, help research legislation, run the office, and help write bills. Not all legislatures provide personal staff, and some states provide staff to one chamber but not the other. The data found in the fourth column of Table XIV-2 represent staff (personal, not shared) provisions among the states. If a state does not provide staff to either chamber it receives a score of 0; if the state provides personal staff to just one of the two chambers it is scored 1; if all legislators in the state have personal staff the state gets a score of 2. On average, the states provide personal staff to at least one chamber of the legislature. In Wisconsin, legislators in both chambers are provided personal staff, placing the Wisconsin legislature among the better-staffed in the country.

Computers. State legislatures, like the rest of society, have felt the impact of the computer revolution. Many tasks previously performed by individuals are now performed by computers. Some examples of these tasks are: calculating local aid formulas, redistricting, maintaining mailing lists, recording roll-call votes, and drafting legislation. The fifth column of data in Table XIV-2 provides a count of the number of legislative functions performed by computers in the states. Some states have clearly been caught up in the tide of new computer technology while other states have been left behind. The average state legislature uses the computer for 16.8 different functions. The range is from 10 computer functions in Arkansas to 21 in Washington. Wisconsin is slightly below average, using the computer for 16 different functions.

Index of Legislative Power. It is possible to create an index of the overall capacity of state legislatures similar to that which was created for governorships. The index of legislative power found in the sixth column of data in Table XIV-2 is created by adding up the number of times each state is above average on each of the five indicators of legislative capacity in Table XIV-2. Doing this yields a measure of legislative strength that is bounded by 0 on the low end and five on the high end, with an average score of 3. The Wisconsin legislature is given a score of 3, indicating that Wisconsin is fairly typical in terms of legislative power.

The Courts

The American court system is complicated by the federal nature of our government. Not only is there a large national court system but there are also 50 different court systems in the states. The state courts, like other institutions, can be differentiated according to a number of different criteria. This section examines differences in judicial salaries, the presence of an intermediate court of appeals, judicial activism, and judicial selection.

Judicial Salaries. Salary is an important indicator of the professionalism of the court system because, just as with the legislatures, high salaries can be used to entice well qualified individuals. Salaries may be even more important for the courts because of the opportunity costs involved in becoming a judge. Because the income potential for attorneys is relatively high, the states have to pay judges a significant amount if they want to attract the best legal minds.

The salary measure presented in Table XIV-3 is the annual salary for state supreme court justices. Comparing these data to the salaries for state legislators, it is clear that judges are better paid than state legislators. The average salary for a state supreme court justice is $93,179. Generally, there are not the vast differences in salary that there were in the legislatures: the lowest salary is $64,452 (Montana) and the highest is $127,267 (California), with a fairly normal distribution in between. Supreme court justices in Wisconsin are paid an average of $94,906, slightly above the national average.

Table XIV-3

CHARACTERISTICS OF THE JUDICIARY

State	Salary	Court of Appeals	Activism	Selection*
Alabama	107125	1	34.5	P
Alaska	105876	1	36.7	M
Arizona	91728	1	12.5	M
Arkansas	93349	1	26.4	P

State	Salary	Court of Appeals	Activism	Selection[a]
California	127267	1	26.0	G
Colorado	84000	1	14.0	M
Connecticut	106553	1	14.3	M
Delaware	105100	0	9.5	G
Florida	103457	1	21.2	M
Georgia	96118	1	15.2	NP
Hawaii	93780	1	28.6	M
Idaho	79183	1	16.3	NP
Illinois	103097	1	19.8	P
Indiana	81000	1	17.6	M
Iowa	90300	1	3.1	M
Kansas	84456	1	15.8	M
Kentucky	78273	1	33.3	NP
Louisiana	94000	1	25.2	NP
Maine	83616	0	18.6	G
Maryland	99000	1	37.9	G
Massachusetts	90450	1	20.0	M
Michigan	111941	1	18.4	NP
Minnesota	94395	1	18.8	NP
Mississippi	90800	0	15.2	P
Missouri	92910	1	18.1	M
Montana	64452	0	31.1	NP
Nebraska	88157	0	15.8	M
Nevada	85000	0	27.8	NP
New Hampshire	95623	0	25.9	G
New Jersey	115000	1	25.0	G
New Mexico	77250	1	11.1	P
New York	125000	1	25.0	G
North Carolina	91855	1	2.9	P
North Dakota	71555	0	25.0	NP
Ohio	101150	1	17.5	NP
Oklahoma	83871	1	32.3	M

State	Salary	Court of Appeals	Activism	Selection[a]
Oregon	83700	1	27.3	NP
Pennsylvania	108045	1	39.1	P
Rhode Island	99431	0	19.0	L
South Carolina	92986	1	46.0	L
South Dakota	72079	0	29.5	M
Tennessee	96348	1	18.2	P
Texas	94685	1	35.7	P
Utah	89300	1	16.9	M
Vermont	73890	0	16.0	M
Virginia	102700	1	18.2	L
Washington	107200	1	36.3	NP
West Virginia	72000	0	38.9	P
Wisconsin	94906	1	32.3	NP
Wyoming	85000	1	4.7	M
Mean	93179	0.76	22.7	--

[a] P = partisan election; NP = nonpartisan election; M = merit; G = gubernatorial appointment; L = legislative appointment.

Source: The data for the courts of appeal and judicial selection are taken from Council of State Governments (1988). The data on salaries are taken from Council of State Governments (1994). The data on judicial activism are taken from Emmert (1988: 15).

Intermediate Court of Appeals. In most states, cases from the lower courts can be challenged in an intermediate appellate court before going to the state supreme court. Not all states have intermediate appellate courts, however. What this means is that anyone wanting to challenge a finding from a lower court has to go to the state supreme court. If there is an appellate level, however, many cases can be weeded out before they get to the supreme court. The presence of appellate courts, therefore, has a strong impact on the state supreme court. In states with appellate courts the supreme courts are able to take their time selecting cases to be heard and consider the merits of each case before the court. Also, the supreme courts in states with an appellate level are less likely to deliver unanimous decisions (Jacob, 1990:258).

The data on appellate courts is presented in the second column of data in table XIV-3. States that have appellate courts are given a score of 1 and states without appellate courts are given a score of 0. Thirty-eight states, including Wisconsin, have appellate courts.

Activism. Although it is difficult to find a single definition of judicial activism, it is usually taken to mean that the court's actions significantly affect public policy (Bowman and Kearney, 1990:303). Frequently what this means is that the court rules against the findings in previous cases or rules that an existing policy is unconstitutional. The data in the third column in Table XIV-3 offer one way of measuring judicial activism in the states. This measure of activism is the percentage of state laws challenged before the state supreme court that were overturned between 1981 and 1985 (Emmert, 1988). The higher this number, the more activist the court. During this time period the average state overturned 22.7 percent of all state laws that were challenged before the supreme court. The range is from 2.9 percent in North Carolina to 46 percent in South Carolina. The Wisconsin supreme court was more activist than the average state supreme court, overturning 32.3 percent of the state laws brought before it during this time period.

Selection. Methods for choosing judges vary a great deal across the states. Some states elect their judges in either partisan or nonpartisan elections. In other states judges are appointed, either by the legislature or by the governor. Still other states use what is sometimes referred to as the merit plan. Under the merit plan, a commission selects a pool of candidates they feel are best qualified to serve on the court and the governor then chooses from among these candidates. It is difficult to say which method produces the "best" judges. Some feel that interpretation of the law should be removed from electoral pressure. Others feel that the people have a right to decide who interprets the law.

The last column in Table XIV-3 presents the methods used in the states for selecting supreme court justices. It should be noted that many states use other methods for the lower courts. The data is coded in the following manner: P=partisan election, NP=nonpartisan election, M=merit, G=gubernatorial appointment, L=legislative appointment. The most common method of selection is the merit plan (17 states), followed by nonpartisan elections (13 states), partisan elections (10 states), gubernatorial appointment (7 states), and Legislative appointment (3 states). Wisconsin uses the nonpartisan election to select its supreme court justices.

A strong court? It is more difficult to judge court systems in terms of overall strength because some concepts, such as method of judicial selection, do not clearly fit into a dimension of strength or capacity. We can, however, tell from the information in Table XIV-3 that Wisconsin has a fairly strong court system: it pays its judges well, it has an appellate division, and the court system is an activist one. The method of judicial selection is not necessarily a very good indicator of the strength of the judicial system. Rather, the fact that Wisconsin uses nonpartisan elections reflects the emphasis on popular participation that is found in progressive, or moralistic, states.

Public Policy

One way to judge the values of a state is to look at the policies produced by state government. For instance, states that spend more on social services probably do so in part because of the political values within the states. This section examines state policy in the areas of consumer protection, social welfare programs, the environment, and taxes.

Consumer protection. Consumer protection is a policy area that exhibits a lot of variation across states. Currently in Wisconsin, the primary enforcer of consumer protection laws is the state attorney general. However, under the 1995-1997 budget, this function will be transferred to the Department of Agriculture, Trade and Consumer Protection (DATCP) on July 1, 1996, with DOJ retaining prosecutorial responsibilities. Still, most of the laws come from the state legislature. Consumer protection laws provide a good example of a liberal policy area; the very nature of consumer protection requires government to intervene in market transactions to protect one of the participants.

The measure of consumer protection found in the first column of data in Table XIV-4 is the total number of specific consumer protection laws enacted by the states up to 1982. The range in laws enacted is from 4 (Arkansas) to 22 (Connecticut and New Jersey), and the average number of laws enacted is 14. Wisconsin comes in significantly above average with 18 pieces of consumer protection legislation enacted.

Table XIV-4

PUBLIC POLICIES IN THE STATES

State	Consumer Protection	AFDC Adequacy	Social Spending	Green Index	Progressive Tax Rank	Policy Index
Alabama	5	4.4	21	50	32	0
Alaska	14	14.5	11	34	--	2
Arizona	13	7.0	22	35	15	2
Arkansas	4	6.4	23	48	28	1
California	20	13.1	30	4	4	5
Colorado	13	8.5	22	16	17	3
Connecticut	22	10.2	24	11	41	4
Delaware	11	7.5	13	24	13	2
Florida	19	6.7	21	18	38	2
Georgia	15	6.7	26	39	25	3
Hawaii	13	11.2	12	12	3	3
Idaho	7	10.0	15	19	24	3
Illinois	13	8.1	26	31	40	1
Indiana	9	7.4	22	43	43	1
Iowa	11	10.2	19	20	34	2
Kansas	8	9.3	18	42	26	0
Kentucky	16	8.0	26	41	30	2
Louisiana	16	5.9	24	49	23	3
Maine	17	11.7	31	2	10	5
Maryland	19	7.9	24	13	14	4
Massachusetts	20	11.0	30	6	11	5
Michigan	18	12.8	26	17	22	5
Minnesota	20	14.2	25	5	2	5
Mississippi	11	4.5	23	47	35	1
Missouri	13	7.6	26	30	33	1
Montana	9	13.0	16	21	7	3
Nebraska	12	9.9	20	29	29	1
Nevada	14	6.2	15	22	44	2
New Hampshire	17	9.6	38	15	46	4

State	Consumer Protection	AFDC Adequacy	Social Spending	Green Index	Progressive Tax Rank	Policy Index
New Jersey	22	7.9	25	14	27	3
New Mexico	8	9.2	15	28	8	1
New York	8	11.4	33	8	12	4
North Carolina	13	8.5	20	23	21	2
North Dakota	13	12.2	18	25	37	2
Ohio	20	8.7	27	37	16	3
Oklahoma	14	8.9	22	40	20	3
Oregon	20	11.6	19	1	1	5
Pennsylvania	15	9.9	32	26	39	3
Rhode Island	21	12.2	23	7	18	5
South Carolina	10	7.4	20	36	19	1
South Dakota	9	9.8	19	27	48	1
Tennessee	18	5.2	29	45	47	2
Texas	15	4.8	24	46	45	2
Utah	12	12.9	16	33	31	1
Vermont	19	14.0	23	3	6	5
Virginia	14	7.7	16	32	36	1
Washington	18	13.4	19	9	42	3
West Virginia	5	8.6	25	44	9	2
Wisconsin	18	14.8	23	10	5	5
Wyoming	7	10.5	11	38	49	0
Mean	14.0	9.5	22	25	25	2.6

Source: The data on consumer protection laws are from the Council of State Governments (1982). The data on AFDC adequacy are taken from Albritton (1990:426-427). The data on tax progressivity are taken from Hansen (1990:347). The data on social spending is from U.S. Bureau of the Census (1993). The data on environmental protection laws is from Hall and Kerr (1991:3).

AFDC Adequacy. Social programs such as Aid to Families with Dependent Children (AFDC) provide another opportunity to evaluate the policy priorities of the states. AFDC is especially suitable because, although the federal government provides significant financial assistance, states also carry a significant burden and have broad discretion in determining benefit levels. Looking at raw expenditures can be deceptive, however, because states have varying financial capacities. One way of comparing AFDC expenditures is to express the AFDC grants as a percent of per capita income in the states. This is a useful measure because per capita income provides us with an indication of what it takes to get by in a state (Albritton, 1990:428) as well as the tax revenues available to help finance the program.

The data on AFDC adequacy is presented in the second column in Table XIV-4 States with high values provide AFDC payments that come closer to per capita income than states with low values. Across the states, the average AFDC grant is 9.5 percent of per capita income. The lowest ratio is 4.4 (Alabama), while the highest ratio, 14.8, is found in Wisconsin. On this measure, then, Wisconsin is found not just above average, but leading the nation.

Social Spending. Another good measure of dedication to social welfare programs is the percent of total state government expenditures that go toward income maintenance and social programs. Measuring social spending in this manner takes into account the fact that some states have much larger budgets and will spend more on social programs because of this. These data are presented in the third column of Table XIV-4, where the range is from 11 percent (Alaska and Wyoming) to 33 percent (New York), and the average is 22 percent. Wisconsin is slightly above average, spending 23 percent of the state budget on social programs.

Environmental Protection. Environmental protection is a policy area that usually involves conflict between industry and agriculture on one side and those who want to protect the environment on the other. As such, it provides a good indicator of progressive policy-making in the states. The fourth column in Table XIV-4 presents state rankings on the "Green Index," which is an index that rates states according to the degree to which they have implemented a number of different environmental policies. Low scores on this ranking indicate that the states have stricter environmental protection laws, and high scores indicate that the states have less strict laws. Wisconsin is ranked fairly high on the green index, coming in tenth among the fifty states.

Tax Progressivity. Taxes are a somewhat different policy area; the issue here is not what the state money is spent on, but where it comes from. There is great variety in the tax policies of the states. Some states rely heavily on an income tax, while others rely heavily on a sales tax, while still others--usually states with significant mineral wealth--rely heavily on severance taxes. Even with these vast differences, state tax policies can be compared on the basis of equity, or progressivity.

A tax is said to be progressive if the proportion of income paid in taxes increases with income. In other words, the wealthy pay a greater share of the income in taxes than do the poor. Flat rate taxes, or taxes that place a heavier burden on the poor are considered less progressive.

The states are ranked according to tax progressivity in the final column of data in Table XIV-4: the higher the number, the less progressive a state's tax policy. According to these data, Oregon is the most progressive state, while Wyoming is the least progressive state. Wisconsin is ranked fifth in tax progressivity, reflecting again the progressive heritage of Wisconsin politics.

Policy Index. Generally, across these policy areas, Wisconsin emerges as one of the most progressive states. To get a sense of how progressive Wisconsin is compared to other states, a policy index is presented in the sixth column of Table XIV-4. This index is a simple count of the number of times a state was above average, in the direction of progressive policy, on the five policy indicators. Wisconsin emerges on this index as one of the most progressive states in the country, ranking above average in all five policy areas. Why is this the case? Part of the answer, which is almost too obvious, is that a state's public policy outputs usually reflect the values of the state's population. Generally speaking, in states where there are progressive, or liberal, policies there is also usually a liberal public (Wright, Erikson, and McIver 1985).

Elections

The electoral arena provides yet another useful point of comparison in state politics. Some states are dominated by the Democratic party, while some are dominated by the Republican party; some states have competitive elections while others do not; some states have restrictive voter registration laws while others have lax registration laws; some states have high rates of voter turnout while others have very low voter turnout.

Comparative data on these aspects of elections in the states are presented in Table XIV-5.

Table XIV-5

PARTIES AND ELECTIONS IN THE STATES

State	Democratic Control	Electoral Competition	Closing Date	Voter Turnout
Alabama	0.666	27.27	10	55.2
Alaska	0.467	53.46	30	65.4
Arizona	0.316	33.90	50	54.1
Arkansas	0.831	9.26	20	53.8
California	0.537	47.29	29	49.1
Colorado	0.438	40.18	25	62.7
Connecticut	0.518	52.81	21	63.8
Delaware	0.519	39.66	17	55.2
Florida	0.594	31.13	30	50.2
Georgia	0.739	16.19	30	46.9
Hawaii	0.814	33.40	30	41.9
Idaho	0.338	35.60	10	65.2
Illinois	0.462	41.61	28	58.9
Indiana	0.518	44.59	29	55.2
Iowa	0.481	48.15	10	65.3
Kansas	0.359	35.81	20	63.0
Kentucky	0.741	27.81	30	53.7
Louisiana	0.828	--	24	59.8
Maine	0.528	45.90	0	72.0
Maryland	0.776	31.00	30	53.4
Massachusetts	0.658	30.39	28	60.2
Michigan	0.421	49.58	30	61.7
Minnesota	0.608	52.44	0	71.6
Mississippi	0.709	16.48	30	52.8
Missouri	0.633	27.12	28	62.0
Montana	0.453	43.34	30	70.1
Nebraska	0.660	54.06	11	63.2

Nevada	0.548	49.60	31	50
New Hampshire	0.259	29.01	10	63.1
New Jersey	0.410	51.81	29	56.3
New Mexico	0.645	37.10	29	51.6
New York	0.530	47.68	30	50.9
North Carolina	0.636	33.42	31	50.1
North Dakota	0.394	56.58	0	67.3
Ohio	0.384	49.61	30	60.6
Oklahoma	0.659	25.49	10	59.7
Oregon	0.534	54.25	21	65.7
Pennsylvania	0.496	40.19	30	54.3
Rhode Island	0.776	39.49	30	58.4
South Carolina	0.550	28.32	30	45.0
South Dakota	0.322	39.19	15	67.0
Tennessee	0.649	26.72	29	52.4
Texas	0.618	21.96	30	49.1
Utah	0.232	45.29	5	65.1
Vermont	0.568	49.16	17	67.5
Virginia	0.617	40.71	31	52.8
Washington	0.568	53.94	30	59.9
West Virginia	0.798	44.97	30	50.6
Wisconsin	0.469	49.13	0	69.0
Wyoming	0.313	30.46	30	62.3
Mean	0.552	38.25	23	58.3

Source: The data on Democratic strength and voter turnout are taken from Bibby and Holbrook (N.d.). The data on closing dates is taken from Council of State Governments (1990). The data on electoral competition are taken from Holbrook and Van Dunk (1993).

Party strength. One convenient way of gauging the electoral tendencies of a state is to examine party strength in state government. Probably the best measure of party strength is one that considers control of the governorship and the state legislature. Just such a measure is presented in the first column of data in table XIV-5. This measure is bound by 0 (complete Republican control) and 1 (complete Democratic control), and is based on success in state legislative and gubernatorial elections from 1989-1994. The average score on this variable is .55, reflecting a slight Democratic advantage in state government. It should be noted, however, that the Democrats have lost some strength in the last two decades: the same variable had an average of .64 during the 1970s and .60 in the 1980s (Bibby et al., 1990:92). The most strongly Democratic states are found in the South and the most Republican states are found in the Plains and Mountain West. Wisconsin, with a score of .469, leans slightly Republican, which

298

represents a change from the 1970s and 1980s, when Wisconsin was more solidly in the Democratic camp. It must be remembered, however, that this measure is based only on control of state government. Wisconsin also displays some Democratic tendencies: both U.S. Senators are Democratic and the state voted with the Democratic candidate in the last two presidential elections.

Electoral Competition. Whether Democratic or Republican, states can also differ in the degree to which their elections are competitive. In some states, candidates are elected and reelected to office with relative ease, whereas in other states there is a high level of competition for elective office. Electoral competition is an important element of the moralistic political culture, which encourages openness and widespread participation in politics. Among other things, electoral competition tends to increase voter turnout and is related to the degree to which states pursue progressive public policies (Holbrook and Van Dunk 1993).

Data on electoral competition are presented in the second column of Table XIV-5. This measure of electoral competition is based on state legislative elections and measures the degree to which winning candidates faced a strong challenge (Holbrook and Van Dunk, 1993). Low values on the competition index indicate low levels of competition and high values indicate high levels of competition. The range in competition is from 9.26 (Arkansas) to 56.58 (North Dakota), and the mean is 38.25. Wisconsin, with a score of 49.13, is among the most competitive states.

Voter Registration Requirements. Voter participation is thought to be invaluable to a system of accountable government. Before one can vote in elections, however, one must fulfill certain legal requirements. In all states except North Dakota, residents must be registered before they are allowed to vote. Although virtually all states require voter registration, the act of registering is more difficult in some states than in others. One factor that affects the ease with which one can register is the closing date for registration; that is, the number of days before the election that one must be registered in order to vote. The earlier the closing date, the less likely it is that unregistered voters will register, largely because most people do not pay much attention to the election until late in the campaign and many people are not aware of the closing date.

Registration closing dates are presented in the third column of data in Table XIV-5, where the average closing date is 23 days. The range in closing dates is from 0 (several states) to 50 (Tennessee) days. Wisconsin is one of four states that allows registration on the day of the election.

Voter turnout. A more direct measure of participation in the states is the rate at which voters turn out to vote. Some states have traditionally produced high rates of voter turnout while other states have traditionally produced lower rates of voter turnout. One measure of turnout, the rate of turnout in the 1992 presidential election, is presented in the last column of Table XIV-5. Turnout in the 1992 presidential election ranged from 47.9 percent in Hawaii 70.1 percent, in Montana, and the average was 58.3 percent. Wisconsin, with a 69 percent turnout rate, was not only above average but was also had one of the highest turnout states in 1992.

Clearly one of the reasons the closing date is important is because it has an influence on the rate of voter turnout. States with early closing dates tend to have lower rates of voter turnout. Also, one of the important consequences of party competition is that it leads to higher rates of voter turnout (Holbrook and Van Dunk, 1993). States with high levels of electoral competition tend to also have relatively high levels of voter turnout. Indeed, part of the explanation for why Wisconsin, or any other state, has the rate of turnout it has can be found in the closing date for registration and the level of electoral competition in the state.

Conclusion

Does Wisconsin's moralistic character reveal itself when compared with the other states? In large part, the answer is yes. First, if we examine political institutions, we find a highly professional state government designed to play an active role in the lives of its citizens. Further evidence of an active state government is found when we look at the public policies of the states. Based on the four policies we looked at, Wisconsin is more redistributive and interventionist in its policies than most of the other states. Finally, in terms of elections, the best evidence of Wisconsin's moralistic political culture is that elections are competitive, voters can register to vote on the day of the election, and voter turnout is higher than in most states.

All in all, then, Wisconsin does emerge as having a moralistic political culture when compared to the other states. This conclusion is based on the evidence amassed in this chapter. No doubt, if other indicators of state politics and culture were to be examined, the results might be somewhat different than those presented here. However, the general conclusion--that Wisconsin fits the moralistic mold quite well--would undoubtedly remain the same.

WISCONSIN GOVERNMENT AND POLITICS:
A SELECTED BIBLIOGRAPHY

I. Political History and Development

Elazar, Daniel J. 1986. *American Federalism: A View from the States*. New York: Harper and Row.

Engler, Jr., Richard E. 1964. *The Challenge of Diversity*. New York: Harper and Row.

Lieske, Joel. 1993. "Regional Subcultures of the United States." *Journal of Politics* 55:888-913

Nesbit, Robert C. 1973. *Wisconsin: A History*. Madison, WI: University of Wisconsin Press.

U.S. Bureau of the Census. 1995. *Statistical Abstract of the United States*. Washington, DC: Government Printing Office.

Wisconsin, State of. 1993, 1995. *Blue Book*. Madison, WI: Wisconsin Legislative Reference Bureau.

II. Wisconsin Constitution

Adrian, Charles R. and Michael R. Fine. 1991. *State and Local Politics*. Chicago: Lyceum/Nelson Hall.

Austin, H. Russell. 1964. *The Wisconsin Story: Building of a Vanguard State*. Third ed. Milwaukee, WI: Milwaukee Journal Co.

Council of State Governments. Various years. *Book of the States*. Lexington, KY: Council of State Governments.

Fine, Michael. 1989. "The Independence of the City: The Legal Constraints on the Tradition of Home Rule." *The Small City and Regional Community*. 8:91-98.

Wisconsin, State of. Various years. *State of Wisconsin: Blue Book*. Madison, WI: Wisconsin Legislative Reference Bureau.

III. Local Government

Advisory Commission on Intergovernmental Relations (ACIR). 1982. *State and Local Roles in the Federal System: A Commission Report*. Washington, DC: Government Printing Office.

----------. 1987. *The Organization of Local Public Economies*. Washington, DC: Government Printing Office.

----------. *Changing Public Attitudes on Governments and Taxes*. Washington, DC: Government Printing Office.

Anchor Savings and Loan v. Madison EOC. 1984. 120 Wis. 2d 291.

Avery v. Midland County. 1968. 390 U.S. 474.

Baker v. Carr. 1962. 369 U.S. 186.

Bowman, Ann and Richard Kearney. 1986. *The Resurgence of the States*. Englewood Cliffs: Prentice-Hall, Inc.

Brown v. Thomson. 1983. 103 S. Ct. 2690.

Crane, Wilder. 1956. "Reflections of a County Board Member." *The County Officer*. 21:20.

Davis v. Grover. 1992. 166 Wis. 2d. 501.

Donoghue, James R. 1979. "Local Government in Wisconsin," In *State of Wisconsin: Blue Book, 1979-1980*. Madison, WI: Wisconsin Legislative Reference Bureau.

Friedrich, C.E. 1989. "Four More Counties Yield to Allure of Sales Tax." *The Milwaukee Journal*. December 3, 1989.

Green, R.K. and A. Reschovsky. 1994. "Fiscal Assistance to Municipal Governments." In *Dollars and Sense: Policy Choices and the Wisconsin Budget*, ed. Donald Nichols. Madison, WI: The Robert M. Lafollette Institute of Public Affairs.

Haferbecker, G.M. 1978. "The New Wisconsin Labor Law: Last-Offer Arbitration for Municipal Employees." In *The Small City and Regional Community Proceedings*, vol. 1, eds. Robert P. Wolensky and Edward J. Miller. Stevens Point, WI: University of Wisconsin Stevens Point Foundation Press.

Hagensick, A. C. 1964. "Influences of Partisanship and Incumbency on a Nonpartisan Election." *Western Political Quarterly*. 17:117-24.

_____. 1968. "'One Man-One Vote' and County Government." *George Washington Law Review*. 36:778.89.

Hanushek, E.A. 1981. "Throwing Money at Schools." *Journal of Policy Analysis and Management*. 1:19-44.

Hawkins, B.W. and R.M. Hendrick. 1994. "Do County Governments Reinforce City-Suburban Inequalities? A Study of City and Suburban Service Allocations." *Social Science Quarterly*. 75:755-71.

Heim, J.P. 1991. "Transferring or Sharing Municipal Services." In *The Small City and Regional Community*, vol. 9, eds. E.J. Miller and R.P. Wolensky. Stevens Point, WI: University of Wisconsin-Stevens Point Foundation Press.

Lampman, R.J. and T.D. McBride. 1988. "Changes in the Pattern of State and Local Revenues and Expenditures in Wisconsin, 1960-1983," In *State Policy Choices: The Wisconsin Experience*, eds. S. Danziger and J.F. Witte. Madison, WI: University of Wisconsin Press.

LeMay, M.C. 1975. *Wisconsin Towns*. Milwaukee, WI: Institute of Governmental Affairs, University of Wisconsin-Extension.

Local Union No. 487 v. Eau Claire. 1989. 147 Wis. 2d 519.

Mac Manus, S. 1978. *Revenue Patterns in U.S. Cities and Suburbs*. New York: Praeger.

Mahan v. Howell. 1973. 93 S.Ct. 979.

Rafuse, R.W. 1991. "Fiscal Disparities in Chicagoland." *Intergovernmental Perspective*. 19:14-19.

Rehfuss, J.A. 1989. *Contracting Out in Government*. San Francisco: Jossey-Bass.

Reynolds v. Sims. 1964. 377 U.S. 533.

Savas, E.S. 1982. *Privatizing the Public Sector*. Chatham, N.J.: Chatham House.

State ex rel. Sonneborn v. Sylvester. 1965. 26 Wis. 2d 43.

Stauber, R. And M. Wyatt. 1990. "Property Tax Relief and Tax Incremental Financing." *In Dollars and Sense: Policy Choices and the Wisconsin Budget*, eds. R.H. Haveman and J. Huddleston. Madison, WI: The Robert M. La Follette Institute of Public Affairs.

Stern, J. et al. 1975. *Fiscal Offer Arbitration*. New York: D.C. Heath and Co.

Vincent, P.E. 1971. "The Fiscal Impact of Commuters." In *Fiscal Pressures of the Central City: The Impact of Commuters, Nonwhites and Overlapping Governments*, eds., W.Z. Hirsch, et al. New York: Praeger.

Walters, W. 1990. "40 of 72 Counties to Collect Sales Tax." *Milwaukee Sentinel*. December, 1990.

Wisconsin Taxpayers Alliance. 1989. "Town Government." *The Wisconsin Taxpayer*. June.

----------. 1993. "Town Government." *The Wisconsin Taxpayer*. December.

----------. 1994. "Town Government." *The Wisconsin Taxpayer*. October.

----------. 1994. "Town Government." *The Wisconsin Taxpayer*. November.

Wisconsin Legislative Council Staff. 1985. "Summary and Analysis of Questionnaire Responses of Mediator-Arbitrators on the Effect of Mediation-Arbitration on Municipal Collective Bargaining." Madison, WI: State of Wisconsin.

Wisconsin, State of. Various years. *State of Wisconsin: Blue Book*. Madison, WI: Wisconsin Legislative Reference Bureau.

Wisconsin, State of. 1848 as Amended. *Wisconsin Constitution*.

IV. Political Parties and Elections

Adamany, David. 1976. "Cross-over Voting and the Democratic Party's Reform Rules." *American Political Science Review*. 70:536-541.

Bibby, John F. And Thomas M. Holbrook. 1996. "Parties and Elections." In *Politics in the American States*, 6th ed., eds. Herbert Jacob and Virginia Gray. Washington, DC: CQ Press.

Cotter, Cornelius P., James L. Gibson, John F. Bibby, and Robert J. Huckshorn. 1984. *Party Organizations in American Politics*. New York: Praeger.

Donoghue, James R. 1974. *How Wisconsin Voted, 1848-1972*. Madison, WI: Institute of Governmental Affairs, University of Wisconsin-Extension.

Dykstra, Robert J. and David R. Reynolds. 1978. "In Search of Wisconsin Progressivism." In *The History of*

American Electoral Behavior, eds. Joel H. Sibley, Allan G. Bogue and William Flanigan. Princeton: Princeton University Press.

Ehrenhalt, Alan. 1989. "How a Party of Enthusiasts Keeps Its Hammerlock on a State Legislature." *Governing*. June:28-33.

Epstein, Leon D. 1986. *Political Parties in the American Mold*. Madison, WI: University of Wisconsin Press.

----------. 1958. *Politics in Wisconsin*. Madison, WI: University of Wisconsin Press.

Fiorina, Morris. P. 1994. "Divided Government in the American States: A Byproduct of Legislative Professionalism?" *American Political Science Review*. 88:304-16.

Gierzynski, Anthony. 1992. *Legislative Party Campaign Committees in the American States*. Lexington: University of Kentucky Press.

Hedlund, Ronald D. and Meredith W. Watts. 1986. "The Wisconsin Open Primary, 1968-1984." *American Politics Quarterly*. 14:55-73.

Herrnson, Paul S. 1995. *Congressional Elections: Campaigning at Home and in Washington*. Washington, DC: CQ Press.

Jewell, Malcolm E. and David Breaux. 1988. "The Effect of Incumbency on State Legislative Elections." *Legislative Studies Quarterly*. 13:495-514.

Loftus, Tom. 1985. "The New 'Political Parties' in State Legislatures." *State Government*. 58:108-109.

Mayer, Kenneth R., and John M. Wood. 1995. "The Impact of Public Financing on Electoral Competitiveness: Evidence from Wisconsin, 1964-1990." *Legislative Studies Quarterly*. 20:69-88.

Millis, Don M. 1989. "The Best Laid Schemes of Mice and Men: Campaign Finance Reform Gone Awry." *Wisconsin Law Review*. 1989:1466-93.

Ranney, Austin and Leon D. Epstein. 1966. "The Two Electorates: Voters and Non-Voters in a Wisconsin Primary." *Journal of Politics*. 28:598-616.

Sorauf, Frank J. 1954. "Extra-Legal Political Parties in Wisconsin." *American Political Science Review*. 48:692-705.

Sundquist, James L. 1983. *Dynamics of the Party System: Alignment and Realignment of Politics Parties in the United States*, Revised Edition. Washington, D.C.: Brookings.

Sykes, Jay G. 1972. *Proxmire*. Washington-New York: Robert B. Luce, Inc.

Thompson, William F. 1988. *The History of Wisconsin, Vol. VI: Continuity and Change, 1940-1965*. Madison, WI: State Historical Society of Wisconsin.

Torelle, Ellen (ed.). 1920. *The Political Philosophy of Robert M. La Follette*. Madison, WI: Robert M. La Follette Co.

Wekken, Gary. 1984. *Democrat Versus Democrat: The National Party's Campaign to Close the Wisconsin Primary*. Columbia: University of Missouri Press.

V. Interest Groups and Public Opinion

Bentley, Arthur F. 1908. *The Process of Government*. Chicago: University of Chicago Press.

Berry, Jeffrey. 1989. *The Interest Group Society*. Illinois: Scott, Foresman/Little, Brown.

Common Cause in Wisconsin. 1987. *Wisconsin-Minnesota Common Cause Survey*. St. Norbert College Survey Center.

Cotter, C.: Gibson, J.; Bibby, J.; and Huckshorn, R. 1984. *Party Organizations in American Politics*. New York: Praeger.

Dye, Thomas R. 1975. *Understanding Public Policy*. New Jersey: Prentice-Hall.

Hamm, Keith. 1986. "The Role of 'Subgovernments' in U.S. Sate Policy Making: An Exploratory Analysis." *Legislative Studies Quarterly*. 11:321-51.

Hedlund, R. 1993. "Interest Groups in Wisconsin: Pressure Politics and a Lingering Progressive Transition." In *Interest Group Politics in the Midwestern States*, eds. R. Hrebenar and C. Thomas.

King, E. 1984. "The Paradoxes of Wisconsin Politics." Unpublished Manuscript.

La Follette, Doug. 1989. *State of Wisconsin Lobbying Manuel*. Madison, WI: Wisconsin Secretary of State.

Lueders, B. 1989. "The Real Scandal." *Isthmus*. 14:1.

Madison, James. 1961. "No. 10" in Alexander Hamilton, James Madison and John Jay, *The Federalist Papers*. New York: The New American Library of World Literature.

Mills, C. Wright. 1956. *The Power Elite*. New York: Oxford University Press.

Morehouse, S.M. 1981. *State Politics, Parties and Policy*. New York: Holt, Reinhart and Winston.

Parenti, Michael. 1988. *Democracy for the Few*. New York: St. Martin's Press.

Radloff, G. 1989a. "Lobbyists Grow From Many Roots." *La Crosse Tribune*. May 7, 1989.

----------. 1989b. "Lobbyists: People You Hire to Tip the Balance." *La Crosse Tribune*. May 7, 1989.

St. Norbert College Survey Center. 1989. *The Wisconsin Survey*.

Thomas, Clive S. and Hrebenar, Ronald J. 1990. "Interest Groups in the States." In *Politics in the American States: A Comparative Analysis*, 5th ed., eds. V. Gray, H. Jacob and R. Albritton. Glenview, IL: Scott, Foresman/Little, Brown Higher Education.

Truman, David B. 1971. *The Governmental Process*. New York: Alfred Knopf.

Walker, J. 1983. "The Origins and Maintenance of Interest Groups in America." *American Political Science Review*. 77:390-406.

Wisconsin Ethics Board. 1994, 1995. *Directory of Registered Lobbying Organizations: 1993-94, 1995-96*. Madison, WI: State of Wisconsin.

----------. 1994, 1995. *Directory of Licensed Lobbyists 1993-94, 1995-96*. Madison, WI: State of Wisconsin.

----------. 1995. *Lobbying Expenditures in Wisconsin: 1993-94 Legislative Session*. Madison, WI: State of Wisconsin.

Wisconsin Secretary of State. 1985-1989. *Lobby Data Reports*. Madison, WI: State of Wisconsin.

Wisconsin State Elections Board. 1985-94. *Wisconsin Biennial Report of Wisconsin State Elections Board: Statistical Report*. Madison, WI: Wisconsin State Elections Board.

VI. Legislature

Bice, Daniel. 1994. "Group Says it's Sorry for Actions: Gave $50 Checks to Lawmakers." *Milwaukee Journal-Sentinel*. January 8, 1994.

----------. 1995a. "George's Efforts to Aid Firm Probed." *Milwaukee Journal-Sentinel*. January 31, 1995.

----------. 1995b. "Budget Session Raises Doubts About Prosser." *Milwaukee Journal-Sentinel*. July 2, 1995.

Buelow, Michael C. 1993. "Lobbyists Cleared for Campaigns." *Wisconsin State Journal*. March 13, 1993.

Daley, Dave. 1993. "Politicians Forced to Ferret out Campaign Money." *Milwaukee Journal-Sentinel*. August 22, 1993.

----------. 1995. "Jensen Warned About Lobbying." *Milwaukee Journal-Sentinel*. February 8, 1995.

----------. 1995. "Jensen Reveals Other Officials' Lobbyist Ties." *Milwaukee Journal-Sentinel*. February 9, 1995.

Hildebrand, Scott. 1995. "Shut Doors at Caucus Don't Help the Public." *Green Bay Press-Gazette*. June 1995.

Jones, Richard P. 1995. "Some in GOP are Concerned About Governor's Veto Power." *Milwaukee Journal-Sentinel*. July 9, 1995.

Jones, Richard P. and Amy Rinard. 1995. "Plan to Limit Debate Angers Democrats." *Milwaukee Journal-Sentinel*. June 16, 1995.

Kelley, Tim. 1994. "Politicians for Sale?" *Wisconsin State Journal*. January 16, 1994.

Loftus, Tom. 1991a. "Art of Legislative Politics."

----------. 1991b. "Ellis Criticizes Chairman's Power." *Milwaukee Journal*. March 15, 1991.

----------. 1991c. "Lawmaker Rips George during his Parting Shot." *Eau Claire Leader Telegram*. April 3, 1992.

Mayer, Kenneth R. and John M. Wood. 1995. "The Impact of Public Financing on Electoral Competitiveness: Evidence from Wisconsin, 1964-1990." *Legislative Studies Quarterly*. 21:69-88.

Mayers, Jeff. 1995a. "Committee Passing into History?" *Wisconsin State Journal*. January 20, 1995.

----------. 1995b. "Lobbying Groups Spend $35.4 million in '93-94." *Wisconsin State Journal*. February 10, 1995.

Miller, Cliff. 1995. "Lessons of History Forgotten in Assembly." *Appleton Post Crescent*. June 20. 1995.

Nicols, John. 1994. "The Special Interests Set the Legislative Agenda." *The Capitol Times*. June 13, 1994.

Pommer, Matt. 1993. "Lawmakers Whittle Budget Bill." *The Capitol Times*. April 29, 1993.

----------. 1994. "High-Tech Campaigns." *The Capitol Times*. June 11, 1994.

Rinard, Amy. 1994. "Kunicki Raps Swoboda Hiring as Move to Help GOP." *Milwaukee Sentinel*. March 29, 1994.

----------. 1995. "'Real Jobs' Proposal Rapped." *Milwaukee Sentinel*. February 2, 1995.

Rowen, James. 1993. "Big Money Flows through gap in Campaign Finance Laws." *Milwaukee Journal*. March 24, 1993.

Van Dunk, Emily. 1994. "Who Runs for State Legislative Office? A Look at Candidate Quality in the 1988 and 1990 State Senate Races in Oregon and Wisconsin." Paper delivered at the 1994 annual meeting of the Wisconsin Political Science Association.

Walters, Steve. 1995a. "Joint Finance Loses Some of Its Clout." *Milwaukee Journal-Sentinel*. June 15, 1995.

----------. 1995b. "Lawmakers Strip 89 Proposals from Thompson's State Budget." *Milwaukee Journal-Sentinel*. March 18, 1995.

Weber, Ronald E., Harvey J. Tucker and Paul Brace. 1991. "Vanishing Marginals in State Legislative Elections." *Legislative Studies Quarterly*. 26:29-47.

VII. Governor

Beyle, T. and R. Dalton. 1983. "The Governor and the State Legislature." In *Being Governor: The View from the Office*, eds. R. L. Beyle and R. Muchmore. Durham: Duke University Press.

Beyle, T. 1990. "Governors." In *Politics in the American States*, eds. V. Gray, H. Jacob, R. Albritton. Glenview, IL: Scott, Foresman and Company.

Bibby, J. F., et al. 1990. "Parties in State Politics." In *Politics in the American States*, eds. V. Gray, H. Jacob, and R. Albritton. Glenview, IL: Scott, Foresman and Company.

Burke, M. 1989. "The Wisconsin Partial Veto: Past, Present and Future." *Wisconsin Law Review*. 6:1395-1432.

Commission for the Study of Administrative Value and Efficiency (SAVE). 1995. *Report*. Madison, WI: State of Wisconsin.

Gosling, J. J. 1985. "Patterns of Influence and Choice in the Wisconsin Budgetary Process." *Legislative Studies Quarterly*. 10:457-82

King, S. 1980. "Executive-Orders of the Wisconsin Governor." *Wisconsin Law Review*. 1980:333-369.

Legislative Reference Bureau. 1989. "Constitutional Amendments Given 'First Consideration Approval' By the 1987 Wisconsin Legislature." Informational Bulletin 89-IB-1. January.

Loftus, T. 1994. *The Art of Legislative Politics*. Washington, DC: Congressional Quarterly.

Rom, M.C. and J. F. Witte. 1988. "Power Versus Participation: The Wisconsin Budget Process." In *State Policy Choices: The Wisconsin Experience*, eds. S. Danziger and J.F. Witte. Madison, WI: The University of Wisconsin Press.

Rosenthal, A. 1990. *Governors and Legislatures: Contending Powers*. Washington: Congressional Quarterly Press.

Sorauf, F.J., Jr. 1953. "The Voluntary Committee System in Wisconsin: An Effort to Achieve Party Responsibility." Unpublished Ph.D. dissertation. University of Wisconsin.

State ex rel., Kleczka v. Contra. 1978. 82 Wis. 2nd 679.

State ex rel., Martin v. Heil. 1942. 242 Wis. 41.

State ex rel., Wisconsin Senate, et al. v. Thompson. 1988. 144 Wis. 2nd 429.

State ex rel., Wisconsin Telephone Co. v. Henry. 1935. 218 Wis. 302, 260 N.W. 486.

Theobald, H. R. 1985. "Rules and Rulings: Parliamentary Procedure from the Wisconsin Perspective." *State of Wisconsin: Blue Book, 1985-86*. Madison, WI: Wisconsin Legislative Reference Bureau.

Wisconsin, State of. 1848. As amended. *Wisconsin Constitution*

VIII. State Administration

Department of Administration. *Budget in Brief 1995 - 1997*. Madison, WI: Department of Administration.

Raney, William Francis. 1940. *Wisconsin: A Story of Progress*. New York: Prentice-Hall.

State ex rel. Reynolds et al. v. Smith. 1964. 22 Wis. (2nd) 516.

State ex rel. Thompson v. Zimmerman. 1954. 264 Wis. 644.

U.S. Bureau of the Census. 1984. *Public Employment in 1983*. Washington, DC: U.S. Government Printing Office.

Wisconsin Legislative Reference Bureau. 1962. *An Analysis of Wisconsin State Government: Its Scope Measured by Civil Service Employment*. Research Bulletin # 136. Madison, WI.

Wisconsin, State of. Various years. *Blue Book*. Madison, WI: Wisconsin Legislative Reference Bureau.

IX. Judiciary

Brace, Paul and Melinda Gann Hall. 1990. "Neo-Institutionalism and Dissent in State Supreme Courts." *Journal of*

Politics. 52:54-70.

Brace, Paul and Melinda Gann Hall. 1993. "Integrated Models of Judicial Dissent." *Journal of Politics*. 55:914-35.

Council of State Governments. 1994. *Book of the States, 1994-95 Edition*. Lexington, KY: Council of State Governments.

Dubois, Philip L. 1980. *From Ballot to Bench: Judicial Elections and the Quest for Accountability*. Austin, TX: University of Texas Press.

Dudley, Robert L. 1994. "The Judicial Career: Tenure an turnover on State High Courts (Some Preliminary Explorations)." Paper presented at the Annual Meeting of the Midwest Political Science Association, Chicago, Illinois.

Emmert, Craig F. 1988. "Judicial Review in State Supreme Courts: Opportunity and Activism." Paper presented at the Annual Meeting of the Midwest Political Science Association, Chicago, Illinois.

Glick, Henry R. 1993. *Courts, Politics & Justice*. New York: McGraw Hill.

Glick, Henry R. and Craig Emmert. 1987. "Selection Systems and Judicial Characteristics: The Recruitment of State Supreme Court Justices." *Judicature*. 70:228-35.

Glick, Henry R. and George W. Pruet, Jr. 1986. "Dissent in State Supreme Courts: Patterns and Correlates of Conflict." In *Judicial Conflict and Consensus: Behavioral Studies of American Appellate Courts*, eds. Sheldon Goldman and Charles Lamb. Lexington, KY: University Press of Kentucky.

Hall, Melinda Gann. 1990. "Opinion Assignment Procedures and Conference Practices in State Supreme Courts." *Judicature*. 73:209-14.

---------- 1992. "Electoral Politics and Strategic Voting in State Supreme Courts." *Journal of Politics*. 54:427-446.

----------. 1995. "Justices as Representatives: Elections and Judicial Politics in the American States." *American Politics Quarterly*. 23:485-503.

National Center for State Courts. 1995. *State Court Caseload Statistics, 1993*. Williamsburg, VA: National Center for State Courts.

Peterson, Steven A. 1981. "Dissent in American Courts." *Journal of Politics*. 43:412-34.

Wisconsin Judicial Commission. 1995. *Annual Report of the Wisconsin Judicial Commission for Calendar Year 1994*. Madison, WI: State of Wisconsin.

Wisconsin, State of. Various years. *State of Wisconsin: Blue Book*. Madison, Wisconsin: Wisconsin Legislative Reference Bureau.

X. Budget and Finance

Associated Press Dispatch (AP Dispatch). 1995a. "Lawmakers Unsure Wisconsin Can Afford Construction Plans." *St. Paul Pioneer Press*. May 18, 1995.

----------. 1995b. "Project Not a Priority, But Gets Funding." *On Wisconsin: Milwaukee Journal-Sentinel* on-line service. June 18, 1995.

----------. 1995c. "Experts Say Party Caucuses a Necessary Evil." *On Wisconsin: Milwaukee Journal-Sentinel* on-line service. June 19, 1995.

----------. 1995d. "Distribution of $1.2 billion Divides Legislature." *On Wisconsin: Milwaukee Journal-Sentinel* on-line service. June 26, 1995.

----------. 1995e. "Gov. Says He'll Sign Budget Bill by End of July." *On Wisconsin: Milwaukee Journal-Sentinel* on-line service. June 30, 1995.

Axelrod, Donald. 1988. *Budgeting for Modern Government.* New York: St. Martin's Press.

Bice, Daniel. 1995. "GOP Would Raise Tax on Cigarettes by a Nickel." *On Wisconsin: Milwaukee Journal-Sentinel* on-line service. June 18, 1995.

Citizens Utility Board v. Thompson. 1995.

Cranford, John. 1989. *Budgeting for America*, 2nd edition. Washington, D.C.: CQ Press.

Dahl, Robert A. and Charles E. Lindblom. 1953, 1963. *Politics, Economics, and Welfare.* New York: Harper and Row, Torchbook Edition.

Daley, Dave. 1993. "Budget Offers Election-Year Boost." *Milwaukee Journal.* August 10, 1993.

Department of Administration. 1987a. *Highlights of the 1985-87 Wisconsin State Budget.* Madison, WI: Department of Administration.

----------. 1989b. *Annual Fiscal Report.* Madison, WI: Department of Administration.

----------. Various years c. *Budget in Brief.* Madison, WI: Department of Administration.

Eggleston, Richard. 1995a. "Democrats Perceive Republicans Funding Home Projects With Ease." St. Paul Pioneer Press. May 29, 1995.

----------. 1995b. "State Assembly Concurs on Portion of State Budget." *On Wisconsin.* June 29, 1995.

Friederich, Charles E. 1987. "Thompson May Try a Democratic Ploy With Partial Veto." *The Milwaukee Journal.* June 21, 1987.

Gosling, James J. 1985. "Patterns of Influence and Choice in the Wisconsin Budgetary Process." *Legislative Studies Quarterly.* 10:457-82.

----------. 1986. "Wisconsin Item-Veto Lessons." *Public Administration Review.* 46:292-300.

----------. 1987. "The State Budget Office and Policy Making." *Public Budgeting and Finance.* 7:51-65.

Hurley, Bill. 1987. "Budget Shows Legislators at Their Best, Worst." *Milwaukee Sentinel.* June 8, 1987.

Jones, Richard P. 1995. "GOP Rebels Wouldn't Compromise on Gas Tax." *On Wisconsin: Milwaukee Journal-Sentinel* on-line service. July 2, 1995.

Legislative Reference Bureau. 1989. "Wisconsin Briefs: Executive Partial Veto of 1989 Senate Bill 31."

----------. 1990. "Wisconsin Briefs: Constitutional Amendment to be Considered by the Wisconsin Electorate."
     April 3, 1990.

Mayers, Jeff. 1991. "Governor Slays Slew of Budget Items." *Wisconsin State Journal*. August 9, 1991.

On Wisconsin, the on-line service of the *Milwaukee Journal Sentinel*. June 1 - July 6, 1995.

Rhodes, Terry A. 1987. *State Budget Process: State of Wisconsin*. Madison, WI: Legislative Fiscal Bureau.

Srb, Arthur L. 1991. "Study Says Wisconsin Tax Bite Regressive." *St. Paul Pioneer Press*. April 23, 1991.

State ex rel Thompson v. Giessel. 1954. 267 Wis. 331.

State ex rel Wisconsin Senate v. Thompson. 1988. 144 Wis. 2d 429.

University of Wisconsin System, Office of University Relations. 1994. "Wisconsin's Property Tax, Budget
     Debate."

Walters, Steven. 1995. "Homeowners, Governor Among Budget Victors." *On Wisconsin*. June 30, 1995.

Walters, Steven and Richard P. Jones. 1995. "State Justices Answer Constitutional Question." *On Wisconsin*. June
     30, 1995.

Wildavsky, Aaron. 1984. *The Politics of the Budgetary Process*, 4th edition. Boston: Little, Brown and Co.

Wisconsin, State of. Various years. *Blue Book*. Madison, WI: Wisconsin Legislative Reference Bureau.

XI. Education

Cibulka, J. 1984. "School Finance Trends in Wisconsin." *Research and Opinion*.

Clancy, D. 1987. "Elementary and Secondary School Aid." Madison: Legislative Fiscal Bureau.

"The Coming Change in School Property Taxes." 1994. *The Wisconsin Taxpayer*. 62: 1-10.

Department of Public Instruction. 1989. "Wisconsin Public School Facts." Madison: Department of Public
     Instruction.

Easton, D. 1965. *A Framework for Political Analysis*. Englewood Cliffs, N. J.: Prentice-Hall.

"Election 1994: Thompson v. Chvala on Education." *Wisconsin School News*. 49:8-17.

Lasswell, H. 1936. *Politics: Who Gets What, When, How*. New York: McGraw-Hill.

Quick, S. 1993. "Battle for the Top Spot." *Wisconsin School News*. 47:8-13.

Shively, N. 1994. "The Politics of School Aid." *Wisconsin School News*. 49: 8-13.

Suchman, D. 1987. "University of Wisconsin System Tuition." Madison: Legislative Fiscal Bureau.

Wisconsin Expenditure Commission. 1986. "Wisconsin Expenditure Commission Report." *The Wisconsin Taxpayer*: 1-8.

Wisconsin, State of. 1987, 1993. *State of Wisconsin, Blue Book, 1987-88, 1993-94.* Madison, WI: Legislative Reference Bureau.

Wisconsin Taxpayers' Alliance. 1994. "1993-94 School Tax Levies and Rates, 1993-1994." *The Wisconsin Taxpayer*. January 1994.

XII. Health and Social Services

Jones, D. "Welfare." 199-207 in Crane, W., Hagensick, and Colleagues. 1987. Wisconsin Government and Politics, Fourth Edition.

Nichols-Casebolt, A., Garfinkel, I., and Wong, P. 1988. "Reforming Wisconsin's Child Support System." 172-186 in S. Danzinger and J.F. Witte, ed. *State Policy Choices, the Wisconsin Experience.* University of Wisconsin Press.

Wisconsin Department of Health & Social Services. 1996. "Proposed Reorganization Plan for the Wisconsin Department of Health and Family Services."

-----. 1995. "Division of Economic Support."

-----. 1995. "Human Services Reporting System."

Wisconsin Division of State Executive Budget and Planning, Department of Administration. 1994. Annual Fiscal Report Appendix.

-----. 1995-97. *Executive Budget.*

-----. 1995-97. *Budget in Brief.* Madison, WI: Department of Administration.

-----. 1987. "Welfare Reform." 21-28 in Executive Budget Policy Issue Papers.

Wisconsin Legislative Fiscal Bureau. 1989. "Aid to Families with Dependent Children" (Informational Paper #49).

-----. 1995. Various Informational Papers.

-----. 1995. Various 1995-1997 Budget Summary Papers.

-----. 1996. "Wisconsin Works (W-2)" (Summary of Provisions in 1995 Wisconsin Act 289).

Wisconsin, State of. 1995. *Blue Book.* Madison, WI: Wisconsin Legislative Fiscal Bureau.

XIII. Natural Resources

Behm, Don. 1989. "Ill Waters: The Fouling of Wisconsin's Lakes and Streams." *The Milwaukee Journal.* November 5-10, 1989.

-----. 1995. "Most Waterways in State Meet Quality Goals." *The Milwaukee Journal.* January 5, 1995.

Bromley, Daniel W. and Barbara J. Irvin. 1991. "Environmental Issues in Wisconsin." In *Dollars and Sense: Policy Choices and the Wisconsin Budget*, vol. 2, eds. James H. Conant, Robert H. Haveman, and Jack Huddleston. Madison, WI: The Board of Regents of the University of Wisconsin System.

Findley, Roger W. and Daniel A. Farber. 1992. *Environmental Law in a Nutshell.* St. Paul: West Publishing Co.

Hardin, Garrett. 1968. "The Tragedy of the Commons." *Science Magazine.* 162:1243-1249.

Haskell, Elizabeth and Victoria Price. 1973. *State Environmental Management: Case Studies of Nine States.* New York: Praeger.

Hays, Samuel P. 1972. *Conservation and the Gospel of Efficiency: The Progressive Conservation Movement, 1890-1920.* New York: Atheneum.

Heberlein, Thomas A. and Thomas M. Beckley. 1990. "Fish and Wildlife Management." In *Dollars and Sense: Policy Choices and the Wisconsin Budget*, vol. 1, eds. Robert H. Haveman and Jack Huddleston. Madison, WI: The Board of Regents of the University of Wisconsin System.

Lester, James P. 1994. "A New Federalism? Environmental Policy in the States." In *Environmental Policy in the 1990s: Toward a New Agenda*, eds. Norman J. Vig and Michael E. Kraft. Washington, D.C.: CQ Press. 2nd ed. 1994.

Parker, Selma. 1973. "Protecting Wisconsin's Environment." In *Blue Book 1973 - 74*, State of Wisconsin. Madison, WI: Wisconsin Legislative Reference Bureau.

Rosenbaum, Walter A. 1995. *Environmental Politics and Policy.* Washington, D.C.: CQ Press.

Segerson, Kathleen and Daniel W. Bromley. 1988. "Natural Resource Policy." In *State Policy Choices: The Wisconsin Experience*, eds. Sheldon Danziger and John F. Witte. Madison, WI: The University of Wisconsin Press.

Smothers, Ronald. 1994. "Study Says Environmental and Economic Health Go Together." *New York Times.* October 19, 1994.

Thomas, Christine L. 1989. "The Role of the Wisconsin Natural Resources Board in Environmental Decision-Making: A Comparison of Perceptions." Diss. The University of Wisconsin-Madison.

Udall, Stewart L. 1963. *The Quiet Crisis.* New York: Holt, Rinehart and Winston.

Vig, Norman J. and Michael E. Kraft, eds. 1994. *Environmental Policy in the 1990s: Toward a New Agenda.* Washington, D.C.: CQ Press.

Wisconsin Department of Natural Resources. 1995. *Voice.* DNR Publication 010. Winter 1995.

Wisconsin Department of Natural Resources. 1995b. "Wisconsin's Environment 1970-1995: An Earth Day Twenty-Fifth Anniversary Commemorative." PUB-1E-200 95.

Wisconsin, State of. Various years. *Blue Book.* Madison, WI: Wisconsin Legislative Reference Bureau.

XIV. Wisconsin Among the States

Albritton, Robert. 1990. "Social Services: Welfare and Health." In *Politics in the American States*, eds. Virginia Gray, Herbert Jacob and Robert Albritton. Glenview, IL: Scott, Foresman.

Beyle, Thad. 1990. "Governors" In *Politics in the American States*, eds. Virginia Gray, Herbert Jacob and Robert Albritton. Glenview, IL: Scott, Foresman.

Bibby, John, Cornelius Cotter, James Gibson and Robert Huckshorn. 1990. "Parties in State Politics." In *Politics in the American States*, eds. Virginia Gray, Herbert Jacob and Robert Albritton. Glenview, IL: Scott Foresman.

Bibby, John, and Thomas Holbrook. Nd. "Parties and Elections in State Politics." In *Politics in the American States*, eds. Virginia Gray and Herbert Jacobs. Washington, DC: CQ Press.

Bowman, Ann, and Richard Kearney. 1990. *State and Local Government*. Boston: Houghton Mifflin.

Council of State Governments, The. Various years. *Book of the States*. Lexington, KY: The Council of State Governments.

Dresang, Dennis L., and James J. Gosling. 1989. *Politics, Policy, and Management in the American States*. New York: Longman.

Elazar, Daniel J. 1984. *American Federalism: A View from the States*. New York: Harper & Row.

Emmert, Craig. 1988. "Judicial Review in State Supreme Courts: Opportunity and Activism." Presented at the Midwest Political Science Association Meeting, April 14-16, 1988, Chicago, IL.

Hall, Bob, and Mary Lee Kerr. 1992. *The 1991-1992 Green Index*. Washington, DC: Island Press.

Hansen, Susan. 1990. "The Politics of State Taxing and Spending." In *Politics in the American States*, eds. Virginia Gray, Herbert Jacob and Robert Albritton. Glenview, IL: Scott, Foresman.

Holbrook, Thomas M., and Emily Van Dunk. 1993. "Electoral Competition in the American States." *American Political Science Review* 87:955-962.

Jacob, Herbert. "Courts: The Least Visible Branch." In *Politics in the American States*, eds. Virginia Gray, Herbert Jacob and Robert Albritton. Glenview, IL: Scott, Foresman.

Nathan, Richard P. 1989. "The Role of the States in American Federalism." In *The State of the States*, ed. Carl Van Horn. Washington, DC: CQ Press.

Wright, Gerald, Robert Erikson, and John McIver. 1985. "Measuring State Partisanship and Ideology." *Journal of Politics* 47:469-489.